Thinking about Democracy

Arend Lijphart has been one of the most innovative and influential thinkers in the field of comparative government and politics for more than three decades. His groundbreaking work on alternative forms of democracy and their suitability for ethnically and religiously divided societies is not only of great theoretical significance, but also of great and growing practical importance – especially in the twenty-first-century world which is rapidly democratizing and in which almost all not-yet-democratic countries are beset by deep ethnic and other cleavages.

This book is a selection of his key essays on the distinction between power sharing and majoritarian forms of democracy and on the two crucial alternatives in constitution-making that guide a democracy in the direction of either power sharing or majoritarianism – the choice of electoral system and the choice between parliamentary and presidential government. The essays include his best known articles and chapters, but also those that have appeared in less accessible journals and books. They are placed in historical and intellectual context by a substantial new introduction outlining the developments in Lijphart's thought.

Thinking about Democracy draws on a lifetime's experience of research and publication in this area and collects together for the first time his most significant and influential work. The book also contains an entirely new introduction and conclusion where Professor Lijphart assesses the development of his thought and the practical impact it has had on emerging democracies. The book will be of enormous interest to all scholars of democracy and comparative politics.

Arend Lijphart is Research Professor Emeritus in Political Science at the University of California, San Diego, USA. His field of specialization is comparative politics, and his current research is focused on the comparative study of democratic institutions. Lijphart has received numerous awards throughout his prestigious career in recognition of his groundbreaking research. In 1989 he was elected to the National Academy of Arts and Sciences and from 1995–96 served as President of the American Political Science Association.

Thinking about Democracy

Power sharing and majority rule
in theory and practice

Arend Lijphart

Routledge
Taylor & Francis Group

LONDON AND NEW YORK

First published 2008
by Routledge
2 Park Square, Milton Park, Abingdon, Oxon, OX14 4RN

Simultaneously published in the USA and Canada
by Routledge
270 Madison Avenue, New York, NY 10016

Routledge is an imprint of the Taylor & Francis Group, an informa business

© 2008 Arend Lijphart

Typeset in Times New Roman by Taylor & Francis Books
Printed and bound in Great Britain by
Antony Rowe Ltd, Chippenham, Wiltshire

British Library Cataloguing in Publication Data
A catalogue record for this book is available from the British Library

Library of Congress Cataloging-in-Publication Data
Lijphart, Arend.
    Thinking about democracy: power sharing and majority rule in theory
and practice/Arend Lijphart.
        p. cm.
    Includes bibliographical references and index. [etc.]
    1. Democracy. I. Title.
    JC423.L524 2007
    321.8 – dc22
            2007012804

ISBN 10: 0-415-77267-2 (hbk)
ISBN 10: 0-415-77268-0 (pbk)
ISBN 10: 0-203-93468-7 (ebk)

ISBN 13: 978-0-415-77267-9 (hbk)
ISBN 13: 978-0-415-77268-6 (pbk)
ISBN 13: 978-0-203-93468-5 (ebk)

Contents

Illustrations

Acknowledgments

I am grateful to the following journals and publishers for permission to reprint the chapters in this collection: *World Politics* and Johns Hopkins University Press for "Consociational Democracy," vol. 21, published in January 1969; *Journal of Democracy* and Johns Hopkins University Press for "Constitutional Design for Divided Societies," vol. 15, no. 2 published in April 2004, "Constitutional Choices for New Democracies," vol. 2, no. 1 published in winter 1991 and "Double-Checking the Evidence," vol. 2, no. 3 published in summer 1991; Johns Hopkins University Press for "Presidentialism and Majoritarian Democracy: Theoretical Observations," in Juan J. Linz and Arturo Valenzuela (eds) *The Failure of Presidential Democracy*, Baltimore MD, 1994; American Political Science Association and the *American Political Science Review* for "Comparative Politics and the Comparative Method," vol. 65, no. 3 published in September 1971; "The Puzzle of Indian Democracy: A Consociational Interpretation," vol. 90, no. 2 published in June 1996; "Unequal Participation: Democracy's Unresolved Dilemma", vol. 91, no. 1 published in March 1997; Editions Yvon Blais for "Self-Determination Versus Pre-Determination of Ethnic Minorities in Power-Sharing Systems" (excerpts), in David Schneiderman (ed.) *Language and the State: The Laws and Politics of Identity*, Cowansville, Quebec, 1991; Yale University Press for "The Quality of Democracy: Consensus Democracy Makes a Difference," chapter 16 of *Patterns of Democracy: Government Forms and Performance in Thirty-Six Countries*, New Haven CT, 1999; Blackwell Publishing and the *International Social Science Journal* for "Majority Rule in Theory and Practice: The Tenacity of a Flawed Paradigm," *International Social Science Journal* vol. 43, no. 3 published in August 1991; Cambridge University Press, "Back to Democratic Basics: Who Really Practices Majority Rule?" in Axel Hadenius (ed.) *Democracy's Victory and Crisis*, Cambridge, 1997; Netherlands Institute for Advanced Studies in the Humanities and Social Sciences (NIAS) for "Europe, the European Union, and Democracy," *NIAS Newsletter*, spring 2002; *Politikon* and Taylor & Francis for "The Alternative Vote: A Realistic Alternative for South Africa?", vol. 18, no. 2, published in June 1991; Oxford University Press for "Electoral Engineering: Limits and Possibilities," chapter 7 of *Electoral Systems and Party Systems: A Study of Twenty-Seven Democracies, 1945–1990*, Oxford, 1994; Odense University Press for "Types of Democracy and Generosity with Foreign Aid: An Indirect Test of the Democratic Peace Proposition" (with Peter J. Bowman), in Erik Beukel, Kurt Klaudi Klausen, and Poul Erik Mouritzen (eds) *Elites, Parties and Democracy*, Odense, Denmark, 1999. Every effort has been made to contact copyright holders for their permission to reprint material in this book. The publishers would be grateful to hear from any copyright holder who is not here acknowledged and will undertake to rectify any errors or omissions in future editions of this book.

Part I
Introduction

1 Introduction
Developments in power sharing theory

The present volume contains articles and chapters written over a period of thirty-five years, from 1969 to 2004, but most of them date from the 1990s. They all evolve around the idea of power sharing democracy, its different forms, alternative democratic institutions, and other closely related topics. In this Introduction, my emphasis will be on the intellectual development of power sharing theory and on the cohesion among its components. The essays that I selected for inclusion in this volume constitute only a small portion of my total scholarly output, and in the Introduction I shall explain why I regard them as the most representative and significant of my work. It will also give me an opportunity to express further thoughts on these topics as well as a few second thoughts that I have had.

Consociational democracy

My article on "Consociational Democracy," published in 1969, is often regarded as the "classic" statement of consociational theory. It is mainly for this reason that I chose it as the first essay to be reprinted in this book (in Chapter 2). It is still frequently cited, and it was selected by the editors of *World Politics* in 1997 as one of the seven most important articles that appeared in the first 50 years of this journal. Strictly speaking, it was not the very first statement of consociational theory. I had already introduced the basic concept in my case study of the Netherlands, *The Politics of Accommodation* (Lijphart 1968a), and it was also included as part of my broad survey of the literature on typologies of democratic systems published in the same year (Lijphart 1968b); in that article, I used the term "consociational" for the first time.

In this connection, I should also point out that neither this term nor the general concept were entirely new. I borrowed the term "consociational" from David Apter's 1961 study of Uganda, and it can actually be traced as far back as Johannes Althusius' writings in the early seventeenth century; Althusius used the Latin *consociatio*. Both of these sources are acknowledged in the "Consociational Democracy" article, as is Gerhard Lehmbruch's 1967 monograph on "proportional democracy" – roughly similar to consociational democracy – which preceded my Dutch case study by one year.[1] I later discovered other precedents: in particular, Sir Arthur Lewis' monograph *Politics in West Africa* (1965) – the first modern scholarly exposition of consociational theory, to which I shall return in the Conclusion – and the writings of the Austro-Marxists Otto Bauer and Karl Renner in the early years of the twentieth century.

In subsequent writings, I gradually refined my analyses in several ways, but my descriptions and definitions have remained stable since the 1990s. One reason for choosing my 1996 case study of India as the next chapter – apart from the intrinsic significance of the Indian case – is that it contains my "final" formulation of consociational theory. Compared with my writings of the late 1960s, I made five significant improvements. One was to define consociational democracy in terms of four basic characteristics – grand coalition, cultural autonomy, proportionality, and minority veto – listed in the first paragraph of the India article and discussed at length later on. Only the first of these was extensively discussed in my 1969 article. Second, I now usually make a distinction between primary and secondary characteristics: grand coalition and autonomy are the most crucial, whereas the other two occupy a somewhat lower position of importance.

Third, I now always emphasize the fact that all four consociational features can assume quite different forms but, at the same time, that these different forms do not work equally well and are not equally to be recommended to multi-ethnic and multi-religious societies that are trying to establish consociational institutions. For instance, in the "Consociational Democracy" article, I describe the varieties of grand coalitions that have been formed, and elsewhere I have described the different ways that the principles of autonomy, proportionality, and minority veto can be implemented. One general recommendation can be made in terms of the traditional categories of constitutional engineering. While consociational democracy is not incompatible with presidentialism, plurality or majority electoral systems, and unitary government, a better constitutional framework is offered by their opposites: parliamentary government, proportional representation (PR), and, for societies with geographically concentrated ethnic or religious groups, federalism. In Chapters 9 through 14, the parliamentary-presidential and plurality-PR contrasts are discussed at greater length. Another general recommendation is that consociational institutions and procedures that follow the principle of what I have called "self-determination" are superior to those that are based on "pre-determination" – discussed at length in Chapter 4.

Fourth, my "Consociational Democracy" article presents only an initial and tentative analysis of the conditions that favor the establishment and survival of consociational systems. On this aspect of consociational theory, my conclusions have undergone a series of adjustments as I explored additional cases and as I listened to the advice of both critics and sympathetic readers. However, from the mid-1980s on, I have settled on a list of nine favorable conditions, which can be found in my article on India. Moreover, I now always list the absence of a solid ethnic or religious majority and the absence of large socioeconomic inequalities among the groups of a divided society as the two most important of these nine favorable factors. Finally, a point that I generally emphasize when recommending consociationalism as a solution to ethnic conflict is that the nine conditions should not be regarded as either necessary or sufficient conditions: an attempt at consociationalism can fail even if all the background conditions are positive, and it is not impossible for it to succeed even if all of these conditions are negative. In short, they must be seen as no more than *favorable* or *facilitating* conditions in the common meanings of these terms.

In my 1969 article, my main examples of consociational and partly (or temporary) consociational systems are the Netherlands, Belgium, Luxembourg, Austria, Switzerland, Lebanon, Nigeria, Colombia, and Uruguay. I have gradually discovered and analyzed other cases, and in my book *Democracy in Plural Societies* (Lijphart 1977), the new cases are Malaysia, Cyprus, Suriname, the Netherlands Antilles, Burundi, Northern Ireland, and the two semi-consociational systems of Canada and Israel. In my article on India as a consociational democracy, I also briefly mention Czecho-Slovakia and South Africa. More recent examples are Fiji, Bosnia-Herzegovina, Macedonia, Kosovo, and Afghanistan.

Of all of these cases, however, India is by far the most important for four reasons: First, it is one of the world's most deeply divided societies, and divided along both religious and linguistic cleavages. Second, it is an almost perfect example of consociational democracy, exhibiting all four of its characteristics in clear and thorough fashion. Third, with the exception of the short authoritarian interlude of the Emergency in 1975–77, it has a longer history of continuous democracy and a better democratic record than any other country in the developing world. Fourth, its large population of more than 1 billion people – larger than the populations of all of the other cases combined – makes it an especially important example. The one qualification is that, as I note toward the end of my analysis of India, consociationalism declined to some extent from the late 1960s on. I made this judgment in 1996 and I clearly feared at that time that consociationalism, and hence also democracy, in India was at risk. I now believe that I was far too pessimistic. In particular, the decline of the Congress Party has actually made the consociational system stronger because the dominant-party system and frequent one-party cabinets have been replaced by an extreme multiparty system and very broad coalition cabinets that often include more than a dozen parties. Moreover, the diminished status of the Congress has made its centralized and hierarchical features less important for the system as a whole, while inside the party these tendencies have also weakened. Federalism has been strengthened a great deal, and minority educational autonomy, separate personal laws, adherence to proportionality, and the minority veto are all still intact.

I have already briefly alluded to my essay on self-determination and pre-determination (Chapter 4). These rival concepts, and my conclusion that self-determination was the more desirable principle on which to organize consociational rules and institutions, were developed as a result of the challenge that I and other consociationalists faced in the 1970s and 1980s to propose an optimal consociational design for the unusual South African conditions: identifying the constituent groups in this country was both objectively difficult and politically controversial. Self-determination may be called the "agnostic" approach to ethnicity and divided societies: they allow us to "agree to disagree" about which groups should be identified as the essential participants in consociations, and even about the contentious issue of whether a country like South Africa can be accurately described as a divided society or not. Election by PR, which is the main self-determination method, permits the emergence and political representation of any group – ethnic or non-ethnic, religious or non-religious – and is not biased for or against ethnic and religious parties. Another advantage is that it promotes the flexible adjustment of power and representation in response to any changes in the strength of ethnic groups, as well as the flexible adjustment to any decline in the overall strength of ethnicity, the growth of a more homogeneous society, and the emergence of non-ethnic and non-religious parties.

Consociational and consensus democracy

In my writings after 1969, I started using the term "power sharing" democracy more and more often as a synonym for consociational democracy. The main reason is that I started to use consociationalism not only as an analytical concept but also as a practical recommendation for deeply divided societies. The term "consociational" worked well enough in scholarly writing, but I found it to be an obstacle in communicating with policy-makers who found it too esoteric, polysyllabic, and difficult to pronounce. Using "power sharing" instead has greatly facilitated the process of communication beyond the confines of academic political science.

I have also often used power sharing as a rough synonym for the concept of "consensus democracy," which grew out of my effort to define and measure consociational democracy more precisely. The result, however, was a new concept that, while still closely related to consociational democracy, is not coterminous with it. Because I use both concepts in my essay on "Constitutional Design for Divided Societies" (Chapter 5) and the concept of consensus democracy exclusively in my chapter on "The Quality of Democracy," taken from my 1999 book *Patterns of Democracy* (Chapter 6), I need to explain the differences between the two concepts here.

The two are closely related in the sense that both are non-majoritarian forms of democracy. The differences can largely be accounted for in terms of how they were derived. As is clear from my "Consociational Democracy" article (Chapter 2), the concept of consociationalism arose out of the analysis of a set of deviant cases where stable democracy was found to be possible in divided societies, and where the explanation of this phenomenon was the application of the principles of grand coalition, autonomy, proportionality, and minority veto – the four defining characteristics of consociational democracy – all of which clearly contrast with majoritarian principles.

In my 1984 book *Democracies* and 1999 *Patterns of Democracy*, I reversed this procedure. I began by enumerating the major characteristics of majoritarian democracy, and subsequently defined each trait of non-majoritarian democracy as a contrast with the corresponding majoritarian trait.[2] I intentionally labeled this non-majoritarian model "consensus democracy" in order not to confuse it with the similar but not identical concept of consociational democracy. The first five majoritarian characteristics are concentration of executive power in single-party majority cabinets, executive-legislative relationships in which the executive is dominant, two-party systems, majoritarian and disproportional electoral systems, and pluralist interest group systems with free-for-all competition among groups. The five contrasting consensus characteristics are executive power sharing in broad multiparty coalitions, executive-legislative balance of power, multiparty systems, proportional representation, and coordinated and "corporatist" interest group systems aimed at compromise and concertation.

These differences are formulated in terms of dichotomous contrasts between the majoritarian and consensus models, but they are all variables on which particular countries may be at either end of the continuum or anywhere in between. These five variables are closely correlated with each other; that is, if a particular country occupies a particular position on one continuum, it is likely to be in a similar position on the other four continua. The five variables can therefore be seen as a single dimension, which for brevity's sake I have called the executives-parties dimension.

A second set of five interrelated variables forms a clearly separate dimension, which I have called the federal-unitary dimension because most of the differences on it are commonly associated with the contrast between federal and unitary government. The majoritarian (unitary) characteristics are unitary and centralized government, concentration of legislative power in a unicameral legislature, flexible constitutions that can be amended by simple majorities, systems in which legislatures have the final word on the constitutionality of their own legislation, and central banks that are dependent on the executive. The five contrasting consensus characteristics are federal and decentralized government, division of legislative power between two equally strong but differently constituted houses, rigid constitutions that can be amended only by super-majorities, systems in which laws are subject to a judicial review of their constitutionality by supreme or constitutional courts, and independent central banks.

An obvious difference between the consociational and consensus models is that the former is defined in terms of four and the latter in terms of ten characteristics. A second clear difference is that the four consociational principles are broader than the consensus traits that appear to be the most similar. For instance, a consociational grand coalition may take the form of a consensual, broadly representative, multiparty coalition cabinet, but it may also take various other forms, like informal advisory arrangements and alternating presidencies (which may be thought of as a sequential "grand coalition"). Moreover, for consociational democracy it is the inclusion of all distinctive population groups rather than all parties that is important when these groups and the parties do not coincide. Federalism is merely one way of establishing group autonomy. The most important aspect of the consociational principle of proportionality is proportional representation (PR), but it also includes proportionality in legislative representation that can occur without formal PR, proportional appointment to the civil service, and proportional allocation of public funds. The minority veto is a broader concept than the mere requirement of extraordinary majorities to amend the constitution. On the other hand, the consensus model's features of bicameralism, judicial review, and independent central banks are not part of the consociational model.

These two differences can be summarized as follows: Consociational and consensus democracy have a large area of overlap, but neither is completely encompassed by the other. This means that consociational democracy cannot be seen as a special form of consensus democracy or vice versa.

A third difference emerges from the discussion of the first two. Where consensus and consociational democracy differ, the former tends to emphasize formal-institutional devices whereas the latter relies to a larger extent on informal practices. Fourth, as already implied earlier, the characteristics of consensus democracy are defined in such a way that they can all be measured in precise quantitative terms – which is not possible for any of the four consociational characteristics.

Finally, although both consociational and consensus democracy are highly suitable forms of democracy for divided societies, consociationalism is the stronger medicine. For instance, while consensus democracy provides many incentives for broad power sharing, consociationalism requires it and prescribes that all significant groups be included in it. Similarly, consensus democracy facilitates but consociational democracy demands group autonomy. Hence for the most deeply divided societies, I recommend a consociational instead of merely a consensus system. At the same time, the differences between them do not entail any conflict, and they are perfectly compatible with each other. My recommendations in "Constitutional Design for Divided Societies" (Chapter 5) combine elements of both.

Chapter 5 attempts to give as straightforward and unequivocal advice as possible to constitution-makers in deeply divided countries, and to make their choices as clear and simple as possible. This entails two other aspects that are worth highlighting. First, it tells them that, without any doubt, they need a consociational solution, and that they should not waste their time on non-consociational alternatives. Second, because consociationalism can assume so many different forms, it tells them clearly which forms are the best and to forget about alternatives that can be regarded as consociational but that are less advantageous. For instance, while a relatively proportional legislature can be engineered without the use of PR, the best method is to use PR – and, in fact, a very specific form of PR: list PR with closed lists and election districts that are not too large.

Consensus democracy

I regard the findings and conclusions of Chapter 6, "The Quality of Democracy: Consensus Democracy Makes a Difference," as probably the most significant of all of my scholarly work, because they clearly demonstrate the superiority of the consensus model. It is the penultimate chapter from my 1999 *Patterns of Democracy*, which contrasts the majoritarian and consensus patterns found in thirty-six democracies.[3] The earlier chapters are devoted to the analysis of each of the ten majoritarian-consensus variables. The most significant finding that emerges from these chapters is that, while there are a large variety of ways to run a democracy, the main institutional rules and practices can all be measured on scales from majoritarianism at one end to consensus on the other. Moreover, as indicated earlier, these institutional characteristics from two distinct clusters and, based on this dichotomous clustering, a two-dimensional "conceptual map" can be drawn on which each of the democracies can be located.

The next, more important, question I asked was: "So what?" Does the difference between majoritarian and consensus democracy make a difference for the operation of democracy, especially for how well democracy works? Especially as far as the executives-parties dimension is concerned, the conventional wisdom is that there is a trade-off between the quality and the effectiveness of democratic government. On the one hand, the conventional wisdom concedes that PR, multiparty systems, and coalition cabinets provide more accurate representation and, in particular, better minority representation and protection of minority interests, a well as broader participation in decision-making. On the other hand, it maintains that the one-party majority governments typically produced by plurality elections are more decisive and hence more effective policy-makers. This logic applies to the federal-unitary dimension, too: federalism, second chambers, rigid constitutions, judicial review, and independent central banks are all likely to inhibit the decisiveness, speed, and coherence of the central government's policy-making.

In the chapter preceding the chapter that is reprinted in this volume (Chapter 6), I analyzed the majoritarians' claim of effectiveness by statistical tests of the effects of the two dimensions of consensus versus majoritarianism on quantitative indicators of macroeconomic performance (economic growth, inflation, unemployment, strike activity, budget deficits, and economic freedom) and control of violence (deaths from political violence and riots), controlling for the level of economic development, population size, and degree of societal division. My original expectation was that the conventional wisdom was at least partly right and that majoritarian democracy (especially on the executives-parties dimension) was indeed likely to produce somewhat more effective government – although I also expected this to be a relatively small advantage that would be offset by the considerably better performance of consensus democracy with regard to democratic quality.

The results turned out to be a great deal more favorable to consensus democracy. On the federal-unitary dimension, there was little difference between the two types of democracy, with one big exception: consensus democracy correlated strongly with lower levels of inflation according to all five indicators of inflation that I used. This is not a surprising finding because consensus on the federal-unitary dimension includes central bank independence, and the most important reason why central banks are made strong and independent is to give them the tools to control inflation. More importantly, on the executives-parties dimension, consensus democracies had a better overall record than majoritarian democracies, especially with regard to the control of inflation but also, albeit much more weakly, with regard to most of the other macroeconomic performance variables and the control of violence. However, these differences were generally not large enough to be statistically significant. This looks like a non-finding, but it actually contains an important conclusion: the fact that consensus democracy has a slight advantage over majoritarian democracy means that majoritarian democracy *cannot claim even a slight advantage.* Contrary to the conventional wisdom, majoritarian democracies are clearly not the better governors.

The big advantages of consensus democracy (on the executives-parties dimension[4]) with regard to the quality of democracy are demonstrated in the next chapter of *Patterns of Democracy*, which is reprinted here as Chapter 6. This chapter also analyzes the degree to which consensus democracy promotes "kinder and gentler" public policies, adjectives borrowed from one of the first President Bush's speeches. Had I written this chapter after the election of the second President Bush, I might have used his favorite term "compassionate" instead. Regardless of whether the two Bushes were serious about seeking such policies, their terms accurately capture the essence of the policy goals. I deliberately distinguished them from the indicators of democratic quality, because people of different political-ideological persuasions may legitimately differ on their desirability. Liberals and conservatives are especially likely to disagree on the degree to which welfare state policies should be promoted. However, on the other three policy goals – responsible environmental performance, a compassionate criminal justice system, and generosity with foreign aid – there is much more widespread agreement. Chapter 6 is subtitled "Consensus Democracy Makes a Difference." In fact, it makes a *huge* difference, both with regard to the quality of democracy and the adoption of compassionate policies. I shall deal with the general question of the strength of the evidence behind consensus and consociational democracy in the concluding chapter, but let me already point out here that all of the evidence presented in Chapter 6 is extraordinarily strong.

There is one final aspect of my work on consensus versus majoritarian democracy that I should like to comment on briefly here. My analyses have focused on ten institutional differences between the two types of democracy. All of these can be described as the most important characteristics of the relevant institutions. Several of these institutions, however, can be explored in greater detail by examining their internal organization and operation. For instance, the only characteristic of legislatures that I analyze is whether they are unicameral or bicameral, and, if bicameral, how the two chambers differ from each other. I do not look at how they organize themselves, even though in this respect there is at least one other variable – the organization of legislative committees – that also fits the majoritarian-consensus contrast: are all of the committee chairs members of the majority party or majority coalition, or are committee chairmanships proportionally allocated among all of the parties in the legislature? Similarly, we can "unpack" cabinets, and ask whether inside the cabinet the prime minister has predominant power or is truly only *primus inter pares* (first among equals[5]) – reflecting, respectively, majoritarian versus consensus patterns.

Another opportunity for this kind of "unpacking" has to do with supreme and constitutional courts. The only aspect of these courts that I analyze in *Patterns of Democracy* is whether they have the right of reviewing the constitutionality of laws enacted by national legislatures, and, if so, their degree of activism in using this judicial review. Additional questions that affect the majoritarian or consensual nature of these courts are the sizes of the courts, the methods of electing justices, their terms of office, and the courts' internal decision rules.[6] The American Supreme Court is highly majoritarian in these respects, while the German Constitutional Court and Indian Supreme Court are examples of more consensual high courts. First, the Supreme Court of the United States has an unusually small membership of only nine justices, compared with sixteen in Germany (although divided in two separate "senates") and twenty-six in India. Obviously larger court memberships offer better opportunities for broad representation of different parties and population groups. Second, election can be by majority vote, which is roughly the American pattern, or by supermajorities, like the two-thirds legislative majorities required in each of the German legislative chambers. Third, new justices can be chosen as vacancies occur, as in the United States – which means that majorities can keep electing their own favorites sequentially; or they can be elected simultaneously or in groups – which makes it more likely that members of minorities will be chosen. Fourth, terms of office can be longer or shorter, and long terms are an obstacle to broad representation. The American Supreme Court is at one extreme of this spectrum: no fixed terms and no mandatory retirement. In Germany, justices have twelve-year terms, and in India they have to retire at age sixty-five. Finally, court decisions can be by regular or by extraordinary majorities. In the United States, a majority of five out of nine suffices, whereas in each of the German "senates," a minimum of five or, in some cases, six votes out of eight are required.

What is especially worth noting here is that the US Supreme Court presents a paradox: it clearly fits the consensus model as far as its strong exercise of judicial review is concerned, but it is highly majoritarian with regard to all five aspects of its selection, composition, and decision rules. We find a similar paradox in the American presidency: separation of powers fits the divided-power character of the second dimension of consensus democracy, but the concentration of executive power in the hands of one person is the very opposite majoritarian characteristic.

Majority rule

Chapters 7 and 8 take a critical look at majority rule. Power sharing democracy (of both the consociational and consensus subtypes) is often described as non-majoritarian, and even anti-majoritarian or counter-majoritarian – and I have used those terms myself, too. In fact, however, power sharing does not deviate much from the basic principle of majority rule. It agrees with that fundamental premise that majority rule is superior to minority rule, but it accepts majority rule merely as a *minimum* requirement: instead of being satisfied with narrow decision-making majorities, it seeks to maximize the size of these majorities. The real contrast is not so much between majoritarian and non-majoritarian as between bare-majority and broad-majority models of democracy.

As Chapter 7 points out, democracy is still most often defined in terms of majority rule – clearly an incomplete definition, especially if "majority" is used in the sense of "bare majority." This chapter then describes majority-rule democracy in terms of a list of nine characteristics (which differ slightly from the list of ten features of majoritarian democracy listed earlier in this Introduction, because they are based on the definitions and data in *Democracies* [1984] instead of *Patterns of Democracy* [1999]). What is striking is that, when these majoritarian criteria are applied to twenty-five democracies, only two – the United Kingdom and New Zealand – qualify as majority-rule systems, and even they deviate to some extent from pure majoritarianism; the other twenty-three all show much greater deviations (see Figure 7.1). This picture does not change when the majoritarian criteria are applied to the larger number of countries covered in *Patterns of Democracy*: of these thirty-six democracies, only the same two have a close fit with majoritarianism. Moreover, New Zealand has been more consensual than majoritarian since 1996, when it changed its electoral system from plurality to PR and, as a result, has also shifted to a multiparty system as well as coalition and minority cabinets.

Of course, if we look only at the executives-parties dimension instead of both dimensions together, several more democracies qualify as majoritarian. Chapter 8 shows, however, that in practice these democracies frequently fail to live up to the majoritarian principle that governments – that is, *executives* – be supported by a majority instead of a minority of the voters. In fact, it is the consensus democracies that have a considerably better record in this respect! Not surprisingly, because consensus democracies aim at broad rather than narrow majority rule, their average cabinet support also tends to be higher than that of majoritarian systems.

As mentioned earlier, majority-rule systems do not have a better record with regard to effective policy-making either. The only strong argument in their favor that remains is their advantage with regard to accountability and identifiability: almost by definition, plurality elections, two-party systems, and one-party cabinets have the edge. If one party is in power and has a governing majority, it can be given credit or blame for specific policies and their implementation. When there are coalition and/or minority cabinets, it is obviously much more difficult to identify who is responsible.

However, the critical question that must be asked is: what is the purpose of accountability and identifiability? Clearly, the main purpose is to keep the government in line with voters' preferences. But when the relative distance between government and the median voters are measured on a left-right scale, it turns out that the distance is actually much smaller in consensus than in majoritarian democracies (see Chapter 6). Another problem is that, while it may be easy to identify the incumbent one-party government as the agent responsible for public policy, it is in practice difficult for the voters – that is, for the majority of the voters – to remove this government. In the United Kingdom since 1945, for instance, all re-elected governments have been re-elected in spite of majorities of voters having voted for opposition parties – and *against* the governing party.

Moreover, the accountability of one-party majority governments is a two-edged sword: it allows citizens to know and judge who is responsible for government policies, but it also provides a clear and tempting target for interest-group pressure. Therefore, especially when special interests are strong and well organized and when the public interest has only weakly organized defenders, it may be easier for multiparty coalition governments with their diffuse accountability to make decisions favoring the public interest over special interests than it is for highly accountable one-party governments (Moosbrugger 2001).

Parliamentary versus presidential government

There is a close connection between the majoritarian-consensus and presidential-parliamentary contrasts. This connection entails two paradoxes.

Presidential government means separation of powers, which would appear to put presidential government in the company of the other divided-power institutions – federalism, bicameralism, separate and independent high courts and central banks – that are at the consensus end of the federal-unitary dimension. As Chapter 9 shows, however, it is (1) on the executives-parties instead of the federal-unitary dimension that presidential government has a strong effect, and (2) this effect is not directed toward consensus and shared power but toward majoritarianism and concentrated power. The only exception that I note is that in some presidential systems, including the United States, presidents are relatively weak and the overall pattern is one of executive-legislative balance of power instead of executive dominance. For the American case, this judgment needs to be qualified. American presidents have particularly strong powers with regard to the conduct of foreign policy, but these powers have not been overly obtrusive because presidents have generally not deviated much from firmly established multilateral and internationalist traditions. However, since 2001 President George W. Bush has embraced a radically different foreign-policy orientation, and the vast and independent foreign-policy powers of the president have become abundantly evident. In addition, as a result of having cohesive and compliant Republican majorities in Congress (until 2007) who backed both his foreign and domestic policies, President Bush exercised in practice almost the same predominant powers as the British prime minister.

This strong tendency toward majoritarianism is one of the four main points in Juan Linz's (1994) famous critique of presidentialism. His other objections are the rigidity of presidentialism, resulting from the fixed terms that presidents serve which cannot be shortened even if a president proves to be incompetent, or becomes seriously ill, or is beset by scandals of various kinds; the tendency of presidential election campaigns to encourage the politics of personality instead of a politics of competing parties and party programs; and the popular election of both president and legislature, which gives both of them democratic legitimacy, and which is therefore likely to lead to stalemate if there are disagreements between them.

An additional small disadvantage is that the so-called voting paradox is more likely to occur in presidential than in parliamentary systems. This problem has been of great concern to democratic political theorists, because it entails a situation in which majority rule does not work and "cyclical majorities" occur. The paradox can occur in any situation where there are at least three players (voters or legislators) and at least three alternatives to choose from. In the following standard example, the preferences A, B, and C of players I, II, and III are:

I   A – B – C
II   B – C – A
III C – A – B

That is, player I's first preference is for A, second preference B, and third C; for player II, the first preference is B; second C; and so on. Given these preference orderings, there is no clear majority: the group of three players, by 2 to 1 margins, prefers A to B, B to C, but C to A. Voting in legislatures usually takes place between two alternatives at one time. If a paradox occurs, this means that there is no winning alternative if all three alternatives are voted on pairwise, or, more problematically, that one of the alternatives wins purely because only two pairwise votes take place – which is the usual parliamentary procedure. The simplest example of three such alternatives is a bill (alternative A), to which an amendment is offered (alternative B is the amended bill), and opposition to the bill with or without amendment (alternative C). Voting is limited to two choices: first between A and B, and then between the winner of either A or B on one hand and C on the other.[7]

What this example shows is, first, that there is a winner only because there is no pairwise vote between C and the loser of the A-B choice. Second, it shows that in the final vote the new entrant (alternative C) inevitably wins – that is, the bill, amended or not, is defeated. Conversely, only when a bill is defeated can a voting paradox possibly have occurred. Here we get to the relevance of this discussion for the parliamentary-presidential contrast. In parliamentary systems, amendments are frequently proposed to bills: in majoritarian democracies, these amendments are usually defeated, whereas in consensus democracies, they are often approved, but in *both* types of parliamentary systems, the bill in its final form is almost always adopted. The conclusion therefore is that voting paradoxes are most unlikely to occur in parliamentary systems – in contrast with presidential systems, where final approval of amended or unamended bills is much less likely.[8]

In the light of all these evident drawbacks of presidential government, it has been very surprising to me that in the discussions of a future constitution for a truly united and sovereign European Union, the proposal of a directly elected president is so frequently mentioned and advocated. This proposal, which in fact means the adoption of a presidential system and which I regard as most unwise, stimulated me to write a brief critique, which is reprinted here as Chapter 10. In this chapter, I summarize not only the inherent flaws of presidentialism, but also point out that presidentialism runs counter to the strong tradition of parliamentary government in most European countries. In addition, I point out their strong commitment to election by PR methods (the subject of the next set of chapters). In short, for a United Europe the combination of parliamentary government and PR is the wisest choice in terms of both its general merits and its conformity with European traditions.

Proportional versus majoritarian electoral systems

The consensus-majoritarian contrast has an even closer connection with the difference between proportional and majoritarian electoral systems than with the parliamentary-presidential difference just discussed. Proportional election results are one of the ten defining characteristics of consensus democracy. They are also an essential component of the general principle of proportionality, which is one of the four fundamental traits of consociational democracy. Quite a bit of my research and writing on electoral systems has been strongly quantitative in nature. Samples of these writings would have been too technical for this volume, and my selections therefore focus on my more accessible analyses of the effects of electoral systems. These do include part of the final chapter of my one thoroughly "technical" book, *Electoral Systems and Party Systems* (Lijphart 1994), but this excerpt summarizes the book's recommendations in non-technical language (Chapter 14).

Chapters 11 and 12 deal with the PR-plurality and parliamentary-presidential choices, which are the most important choices for constitution-makers. Because my empirical data are limited to the firmly established Western democracies and because I exclude a few democracies that do not unambiguously fit the four categories, only fourteen cases are available for analysis. Moreover, because there are no presidential-PR systems and only one presidential-plurality system (the United States), the comparison becomes mainly one of nine PR cases versus four plurality cases in thirteen parliamentary systems. The evidence of how the two types of systems work is similar to that in Chapter 6: effective policy-making (measured in terms of macroeconomic performance) and the quality of democracy. On all of the indicators, the performance of the parliamentary-PR cases is uniformly superior. I repeated the analysis eight years later with all thirty-six cases and the much more extensive data collected for *Patterns of Democracy*. Instead of consensus democracy, my independent variable was now the average degree of electoral proportionality in the thirty-six democracies. The results are very similar to my findings for the effect of consensus democracy – not all that surprising because proportionality is one of the five ingredients of which consensus democracy consists (on the executives-parties dimension). To the extent that differences appear, the effects of proportionality are even somewhat more impressive, and often more significant statistically, than the effects of consensus democracy (Lijphart 1999b).

The findings of my original analysis in Chapter 11 were reinforced even more by the critiques of it that were written by Guy Lardeyret and Quentin L. Quade, which alerted me to several issues that I should have dealt with in the first place. When I did examine their criticisms carefully, in the article reprinted here as Chapter 12, I found that double-checking my evidence made my original conclusions even stronger.[9] Overall, the evidence in favor of PR is impressively robust.

Chapter 13 discusses the alternative vote (AV), now more frequently called the instant-runoff vote (IRV), which is a more accurately descriptive term. It is a rarely used majoritarian electoral system, in which voters are asked to rank-order the candidates. The main example at the national level is its use for the election of the Australian House of Representatives (where it is known by still another term as the "majority-preferential method"). However, it has achieved prominence in the debate on how best to handle the problems of deeply divided countries, because Donald L. Horowitz, a well known expert on divided societies, has championed it as his favorite solution. In 1991, he published a book on South Africa in which he strongly recommended the adoption of AV. This happened at a delicate stage of the negotiations on the new constitution for a democratic South Africa. Because I disagreed strongly with Horowitz's AV proposal, and in fact regarded it as very dangerous for South Africa, I was moved to write a critique of AV as a suitable electoral system for divided societies in general, and South Africa in particular. Fortunately, the South Africans disregarded Horowitz's advice and adopted a highly proportional PR system for their first democratic elections in 1994.

My main disagreement with Horowitz is that AV is a majoritarian method and that I strongly prefer PR to any majoritarian election method in divided societies. In fact, my stance is that PR and consensus democracy work better for all countries, even for more homogeneous ones. Horowitz and I agree, however, when we look exclusively at majoritarian methods: plurality (often, especially in Britain and former British dependencies, also called "first past the post" or FPTP), majority-runoff, two-ballot majority-plurality, and AV.[10] In plurality systems, the candidate with the most votes wins regardless of whether his or her votes constitute a majority or not. In majority-runoff systems, an absolute majority of 50 percent plus one is required on the first ballot; if no candidate receives this majority, the top two candidates compete in a subsequent runoff election. Majority-plurality is a variant, used in France, where more than two candidates can compete on the second ballot and a plurality suffices to win. My overall assessment is that both AV and majority-runoff have the great advantage that winners are chosen by majorities instead of merely the largest minorities, and that AV is superior to majority-runoff for two reasons: it does not require two separate elections, which tend to depress turnout (see Chapter 15), and it is more accurate than majority-runoff because, when there are more than three candidates, it does not immediately eliminate candidates that are in third or lower places in the first round of counting when first preferences are counted (see the illustration in note 4 of Chapter 13). Therefore, if I were forced to choose among majoritarian methods, my choice would be AV as the least unattractive of these methods.

Chapter 14 presents the five major recommendations for electoral reform that I formulated on the basis of the findings of my twenty-seven-nation study *Electoral Systems and Party Systems* (1994). The first recommendation of two-tier districting in PR systems and the third recommendation of using national electoral thresholds were already briefly previewed in the discussion of the Danish model of elections in Chapter 5. The fourth recommendation involves a comparison of the single transferable vote (STV) and the single non-transferable vote (SNTV). STV is defined in the penultimate section of Chapter 13, and SNTV is simply STV without any vote transfers, that is, a hypothetical STV system where all voters express only first preferences and no second or lower preferences.[11] The term *apparentement* in the last recommendation is the technical name of what can also be called "connected lists," as I do in the penultimate section of Chapter 13. My second recommendation is probably the most unusual, because it seeks to improve majoritarian systems, of which I am not a proponent. However, if the choice is limited to majoritarian election systems, I am more than willing to suggest the "least bad" options: the alternative vote (AV), as stated earlier, and, in addition, two-tier districting (of which there are no empirical examples), which has the potential of alleviating some of the more serious deficiencies of majoritarian systems. A great deal of fine-tuning of election rules is common in PR systems, but quite rare in majoritarian systems, particularly in those that use plurality.

Voter turnout, democratic peace, and the comparative method

The last three chapters are also linked to this volume's theme of power sharing versus majority rule, but not as directly linked with each other. In Chapter 15 (my presidential address to the American Political Science Association in 1996), I argue that broad voter participation is crucial in democracies because, although the ideal of complete political equality is probably impossible to attain, high voter turnout reduces political *in*equality. Turnout levels are strongly influenced by election rules and practices. In particular, PR systems tend to have considerably higher levels of turnout than majoritarian systems. As Chapter 6 has shown, turnout is higher in consensus than in majoritarian democracies, mainly because of the proportionality of their electoral systems.

One rule has the greatest positive effect: mandatory voting. This rule is not a typical component of either consensus or majoritarian systems (measured along the executives-parties dimension); in fact, the best known examples of compulsory voting, combined with strict enforcement, are consensual Belgium and majoritarian Australia. Conceptually, however, mandatory voting has a close fit with the consensus ideal of inclusiveness and broad participation. If, in the future, more democracies will adopt it, my prediction is that these are more likely to be consensus than majoritarian countries. On the other hand, of course, majoritarian democracies with their lower voter turnouts actually have a greater need for mandatory voting. I should therefore add it to my set of recommendations for majoritarian electoral systems: AV, two-tier districting, and also compulsory voting! It is worth noting that the most prominent recent appeals for instituting mandatory voting have come from citizens of the majoritarian United Kingdom and United States. The British Institute for Public Policy Research published a policy paper entitled *A Citizen's Duty: Voter Inequality and the Case for Compulsory Turnout* in May 2006 (Keany and Rogers 2006). After encountering mandatory voting on a visit to Australia, Norman Ornstein (2006), resident scholar at the American Enterprise Institute, published an op-ed piece in the *New York Times* recommending it for the United States, entitled "Vote – or Else." Martin P. Wattenberg (2007, 6), a political scientist at the University of California, Irvine, studied the steadily decreasing turnout especially among young people; his book's main conclusion is that "only the institution of compulsory election attendance has proven to be a cure-all for the problem of unequal political participation."

The democratic peace proposition states that democracies are more peaceful than non-democracies, especially in their relations with each other. For several reasons, as Chapter 16 points out, it has been very difficult to test this proposition, and most tests have been indirect ones. This chapter, which I co-authored with Peter J. Bowman, offers another test of this kind, based on data from *Patterns of Democracy*. The usual explanation of the democratic peace is that it is produced by the compromise-oriented cultures and structures of democracies. A proposition that can be derived from it is that we can also expect consensus democracies with their especially strong inclination toward compromise to be more likely to pursue peaceful foreign policies – which we measure in terms of levels of foreign aid and military spending – than majoritarian democracies. It is this second proposition that we test and find to be valid. Indirectly, it provides additional support for the democratic peace proposition.

Based on this indirect test as well as my reading of the extensive literature on the democratic peace proposition, I am persuaded that the proposition is essentially correct. If it is indeed correct, the world will become more peaceful as more countries become democratic – especially, as suggested by our test, if these democratic countries adopt a consensus instead of a majoritarian form of democracy. The "kinder and gentler" nature of consensus democracy appears to be an advantage not only for its own citizens but also for the cause of world peace.

Chapter 17 on the comparative method was originally published in 1971 and is the second oldest article reprinted here. Like my "Consociational Democracy" (1969) article, it has achieved the status of something like a "classic" and is still frequently cited. It defines the comparative method by comparing and contrasting it with the statistical and case study methods, and, at the end of the chapter, offers a classification of six types of case studies. Because the statistical analysis of many cases is better able to establish controls than the comparative analysis of relatively few cases, the latter emerges as merely a "second best" solution. I developed second thoughts about this characterization, and I wrote a subsequent article in which I presented several distinct advantages of the comparative method (Lijphart 1975a). In particular, when one analyzes a relatively small number of cases, one can be more thorough and more attentive to details that are likely to be overlooked in statistical analysis: one can make sure that the data are as reliable as possible, that the indicators are valid, that the concepts are not stretched, and that the cases are really independent of each other. Moreover, when relatively few, but carefully selected, "comparable" cases are analyzed, it is more likely that these comparable cases will include subnational as well as national cases – in contrast with statistical analyses in comparative politics which almost always focus exclusively on national cases.

In my own research, however, I have tended to move from case studies (like my 1968 case study of the Netherlands in *The Politics of Accommodation*) to the comparative method (as in my 1969 "Consociational Democracy" and 1977 *Democracy in Plural Societies*), and finally mainly to the statistical method (in my 1984 *Democracies* and 1999 *Patterns of Democracy*). In *Patterns of Democracy*, I analyze as many as thirty-six cases – a large number, but still small enough to allow me to be sufficiently familiar with the details of each case. This number is also obviously more than large enough to permit statistical analysis. As useful as the comparative method may be in many situations, it can never offer the kind of strong and convincing evidence that statistical analysis provides – for instance, in Chapter 6, in favor of the desirable qualities of consensus democracy. In the conclusion, I shall return to the general question of the strength of the evidence that we have concerning power sharing.

Notes

1 See notes 15 and 24 in Chapter 2.
2 There are slight differences between the lists of majoritarian-consensus variables in the two books. The ten described here are from my 1999 *Patterns of Democracy*.
3 The thirty-six democracies are all of the countries (with populations of at least a quarter of a million) that were democratic in 1996 and that had been continuously democratic since 1977 or earlier: the three large Northwest European countries (the United Kingdom, Germany, and France); six smaller countries in the same area (Ireland, the Netherlands, Belgium, Luxembourg, Switzerland, and Austria); the five Nordic countries (Sweden, Norway, Denmark, Finland, and Iceland); five Southern European countries (Spain, Portugal, Italy, Greece, and Malta); nine countries in the Americas (the United States, Canada, Colombia, Venezuela, Costa Rica, Jamaica, Trinidad and Tobago, the Bahamas, and Barbados); six countries in Asia and the Pacific (India, Japan, Israel, Australia, New Zealand, and Papua New Guinea); and two African countries (Botswana and Mauritius).
4 As indicated in Chapter 6, the results with regard to the federal-unitary dimension were generally weak and inconclusive.
5 British prime ministers are often called "first among equals," but they are in fact examples of very powerful prime ministers. I have a brief discussion of the possibility of comparing prime ministerial powers, and I cite some preliminary results, in *Patterns of Democracy*, pp. 113–15.
6 I am indebted to Isaac Herzog for suggesting these differences among high courts.
7 This is the procedure that Bjørn Erik Rasch (2000) terms the "amendment" method, in contrast with the "successive" procedure, in which the alternatives are voted on sequentially (that is, one by one, instead of pairwise), until one of the alternatives receives a majority. With the latter method, B and C have equal chances of being the winner if a voting paradox occurs.

8 I presented this argument in a short article in the Dutch political science journal *Acta Politica* a long time ago (Lijphart 1975b), but, to my knowledge, it has not been cited or commented on in the English-language literature on the voting paradox.

9 For reasons of space, the articles by Lardeyret and Quade are not reproduced in this volume, but Chapter 12 reports their criticisms in detail.

10 All of these methods may be used in multi-member as well as single-member districts, but multi-member districts, which tend to aggravate the disproportionality of majoritarian methods, have become increasingly rare.

11 A more detailed explanation is as follows. In an SNTV system (as used in Japan until 1993), each voter casts one vote in a multi-member district, and the candidates receiving the most votes win. For instance, if in a three-member district, five candidates receive 30, 30, 25, 10, and 5 percent of the vote, the top three candidates are elected. SNTV offers good opportunities for minority representation – in the above example 25 percent of the voters elect one of the three representatives – but it can also lead to distorted outcomes; for instance, if five candidates receive 70, 10, 10, 5, and 5 percent of the vote in the same district, the top candidate wins with a lot of wasted votes, and two candidates win with very low vote totals.

References

Apter, David E. 1961. *The Political Kingdom in Uganda: A Study in Bureaucratic Nationalism*. Princeton NJ: Princeton University Press.

Horowitz, Donald L. 1991. *A Democratic South Africa? Constitutional Engineering in a Divided Society*. Berkeley CA: University of California Press.

Keaney, Emily, and Ben Rogers. 2006. *A Citizen's Duty: Voter Inequality and the Case for Compulsory Turnout*. London: Institute for Public Policy Research.

Lehmbruch, Gerhard. 1967. *Proporzdemokratie: Politisches System und politische Kultur in der Schweiz und in Österreich*. Tübingen: Mohr.

Lewis, W. Arthur. 1965. *Politics in West Africa*. London: Allen and Unwin.

Lijphart, Arend. 1968a. *The Politics of Accommodation: Pluralism and Democracy in the Netherlands*. Berkeley CA: University of California Press.

——1968b. "Typologies of Democratic Systems." *Comparative Political Studies* 1, 1 (April): 3–44.

——1975a. "The Comparable-Cases Strategy in Comparative Research." *Comparative Political Studies* 8, 2 (July): 158–77.

——1975b. "De paradox van Condorcet en de Nederlandse parlementaire praktijk." *Acta Politica* 10, 2 (April): 188–98.

——1977. *Democracy in Plural Societies: A Comparative Exploration*. New Haven CT: Yale University Press.

——1984. *Democracies: Patterns of Majoritarian and Consensus Government in Twenty-One Countries*. New Haven CT: Yale University Press.

——1994. *Electoral Systems and Party Systems: A Study of Twenty-Seven Democracies, 1945–1990*. Oxford: Oxford University Press.

——1999a. *Patterns of Democracy: Government Forms and Performance in Thirty-Six Countries*. New Haven CT: Yale University Press.

——1999b. "Australian Democracy: Modifying Majoritarianism?" *Australian Journal of Political Science* 34, 3 (November): 313–26.

Linz, Juan J. 1994. "Presidential or Parliamentary Democracy: Does It Make a Difference?" In Juan J. Linz and Arturo Valenzuela (eds) *The Failure of Presidential Democracy*, pp. 3–87. Baltimore MD: Johns Hopkins University Press.

Moosbrugger, Lorelei. 2001. *Institutions with Environmental Consequences: The Politics of Agrochemical Policy-Making.* Doctoral dissertation, University of California, San Diego.

Ornstein, Norman. 2006. "Vote – or Else." *New York Times,* 10 August.

Rasch, Bjørn Erik. 2000. "Parliamentary Floor Voting Procedures and Agenda Setting in Europe." *Legislative Studies Quarterly* 25, 1 (February): 3–23.

Wattenberg, Martin P. 2007. *Is Voting for Young People?* New York: Pearson Longman.

Part II

Consociational and consensus democracy

2 Consociational democracy

Types of Western democratic systems

In Gabriel A. Almond's famous typology of political systems, first expounded in 1956, he distinguishes three types of Western democratic systems: Anglo-American political systems (exemplified by Britain and the United States), Continental European political systems (France, Germany, and Italy), and a third category consisting of the Scandinavian and Low Countries. The third type is not given a distinct label and is not described in detail; Almond merely states that the countries belonging to this type "combine some of the features of the Continental European and the Anglo-American" political systems, and "stand somewhere in between the Continental pattern and the Anglo-American."[1] Almond's threefold typology has been highly influential in the comparative analysis of democratic politics, although, like any provocative and insightful idea, it has also been criticized. This research note will discuss the concept of "consociational democracy" in a constructive attempt to refine and elaborate Almond's typology of democracies.[2]

The typology derives its theoretical significance from the relationship it establishes between political culture and social structure on the one hand and political stability on the other hand. The Anglo-American systems have a "homogeneous, secular political culture" and a "highly differentiated" role structure, in which governmental agencies, parties, interest groups, and the communications media have specialized functions and are autonomous, although interdependent. In contrast, the Continental European democracies are characterized by a "fragmentation of political culture" with separate "political sub-cultures." Their roles "are embedded in the sub-cultures and tend to constitute separate sub-systems of rôles."[3] The terms "Anglo-American" and "Continental European" are used for convenience only and do not imply that geographical location is an additional criterion distinguishing the two types of democratic systems. This point deserves special emphasis, because some of Almond's critics have misinterpreted it. For instance, Arthur L. Kalleberg states that the two types "are based on criteria of geographic location and area," and that "Almond does not come out and specify that these *are* his criteria of classification; we have to infer them from the titles and descriptions he gives of each of his groups of states."[4] Actually, Almond does indicate clearly what his criteria are, and he also specifically rejects the criterion of geography or region as irrelevant, because it is not based "on the properties of the political systems."[5]

Political culture and social structure are empirically related to political stability. The Anglo-American democracies display a high degree of stability and effectiveness. The Continental European systems, on the other hand, tend to be unstable; they are characterized by political immobilism, which is "a consequence of the [fragmented] condition of the political culture." Furthermore, there is the "ever-present threat of what is often called the 'Caesaristic' breakthrough" and even the danger of a lapse into totalitarianism as a result of this immobilism.[6]

The theoretical basis of Almond's typology is the "overlapping memberships" proposition formulated by the group theorists Arthur F. Bentley and David B. Truman and the very similar "crosscutting cleavages" proposition of Seymour Martin Lipset. These propositions state that the psychological cross-pressures resulting from membership in different groups with diverse interests and outlooks lead to moderate attitudes. These groups may be formally organized groups or merely unorganized, categoric, and, in Truman's terminology, "potential" groups. Cross-pressures operate not only at the mass but also at the elite level: the leaders of social groups with heterogeneous and overlapping memberships will tend to find it necessary to adopt moderate positions. When, on the other hand, a society is divided by sharp cleavages with no or very few overlapping memberships and loyalties – in other words, when the political culture is deeply fragmented – the pressures toward moderate middle-of-the-road attitudes are absent. Political stability depends on moderation and, therefore, also on overlapping memberships. Truman states this proposition as follows: "In the long run a complex society may experience revolution, degeneration, and decay. If it maintains its stability, however, it may do so in large measure because of the fact of multiple memberships."[7] Bentley calls compromise "the very process itself of the criss-cross groups in action."[8] And Lipset argues that "the chances for stable democracy are enhanced to the extent that groups and individuals have a number of crosscutting, politically relevant affiliations."[9] Sometimes Almond himself explicitly adopts the terminology of these propositions: for instance, he describes the French Fourth Republic as being divided into "three main ideological families or subcultures," which means that the people of France were "exposed to few of the kinds of 'cross-pressures' that moderate [their] rigid political attitudes," while, on the other hand, he characterizes the United States and Britain as having an "overlapping pattern" of membership.[10]

In his later writings, Almond maintains both the threefold typology of Western democracies and the criteria on which it is based, although the terms that he uses vary considerably. In an article published in 1963, for instance, he distinguishes between "stable democracies" and "immobilist democracies." The latter are characterized by "fragmentation, both in a cultural and structural sense" and by the absence of "consensus on governmental structure and process" (i.e. the Continental European systems). The former group is divided into two sub-classes: one includes Great Britain, the United States, and the Old Commonwealth democracies (i.e. the Anglo-American systems), and the other "the stable multi-party democracies of the European continent – the Scandinavian and Low Countries and Switzerland."[11] And in *Comparative Politics: A Developmental Approach*, published in 1966, a distinction is drawn between modern democratic systems with "high subsystem autonomy" (the Anglo-American democracies) and those with "limited subsystem autonomy" and fragmentation of political culture (the Continental European democracies). The third type is not included in this classification.[12]

In what respects are Switzerland, Scandinavia, and the Low Countries "in between" the Anglo-American and Continental European democracies? Here, too, Almond consistently uses the two criteria of role structure and political culture. A differentiated role structure (or a high degree of subsystem autonomy) is related to the performance of the political aggregation function in a society. The best aggregators are parties in two-party systems like the Anglo-American democracies, but the larger the number and the smaller the size of the parties in a system, the less effectively the aggregation function will be performed; in the Continental European multiparty systems only a minimum of aggregation takes place. The "working multiparty systems" of the Scandinavian and Low Countries differ from the French-Italian "crisis" systems in that some, though not all, of their parties are "broadly aggregative." Almond gives the Scandinavian socialist parties and the Belgian Catholic and socialist parties as examples.[13] This criterion does not distinguish adequately between the two types of democracies, however: if one calls the Belgian Catholic party broadly aggregative, the Italian Christian Democrats surely also have to be regarded as such. On the other hand, none of the Dutch and Swiss parties can be called broadly aggregative.

Instead of using the extent of aggregation performed by political parties as the operational indicator of the degree of subsystem autonomy, it is more satisfactory to examine the system's role structure directly. Like the Anglo-American countries, the Scandinavian states have a high degree of subsystem autonomy. But one finds a severely limited subsystem autonomy and considerable interpenetration of parties, interest groups, and the media of communication in the Low Countries, Switzerland, and also in Austria. In fact, subsystem autonomy is at least as limited in these countries as in the Continental European systems. According to the criterion of role structure, therefore, one arrives at a dichotomous rather than a threefold typology: the Scandinavian states must be grouped with the Anglo-American systems, and the other "in-between" states with the Continental European systems.

The application of the second criterion – political culture – leads to a similar result. Almond writes that the political culture in the Scandinavian and Low Countries is "more homogeneous and fusional of secular and traditional elements" than that in the Continental European systems.[14] This is clearly true for the Scandinavian countries, which are, in fact, quite homogeneous and do not differ significantly from the homogeneous Anglo-American systems. But again, the other "in-between" countries are at least as fragmented into political subcultures – the *familles spirituelles* of Belgium and Luxembourg, the *zuilen* of the Netherlands, and the *Lager* of Austria – as the Continental European states. Therefore, on the basis of the two criteria of political culture and role structure, the Western democracies can be satisfactorily classified into two broad but clearly bounded categories: (1) the Anglo-American, Old Commonwealth, and Scandinavian states; (2) the other European democracies, including France, Italy, Weimar Germany, the Low Countries, Austria, and Switzerland.

Fragmented but stable democracies

The second category of the above twofold typology is too broad, however, because it includes both highly stable systems (e.g. Switzerland and Holland) and highly unstable ones (e.g. Weimar Germany and the French Third and Fourth Republics). The political stability of a system can apparently not be predicted solely on the basis of the two variables of political culture and role structure. According to the theory of crosscutting cleavages, one would expect the Low Countries, Switzerland, and Austria, with subcultures divided from each other by mutually reinforcing cleavages, to exhibit great immobilism and instability. But they do not. These deviant cases of fragmented but stable democracies will be called "consociational democracies."[15] In general, deviant case analysis can lead to the discovery of additional relevant variables, and in this particular instance, a third variable can account for the stability of the consociational democracies: the behavior of the political elites. The leaders of the rival subcultures may engage in competitive behavior and thus further aggravate mutual tensions and political instability, but they may also make *deliberate efforts to counteract the immobilizing and unstabilizing effects of cultural fragmentation*. As a result of such overarching cooperation at the elite level, a country can, as Claude Ake states, "achieve a degree of political stability quite out of proportion to its social homogeneity."[16]

The clearest examples are the experiences of democratic Austria after the First World War and of pre-democratic Belgium in the early nineteenth century. The fragmented and unstable Austrian First Republic of the interwar years was transformed into the still fragmented but stable Second Republic after the Second World War by means of a consociational solution. As Frederick C. Engelmann states, "the central sociopolitical fact in the life of post-1918 Austria [was that] the Republic had developed under conditions of cleavage so deep as to leave it with a high potential for – and a sporadic actuality of – civil war." The instability caused by the deep cleavage and antagonism between the Catholic and socialist *Lager* (subcultures) spelled the end of democracy and the establishment of a dictatorship. The leaders of the rival subcultures were anxious not to repeat the sorry experience of the First Republic, and decided to join in a grand coalition after the Second World War. According to Engelmann, "critics and objective observers agree with Austria's leading politicians in the assessment that the coalition was a response to the civil-war tension of the First Republic."[17] Otto Kirchheimer also attributes the consociational pattern of Austria's post-1945 politics (until early 1966) to "the republic's historical record of political frustration and abiding suspicion."[18] Val R. Lorwin describes how the potential instability caused by subcultural cleavage was deliberately avoided at the time of the birth of independent Belgium: the Catholic and Liberal leaders had learned

> the great lesson of mutual tolerance from the catastrophic experience of the Brabant Revolution of 1789, when the civil strife of their predecessors had so soon laid the country open to easy Habsburg reconquest. It was a remarkable and *self-conscious "union of the oppositions"* that made the revolution of 1830, wrote the Constitution of 1831, and headed the government in its critical years.[19]

The grand coalition cabinet is the most typical and obvious, but not the only possible, consociational solution for a fragmented system. The essential characteristic of consociational democracy is not so much any particular institutional arrangement as the deliberate joint effort by the elites to stabilize the system. Instead of the term "grand coalition" with its rather narrow connotation, one could speak of universal participation, or as Ralf Dahrendorf does, of a "cartel of elites."[20] A grand coalition cabinet as in Austria represents the most comprehensive form of the cartel of elites, but one finds a variety of other devices in the other Western consociational democracies and, outside Western Europe, in the consociational politics of Lebanon, Uruguay (until early 1967), and Colombia. Even in Austria, not the cabinet itself but the small extra-constitutional "coalition committee," on which the top socialist and Catholic leaders were equally represented, made the crucial decisions. In the Swiss system of government, which is a hybrid of the presidential and the parliamentary patterns, all four major parties are represented on the multi-member executive. In Uruguay's (now defunct) governmental system, fashioned after the Swiss model, there was *coparticipación* of the two parties on the executive.

In the Colombian and Lebanese presidential systems, such a sharing of the top executive post is not possible because the presidency is held by one person. The alternative solution provided by the Lebanese National Pact of 1943 is that the President of the Republic must be a Maronite and the President of the Council a Sunni, thus guaranteeing representation to the country's two major religious groups. In Colombia, the Liberal and Conservative parties agreed in 1958 to join in a consociational arrangement in order to deliver the country from its recurrent civil wars and dictatorships. The agreement stipulated that the presidency would be alternated for four-year terms between the two parties and that there would be equal representation (*paridad*) on all lower levels of government. In the Low Countries, the cabinets are usually broadly based coalitions, but not all major subcultures are permanently represented. The typical consociational devices in these democracies are the advisory councils and committees, which, in spite of their very limited formal powers, often have decisive influence. These councils and committees may be permanent organs, such as the powerful Social and Economic Council of the Netherlands – a perfect example of a cartel of economic elites – or *ad hoc* bodies, such as the cartels of top party leaders that negotiated the "school pacts" in Holland in 1917 and in Belgium in 1958.

The desire to avoid political competition may be so strong that the cartel of elites may decide to extend the consociational principle to the electoral level in order to prevent the passions aroused by elections from upsetting the carefully constructed, and possibly fragile, system of cooperation. This may apply to a single election or to a number of successive elections. The *paridad* and *alternación* principles in Colombia entail a controlled democracy for a period of sixteen years, during which the efficacy of the right to vote is severely restricted. Another example is the Dutch parliamentary election of 1917, in which all of the parties agreed not to contest the seats held by incumbents in order to safeguard the passage of a set of crucial constitutional amendments; these amendments, negotiated by cartels of top party leaders, contained the terms of the settlement of the sensitive issues of universal suffrage and state aid to church schools. A parallel agreement on the suffrage was adopted in Belgium in 1919 without holding the constitutionally prescribed election at all.

Consociational democracy violates the principle of majority rule, but it does not deviate very much from normative democratic theory. Most democratic constitutions prescribe majority rule for the normal transaction of business when the stakes are not too high, but extraordinary majorities or several successive majorities for the most important decisions, such as changes in the constitution. In fragmented systems, many other decisions in addition to constituent ones are perceived as involving high stakes, and therefore require more than simple majority rule. Similarly, majority rule does not suffice in times of grave crisis in even the most homogeneous and consensual of democracies. Great Britain and Sweden, both highly homogeneous countries, resorted to grand coalition cabinets during the Second World War. Julius Nyerere draws the correct lesson from the experience of the Western democracies, in which, he observes, "it is an accepted practice in times of emergency for opposition parties to sink their differences and join together in forming a national government."[21] And just as the formation of a national unity government is the appropriate response to an external emergency, so the formation of a grand coalition cabinet or an

alternative form of elite cartel is the appropriate
crisis of fragmentation into hostile subcultures.

Furthermore, the concept of consociationa¹
ment with the empirical "size principle," foῐ
This principle, based on game-theoretic assu.
situations similar to *n*-person, zero-sum games wiι.
agreements about the division of the payoff], particip.
just as large as they believe will ensure winning and no
dency will be toward a "minimum winning coalition," which ι.
will be a coalition with bare majority support – but only undeι
tions specified in the size principle. The most important conditio.
zero-sum assumption: "only the direct conflicts among participants
included and common advantages are ignored."[22] Common advantages wι.
be completely ignored only in two diametrically opposite kinds of situations: (1) when the participants in the "game" do not perceive any common
advantages, and when, consequently, they are likely to engage in unlimited
warfare; and (2) when they are in such firm agreement on their common
advantages that they can take them for granted. In the latter case, politics
literally becomes a game. In other words, the zero-sum condition and the
size principle apply only to societies with completely homogeneous political
cultures and to societies with completely fragmented cultures. To the extent
that political cultures deviate from these two extreme conditions, pressures
will exist to fashion coalitions and other forms of cooperation that are more
inclusive than the bare "minimum winning coalition" and that may be all-
inclusive grand coalitions.

Almond aptly uses the metaphor of the game in characterizing the Anglo-
American systems:

> Because the political culture tends to be homogeneous and pragmatic,
> [the political process] takes on some of the atmosphere of a game. A
> game is a good game when the outcome is in doubt and when the stakes
> are not too high. When the stakes are too high, the tone changes from
> excitement to anxiety.[23]

Political contests in severely fragmented societies are indeed not likely to be
"good games." But the anxieties and hostilities attending the political process may be countered by removing its competitive features as much as
possible. In consociational democracies, politics is treated not as a game but
as a serious business.

Factors conducive to consociational democracy

Consociational democracy means government by elite cartel designed to
turn a democracy with a fragmented political culture into a stable democracy. Efforts at consociationalism are not necessarily successful, of course:

tional designs failed in Cyprus and Nigeria, and Uruguay aban-
its Swiss-style consociational system. Successful consociational
racy requires: (1) That the elites have the ability to accommodate the
gent interests and demands of the subcultures. (2) This requires that
y have the ability to transcend cleavages and to join in a common effort
th the elites of rival subcultures. (3) This in turn depends on their com-
mitment to the maintenance of the system and to the improvement of its
cohesion and stability. (4) Finally, all of the above requirements are based
on the assumption that the elites understand the perils of political fragmentation. These four requirements are logically implied by the concept of
consociational democracy as defined in this paper. Under what conditions
are they likely to be fulfilled? An examination of the successful consociational democracies in the Low Countries, Switzerland, Austria, and Lebanon suggests a number of conditions favorable to the establishment and the
persistence of this type of democracy. These have to do with inter-subcultural relations at the elite level, inter-subcultural relations at the mass
level, and elite-mass relations within each of the subcultures.

Relations among the elites of the subcultures

It is easier to assess the probability of continued success of an already
established consociational democracy than to predict the chance of success
that a fragmented system would have if it were to attempt consociationalism. In an existing consociational democracy, an investigation of
the institutional arrangements and the operational code of inter-elite
accommodation can throw light on the question of how thorough a commitment to cooperation they represent and how effective they have been in
solving the problems caused by fragmentation. *The length of time a consociational democracy has been in operation* is also a factor of importance.
As inter-elite cooperation becomes habitual and does not represent a deliberate departure from competitive responses to political challenges, consociational norms become more firmly established. And, as Gerhard
Lehmbruch states, these norms may become an important part of "the
political socialization of elites and thus acquire a strong degree of persistence through time."[24]

There are three factors that appear to be strongly conducive to the
establishment or maintenance of cooperation among elites in a fragmented
system. The most striking of these is the existence of *external threats* to the
country. In all of the consociational democracies, the cartel of elites was
either initiated or greatly strengthened during periods of international crisis,
especially the First and Second World Wars. During the First World War,
the comprehensive settlement of the conflict among Holland's political
subcultures firmly established the pattern of consociational democracy.
"Unionism" – i.e. Catholic-Liberal grand coalitions – began during Belgium's struggle for independence in the early nineteenth century, but lapsed

when the country appeared to be out of danger. As a result of the First World War, unionism was resumed and the socialist leaders were soon admitted to the governing cartel. The Second World War marked the beginning of consociational democracy in Lebanon: the National Pact – the Islamo-Christian accord that provided the basis for consociational government for the country – was concluded in 1943. In Switzerland, consociational democracy developed more gradually, but reached its culmination with the admission of the socialists to the grand coalition of the Federal Council, also in 1943. The Austrian grand coalition was formed soon after the Second World War, when the country was occupied by the Allied forces. In all cases, the external threats impressed on the elites the need for internal unity and cooperation. External threats can also strengthen the ties among the subcultures at the mass level and the ties between leaders and followers within the subcultures.

A second factor favorable to consociational democracy, in the sense that it helps the elites to recognize the necessity of cooperation, is a *multiple balance of power among the subcultures* instead of either a dual balance of power or a clear hegemony by one subculture. When one group is in the majority, its leaders may attempt to dominate rather than cooperate with the rival minority. Similarly, in a society with two evenly matched subcultures, the leaders of both may hope to achieve their aims by domination rather than cooperation, if they expect to win a majority at the polls. Robert Dahl argues that for this reason it is doubtful that the consociational arrangement in Colombia will last, because "the temptation to shift from coalition to competition is bound to be very great."[25] When political parties in a fragmented society are the organized manifestations of political subcultures, a multiparty system is more conducive to consociational democracy and therefore to stability than a two-party system. This proposition is at odds with the generally high esteem accorded to two-party systems. In an already homogeneous system, two-party systems may be more effective, but a moderate multiparty system, in which no party is close to a majority, appears preferable in a consociational democracy. The Netherlands, Switzerland, and Lebanon have the advantage that their subcultures are all minority groups. In the Austrian two-party system, consociational politics did work, but with considerable strain. Lehmbruch states: "Austrian political parties are strongly integrated social communities ... and the bipolar structure of the coalition reinforced their antagonisms."[26] The internal balance of power in Belgium has complicated the country's consociational politics in two ways. The Catholic, socialist, and Liberal subcultures are minorities, but the Catholics are close to majority status. The Catholic party actually won a legislative majority in 1950, and attempted to settle the sensitive royal question by majority rule. This led to a short civil war, followed by a return to consociational government. Moreover, the Belgian situation is complicated as a result of the linguistic cleavage, which cuts across the three spiritual families. The linguistic balance of power is a dual balance in which the Walloons fear the numerical majority of the Flemings, while the Flemings resent the economic and social superiority of the Walloons.

Consociational democracy presupposes not only a willingness on the part of elites to cooperate but also a capability to solve the political problems of their countries. Fragmented societies have a tendency to immobilism, which consociational politics is designed to avoid. Nevertheless, decision-making that entails accommodation among all subcultures is a difficult process, and consociational democracies are always threatened by a degree of immobilism. Consequently, a third favorable factor to inter-elite cooperation is a *relatively low total load on the decision-making apparatus*. The stability of Lebanon is partly due to its productive economy and the social equilibrium it has maintained so far, but it may not be able to continue its successful consociational politics when the burdens on the system increase. Michael C. Hudson argues that the Lebanese political system is "attuned to incessant adjustment among primordial groups rather than policy planning and execution." As a result, its "apparent stability ... is deceptively precarious: social mobilization appears to be overloading the circuits of the Lebanese political system."[27] In general, the size factor is important in this respect: the political burdens that large states have to shoulder tend to be disproportionately heavier than those of small countries. Ernest S. Griffith argues that "democracy is more likely to survive, other things being equal, in small states. Such states are more manageable."[28] In particular, small states are more likely to escape the onerous burdens entailed by an active foreign policy. Lehmbruch states that the Swiss, Austrian, and Lebanese cases "show that the preservation of the inner equilibrium presupposes a reduction of external demands to the political system." And he even goes so far as to conclude that the type of politics found in these three countries "seems to work in small states only."[29]

Inter-subcultural relations at the mass level

The political cultures of the countries belonging to Almond's Continental European type and to the consociational type are all fragmented, but the consociational countries have even clearer boundaries among their subcultures. Such *distinct lines of cleavage* appear to be conducive to consociational democracy and political stability. The explanation is that subcultures with widely divergent outlooks and interests may coexist without necessarily being in conflict; conflict arises only when they are in contact with each other. As Quincy Wright states: "Ideologies accepted by different groups within a society may be inconsistent without creating tension; but if ... the groups with inconsistent ideologies are in close contact ... the tension will be great."[30] David Easton also endorses the thesis that good social fences may make good political neighbors, when he suggests a kind of voluntary *apartheid* policy as the best solution for a divided society: "Greater success may be attained through steps that conduce to the development of a deeper sense of mutual awareness and responsiveness among *encapsulated cultural units.*" This is "the major hope of avoiding stress."[31] And Sidney Verba follows the same line of reasoning when he argues that political and economic modernization in Africa is bringing "differing subcultures into contact with each other and *hence* into conflict."[32]

This argument appears to be a direct refutation of the overlapping-memberships proposition, but by adding two amendments to this proposition the discrepancy can be resolved. In the first place, the basic explanatory element in the concept of consociational democracy is that political elites may take joint actions to counter the effects of cultural fragmentation. This means that the overlapping-memberships propositions may become a self-denying hypothesis under certain conditions. Second, the view that any severe discontinuity in overlapping patterns of membership and allegiance is a danger to political stability needs to be restated in more refined form. A distinction has to be made between essentially homogeneous political cultures, where increased contacts are likely to lead to an increase in mutual understanding and further homogenization, and essentially heterogeneous cultures, where close contacts are likely to lead to strain and hostility. This is the distinction that Walker Connor makes when he argues that "increased contacts help to dissolve regional cultural distinctions within a state such as the United States. Yet, if one is dealing not with minor variations of the same culture, but with two quite distinct and self-differentiating cultures, are not increased contacts between the two apt to increase antagonisms?"[33] This proposition can be refined further by stating both the degree of homogeneity and the extent of mutual contacts in terms of continua rather than dichotomies. In order to safeguard political stability, the volume and intensity of contacts must not exceed the commensurate degree of homogeneity. Karl W. Deutsch states that stability depends on a "balance between transaction and integration" because "the number of opportunities for possible violent conflict will increase with the volume and range of mutual transactions."[34] Hence, it may be desirable to keep transactions among antagonistic subcultures in a divided society – or, similarly, among different nationalities in a multinational state – to a minimum.

Elite–mass relations within the subcultures

Distinct lines of cleavage among the subcultures are also conducive to consociational democracy because they are likely to be concomitant with a high degree of *internal political cohesion of the subcultures.* This is vital to the success of consociational democracy. The elites have to cooperate and compromise with each other without losing the allegiance and support of their own rank and file. When the subcultures are cohesive political blocs, such support is more likely to be forthcoming. As Hans Daalder states, what is important is not only "the extent to which party leaders are more tolerant than their followers" but also the extent to which they "are yet able to carry them along."[35]

A second way in which distinct cleavages have a favorable effect on elite-mass relations in a consociational democracy is that they make it more likely that the parties and interest groups will be the organized representatives of the political subcultures. If this is the case, the political parties may not be the best aggregators, but there is at least an *adequate articulation of the interests of the subcultures*. Aggregation of the clearly articulated interests can then be performed by the cartel of elites. In Belgium, the three principal parties represent the Catholic, Socialist, and Liberal spiritual families, but the linguistic cleavage does not coincide with the cleavages dividing the spiritual families, and all three parties have both Flemings and Walloons among their followers. Lorwin describes the situation as follows: "The sentimental and practical interests of the two linguistic communities are not effectively organized, and the geographical regions have no administrative or formal political existence. There are no recognized representatives qualified to formulate demands, to negotiate, and to fulfill commitments."[36] The religious and class issues have been effectively articulated by the political parties and have by and large been resolved, but the linguistic issue has not been clearly articulated and remains intractable. In Switzerland, the parties also represent the religious-ideological groups rather than the linguistic communities, but much of the country's decentralized political life takes place at the cantonal level, and most of the cantons are linguistically homogeneous.

A final factor which favors consociational democracy is *widespread approval of the principle of government by elite cartel*. This is a very obvious factor, but it is of considerable importance and deserves to be mentioned briefly. For example, Switzerland has a long and strong tradition of grand coalition executives, and this has immeasurably strengthened Swiss consociational democracy. On the other hand, the grand coalition in Austria was under constant attack by critics who alleged that the absence of a British-style opposition made Austrian politics "undemocratic." This attests to the strength of the British system as a normative model even in fragmented political systems, where the model is inappropriate and undermines the attempt to achieve political stability by consociational means.

Centripetal and centrifugal democracies

An examination of the other two types of the threefold typology of democracies in the light of the distinguishing characteristics of consociational democracy can contribute to the clarification and refinement of all three types and their prerequisites. In order to avoid any unintended geographical connotation, we shall refer to the homogeneous and stable democracies as the centri*petal* (instead of the Anglo-American) democracies, and to the fragmented and unstable ones as the centri*fugal* (instead of the Continental European) democracies. The centrifugal democracies include the French Third and Fourth Republics, Italy, Weimar Germany, the Austrian First Republic, and the short-lived Spanish Republic of the early 1930s. The major examples of centripetal democracy are Great Britain, the Old Commonwealth countries, the United States, Ireland, the Scandinavian states, and the postwar Bonn Republic in Germany.

The French Fourth Republic is often regarded as the outstanding example of unstable, ineffective, and immobilist democracy, but the explanation of its political instability in terms of cultural fragmentation has been criticized on two grounds. In the first place, Eric A. Nordlinger rejects the argument that the "ideological inundation of French politics" and its "fragmented party system" were responsible for its chronic instability; he states that this explanation conveniently overlooks

> the way in which the game of politics is actually played in France. Although ideologism pervades the parties' electoral and propaganda efforts, this public ideological posturing of French politicians does not prevent them from playing out their game of compromise in the Assembly and its *couloirs*. In fact, the political class thinks of compromise as a positive principle of action, with parliamentary activity largely revolving around nonideological squabbles.[37]

The elites of the center parties that supported the Republic fulfilled to some extent all of the logical prerequisites for consociational democracy except the most important one: they lacked the ability to forge effective and lasting solutions to pressing political problems. They indeed played a nonideological game, but, as Nathan Leites observes, with a "well-developed capacity for avoiding their responsibility."[38] In other words, they were nonideological, but not constructively pragmatic. To turn a centrifugal into a consociational democracy, true statesmanship is required. Moreover, it is incorrect to assume that, because the elites were not divided by irreconcilable ideological differences, mass politics was not ideologically fragmented either.[39]

The second criticism of the cultural fragmentation thesis alleges, on the basis of independent evidence, that not only at the elite level but also at the mass level, ideology played a negligible role in France. Philip E. Converse and Georges Dupeux demonstrate that the French electorate was not highly politicized and felt little allegiance to the political parties.[40] But the lack of stable partisan attachments does not necessarily indicate that the political culture was not fragmented. Duncan MacRae argues persuasively that political divisions did extend to the electorate as a whole in spite of the apparent "lack of involvement of the average voter." Even though political allegiances were diffuse, there were "relatively fixed and non-overlapping *social* groupings" to which "separate leaders and separate media of communication had access."[41] The combination of fragmentation into subcultures and low politicization can in turn be explained by the negative

French attitude toward authority. Stanley Hoffmann speaks of "potential insurrection against authority," and Michel Crozier observes that this attitude makes it "impossible for an individual of the group to become its leader."[42]

Strong cohesion within the subcultures was mentioned earlier as a factor conducive to consociational democracy; the lack of it in France can explain both that the French people were fragmented but at the same time not politically involved, and that the political elites did not have the advantage of strong support from the rank and file for constructive cooperation.

On the other hand, the example of France also serves to make clear that the lack of problem-solving ability as a cause of political instability must not be overstated. After all, as Maurice Duverger points out, in spite of all of the Fourth Republic's flaws and weaknesses, it "would have continued to exist if it had not been for the Algerian war."[43] The critical factor was the too-heavy burden of an essentially external problem on the political system. Similarly, the fragmented Weimar Republic might have survived, too, if it had not been for the unusually difficult problems it was faced with.

Germany's experience with democracy also appears to throw some doubt on our threefold typology and the theory on which it is based. Weimar Germany was a centrifugal democracy but the Bonn Republic can be grouped with the centripetal democracies. In explaining this extraordinary shift, we have to keep in mind that cultural fragmentation must be measured on a continuum rather than as a dichotomy, as we have done so far. The degree of homogeneity of a political culture can change, although great changes at a rapid pace can normally not be expected. Three reasons can plausibly account for the change from the fragmented political culture of the unstable Weimar Republic to the much more homogeneous culture of the Bonn Republic: (1) the traumatic experiences of totalitarianism, war, defeat, and occupation; (2) "conscious manipulative change of fundamental political attitudes," which, as Verba states, added up to a "remaking of political culture";[44] (3) the loss of the eastern territories, which meant that, as Lipset argues, "the greater homogeneity of western Germany now became a national homogeneity."[45]

The degree of competitive or cooperative behavior by elites must also be seen as a continuum. Among the consociational democracies, some are more consociational than others; and many centripetal democracies have some consociational features. The phenomenon of war-time grand coalition cabinets has already been mentioned. The temporary Christian Democratic-socialist grand coalition under Chancellor Kiesinger falls in the same category. In fact, the stability of the centripetal democracies depends not only on their essentially homogeneous political cultures but also on consociational devices, to the extent that a certain degree of heterogeneity exists. The alternation of English-speaking and French-speaking leaders of the Liberal party in Canada may be compared with the Colombian device of *alternación*. In the United States, where, as Dahl states, "the South has for nearly two centuries formed a distinctive regional subculture,"[46] cultural fragmentation led to secession and civil war. After the Civil War, a consociational arrangement developed that gave to the South a high degree of autonomy and to the Southern leaders – by such means as chairmanships of key Congressional committees and the filibuster – a crucial position in federal decision-making. This example also shows that, while consociational solutions may increase political cohesion, they also have a definite tendency to lead to a certain degree of immobilism.

Even in Denmark, which is among the most homogeneous of the centripetal democracies, one finds considerable consociationalism. This does not appear in grand coalition cabinets – in fact, Denmark is known for its long periods of government by minority cabinets – but in the far-reaching search for compromise in the legislature. The rule of the game prescribes that the top leaders of all four major parties do their utmost to reach a consensus. This is *glidningspolitik,* which Gerald R. McDaniel translates as the "politics of smoothness"[47] – an apt characterization of consociational politics.

Notes

1 Gabriel A. Almond, "Comparative Political Systems," *Journal of Politics*, XVIII (August 1956), 392–93, 405.
2 This note represents an intermediate stage of a research project concerning political stability in democratic systems. An earlier and briefer discussion of the concept of consociational democracy, in the context of a critical analysis of the utility of typologies in comparative politics, appeared in the author's "Typologies of Democratic Systems," *Comparative Political Studies*, I (April 1968), 3–44. The author is indebted to the Institute of International Studies, Berkeley, for financial support.
3 Almond, 398–99, 405–7 (italics omitted).
4 Kalleberg, "The Logic of Comparison: A Methodological Note on the Comparative Study of Political Systems," *World Politics*, XIX (October 1966), 73–74. Hans Daalder's critical question "Why should France, Germany, and Italy be more 'continental,' than Holland, or Switzerland, or more 'European' than Britain?" seems to be based on a similar erroneous interpretation; see his "Parties, Elites, and Political Developments in Western Europe," in Joseph LaPalombara and Myron Weiner, eds, *Political Parties and Political Development* (Princeton NJ 1966), 43n.
5 Almond, 392. There is also no reason, therefore, to call the exclusion of Scandinavia and the Low Countries from the "Continental European" systems an "artificial qualifier," as Kalleberg does, 74.
6 Almond, 408.
7 David B. Truman, *The Governmental Process: Political Interests and Public Opinion* (New York 1951), 508, 511.
8 Arthur F. Bentley, *The Process of Government: A Study of Social Pressures*, 4th edn (Evanston IL 1955), 208.
9 Seymour Martin Lipset, *Political Man: The Social Bases of Politics* (Garden City NY 1960), 88–89.
10 Almond and G. Bingham Powell, Jr., *Comparative Politics: A Developmental Approach* (Boston MA 1966), 122, 263; Almond and Sidney Verba, *The Civic Culture: Political Attitudes and Democracy in Five Nations* (Princeton NJ 1963), 134.

11 "Political Systems and Political Change," *American Behavioral Scientist*, VI (June 1963), 9–10.
12 Almond and Powell, 259 (italics omitted).
13 Almond, rapporteur, "A Comparative Study of Interest Groups and the Political Process," *American Political Science Review*, LII (March 1958), 275–77; Almond, "A Functional Approach to Comparative Politics," in Almond and James S. Coleman, eds, *The Politics of the Developing Areas* (Princeton NJ 1960), 42–43. See also Göran G. Lindahl, "Gabriel A. Almond's funktionella kategorier: En kritik," *Statsvetenskaplig Tidskrift*, no. 4 (1967), 263–72; and Constance E. van der Maesen and G. H. Scholten, "De functionele benadering van G. A. Almond bij het vergelijken van politieke stelsels," *Acta Politica*, I (1965–66), 220–26.
14 "A Functional Approach," 42.
15 Cf. Johannes Althusius' concept of *consociatio* in his *Politica Methodice Digesta*, and the term "consociational" used by David E. Apter, *The Political Kingdom in Uganda: A Study in Bureaucratic Nationalism* (Princeton NJ 1961), 24–25.
16 Claude Ake, *A Theory of Political Integration* (Homewood IL 1967), 113. This possibility exists not only in the fragmented democracies, but also in fragmented predemocratic or nondemocratic systems, of course. See also Arend Lijphart, *The Politics of Accommodation: Pluralism and Democracy in the Netherlands* (Berkeley CA 1968), 1–15, 197–211.
17 Frederick C. Engelmann, "Haggling for the Equilibrium: The Renegotiation of the Austrian Coalition, 1959," *American Political Science Review*, LVI (September 1962), 651–52.
18 Kirchheimer, "The Waning of Opposition in Parliamentary Regimes," *Social Research*, XXIV (summer 1957), 137.
19 Lorwin, "Constitutionalism and Controlled Violence in the Modern State: The Case of Belgium" (paper presented at the annual meeting of the American Historical Association, San Francisco, 1965), 4 (italics added). For a description of the establishment of consociational democracy in the Netherlands, see Lijphart, *The Politics of Accommodation*, 103–12.
20 Dahrendorf, *Society and Democracy in Germany* (Garden City NY 1967), 276.
21 Nyerere, "One-Party Rule," in Paul E. Sigmund, Jr., ed., *The Ideologies of the Developing Nations* (New York 1963), 199.
22 William H. Riker, *The Theory of Political Coalitions* (New Haven CT 1962), 29, 32–33.
23 Almond, "Comparative Political Systems," 398–99.
24 Lehmbruch, "A Non-Competitive Pattern of Conflict Management in Liberal Democracies: The Case of Switzerland, Austria and Lebanon" (paper presented at the Seventh World Congress of the International Political Science Association, Brussels, 1967), 6. See also Lehmbruch, *Proporzdemokratie: Politisches System und politische Kultur in der Schweiz und in Österreich* (Tübingen 1967).
25 Dahl, *Political Oppositions in Western Democracies* (New Haven CT 1966), 337.
26 Lehmbruch, 8.
27 Hudson, "A Case of Political Underdevelopment," *Journal of Politics*, XXIX (November 1967), 836.
28 Griffith, "Cultural Prerequisites to a Successfully Functioning Democracy," *American Political Science Review*, L (March 1956), 102.
29 Lehmbruch, 9.
30 Wright, "The Nature of Conflict," *Western Political Quarterly*, IV (June 1951), 196.
31 Easton, *A Systems Analysis of Political Life* (New York 1965), 250–51 (italics added). See also G. H. Scholten, "Het vergelijken van federaties met behulp van systeem-analyse," *Acta Politica*, II (1966–67), 51–68.
32 Verba, "Some Dilemmas in Comparative Research," *World Politics*, XX (October 1967), 126 (italics added).

33 Connor, "Self-Determination: The New Phase," *World Politics*, XX (October 1967), 49–50.

34 Deutsch, *Political Community at the International Level* (Garden City NY 1954), 39.

35 Daalder, 69.

36 Lorwin, "Belgium: Religion, Class, and Language in National Politics," in Dahl, ed., *Political Oppositions in Western Democracies*, 174.

37 Nordlinger, "Democratic Stability and Instability: The French Case," *World Politics*, XVIII (October 1965), 143.

38 Leites, *On the Game of Politics in France* (Stanford CA 1959), 2.

39 Nor does the reverse assumption hold true. Giovanni Sartori relates the instability of Italian democracy to "poor leadership, both in the sense that the political elites lack the ability for problem-solving and that they do not provide a generalized leadership." This weakness of leadership, he continues, "is easily explained by the fragmentation of the party system and its ideological rigidity." ("European Political Parties: The Case of Polarized Pluralism," in LaPalombara and Weiner, eds, *Political Parties and Political Development*, 163.) The example of the consociational democracies shows that this is not a sufficient explanation.

40 Converse and Dupeux, "Politicization of the Electorate in France and the United States," *Public Opinion Quarterly*, XXVI (spring 1962), 1–23.

41 MacRae, *Parliament, Parties, and Society in France: 1946–1958* (New York 1967), 333.

42 Hoffmann and others, *In Search of France* (Cambridge 1963), 8 (italics omitted); Crozier, *The Bureaucratic Phenomenon* (Chicago IL 1964), 220.

43 Duverger, "The Development of Democracy in France," in Henry W. Ehrmann, ed., *Democracy in a Changing Society* (New York 1964), 77.

44 Verba, "Germany: The Remaking of Political Culture," in Lucian W. Pye and Verba, eds, *Political Culture and Political Development* (Princeton NJ 1965), 133.

45 Lipset, *The First New Nation: The United States in Historical and Comparative Perspective* (New York 1963), 292.

46 Dahl, 358.

47 McDaniel, "The Danish Unicameral Parliament" (unpublished PhD dissertation, University of California, Berkeley 1963), iv.

3 The puzzle of Indian democracy
A consociational interpretation

India has been the one major deviant case for consociational (power sharing) theory, and its sheer size makes the exception especially damaging. A deeply divided society with, supposedly, a mainly majoritarian type of democracy, India nevertheless has been able to maintain its democratic system. Careful examination reveals, however, that Indian democracy has displayed all four crucial elements of power sharing theory. In fact, it was a perfectly and thoroughly consociational system during its first two decades. From the late 1960s on, although India has remained basically consociational, some of its power sharing elements have weakened under the pressure of greater mass mobilization. Concomitantly, in accordance with consociational theory, intergroup hostility and violence have increased. Therefore, India is not a deviant case for consociational theory but, instead, an impressive confirming case.

India has long been a puzzle for students of comparative democratic politics. Its success in maintaining democratic rule since independence in 1947 (excluding the brief authoritarian interlude of the 1975–77 Emergency) in the world's largest and most heterogeneous democracy runs counter to John Stuart Mill's (1958, 230) proposition that democracy is "next to impossible" in multiethnic societies and completely impossible in linguistically divided countries.[1] And it confounds Selig S. Harrison's prediction (1960, 338), in line with Mill's argument, of India's democratic failure and/ or territorial disintegration: "The odds are almost wholly against the survival of freedom and ... the issue is, in fact, whether any Indian state can survive at all." The Indian puzzle is even more troublesome for consociational (power sharing) theory. In contrast with Mill's and Harrison's thinking, power sharing theory holds that democracy is possible in deeply divided societies but only if their type of democracy is consociational, that is, characterized by (1) grand coalition governments that include representatives of all major linguistic and religious groups, (2) cultural autonomy for these groups, (3) proportionality in political representation and civil service appointments, and (4) a minority veto with regard to vital minority rights and autonomy. In contrast, under majoritarian winner-take-all democracy – characterized by the concentration of power in bare-majority one-party governments, centralized power, a disproportional electoral system, and absolute majority rule – consociational theory regards stable democracy in deeply divided societies as highly unlikely. In other words, consociational theory maintains that power sharing is a necessary (although not a sufficient) condition for democracy in deeply divided countries.

Consociational theory has had a strong influence on comparative politics, and it has spawned a vast literature. Soon after it was formulated, Daalder (1974, 609) spoke of "an incipient school" of consociationalism, and, a few years later, Powell (1979, 295) proclaimed the theory "among the most influential contributions to comparative politics." It has become a widely accepted paradigm for the analysis of democracies that can be regarded as the prototypes of power sharing, such as the Netherlands (Daalder and Irwin 1989; Mair 1994), Belgium (Huyse 1987; Zolberg 1977), Austria (Powell 1970; Luther and Müller 1992), Switzerland (Lehmbruch 1993; Linder 1994; Steiner 1990), Lebanon (Dekmejian 1978; Messarra 1994), Malaysia (Von Vorys 1975; Zakaria 1989), and Colombia (Dix 1980; Hartlyn 1988). And it has been used for the interpretation of many other political systems, from tiny Liechtenstein (Batliner 1981) to the European Union (Chryssochoou 1994; Gabel 1994; Hix 1994; Lindberg 1974); in all parts of the world, for instance, Canada (Cannon 1982), Venezuela (Levine 1973), Suriname (Dew 1994), Italy (Graziano 1980), Nigeria (Chinwuba 1980), Gambia (Hughes 1982), Kenya (Berg-Schlosser 1985), and Sri Lanka (Chehabi 1980); and not only democracies but also such nondemocratic states as the former Yugoslavia (Goldman 1985; Vasovic 1992) and the former Soviet Union (Van den Berghe 1981, 190–91). Furthermore, consociational democracy has been proposed as a normative model for many ethnically divided countries, and it had a decisive influence in the shaping of South Africa's 1994 power sharing constitution (Huntington 1988; Lijphart 1994; Worrall 1981). Given its prominent status, consociational theory has received a commensurate amount of criticism (e.g. Barry 1975; Halpern 1986; Horowitz 1985; Taylor 1992), but it has successfully held its own, partly by rebutting its critics and partly by incorporating many of the critics' concerns (Lehmbruch 1993; Lijphart 1985, 83–117; Steiner and Dorff 1980).

Nevertheless, consociational theory has remained vulnerable on one major count: the glaring exception of India to its otherwise unblemished empirical validity. Indian democracy has worked despite the fact that, according to the usual interpretation (Pathak 1993, 36; Weiner 1989, 78), the Indian political system devised by the founding fathers was patterned after the majoritarian and adversarial Westminster model. B. K. Nehru (1986, 74) writes that the Indian mind was "completely conditioned to believing that whatever was British was best" and calls it no wonder that the Indian Constitution is but an "amended version" of the 1935 Government of India Act. And Paul R. Brass (1991, 342) states that "the consociationalists ... consistently ignore the experience of India, the largest, most culturally diverse society in the world that has ... functioned with a highly competitive and distinctly adversarial system of politics." A theory with only one disconfirming case comes close to perfect validity, of course,[2] but one cannot simply shrug off a deviant case that looms as large as India's huge democracy, with its 900 million inhabitants.

In the admittedly rare attempts to come to terms with the Indian exception, consociational scholars have conceded that India's democracy is, in line with the usual interpretation, mainly majoritarian because of the frequency of one-party majority cabinets, the highly centralized federal system that K. C. Wheare (1964, 28) considers only "quasi-federal," and a highly disproportional electoral system that has regularly enabled the Congress Party to win parliamentary majorities without ever winning a majority of the popular vote. Yet, they have claimed that India is not completely majoritarian, citing Rajni Kothari's (1970, 421) description of the Indian political system as a "coalitional arena," akin to a grand coalition, and the autonomy for the major linguistic groups provided by the coinciding linguistic and state boundaries of India's federal design, and they have equivocated between calling India nonconsociational (Lijphart 1977, 181, 225) and semiconsociational (Lijphart 1979, 513; Powell 1982, 215). In other words, the argument was that, while India remained a deviant case, its negative significance for consociational theory was relatively mild.

This argument can be taken much farther, however, on the basis of a more thorough examination of the Indian case. The evidence clearly shows that India has always had a power sharing system of democracy, especially strongly and unmistakably during its first two decades of independence, from 1947 to 1967, but continuing, albeit in somewhat attenuated form, after about 1967. As Indian democracy has become less firmly consociational, intergroup tensions and violence have increased. If this reinterpretation is correct, as I shall try to demonstrate, then India is no longer a deviant case for consociational theory and, in fact, becomes an impressive confirming case.[3]

The four elements of power sharing in India

Indian democracy has clearly exhibited all four of the defining characteristics of power sharing also found in the other prominent examples of consociational systems: Canada from 1840 to 1867 (strictly speaking, a consociational *pre*democracy), the Netherlands from 1917 to 1967, Lebanon from 1943 to 1975 and again after the 1989 Taif Accord, Switzerland since 1943, Austria from 1945 to 1966, Malaysia since 1955 with a temporary breakdown from 1969 to 1971, Colombia from 1958 to 1974, Cyprus from 1960 to 1963, Belgium since 1970, Czecho-Slovakia from 1989 until the 1993 partition of the country, and South Africa according to its 1994 interim constitution (Lijphart 1977, 1992, 1994; Olson 1994).

Grand coalition

Government by grand coalition can take many different forms. The modal form is an inclusive cabinet coalition of ethnic, linguistic, or religious parties, as in the Austrian, Malaysian, and South African power sharing systems, but there are many other possibilities. One entails the formation of grand governing coalitions in sites other than the cabinet, such as the Dutch pattern of permanent or *ad hoc* "grand" councils or committees with much greater influence than their formal advisory role. Another entails grand coalitions in cabinets, defined not in partisan terms but more broadly in terms of the representation of linguistic or other groups in a predetermined ratio; for instance, Belgian cabinets have rarely been coalitions of all significant parties, but they have been ethnically "grand" because of the constitutional rule that cabinets must consist of equal numbers of Dutch-speakers and French-speakers. Yet another option entails neither cabinets nor parties: the allocation of top governmental offices – such as the presidency, prime ministership, and assembly speakership in Lebanon, and the presidency and vice-presidency in Cyprus – to specified ethnic or religious groups.

The Indian case adds even greater variety. Its main vehicle for grand coalition is the cabinet, which is not an exceptional form, but the unique aspect in India is that cabinets are produced by the broadly representative and inclusive nature of a single, dominant party, the Congress Party. In a seminal article, originally published in 1964, Kothari (1989, 21–35) tried to analyze the Indian party system from the comparative perspective of the distinction between one-, two-, and multiparty systems. He found that the intermediate category of one-party dominance provides a reasonably good fit but that Indian one-party dominance is still quite different from the authoritarian type in a country like Ghana. The Congress Party's location in the center means that minor parties surround it on all sides. These, in turn, which Kothari (1989, 22–23) calls "parties of pressure," perform the role of preventing the ruling "party of consensus" from straying too far from "the balance of effective public opinion." Hence, he assigns a separate conceptual category to India's party system, uniquely occupied by the Indian case: the "Congress system."[4] One important conclusion that emerges from this classificatory exercise is to highlight the vast differences between the Congress system, with virtually permanent rule by a centrist party, and the Westminster-style two-party system, with alternation in office by right-wing and left-wing parties.

The second major conclusion is that the Congress system has served as the foundation for a consociational grand coalition. Despite never winning a majority of the popular vote in parliamentary elections, the Congress Party has been balanced in the political center and has encompassed "all the major sections and interests of society" (Kothari 1989, 27). Prior to independence the Congress was already an internally federal organization with a high degree of intraparty democracy and a strong penchant for consensus. This "historical consensus" Kothari (1989, 23, 51) writes, was successfully transformed into a "consensus of the present," and he comes close to using consociational terminology in describing Indian democracy as a "consensus system which operates through the institution of a party of consensus," namely, the Congress Party. Crawford Young (1976, 314) makes the same point in explicitly consociational language: "Lijphart's theory of consociational democracy has application to the Indian pattern of integration. ... At the summit is a national political elite who are committed to reconciling differences through bargaining amongst themselves." The combination of the Congress Party's inclusive nature and political dominance has generated grand coalition cabinets with ministers belonging to all the main religious, linguistic, and regional groups.

Cultural autonomy

Cultural autonomy for religious and linguistic groups has taken three main forms in power sharing democracies: (1) federal arrangements in which state and linguistic boundaries largely coincide, thus providing a high degree of linguistic autonomy, as in Switzerland, Belgium, and Czecho-Slovakia; (2) the right of religious and linguistic minorities to establish and administer their own autonomous schools, fully supported by public funds, as in Belgium and the Netherlands; and (3) separate "personal laws" – concerning marriage, divorce, custody and adoption of children, and inheritance – for religious minorities, as in Lebanon and Cyprus. Indian democracy has had all these three forms, the last two from the very beginning and linguistic federalism since the 1950s.

The British colonial rulers of India drew the administrative divisions of the country without much regard for linguistic or cultural cohesion. The Congress movement was opposed to this policy and committed itself to a thorough redrawing of the boundaries along linguistic lines; from 1921 on, it also based its own organization on linguistically homogeneous units, the so-called Pradesh Committees. Jawaharlal Nehru and other Congress leaders had second thoughts, however, and the Constituent Assembly, following the advice of its Linguistic Provinces Commission, decided not to incorporate the linguistic principle into the new Constitution. Pressures from below forced a complete change of policy in the 1950s. After the state of Madras was divided into the separate Tamil-speaking and Telugu-speaking states of Tamil Nadu and Andhra Pradesh in 1953, the States Reorganization Commission embraced the linguistic principle and recommended drastic revisions in state boundaries along linguistic lines in 1955. These were quickly implemented in 1956, followed by the creation of several additional states in later years.

Linguistic federalism has not fully satisfied the minorities' desire for autonomy and security. The balance of power in the Indian federal system was asymmetrical in favor of the central government from the beginning, and further centralization has occurred from the late 1960s on, a subject to which I shall return below. As a result, many states have been demanding greater autonomy. The special autonomous status constitutionally granted to Kashmir, the one Muslim-majority state, was in practice also soon undermined, and smaller linguistic minorities without statehood have agitated for the creation of new states. But the leadership's initial fears that linguistic federalism would strengthen fissiparous tendencies have not been realized, and, in retrospect, the policy is regarded as a success by most observers. As consociational theory would have predicted, the "rationalizing [of] the political map of India" has made language "a cementing and integrating influence" instead of a "force for division" (Kothari 1970, 115; see also Banerjee 1992).

The crucial feature of educational autonomy is not just the minorities' right to set up and run their own schools but the ability to make this right effective through full government financial support of these schools. Dutch and Belgian religious minorities had to fight hard to obtain this right, and, while full educational autonomy was granted in the Netherlands in 1917, it was not instituted in Belgium until 1958. In India, however, the constitution provided this right from the outset. Article 30 states that "all minorities, whether based on religion or language, shall have the right to establish and administer educational institutions of their choice" and, more important, that "the State shall not, in granting aid to educational institutions, discriminate against any educational institution on the ground that it is under the management of a minority, whether based on religion or language."

Separate personal laws for Hindus, Muslims, and smaller religious minorities already existed under British rule, and they were carried forward and sometimes amended or replaced by similar new laws in independent India. Examples are the 1955 Hindu Marriages Act, the 1956 Hindu Succession (that is, inheritance) Act, the 1937 Muslim Personal Law (Shariat) Application Act, the 1939 Dissolution of Muslim Marriages Act, and the 1872 Indian Christian Marriage Act (Fyzee 1964; Engineer 1987). These statutes were enacted by parliamentary majorities but, when intended for one of the minorities, were drafted in conformity with the minority's wishes. For instance, after the controversial 1985 Shah Bano decision by the Supreme Court (involving the right of a divorced Muslim woman to financial support from her former husband), a new Muslim Women (Protection of Right on Divorce) Act was adopted in 1986, largely in line with the wishes of the Muslim Personal Law Board. And the new 1993 Christian Marriage Act was proposed by the government after extensive consultations with and the final approval of all Christian churches, albeit only reluctant endorsement by the Roman Catholic church.

The Constituent Assembly explicitly considered the question of whether separate personal laws ought to be continued in independent, democratic India. An amendment to the draft constitution was proposed that would have ended this form of religious autonomy: "The Union or the State shall not undertake any legislation or pass any law ... applicable to some particular community or communities and no other" (cited in Luthera 1964, 83). Significantly, such a clause was *not* included in the constitution. A year later, Law Minister B. R. Ambedkar, replying to accusations of discrimination on the ground of religion during a parliamentary debate, again emphatically endorsed the principle of minority personal laws: "The Constitution permits us to treat different communities differently and if we treat them differently, nobody can charge the Government with practising discrimination" (cited in Luthera 1964, 86).

Proportionality

In accordance with the principle of proportionality, the normal electoral system in power sharing democracies is proportional representation (PR). The plurality (first-past-the-post) and other majoritarian methods have the tendency to overrepresent majorities and large parties and to discriminate against smaller minority parties, as well as the corollary tendency to create artificial parliamentary majorities for parties that fall considerably short of winning popular vote majorities, what Rae (1967, 74–77) has called "manufactured majorities." It is not impossible, however, for power sharing systems to circumvent these disproportional effects. For instance, despite Malaysia's plurality elections, the interethnic coalition has succeeded in guaranteeing a nearly proportional share of parliamentary seats to the minority Chinese and Indian parties by giving them the coalition's exclusive nomination in a number of districts.

In India, too, power sharing has managed to coexist with the plurality electoral system inherited from the British. One reason is that plurality does not disfavor geographically concentrated minorities, and India's linguistic minorities are regionally based. Another is that the Congress Party's repeated manufactured majorities have not come at the expense of India's many minorities due to its special status as the "party of consensus," which has been deliberately protective of the various religious and linguistic minorities. Indian cabinets, which have been mainly Congress cabinets, also have accorded shares of ministerships remarkably close to proportional, especially given the constraint of only about twenty positions usually available, to the Muslim minority of about 12 percent and even the much smaller Sikh minority (roughly 2 percent), as well as to the different linguistic groups, states, and regions of the country (Pai Panandiker and Mehra 1996). In addition, a special feature of the electoral law guarantees the so-called Scheduled Castes (untouchables) and Scheduled Tribes (aboriginals) proportional shares of parliamentary representation by means of "reserved seats," that is, seats for which only members of these groups are allowed to be candidates. Finally, these scheduled groups and the so-called Other Backward Classes have benefited from other quotas – so-called reservations – with regard to public service employment and university admissions (Mehta 1991; Prasad 1991; Srinivasavaradan 1992, 105–33).[5]

Minority veto

The minority veto in power sharing democracies usually consists of merely an informal understanding that minorities can effectively protect their autonomy by blocking any attempts to eliminate or reduce it. The major exception is countries in which one or a few minorities face a solid majority (such as Belgium, Cyprus, and the former Czecho-Slovakia), and the minority veto is formally entrenched in the constitution. India has a numerical Hindu majority of about 83 percent, but the Hindus are so thoroughly divided by language, caste, and sect that they do not form a political majority. A good example of the informal veto in Indian politics is the 1965 agreement by the central government that Hindi would not be made the exclusive official language without the concurrent approval of the major non-Hindi speaking regions, in effect giving a veto to the southern states, which had opposed dropping English as a language of administration. The provision works best if the minority veto does not have to be used very often in order to protect minority rights and autonomy, and this has been the case in India. No attempts have been made to reverse linguistic federalism, and, while opposition to educational autonomy has been increasing, no governmental actions to weaken or abolish it have been undertaken. The one clear instance of the actual use of the minority veto occurred in the mid-1980s in connection with the separate personal laws: The Muslim minority saw the Supreme Court decision in the Shah Bano case as an attack on Muslim personal law, and it succeeded in vetoing this decision by persuading the government to propose, and parliament to enact, a law reversing the court's judgment.

The one respect in which India does seem to differ from the other consociational democracies is that power sharing was not instituted by a deliberate and comprehensive agreement, such as the 1917 Pacification in the Netherlands, the 1943 National Pact in Lebanon, the 1945 Grand Coalition accord in Austria, and the Malayan Alliance of the early 1950s. But not all consociational democracies have been established by a compact of this kind of comprehensiveness and intentionality; in Belgium and Switzerland, for instance, power sharing developed in a slow step-by-step fashion over more than a century, and Daalder (1974) has argued that even the Dutch Pacification should be seen as merely one step in a long incremental process. This means that India's incremental and sometimes haphazard development of power sharing is somewhat unusual among consociational democracies but not at all unique.

In the face of overwhelming evidence concerning the consociational character of India's democratic system, how can we explain the explicit and complete rejection by Brass (1991, 342–43) of the applicability of consociational theory to India? Brass claims that India is not at all a consociational democracy and, on the contrary, has "functioned with a highly competitive and distinctly adversarial system of politics." One explanation is that he defines power sharing in much too narrow terms. His main point is that India has had a variety of interethnic and intercommunal as well as monoethnic parties and sometimes coalitions among these. The implication is that only cabinet coalitions of monoreligious and monoethnic political parties deserve to be regarded as grand coalitions, which is obviously incorrect in view of the great variety of forms that grand coalitions can assume. Moreover, by focusing exclusively on parties and coalitions, Brass completely ignores the evidence with regard to autonomy, proportionality, and the minority veto.

Brass (1991, 343) concedes that India "has adopted many consociational devices, some permanently, some temporarily," but he fails to see that *together* these devices add up to a fully consociational system. Compared to India, the other consociational democracies do not have any additional or stronger methods of power sharing. The final explanation of Brass's disagreement with my interpretation may be that he focuses on India's more recent democratic experience, when its consociational character has not been as strong as in the first two decades, a subject that I shall treat at greater length later. But even in more recent decades India has remained basically consociational rather than "not consociational at all."

India's power sharing system: how much of a surprise?

Categorizing India as one of the consociational democracies, completely on a par with the other well known cases, is a novel interpretation, although several scholars have identified particular instances of power sharing in India (even Brass 1991; Kothari 1989; Young 1976; see also Hardgrave 1993; Weiner 1969). What needs to be emphasized, however, is that, from the perspective of consociational theory, the adoption of power sharing by India and its maintenance for nearly half a century is not at all unexpected or surprising. For one thing, consociational theory places great emphasis on the contribution of prudent and constructive leadership in the development of successful power sharing systems. Jawaharlal Nehru is an almost perfect example of such leadership. He was prime minister from 1947 until his death in 1964, during the heyday of Indian power sharing. Kothari (1976, 15–16) comments that in India

> it is essential that the institutional system provides for widespread diffusion of power. That this happened to a significant degree under Nehru, and that this trend even appeared to grow stronger in the later part of his career, is a tribute [mainly] to the democratic values, vision, and self-confidence of one man.

That Nehru was not a fully convinced consociational thinker is shown by his initial opposition to the principle of linguistic federalism. But his leadership combined firmness and self-confidence with flexibility and tolerance, and he unfailingly respected and promoted the internally democratic and federal nature of the Congress Party. Even on the issue of linguistic federalism, he turned out in the end to be a consociational practitioner. In Kothari's (1970, 157) words once again, "Nehru's understanding of the consensus framework represented by the Congress was better than that of most of his contemporaries," although he operated "more on the intuition of a pragmatic politician than on any intellectual grasp of the logic of the system."

Furthermore, consociational theory tries to explain the probability that power sharing will be instituted and maintained in divided societies in terms of nine background factors that may favor or hinder it. Since most of these conditions are favorable in India, it is again not very surprising that consociational democracy was established and has worked quite well. The following brief review of the nine factors rates India on each; the two most important factors are listed first.

1 The most serious obstacle to power sharing in divided societies is the presence of a solid majority that, understandably, prefers pure majority rule to consociationalism; this factor was mainly responsible for the 1963 failure of the Cypriot consociational system, for instance. As indicated earlier, India's numerical Hindu majority is internally divided to such an extent that the country consists of minorities only.

2 The second major factor is the absence or presence of large socioeconomic differences among the groups of a divided society. In India, there are disparities of this kind among regions and, hence, among linguistic groups, as well as and more important between Hindus and Muslims. But even the latter difference is not as great as is often assumed. In a country such as India, where illiteracy is still quite high, literacy rates are good indicators of different levels of socioeconomic development. In rural areas – and India is still mainly rural – there is very little difference in the literacy rates of Hindus and Muslims; in urban areas, about two thirds of Hindus are literate compared with one half of Muslims (Sharif 1993). Linguistic-regional variations in socioeconomic development are mitigated by the fact that the poorer Hindi-speaking areas have historically exercised more power in the central government than the rest of the country, similar to the trade-off between the economically dominant Chinese and the politically dominant Malays in consociational Malaysia (Esman 1972, 25). Finally, socioeconomic differences within religious and linguistic groups are so much larger that they overshadow intergroup disparities.

3 If there are too many groups, then negotiations among them will be too difficult and complex. India, with its extremely large number of groups, including fourteen major languages, receives an unfavorable rating on this factor.

4 If the groups are of roughly the same size, then there is a balance of power among them. India's division into very many minorities, without any clearly predominant groups, achieves such a rough balance.

5 If the total population is relatively small, then the decision-making process is less complex (Dahl and Tufte 1973, 40). Since India is the world's second most populous country, there appears to be no doubt that its score on this factor should be negative. Weiner (1989, 35–36) suggests, however, that India's success in sustaining democracy despite growing tensions and violence can be explained, first, in terms of its federal system (essentially a consociational explanation, because India's linguistic federalism is a key element of its power sharing system) and, second, in terms of the size of the country, which means that much of the conflict remains localized and does not directly endanger the central authority. Weiner's second argument is also highly plausible and suggests that the relationship between size and the chances for power sharing is curvilinear instead of linear; as size increases, conditions for power sharing worsen initially, but beyond a certain critical point the tendency is reversed.

6 External dangers promote internal unity. The long struggle against British colonial rule was such a unifying factor in India, as was the 1962 war with China. The wars with Pakistan had the potential of inflaming internal Hindu-Muslim tensions but did not produce this negative effect.

7 Overarching loyalties reduce the strength of particularistic loyalties. Indian nationalism, powerfully stimulated by the Indian National Congress in the period before independence, has been such a unifying force (Khilnani 1992; Masselos 1985; Suntharalingam 1983). The only serious challenge came from the Muslim League, which claimed that India's Muslims constituted a separate "nation," but this challenge was effectively removed by the 1947 partition.

8 If groups are geographically concentrated, then federalism can be used to promote group autonomy. Although India's religious groups are territorially intermixed, the geographical concentration of linguistic groups has made India's highly successful linguistic federalism possible. Hence, on balance, a positive rating is justified.

9 Traditions of compromise and accommodation foster consociationalism. The Indian National Congress was a movement based on consensus before it became the party of consensus in 1947. More generally, too, as Austin (1966, 315) writes, "consensus has deep roots in India. Village panchayats traditionally reached decisions in this way. ... Indians prefer lengthy discussions of problems to moving quickly to arbitrary decisions."

In sum, India rates favorably on seven of the nine conditions for power sharing, or on eight if we accept Weiner's reasoning. These include the two most important factors. Among the other consociational democracies, such a favorable predisposition is matched only by Switzerland and the

Netherlands. Perhaps it would have been more surprising if India had *not* adopted and maintained a power sharing system!

The weakening of power sharing after the late 1960s

Indian power sharing from independence to the present can be divided into two periods: the two decades after 1947, when consociationalism was full-fledged and complete, and the period beginning in the late 1960s, when power sharing continued but in slightly weaker form. How can we account for this shift? Generally speaking, the main reason for the decline (and sometimes failure) of power sharing systems is an inherent deep-seated tension. Political leaders have to perform a difficult balancing act between compromises with rivals and maintaining the support of their own followers, both activists and voters. Pleasing other elites will tend to displease their own supporters, and vice versa, and the search for compromise is a time-consuming task that may lead to a degree of immobilism, which is also likely to discontent supporters, who expect and demand effective and decisive government action.[6] It is therefore easier for political elites to share power successfully if their followers are relatively passive and deferential, as shown in particular by the Dutch case (Lijphart 1968, 139–77). This also means that strong pressures from below will increase the elites' tendencies to concentrate and centralize power rather than to share it.

The weakening of power sharing in India after the late 1960s fits this explanatory framework very well. As many scholars have pointed out, the 1960s marked the beginning of mounting democratic activism by previously quiet groups, especially the middle peasants (Brass 1990; Frankel 1988; Kohli 1990; Rudolph and Rudolph 1987). The resulting pressures for more decisive and less consensual government action have prompted greater concentration and centralization of power, especially in the Congress Party and the federal system. Four factors contributed to this weakening.

First, under the leadership of Indira Gandhi, who became prime minister in 1966 (after the brief interregnum of Lal Bahadur Shastri, who succeeded Nehru after his death in 1964), the Congress Party was transformed from an internally democratic, federal, and consensual organization to a centralized and hierarchical party. According to Varshney (1993a, 243),

> Nehru had used his charisma to promote intraparty democracy, not to undermine it, strengthening the organization in the process. Indira Gandhi used her charisma to make the party utterly dependent on her, suspending intraparty democracy and debate, and weakening the organization as a result.

In very similar terms, Das Gupta (1989, 71) describes the new Congress Party as "less a national institution of interest reconciliation than a central organization for mobilizing endorsement for the leadership and its hierarchical apparatus." It has remained a broadly inclusive party, but less by means of *representation* from the bottom up than by *representativeness* from the top down.

Second, the federal system, never highly decentralized, was centralized even more. One instrument was the increasingly frequent use of the so-called President's Rule for partisan purposes. The founding fathers had given the central government the right to dismiss state governments and to replace them with direct rule from the center for the purpose of dealing with grave emergencies, not foreseeing that the central government "would resort to devices intended to safeguard unity and cohesion for undermining democratically elected [state] governments and seeking to diminish their role and importance" (Arora and Mukarji 1992, 8). President's Rule was invoked ten times before the end of 1967 but sixty-six times in the only slightly longer period from 1968 to early 1989 (Kathuria 1990, 339). Like the centralization of the Congress Party, the similar trend in the federal system is often attributed to Indira Gandhi. It would be wrong, however, to interpret these trends primarily in terms of the – admittedly starkly contrasting – leadership propensities of Nehru and his daughter. For one thing, they can be explained more convincingly in terms of the structural tensions inherent in power sharing. For another, Indira Gandhi's two main successors reverted to a less confrontational and more consensual style of leadership (Rajiv Gandhi intermittently and P. V. Narasimha Rao more consistently) without, however, undoing either the party's or the federation's centralization.

The third source of weakness is that the pressures from below have specifically included calls for the abolition of crucial consociational rules put in place by power sharing compromises: separate personal laws, minority educational autonomy, and Kashmir's constitutionally privileged (although no longer actually implemented) autonomous status. Not all the criticism of the 1986 Muslim Women (Protection of Right on Divorce) Act necessarily entailed a wholesale condemnation of personal law; many critics objected mainly to the specific provisions of the new law, calling it "a primitive anti-woman bill" (Iyer 1987, xvi). But the Supreme Court judgment in the Shah Bano case explicitly called for the elimination of separate personal laws and their replacement by a "uniform civil code," arguing in a clearly anti-consociational vein that "a common civil code will help the cause of national integration by removing disparate loyalties to laws which have conflicting ideologies" (cited in Engineer 1987, 33). The reversal of the court's decision gave new ammunition to the foes of separate personal laws.

In an examination of the claim that minorities enjoy more rights than the Hindu majority, Sharma (1993, 102, 106) argues that it is valid as far as the minorities' educational autonomy is concerned: Their schools are not "subject to governmental control in the way similar institutions run by the majority community are. The minorities in this respect do in fact enjoy rights not available to the majority community." He concludes that "this in effect means that the majority community subsidizes the educational system of the minority communities." Sharma captures the growing criticism of minority educational autonomy very well, including the tendentious argument that it is the "majority," instead of society as a whole, that does the subsidizing. One way to solve the problem would be to make educational autonomy available to any group, regardless of its majority or minority status and regardless of whether it is a religious, linguistic, or any other kind of group, such as a group of people espousing a particular educational philosophy like Montessori. Instead of such an improvement of the system along consociational lines, as in the Netherlands, for instance, the prevailing tendency among the critics is the anti-consociational one of abolition.

The Bharatiya Janata Party (BJP) has made itself the main mouthpiece against the government's alleged pandering to minorities, what its leader L. K. Advani calls "minorityism" (Varshney 1993a, 252). The BJP, usually described as a "Hindu nationalist party," is clearly anticonsociational, and its growing strength represents a major potential danger to power sharing in India.[7] The 1991 state elections brought the BJP to power in India's largest state, Uttar Pradesh, with one sixth of the country's population, as well as in Madhya Pradesh, Rajasthan, and Himachal Pradesh. After the imposition of President's Rule and new elections in November 1993, the BJP retained control only in Rajasthan, but it also won the election in the union territory (and capital city) of Delhi. In the February 1995 state elections, it extended its influence from the northern Hindi-speaking heartland to the western part of the country by winning elections in Gujarat and, allied with the Hindu fundamentalist party Shiv Sena, in Maharashtra.

The fourth and final source of weakness derives from a combination of the inherent tensions of power sharing and the unique Indian form of grand coalition, based on the predominance of a broadly representative party. All the pressures from below make it especially difficult to maintain broad support for a party explicitly committed to power sharing and minority rights. The Congress Party has never won a majority of the popular vote, and in 1967 its plurality fell to only slightly more than 40 percent. It lost the 1977 and 1989 elections outright, and because it gained a mere plurality of seats in 1991 it could only form a minority cabinet. In fact, the 1989 and 1991 election results show that India has shifted from a dominant- to a multi-party system. The shift in the effective number of parliamentary parties – the number of parties in parliament weighted by their size (Taagepera and Shugart 1989, 77–91) – is instructive in this respect: The eight elections from 1951 to 1984 yielded eight manufactured majorities (seat majorities won without vote majorities) and an average effective number of 2.2 parties, typical of either a two-party or dominant-party system; the elections in 1989 and 1991 failed to produce a majority party, and the average effective number of parties increased to 3.8, clearly a multiparty system.

These weaknesses do not signify that power sharing has ended or is ending in India. Congress Party cabinets have continued to be broadly representative, and non-Congress cabinets have been only marginally less so during their two brief periods in power. Federalism has weakened but is far from dead, and the principle of linguistic federalism is very much alive. Minority educational autonomy and separate personal laws are under attack, but they have so far survived, along with the minority veto and the proportionality principle.

The above description of continued, although weakened, power sharing in India fits consociational theory in two other respects. The theory states that power sharing is a necessary condition for the survival of democracy in divided societies; indeed, Harrison's (1960, 338) dire prediction of India's democratic failure, quoted at the beginning of this article, is not shared by any knowledgeable observer of Indian politics today (see especially Varshney 1995). At the same time, while Indian democracy is quite stable in this fundamental sense, the weakening of power sharing should be expected to be accompanied by increases in intergroup tensions and violence, which clearly has been the case in India. The official figures, which tend to be on the conservative side, on Hindu-Muslim violence in the 1954–85 period presented in P. R. Rajgopal's (1987, 16–17) study show an alarming trend. When the first five years (1954–58) are compared with the last five years (1981–85), the number of violent incidents rose from 339 to 2,290, the number of persons killed from 112 to 2,350, and the number of persons injured from 2,229 to 17,791. This trend, Rajgopal observes, "shows no signs of being reversed." Indeed, in the aftermath of the destruction of the mosque at Ayodhya in December 1992, rioting in many parts of India led to about 1,200 deaths in one month, and more than 600 people were killed in anti-Muslim rioting in Bombay in January 1993 (Hardgrave 1993, 64–65).

The causal link between the weakening of power sharing and these problems of governance has also been noted by scholars not explicitly belonging to the consociational school. For instance, Weiner (1989, 11) writes that "conflict management has become more difficult with the decline of the Congress party organization and the weakening of the federal structure." Varshney (1993b, 17–18) finds it

> not surprising that the attempt by the post-Nehru leadership of the Congress party to centralize an essentially diverse and federal polity has co-existed with some of the worst stresses that the polity has experienced, including the insurgenc[ies] in Punjab and Kashmir.

A return to full-fledged power sharing?

A final piece of evidence about the close fit between the Indian case and consociational theory is provided by the proposals for political and constitutional reform. If the consociational interpretation of India's democracy is correct, that is, if the survival of Indian democracy can be explained by its power sharing character and if its increasing turbulence after the 1960s can be explained in terms of the weakening of power sharing, we should expect these proposals to have two characteristics. First, all or most of them should be aimed at strengthening the consociational aspects of the political system. Second, given the growth in intergroup tensions and violence and the growing opposition to the very principle of power sharing, they can be expected to call for far-reaching reform with a sense of urgency.

Both expectations are correct. Although there is no vigorous public debate about or widespread demand for political change, Indians who do call for reform have in mind drastic measures, indeed. For instance, Abid Hussain (1993, 11) asserts that India's "deformed polity" is "in need of drastic surgery." In a volume entitled *Reforming the Constitution*, others have called for "fundamental changes" (Reddy 1992) and "major amendments" (Vira 1992) to the constitution, or even for the election of a new constituent assembly (Malaviya 1992) that should draft an entirely "new constitution" (Rao 1992) as the foundation for a "Second Republic" (Jaisingh 1992). Significantly, the substantive thrust of all but one of the major reform plans is in the direction of stronger power sharing. The one exception, which is only a partial exception, is the frequently voiced suggestion that India should adopt an American-style or French-style presidential system (Pathak 1993; Rao 1992; Sathe 1991, 37–38; Trehan 1993; see also Noorani 1989). From the consociational perspective, the problem with presidentialism is its concentration of executive power in the hands of one person, who, in a divided society, is inevitably a member of one particular group; power sharing requires joint rule by the representatives of all major groups in a collegial decision-making body, ideally provided by cabinets in parliamentary systems. The most prominent and detailed presidentialist proposal for India, however, put forward by B. K. Nehru, explicitly recognizes this disadvantage and tries to compensate for it by recommending a special form of presidentialism, used in Nigeria and also recommended by Horowitz (1985, 635–38) for ethnically heterogeneous societies elsewhere. Nehru's (1992, 138) proposal is to

> divide the country into four zones – east, west, south, and north – and require a successful candidate for the Presidency not only to get an overall majority of the votes cast throughout the country but also a specific, relatively small, percentage of votes in all the zones, before he can be declared elected.

This would ensure that the winning candidate has at least a minimum of support in regions other than his or her own.[8]

The other major reform proposals, entailing the strengthening of the federal system and the adoption of a proportional representation (PR) election system, are all fully consonant with power sharing. There appears to be almost universal agreement that India's federal system should be decentralized; this is the tenor of the 1988 report of the Sarkaria Commission on Union-State Relations, which Mukarji and Mathew (1992, 280) call "conservative but constructive," since they and other reformers would prefer to go much farther. An especially interesting proposal by Mukarji and Arora (1992, 270) is to establish a three-level federalism, with each state becoming a federation, or even a more radical multilevel federalism. They call such a system a "cascading federalism: a federation of federations." One reason this kind of reform is so attractive is that the Indian states are inordinately large; not counting the seven union territories, the *average* population of the twenty-five states is about 35 million, larger than California, the most populous state in the United States.

Another and more straightforward solution to the problem of unwieldy state size would be to increase the number of states. Kothari (1976, 81) suggests about forty, and a detailed proposal by Khan (1992, 108–22) specifies fifty-eight, six of which would be carved out of the huge state of Uttar Pradesh, with a population of almost 150 million. Similarly, Kashyap (1992, 32–33) recommends the creation of "50 to 60 States of almost equal size." A considerable increase in the number of states also offers an opportunity for further fine-tuning of linguistic homogeneity.

Finally, many reformers have proposed the adoption of PR for parliamentary elections (Bhambhri 1971; Nehru 1992). The German system, which combines first-past-the-post elections for half the parliamentary seats with overall proportionality for all seats by means of list PR, is the most frequently mentioned specific suggestion (Hegde 1986, 107; Seth 1971; Singh 1986, 120; see also Vanhanen 1987). PR is based on the consociational principle of proportionality, and, as comparative studies of democratic systems show, it is conducive to multiparty systems, which in turn are conducive to broad multiparty cabinets (Lijphart 1984), although there is no guarantee, of course, that coalitions larger than a bare majority will be formed. In the case of India, even a narrow coalition of parties elected by PR is likely to be based on at least a popular majority, which means that it would be more broadly based than any Indian cabinet so far.

One reform that PR almost certainly would preclude is a return to the "Congress system," which Kothari (1989, 304–6) appears to favor and which, it should be noted, is also consociational in orientation, with either the Congress Party itself or another party becoming the new party of consensus. Without a majority-manufacturing electoral system, it would be difficult for such a party to develop. But it is unlikely anyway that a new party of consensus could form without the advantage of the unique historical circumstances of 1947, when the ruling party emerged from an enormously effective and successful national liberation movement, and without Jawaharlal Nehru's unusually high quality of leadership. Moreover, instead of helping the moderate and centrist Congress Party, first-past-the-post might well bring an anti-consociational party like the BJP to power with a manufactured majority.

Conclusion

The big puzzle of Indian democracy – its survival despite the country's deep ethnic and communal divisions – is solved by the consociational interpretation presented in this article. India has had a power sharing system of democracy during its almost fifty years of independence, and an especially full and thorough form of it during its first two decades, displaying all four of the essential elements of power sharing as clearly as Austria, the Netherlands, Switzerland, Lebanon, Malaysia, and the other well known examples of consociational democracy. That newly independent India embraced power sharing and has maintained it ever since is not even very surprising, because most of the conditions found to be conducive to it in these other countries are also favorable in the Indian case. After the late 1960s, as a result of greater mass mobilization and activation, power sharing became less strong and pervasive, evidenced by the centralization of the Congress Party and the federal system, the decline of the Congress Party's electoral strength, the attack on minority rights, and the rise of the BJP. As consociational theory would have predicted, Indian democracy has remained basically stable, but the weakening of power sharing has been accompanied by an increase in intergroup hostility and violence. Concern about these trends is reflected in the consociational thrust of the major proposals for political and constitutional change by reform-minded Indians.

The consociational interpretation of India strengthens our understanding of the Indian case by providing a theoretically coherent explanation of the main patterns and trends in its political development. Furthermore, it strengthens consociational theory by removing the one allegedly deviant case and by showing that, instead, the crucial case of India is unmistakably a confirming case.

Acknowledgments

Earlier versions of this article were presented as seminar or conference papers at the Centre for the Study of Developing Societies, Delhi, on 3 December 1993; the Department of Political Science at Delhi University, South Campus, on 8 December 1993; "Regime Transformation and Democratization in Comparative Perspective," University of California, Los Angeles, 20–21 May 1994; and the Department of Political Science, University of California, Santa Barbara, 15 May 1995. A preliminary version was published as an occasional paper by the Rajiv Gandhi Institute for Contemporary Studies in New Delhi (RGICS Paper no. 18, 1994). It is part of a collaborative and comparative US-Indian research project, directed by K. S. Bajpai and supported by the Ford Foundation and the Rajiv Gandhi Foundation. I would like to acknowledge the valuable assistance of the Centre for Policy Research in New Delhi and its director, V. A. Pai Panandiker, and of the Library of the India International Centre, New Delhi. For helpful comments on earlier drafts, I am grateful to Kanti Bajpai, Paul R. Brass, Pradeep K. Chhibber, Jyotirindra Das Gupta, Henry W. Ehrmann, Dipak K. Gupta, Thomas A. Koelble, Victor V. Magagna, G. Bingham Powell, Jr., V. Ramachandran, Varun Sahni, Ashutosh Varshney, and three anonymous referees.

Notes

1 Two other puzzles are posed by Indian democracy. The first is its survival despite widespread poverty and illiteracy (Dahl 1989, 253), which casts grave doubts on the hypothesized link between the level of socioeconomic development and stable democracy, further weakened by the fact that several other Third World democracies have by now established stable democratic rule (e.g. Barbados, Botswana, Costa Rica, Jamaica, Malta, Mauritius, and Papua New Guinea). The second, which I shall discuss later, is Myron Weiner's (1989, 9) "Indian paradox," that is, "the far more puzzling contradiction between India's high level of political violence and its success at sustaining a democratic political system."

2 Three other counterexamples mentioned by Powell (1979, 296) are Sri Lanka, Trinidad, and the Philippines, but the first two are cases of majority "control" instead of genuinely democratic majority rule with alternating majorities, in Ian Lustick's (1979) sense of the term. Lustick argues that power sharing is not the only method that can maintain stability in divided societies; the alternative is a system of control in which a dominant group uses its superior power to keep the other group or groups subordinate. In control democracies, power is almost permanently in the hands of the majority group (Sinhalese in Sri Lanka, Africans in Trinidad, and, until 1972, Protestants in Northern Ireland), and the minorities are excluded from power and often discriminated against. In the case of the Philippines, it is doubtful that we can speak of a true deeply divided society, and, in any case, democracy broke down in 1972 and was not restored for many years (see Lijphart 1985, 103).

3 India obviously remains deviant in terms of Mill's and Harrison's nonconsociational thinking, mentioned earlier.

4 A further comparison with Japan, not yet so obvious in the early 1960s, reveals the additional contrast between India's centrist Congress Party and Japan's right-of-center Liberal Democrats. Mexico's Institutional Revolutionary Party (PRI) is probably the closest parallel to the centrist Congress Party, except that it does not operate in a fully competitive democratic setting.

5 Clearly, the consociational interpretation does not fit India's caste conflict as well as it fits the linguistic and religious divisions. In the early years, an accommodation with the Scheduled Castes was reached, but further accommodation with the backward castes came about only later and mainly in parts of southern India. Especially in northern India, where there has been little intercaste accommodation, caste conflict is the most serious (see Frankel 1988).

6 Other possible causes of the decline of power sharing are the emergence of new and unforeseen problems, such as the international crisis that can explain much of the collapse of Lebanese power sharing in the 1970s (Lijphart 1985, 91–92), and the improvement in intergroup relations by successful power sharing to such an extent that full-fledged power sharing becomes superfluous, as in the Austrian and Dutch cases after 1966 and 1967, respectively.

7 The BJP also can be called a majority-control party in the sense that Lustick (1979) uses the term *control*; see note 2 above.

8 A serious drawback of the Nigerian system, used in 1979 and 1983 (in which the winner needs a nationwide plurality plus at least 25 percent of the vote in no fewer than two thirds of the states) is that it can easily result in none of the candidates being elected. This is not a problem in Nehru's (1992, 137) plan because he proposes the indirect election of the president – by an electoral college of national, state, and local legislators – in which repeated ballots can be conducted until a winner emerges. Of course, consociationalists would still prefer a broadly *representative* collegial executive to a broadly *supported* presidency.

References

Arora, Balveer, and Nirmal Mukarji. 1992. "Introduction: The Basic Issues." In *Federalism in India: Origins and Development*, eds Nirmal Mukarji and Balveer Arora. New Delhi: Vikas.

Austin, Granville. 1966. *The Indian Constitution: Cornerstone of a Nation*. Bombay: Oxford University Press.

Banerjee, Ashis. 1992. "Federalism and Nationalism: An Attempt at Historical Interpretation." In *Federalism in India: Origins and Development*, eds Nirmal Mukarji and Balveer Arora. New Delhi: Vikas.

Barry, Brian. 1975. "Political Accommodation and Consociational Democracy." *British Journal of Political Science* 5 (October): 477–505.

Batliner, Gerard. 1981. *Zur heutigen Lage des liechtensteinischen Parlaments*. Vaduz: Verlag der Liechtensteinischen Akademischen Gesellschaft.

Berg-Schlosser, Dirk. 1985. "Elements of Consociational Democracy in Kenya." *European Journal of Political Research* 13 (March): 95–109.

Bhambhri, C. P. 1971. "Electoral Reform and Party System in India: A Plea for Proportional Representation." In *Elections and Electoral Reform in India*, ed. Subhash C. Kashyap. New Delhi: Institute for Constitutional and Parliamentary Studies.

Brass, Paul R. 1990. *The Politics of India Since Independence*. Cambridge: Cambridge University Press.

——1991. *Ethnicity and Nationalism: Theory and Comparison*. New Delhi: Sage.

Cannon, Gordon E. 1982. "Consociationalism vs. Control: Canada as a Case Study." *Western Political Quarterly* 35 (March): 50–64.

Chehabi, H. E. 1980. "The Absence of Consociationalism in Sri Lanka." *Plural Societies* 11 (winter): 55–65.

Chinwuba, Felix Aneze. 1980. "Consociationalism as an Approach to Political Integration: The Case of the Federal Republic of Nigeria." PhD dissertation, Tulane University.

Chryssochoou, Dimitris N. 1994. "Democracy and Symbiosis in the European Union: Towards a Confederal Consociation?" *West European Politics* 17 (October): 1–14.

Daalder, Hans. 1974. "The Consociational Democracy Theme." *World Politics* 26 (July): 604–21.

Daalder, Hans, and Galen A. Irwin, eds. 1989. Special issue on "Politics in the Netherlands: How Much Change?" *West European Politics* 12 (January): 1–185.

Dahl, Robert A. 1989. *Democracy and Its Critics*. New Haven CT: Yale University Press.

Dahl, Robert A., and Edward R. Tufte. 1973. *Size and Democracy*. Stanford CA: Stanford University Press.

Das Gupta, Jyotirindra. 1989. "India: Democratic Becoming and Combined Development." In *Democracy in Developing Countries: Asia*, eds Larry Diamond, Juan J. Linz, and Seymour Martin Lipset. Boulder CO: Lynne Rienner.

Dekmejian, Richard Hrair. 1978. "Consociational Democracy in Crisis: The Case of Lebanon." *Comparative Politics* 10 (January): 251–65.

Dew, Edward M. 1994. *The Trouble in Suriname, 1975–1993*. Westport CT: Praeger.

Dix, Robert H. 1980. "Consociational Democracy: The Case of Colombia." *Comparative Politics* 12 (April): 303–21.

Engineer, Asghar Ali, ed. 1987. *The Shah Bano Controversy*. Hyderabad, India: Orient Longman.

Esman, Milton J. 1972. *Administration and Development in Malaysia: Institution-Building and Reform in a Plural Society*. Ithaca NY: Cornell University Press.

Frankel, Francine R. 1988. "Middle Classes and Castes in India's Politics: Prospects for Political Accommodation." In *India's Democracy: An Analysis of Changing State-Society Relations*, ed. Atul Kohli. Princeton NJ: Princeton University Press.

Fyzee, Asaf A. A. 1964. *Outlines of Muhammadan Law*. 3rd edn. London: Oxford University Press.

Gabel, Matthew J. 1994. "Balancing Democracy and Stability: Considering the Democratic Deficit in the EU from a Consociational Perspective." Presented at the Joint Sessions of Workshops of the European Consortium for Political Research, Madrid.

Goldman, Joseph Richard. 1985. "Consociational Authoritarian Politics and the 1974 Yugoslav Constitution: A Preliminary Note." *East European Quarterly* 19 (June): 241–49.

Graziano, Luigi. 1980. "The Historic Compromise and Consociational Democracy: Toward a 'New Democracy'?" *International Political Science Review* 1 (3): 345–68.

Halpern, Sue M. 1986. "The Disorderly Universe of Consociational Democracy." *West European Politics* 9 (April): 181–97.

Hardgrave, Robert L., Jr. 1993. "India: The Dilemmas of Diversity." *Journal of Democracy* 4 (October): 54–68.

Harrison, Selig S. 1960. *India: The Most Dangerous Decades*. Princeton NJ: Princeton University Press.

Hartlyn, Jonathan. 1988. *The Politics of Coalition Rule in Colombia*. Cambridge: Cambridge University Press.

Hegde, Ramakrishna. 1986. *Electoral Reforms: Lack of Political Will*. Bangalore: Karnataka State Janata Party.

Hix, Simon. 1994. "Approaches to the Study of the EC: The Challenge to Comparative Politics." *West European Politics* 17 (January): 1–30.

Horowitz, Donald L. 1985. *Ethnic Groups in Conflict*. Berkeley CA: University of California Press.

Hughes, Arnold. 1982. "The Limits of 'Consociational Democracy' in the Gambia." *Civilisations* 32 (2): 65–92.

Huntington, Samuel P. 1988. "One Soul at a Time: Political Science and Political Reform." *American Political Science Review* 82 (March): 3–10.

Hussain, Abid. 1993. *India: Challenges and Changes*. New Delhi: Rajiv Gandhi Institute for Contemporary Studies.

Huyse, Luc. 1987. *De verzuiling voorbij*. Louvain: Kritak.

Iyer, V. R. Krishna. 1987. *The Muslim Women (Protection of Rights on Divorce) Act, 1986*. Lucknow: Eastern Book Company.

Jaisingh, Hari. 1992. "Time for a Second Republic." In *Reforming the Constitution*, ed. Subhash C. Kashyap. New Delhi: UBSPD.

Kashyap, Subhash C. 1992. "Constitution, Its Working and Need for Reforms." In *Reforming the Constitution*, ed. Subhash C. Kashyap. New Delhi: UBSPD.

Kathuria, Harbir Singh. 1990. *President's Rule in India, 1967–89*. New Delhi: Uppal.

Khan, Rasheeduddin. 1992. *Federal India: A Design for Change*. New Delhi: Vikas.

Khilnani, Sunil. 1992. "India's Democratic Career." In *Democracy: The Unfinished Journey, 508 BC to AD 1993*, ed. John Dunn. Oxford: Oxford University Press.

Kohli, Atul. 1990. *Democracy and Discontent: India's Growing Crisis of Governability*. Cambridge: Cambridge University Press.

Kothari, Rajni. 1970. *Politics in India*. Boston MA: Little, Brown.

——1976. *Democratic Polity and Social Change in India: Crisis and Opportunities*. Bombay: Allied.

——1989. *Politics and the People: In Search of a Humane India*. Delhi: Ajanta.

Lehmbruch, Gerhard. 1993. "Consociational Democracy and Corporatism in Switzerland." *Publius* 23 (spring): 43–60.

Levine, Daniel H. 1973. *Conflict and Political Change in Venezuela*. Princeton NJ: Princeton University Press.

Lijphart, Arend. 1968. *The Politics of Accommodation: Pluralism and Democracy in the Netherlands*. Berkeley CA: University of California Press.

——1977. *Democracy in Plural Societies: A Comparative Exploration*. New Haven CT: Yale University Press.

——1979. "Consociation and Federation: Conceptual and Empirical Links." *Canadian Journal of Political Science* 12 (September): 499–515.

——1984. *Democracies: Majoritarian and Consensus Patterns of Government in Twenty-One Countries*. New Haven CT: Yale University Press.

——1985. *Power sharing in South Africa*. Berkeley CA: Institute of International Studies, University of California.

——1992. "Democratization and Constitutional Choices in Czecho-Slovakia, Hungary, and Poland," *Journal of Theoretical Politics* 4 (April): 207–33.

——1994. "Prospects for Power sharing in the New South Africa." In *Election '94 South Africa: The Campaigns, Results and Future Prospects*, ed. Andrew Reynolds. New York: St. Martin's Press.

Lindberg, Leon N. 1974. "The Political System of the European Community." In *Politics in Europe: Structures and Processes in Some Postindustrial Democracies*, ed. Martin O. Heisler. New York: David McKay.

Linder, Wolf. 1994. *Swiss Democracy: Possible Solutions to Conflict in Multicultural Societies*. New York: St. Martin's Press.

Lustick, Ian. 1979. "Stability in Deeply Divided Societies." *World Politics* 31 (April): 325–44.

Luther, Kurt Richard, and Wolfgang Müller, eds. 1992. Special Issue on "Politics in Austria: Still a Case of Consociationalism?" *West European Politics* 15 (January): 1–226.

Luthera, Ved Prakash. 1964. *The Concept of the Secular State and India*. London: Oxford University Press.

Mair, Peter. 1994. "The Correlates of Consensus Democracy and the Puzzle of Dutch Politics." *West European Politics* 17 (October): 97–123.

Malaviya, S. P. 1992. "Case for a Constituent Assembly." In *Reforming the Constitution*, ed. Subhash C. Kashyap. New Delhi: UBSPD.

Masselos, Jim. 1985. *Indian Nationalism: An History*. New Delhi: Sterling.

Mehta, Piarey Lal. 1991. *Constitutional Protection to Scheduled Tribes in India: In Retrospect and Prospects*. Delhi: H. K. Publishers.

Messarra, Antoine Nasri. 1994. *Théorie générale du système politique libanais*. Paris: Cariscript.

Mill, John Stuart. 1958 [1861]. *Considerations on Representative Government*. New York: Liberal Arts Press.

Mukarji, Nirmal, and Balveer Arora. 1992. "Conclusion: Restructuring Federal Democracy." In *Federalism in India: Origins and Development*, eds Nirmal Mukarji and Balveer Arora. New Delhi: Vikas.

Mukarji, Nirmal, and George Mathew. 1992. "Epilogue: Federal Issues, 1988–90." In *Federalism in India: Origins and Development*, eds Nirmal Mukarji and Balveer Arora. New Delhi: Vikas.

Nehru, B. K. 1986. *Thoughts on Our Present Discontents*. New Delhi: Allied.

——1992. "A Fresh Look at the Constitution." In *Reforming the Constitution*, ed. Subhash C. Kashyap. New Delhi: UBSPD.

Noorani, A. G. 1989. *The Presidential System: The Indian Debate*. New Delhi: Sage.

Olson, David M. 1994. "The Sundered State: Federalism and Parliament in Czechoslovakia." In *Parliaments in Transition: The New Legislative Politics in the Former USSR and Eastern Europe*, ed. Thomas F. Remington. Boulder CO: Westview Press.

Pai Panandiker, V. A., and Ajay Mehra. 1996. *The Indian Cabinet and Governance of India*. New Delhi: Konark.

Pathak, Bindeshwar. 1993. "Facets of the System: Presidential vs. Parliamentary." In *Perspectives on the Constitution*, ed. Subhash S. Kashyap. Delhi: Shipra.

Powell, G. Bingham, Jr. 1970. *Social Fragmentation and Political Hostility: An Austrian Case Study*. Stanford CA: Stanford University Press.

——1979. Book review of Arend Lijphart's *Democracy in Plural Societies*. In *American Political Science Review* 73 (March): 295–97.

——1982. *Contemporary Democracies: Participation, Stability, and Violence*. Cambridge MA: Harvard University Press.

Prasad, Anirudh. 1991. *Reservation Policy and Practice in India: A Means to an End*. New Delhi: Deep & Deep Publications.

Rae, Douglas W. 1967. *The Political Consequences of Electoral Laws*. New Haven CT: Yale University Press.

Rajgopal, P. R. 1987. *Communal Violence in India*. New Delhi: Uppal.

Rao, S. Ramachandra. 1992. "Plea for a New Constitution." In *Reforming the Constitution*, ed. Subhash C. Kashyap. New Delhi: UBSPD.

Reddy, K. Brahmananda. 1992. "Case for Fundamental Changes." In *Reforming the Constitution*, ed. Subhash C. Kashyap. New Delhi: UBSPD.

Rudolph, Lloyd I., and Susanne Hoeber Rudolph. 1987. *In Pursuit of Lakshmi: The Political Economy of the Indian State*. Chicago IL: University of Chicago Press.

Sathe, Vasant. 1991. *National Government: Agenda for a New India*. New Delhi: UBS.

Seth, J. D. 1971. "Towards a New Electoral Law." In *Elections and Electoral Reforms in India*, ed. Subhash C. Kashyap. New Delhi: Institute of Constitutional and Parliamentary Studies.

Sharif, Abu Saleh. 1993. *Some Socio-Economic and Demographic Aspects of Population According to Religion in India*. Bombay: Centre for the Study of Society and Secularism.

Sharma, Arvind. 1993. "Minority vs. Majority Rights." In *Perspectives on the Constitution*, ed. Subhash C. Kashyap. Delhi: Shipra.

Singh, L.P. 1986. *Electoral Reform: Problems and Suggested Solutions.* New Delhi: Uppal.

Srinivasavaradan, T. C. A. 1992. *Federal Concept: The Indian Experience.* New Delhi: Allied.

Steiner, Jürg. 1990. "Power sharing: Another Swiss 'Export Product'?" In *Conflict and Peacemaking in Multiethnic Societies*, ed. Joseph V. Montville. Lexington MA: Lexington Books.

Steiner, Jürg, and Dorff, Robert H. 1980. *A Theory of Political Decision Modes: Intraparty Decision Making in Switzerland.* Chapel Hill NC: University of North Carolina Press.

Suntharalingam, R. 1983. *Indian Nationalism: An Historical Analysis.* New Delhi: Vikas.

Taagepera, Rein, and Matthew Soberg Shugart. 1989. *Seats and Votes: The Effects and Determinants of Electoral Systems.* New Haven CT: Yale University Press.

Taylor, Rupert. 1992. "South Africa: A Consociational Path to Peace?" *Transformation* 17: 1–11.

Trehan, Virender M. 1993. "Need for Change." In *Perspectives on the Constitution*, ed. Subhash C. Kashyap. Delhi: Shipra.

Van den Berghe, Pierre L. 1981. *The Ethnic Phenomenon.* New York: Elsevier.

Vanhanen, Tatu. 1987. "What Kind of Electoral System for Plural Societies? India as an Example." In *The Logic of Multiparty Systems*, ed. Manfred J. Holler. Dordrecht: Kluwer.

Varshney, Ashutosh. 1993a. "Contested Meanings: India's National Identity, Hindu Nationalism, and the Politics of Anxiety." *Daedalus* 122 (summer): 227–61.

——1993b. "India's Democratic Exceptionalism and Its Troubled Trajectory." Revised version of paper presented at the 1990 annual meeting of the American Political Science Association, San Francisco.

——1995. "The Self-Correcting Mechanisms of Indian Democracy." *Seminar* (Delhi) 425 (January): 38–41.

Vasovic, Vucina. 1992. "A Plea for Consociational Pluralism." In *The Tragedy of Yugoslavia: The Failure of Democratic Transformation*, eds Jim Seroka and Vukasin Pavlovic. Armonk NY: M. E. Sharpe.

Vira, Dharma. 1992. "Inadequacy and Impracticability of the Present Constitution: Case for Major Amendments." In *Reforming the Constitution*, ed. Subhash C. Kashyap. New Delhi: UBSPD.

Von Vorys, Karl. 1975. *Democracy Without Consensus: Communalism and Political Stability in Malaysia.* Princeton NJ: Princeton University Press.

Weiner, Myron. 1969. *Party Building in a New Nation: The Indian National Congress.* Chicago IL: University of Chicago Press.

——1989. *The Indian Paradox: Essays in Indian Politics.* New Delhi: Sage.

Wheare, K. C. 1964. *Federal Government.* 4th edn. New York: Oxford University Press.

Worrall, Denis. 1981. "The Constitutional Committee of the President's Council." *Politikon* 8 (December): 27–34.

Young, Crawford. 1976. *The Politics of Cultural Pluralism.* Madison WI: University of Wisconsin Press.

Zakaria, Haji Ahmad. 1989. "Malaysia: Quasi Democracy in a Divided Society." In *Democracy in Developing Countries: Asia*, eds Larry Diamond, Juan J. Linz, and Seymour Martin Lipset. Boulder CO: Lynne Rienner.

Zolberg, Aristide R. 1977. "Splitting the Difference: Federalization Without Federalism in Belgium." In *Ethnic Conflict in the Western World*, ed. Milton J. Esman. Ithaca NY: Cornell University Press.

4 Self-determination versus pre-determination of ethnic minorities in power sharing systems

Introduction

In this paper, I want to make three main points. The first of these is that the basic principles of consociational democracy – or power sharing democracy – are so obviously the appropriate answer to the problems of deeply divided (plural) societies that both politicians and social scientists have repeatedly and independently re-invented and rediscovered them. Second, these principles must be thought of as broad guidelines that can be implemented in a variety of ways – not all of the which, however, are of equal merit and can be equally recommended to divided societies. My third and most important point will be that an especially important set of alternatives in applying the consociational principles is the choice between self-determination and pre-determination of the constituent groups in the power sharing system, that is, the groups that will be the collective actors among whom power will be shared.

To give a brief preview of the last proposition, the terms "self-determination" and "pre-determination" describe the alternatives very well and in an almost self-explanatory way, but my use of the former differs from the most common usage. Self-determination deviates from the concept of "*national* self-determination" – the idea that nations should have the right to form separate sovereign states – in two fundamental respects. It refers to a method or process that gives various rights to groups *within* the existing state – for instance, autonomy rather than sovereignty – and it allows these groups to manifest themselves instead of deciding in advance on the identity of the groups. Needless to say, my concept of pre-determination is completely unrelated to the superficially similar theological concept of pre-destination. Like self-determination, it refers to an internal process, but in contrast with self-determination, it means that the groups that are to share power are identified in advance. Both in contemporary and historical cases of consociationalism, pre-determination is more common, but I shall argue that self-determination has a number of great advantages and ought to be given much more attention by constitutional engineers who are trying to devise solutions for divided societies.

As a final introductory remark, let me define a few other basic concepts. I shall use the terms *deeply divided society* and *plural society* as synonyms. A plural society is a society that is sharply divided along religious, ideological, linguistic, cultural, ethnic, or racial lines into virtually separate subsocieties with their own political parties, interest groups, and media of communication. These subsocieties will be referred to as *segments*. As the definition of plural society indicates, the segments can differ from each other in several ways: in terms of religion, language, ethnicity, race, and so on. The most common of these is *ethnicity*, but the different categories overlap considerably. Ethnic differences imply cultural differences and often linguistic differences as well. Furthermore, cultural differences frequently include religious differences. Even when, as in the plural societies of Lebanon and Northern Ireland, the segments are mainly described in religious terms, the differences between them encompass a great deal more and can also be legitimately described as ethnic differences. I shall therefore make the general assumption that segments are ethnic segments and, in particular, ethnic minorities. Finally, let me emphasize that I shall use the terms *consociational* democracy and *power sharing* democracy synonymously and interchangeably. [...]

Varieties of power sharing

In my previous writings, I have emphasized that consociational democracy does not mean one specific set of rules and institutions.[1] Instead, it means a general type of democracy defined in terms of four broad principles, all of which can be applied in a variety of ways. For instance, as indicated earlier, the grand coalition can be a cabinet in a parliamentary system or a coalitional arrangement of a president and other top office-holders in a presidential system of government. The Swiss seven-member federal executive, which is based on a hybrid of parliamentary and presidential principles, is an additional example. Segmental autonomy may take the role of territorial federalism or of autonomy for segments that are not defined in geographical terms. Proportional results in elections may be achieved by the various systems of formal proportional representation (PR) or by several non-PR methods, such as Lebanon's method of requiring ethnically balanced slates in multi-member district plurality elections.[2] The minority veto can be either an absolute or a suspensive veto, and it may be applied either to all decisions or to only certain specified kinds of decisions, such as matters of culture and education. There is also the general difference, applicable to all four consociational principles, between laying down the basic rules of power sharing in formal documents – such as constitutions, laws, or semi-public agreements – and relying on merely informal and unwritten agreements and understandings among the leaders of the segments.

I have come to believe that one of the most important differences between consociational arrangements – and also one of the most important choices that consociational engineers have to make – is the difference between pre-determination and self-determination of the segments of a plural society. Should these segments be identified in advance, and should power sharing be implemented as a system in which these pre-determined segments share power? This appears to be the simplest way of instituting consociationalism, although, as I shall show below, it entails several problems and drawbacks. The alternative, which is necessarily somewhat more complicated, is to set up a system in which the segments are allowed, and even encouraged, to emerge spontaneously – and hence to define themselves instead of being pre-defined.

The crucial importance of this set of alternatives has become especially clear to me as a result of my thinking about the best way of setting up a democratic power sharing system in South Africa. The first problem, of course, is to induce the different groups in South Africa to start negotiations on a peaceful and democratic solution for their country, and the second problem will be to secure agreement on the principle of power sharing. Assuming that these problems can be solved, I have tried to address the next question: what kind of power sharing system should be adopted? Here the main problem is that, while there is broad agreement that South Africa is a plural society, the identification of the segments is both objectively difficult and politically controversial. The root of this problem is that the South African system of minority rule has long relied on an official and strict classification of its citizens in four racial groups (African, White, Coloured, and Asian) and the further classification of the Africans into about a dozen ethnic groups. The racial classification has served the allocation of basic rights: for instance, the current "tricameral" system allows Whites, Coloureds, and Asians to elect separate chambers of parliament, and excludes Africans from the national franchise. The ethnic classification has been the basis of the "grand apartheid" system of setting up, and encouraging the eventual independence, of a series of ethnic homelands (formerly called Bantustans).

As a result of this policy of artificially forcing people into racial and ethnic categories, it has become quite unclear what the true dividing lines in the society are. The South African government appears to continue to think mainly in terms of race when it speaks of group rights and a sharing of power among groups. My own feeling is that the ethnic groups, including the two White ethnic groups of Afrikaners and English-speakers, are the strongest candidates to be considered the segments of the South African plural society, but I admit right away that the situation is more complicated. For instance, the English-speaking Whites appear to be a residual group rather than a cohesive and self-conscious ethnic segment. Another example concerns the Coloureds: should they be considered a separate segment or, since most of them speak Afrikaans and have an Afrikaans cultural background, do they form a single ethnic segment together with the White Afrikaners? Others have argued that modernization, industrialization, and urbanization have had a "melting pot" effect, and that South Africa today is no longer a plural society and has become a "common society".[3]

Furthermore, the White government's insistence on African ethnic differences in connection with its widely despised homelands policy has had the ironic effect of making ethnicity highly suspect among most Africans. This sentiment is expressed clearly in Archbishop Desmond Tutu's statement: "We Blacks (most of us) execrate ethnicity with all our being."[4] Similarly, the African National Congress, the most powerful Black party in South Africa (although officially banned), both rejects ethnicity, since it regards ethnicity as a White divide-and-rule policy, and denies even its existence and hence its political relevance.

How can we resolve these disagreements about the identity of the segments and about whether South Africa is a plural society or not? My answer is that these disagreements do not need to be resolved, since we can design a consociational system on the basis of self-determined segments. First of all, I recommend elections by a relatively pure form of PR which will allow representation for even very small parties. Its rationale is based on the definition of a plural society that I gave earlier. This definition implies that one of the tests of whether a society is genuinely plural is whether or not its political parties are organized along segmental lines. We can turn this logic around: if we know that a society is plural but cannot identify the segments with complete confidence, we can take our cue from the political parties that form under conditions of free association and competition. PR is the optimal electoral system for allowing the segments to manifest themselves in the form of political parties. The beauty of PR is not just that it yields proportional results and permits minority representation – two important advantages from a consociational perspective – but also that it permits the segments to define themselves. Hence the adoption of PR obviates the need for any prior sorting of divergent claims about the segmental composition of South Africa or any other plural society. The proof of segmental identity is electoral success. We can go one step further: PR elections can also provide an answer to the question of whether South Africa is a plural society or not. If it is a plural society, the successful parties will be mainly segmental (and presumably ethnic) parties; if it is not a plural society, the parties that will emerge will be non-segmental policy-oriented parties. PR treats all groups, segmental or non-segmental, in a completely equal and even-handed way.

All of the consociational principles can now be instituted on the basis of self-determination. A grand coalition can be prescribed by requiring that the cabinet be composed of all parties of a specified minimum size in parliament; since these will be segmental parties, the cabinet will automatically be an inter-segmental grand coalition. The proportional allocation of public service jobs and public funds can also be based on the relative strengths that the several segments have demonstrated in the PR elections. And instead of granting a minority veto to all pre-determined segments, such a veto can be given to any group of legislators above a certain specified percentage.

Segmental autonomy can be organized along similar lines. Any cultural group that wishes to have internal autonomy can be given the right to establish a "cultural council," a publicly recognized body equivalent to a state in a federation. One of its main responsibilities will be the administration of schools for those who wish to receive an education according to the group's linguistic and cultural traditions. The voluntary self-segregation that such schools entail is acceptable as long as the option of multicultural and multiethnic education is also made available and provided that all schools are treated equally. It should be emphasized that this kind of non-territorial self-determined segmental autonomy can either be an alternative or an addition to geographically based federalism. The two are eminently compatible. In the South African case, territorial federalism makes a great deal of sense because many of the ethnic segments have clear geographical strongholds and also because of the great diversity of the country in other respects. At the same time, however, there is so much group inter-mixture that territorial federalism by itself is insufficient to satisfy the demands of segmental autonomy.

In their book *South Africa Without Apartheid* Heribert Adam and Kogila Moodley make similar recommendations.[5] And such proposals have also been formally placed on the political agenda of South Africa by the Progressive Federal Party (PFP). In its constitutional plan adopted in 1978, the PFP proposes the following procedure to effect a grand coalition cabinet: The lower house of a bicameral legislature will be elected by PR, and the lower house will in turn elect the prime minister by majority vote. Then a power sharing cabinet will be formed by requiring that the prime minister appoint cabinet members "proportional to the strength of the various political parties" in the lower house and that "in doing so the Prime Minister will have to negotiate with the leaders of the relevant parties." Segmental autonomy is proposed by the PFP in the following self-determined form: "A cultural group may establish a Cultural Council to assist in maintaining and promoting its cultural interests and apply to have that council registered with the Federal Constitutional Court." These cultural councils will be publicly recognized bodies almost on a par with the states in the federal system that the PFP recommends; in the federal senate, where the states will be represented by equal numbers of senators, each cultural council will be able to name one senator, too.[6]

The PFP proposal of cultural councils was inspired by the Belgian example of non-territorial federalism (or, more accurately, partly non-territorial federalism), but it differs significantly from the Belgian model in that the Belgian cultural councils are based on pre-determination: three, and only three, councils – Dutch, French and German – were established. Similarly, the Belgian constitution prescribes that the cabinet be composed of equal numbers of Dutch-speakers and French-speakers – again an example of pre-determination of segments. There are a number of other well known examples of pre-determined segments, particularly the Greek and Turkish segments which are explicitly specified in the 1960 Cypriot constitution, and Maronites, Sunnis, Shiites, and other religious sects recognized in the 1943 National Pact in Lebanon. However, the pre-1970 Belgian system of inter-religious and inter-ideological consociationalism was largely of the self-determined kind. The same generalization applies to the Dutch, Swiss and Austrian cases of consociational democracy.

A final, particularly interesting, but much less well known example of self-determination is the 1925 Law of Cultural Autonomy in Estonia. Under its terms, each ethnic minority with more than 3,000 formally registered members had the right to establish autonomous institutions under the authority of a cultural council elected by the minority. This council could organize, administer, and supervise minority schools and other cultural institutions such as libraries and theaters, and it could issue decrees and raise taxes for these purposes. The councils also received state and local subsidies, and public funding was provided for the minority schools at the same level as for Estonian schools. The German and Jewish minorities quickly took advantage of the law and set up their own autonomous cultural authorities. As Georg von Rauch writes, "these cultural authorities soon proved their worth, and the Estonian government was able to claim, with every justification, that it had found an exemplary solution to the problem of its minorities."[7]

Advantages of self-determination

In the case of South Africa, because of special South African conditions and circumstances, self-determination of the segments is almost certainly the only way in which a consociation can be successfully established and operated. In most other cases, self-determination and pre-determination may both be reasonable options for consociational engineers. I would argue, however, that self-determination has a number of great advantages over pre-determination and hence that, unless there are compelling reasons to opt for pre-determination, the presumption should be in favor of self-determination. In this final section of my paper, let me list the advantages of self-determination:

1   The very first point in favor of self-determination is that it avoids the problem of invidious comparisons and discriminatory choices. Deciding which groups are to be the recognized segments in a power sharing system necessarily entails the decision of which groups are not going to be recognized. In Lebanon, for instance, should the Moslem and Christian communes or the Maronites, Sunni, Shiite, Greek Orthodox, etc., sub-communes be made into the basic building blocks of the power sharing system? In Belgium, since the small German-speaking minority

was given its own cultural council, should not the Spanish, Turkish, and Moroccan minorities be given the same privilege? Even in cases that appear to be completely clear and uncontroversial, I would still argue that self-determination has no disadvantages compared with pre-determination in this respect.

2 The problem of potential discrimination is especially serious in countries where there are two or more large segments, which will obviously be recognized as participants in the power sharing system, but also one or more very small minorities. These minorities run the risk of being overlooked, disregarded, or worse. Cyprus provides a good illustration. During the negotiations about the constitution and the electoral law, the question of how to define membership in the Greek majority community and in the Turkish minority community and the question of how to deal with the other, much smaller, minorities such as the Armenians and Maronites were discussed with "extraordinary intensity," as S. G. Xydis reports. Xydis speculates that the Turkish Cypriots may have been "anxious to prevent any other minority in Cyprus from acquiring the status similar to that of the Turkish community with all its political implications."[8]

3 Pre-determination entails not only potential discrimination against groups but, as a rule, also the assignment of individuals to specific groups. Individuals may well object to such labeling. In fact, the very principle of officially registering individuals according to ethnic or other group membership may be controversial, offensive, or even completely unacceptable to many citizens. Self-determination avoids the entire problem of placing people in groups and of establishing procedures for making decisions in individual cases. The New Zealand system of guaranteed Maori representation in parliament can serve as an example here. For many years, Maoris were placed on separate voter registers and voted for Maori candidates in four exclusively Maori districts. This entailed the problem of deciding whether particular individuals should be placed on Maori or the general voter registers and the additional problem that many Maoris preferred not to be singled out for this special treatment. In order to alleviate these problems, it was decided that the special Maori seats would be retained but that, for Maoris, registration on the Maori register would be optional. Clearly the entire problem could be solved by the introduction of PR; reserved Maori seats would no longer be necessary. This is what New Zealand's Royal Commission on the Electoral System proposed in 1986.[9]

4 Self-determination gives equal chances not only to all ethnic or other segments, large or small, in a plural society but also to groups and individuals who explicitly reject the idea that society should be organized on a segmental basis. In the Lebanese case, Theodor Hanf has suggested that the consociational arrangement could be strengthened considerably if secularly oriented groups and individuals could be recognized on a par with the traditional religious communities:

A formula which makes group membership optional instead of obligatory could perhaps reduce the fear of those who wish to preserve their group identity, and perhaps prevent pressure being exerted upon those who do not wish to define themselves as members of a specific community but as Lebanese.[10]

A system of self-determination would obviously make this possible. In the Netherlands, the self-determined system of segmental schools, primarily designed to accommodate the main religious groups, has also been taken advantage of by small secular groups interested in particular educational philosophies to establish, for instance, Montessori schools.

5 In systems of pre-determination, there is a strong temptation to fix the relative shares of representation and other privileges for the segments on a permanent or semi-permanent basis. Examples are the 1:1 (Dutch-French) ratio of representation in the Belgian cabinet, the 7:3 (Greek-Turkish) ratio in the Cypriot cabinet and legislature, and the 6:5 (Christian-Moslem) ratio in the Lebanese parliament. Especially in Lebanon, this fixed ratio has become extremely controversial and it is one of the underlying causes of the breakdown of consociationalism in that country. Self-determination has the advantage of being completely flexible, since it is based on the numbers of people supporting the different parties and registering as members of cultural groups. It is naturally and continually self-adjusting.

6 Even when ethnic groups are geographically concentrated, the boundaries between different ethnic groups never perfectly divide these groups from each other. This means that territorial federalism can never be a perfect answer to the requirements of ethnic and cultural autonomy. And, if we opt for autonomy on a non-territorial – that is, individual – basis, the most satisfactory method is to let the individuals determine their group membership for themselves. This consideration is becoming more and more important as individual mobility in modern societies increases and dilutes the geographical concentration of ethnic groups.

7 Finally, let me make an argument which is partly at variance with the main thrust of my reasoning so far. In many cases, the main segments of a plural society may be absolutely clear and uncontroversial, and these segments may want to be recognized as formally and specifically as possible. In these circumstances, it may make sense to use a combination of pre-determination and self-determination: for instance, a two-tier system of pre-determination of the large segments and self-determination of any other group that may aspire to similar, though not necessarily identical, rights of representation and autonomy. While my main argument remains that self-determination is to be preferred to pre-determination, many of the advantages of self-determination can be attained by using self-determination as a complementary method to pre-determination.

Are there any disadvantages to self-determination? The only genuine drawback is that it precludes the application of the principle of minority overrepresentation. As indicated earlier, the principle of proportionality is already favorable to minorities, especially small minorities, but it may be extended even further by giving minorities more than proportional representation. The 7:3 ratio in Cyprus is an example of such overrepresentation, since the actual population ratio of the Greek and Turkish segments is closer to 8:2. The advantage that minorities derive from overrepresentation should not be exaggerated, however. The stronger protection for minorities in power sharing systems is provided by guaranteed representation, guaranteed autonomy, and, if necessary, the use of the minority veto. Compared with these strong weapons, overrepresentation is no more than a marginal benefit.

Notes

1 See Arend Lijphart, "Consociation: The Model and Its Applications in Divided Societies," in Desmond Rea, ed., *Political Co-operation in Divided Societies: A Series of Papers Relevant to the Conflict in Northern Ireland* (Dublin: Gill and Macmillan, 1982) at 166–86. See also Heinz Kloss, "Territorial prinzip, Bekenntnisprinzip, Verfügungsprinzip: Über die Möglichkeiten der Abgrenzung der Volklichen Zugehörigkeit" (1965) 22 *Europa Ethnica* at 52–73.

2 Arend Lijphart, "Proportionality by Non-PR Methods: Ethnic Representation in Belgium, Cyprus, Lebanon, New Zealand, West Germany, and Zimbabwe" in Bernard Grofman and Arend Lijphart, eds, *Electoral Laws and Their Political Consequences* (New York: Agathon Press, 1986) at 113–23.

3 Heribert Adam and Kogila Moodley, *South Africa Without Apartheid: Dismantling Racial Domination* (Berkeley CA: University of California Press, 1986) esp. at 196–214.

4 Desmond Mpilo Tutu, *Hope and Suffering: Sermons and Speeches* (Grand Rapids MI: Eerdmans, 1984) at 121.

5 *Supra*, note 3 at 215–63.

6 Arend Lijphart, *Power-Sharing in South Africa* (Berkeley CA: Institute of International Studies, University of California, 1985) at 66–73.

7 Georg von Rauch, *The Baltic States: Estonia, Latvia, Lithuania – The Years of Independence 1917–1940* (Berkeley CA: University of California Press, 1974) at 141–42.

8 Stephen G. Xydis, *Cyprus: Reluctant Republic* (The Hague: Mouton, 1973) at 490–92.

9 Arend Lijphart, "The Demise of the Last Westminster System? Comments on the Report of New Zealand's Royal Commission on the Electoral System" (August 1987) 6:2 *Electoral Studies* at 97–103.

10 Theodor Hanf, "The 'Political Secularization' Issue in Lebanon" in *The Annual Review of the Social Science of Religion,* vol. 5 (Amsterdam: Mouton, 1981) at 249.

5 Constitutional design for divided societies[1]

Over the past half-century, democratic constitutional design has undergone a sea change. After the Second World War, newly independent countries tended simply to copy the basic constitutional rules of their former colonial masters, without seriously considering alternatives. Today, constitution writers choose more deliberately among a wide array of constitutional models, with various advantages and disadvantages. While at first glance this appears to be a beneficial development, it has actually been a mixed blessing: Since they now have to deal with more alternatives than they can readily handle, constitution writers risk making ill advised decisions. In my opinion, scholarly experts can be more helpful to constitution writers by formulating specific recommendations and guidelines than by overwhelming those who must make the decision with a barrage of possibilities and options.

This essay presents a set of such recommendations, focusing in particular on the constitutional needs of countries with deep ethnic and other cleavages. In such deeply divided societies the interests and demands of communal groups can be accommodated only by the establishment of power sharing, and my recommendations will indicate as precisely as possible which particular power sharing rules and institutions are optimal and why. (Such rules and institutions may be useful in less intense forms in many other societies as well.)

Most experts on divided societies and constitutional engineering broadly agree that deep societal divisions pose a grave problem for democracy, and that it is therefore generally more difficult to establish and maintain democratic government in divided than in homogeneous countries. The experts also agree that the problem of ethnic and other deep divisions is greater in countries that are not yet democratic or fully democratic than in well established democracies, and that such divisions present a major obstacle to democratization in the twenty-first century. On these two points, scholarly agreement appears to be universal.

A third point of broad, if not absolute, agreement is that the successful establishment of democratic government in divided societies requires two key elements: power sharing and group autonomy. Power sharing denotes the participation of representatives of all significant communal groups in political decision-making, especially at the executive level; group autonomy means that these groups have authority to run their own internal affairs, especially in the areas of education and culture. These two characteristics are the primary attributes of the kind of democratic system that is often referred to as power sharing democracy or, to use a technical political-science term, "consociational" democracy.[2] A host of scholars have analyzed the central role of these two features and are sympathetic to their adoption by divided societies.[3] But agreement extends far beyond the consociational school. A good example is Ted Robert Gurr, who in *Minorities at Risk: A Global View of Ethnopolitical Conflicts* clearly does not take his inspiration from consociational theory (in fact, he barely mentions it), but based on massive empirical analysis reaches the conclusion that the interests and demands of communal groups can usually be accommodated "by some combination of the policies and institutions of *autonomy* and *power sharing*."[4]

The consensus on the importance of power sharing has recently been exemplified by commentators' reactions to the creation of the Governing Council in Iraq: the Council has been criticized on a variety of grounds, but no one has questioned its broadly representative composition. The strength of the power sharing model has also been confirmed by its frequent practical applications. Long before scholars began analyzing the phenomenon of power sharing democracy in the 1960s, politicians and constitution writers had designed power sharing solutions for the problems of their divided societies (for example, in Austria, Canada, Colombia, Cyprus, India, Lebanon, Malaysia, the Netherlands, and Switzerland). Political scientists merely discovered what political practitioners had repeatedly – and independently of both academic experts and one another – invented years earlier.

Critics of power sharing

The power sharing model has received a great deal of criticism since it became a topic of scholarly discourse three decades ago. Some critics have argued that power sharing democracy is not ideally democratic or effective; others have focused on methodological and measurement issues.[5] But it is important to note that very few critics have presented serious alternatives to the power sharing model. One exception can be found in the early critique by Brian Barry, who in the case of Northern Ireland recommended "cooperation without cooptation" – straightforward majority rule in which both majority and minority would simply promise to behave moderately.[6] Barry's proposal would have meant that Northern Ireland's Protestant majority, however moderate, would be in power permanently, and that the Catholic minority would always play the role of the "loyal" opposition. Applied to the case of the Iraqi Governing Council, Barry's alternative to power sharing would call for a Council composed mainly or exclusively of moderate members of the Shi'ite majority, with the excluded Sunnis and Kurds in opposition. This is a primitive solution to ethnic tensions and extremism, and it is naive to expect minorities condemned to permanent opposition to remain loyal, moderate, and constructive. Barry's suggestion therefore cannot be – and, in practice, has not been – a serious alternative to power sharing.

The only other approach that has attracted considerable attention is Donald L. Horowitz's proposal to design various electoral mechanisms (especially the use of the "alternative vote" or "instant runoff") that would encourage the election of moderate representatives.[7] It resembles Barry's proposal in that it aims for moderation rather than broad representation in the legislature and the executive, except that Horowitz tries to devise a method to induce the moderation that Barry simply hopes for. If applied to the Iraqi Governing Council, Horowitz's model would generate a body consisting mainly of members of the Shi'ite majority, with the proviso that most of these representatives would be chosen in such a way that they would be sympathetic to the interests of the Sunni and Kurdish minorities. It is hard to imagine that, in the long run, the two minorities would be satisfied with this kind of moderate Shi'ite representation, instead of representation by members of their own communities. And it is equally hard to imagine that Kurdish and Sunni members of a broadly representative constituent assembly would ever agree to a constitution that would set up such a system.

Horowitz's alternative-vote proposal suffers from several other weaknesses, but it is not necessary to analyze them in this article.[8] The main point that is relevant here is that it has found almost no support from either academic experts or constitution writers. Its sole, and only partial, practical application to legislative elections in an ethnically divided society was the short-lived and ill fated Fijian constitutional system, which tried to combine the alternative vote with power sharing; it was adopted in 1999 and collapsed in 2000.[9] With all due respect to the originality of his ideas and the enthusiasm with which he has defended them, Horowitz's arguments do not seem to have sparked a great deal of assent or emulation.[10]

"One size fits all"?

In sum, power sharing has proven to be the only democratic model that appears to have much chance of being adopted in divided societies, which in turn makes it unhelpful to ask constitution writers to contemplate alternatives to it. More than enough potential confusion and distraction are already inherent in the consideration of the many alternatives *within* power sharing. Contrary to Horowitz's claim that power sharing democracy is a crude "one size fits all" model,[11] the power sharing systems adopted prior to 1960 (cited earlier), as well as more recent cases (such as Belgium, Bosnia, Czecho-Slovakia, Northern Ireland, and South Africa), show enormous variation. For example, broad representation in the executive has been achieved by a constitutional requirement that it be composed of equal numbers of the two major ethnolinguistic groups (Belgium); by granting all parties with a minimum of 5 percent of the legislative seats the right to be represented in the cabinet (South Africa, 1994–99); by the equal representation of the two main parties in the cabinet and an alternation between the two parties in the presidency (Colombia, 1958–64); and by permanently earmarking the presidency for one group and the prime ministership for another (Lebanon).

All of these options are not equally advantageous, however, and do not work equally well in practice, because the relative success of a power sharing system is contingent upon the specific mechanisms devised to yield the broad representation that constitutes its core. In fact, the biggest failures of power sharing systems, as in Cyprus in 1963 and Lebanon in 1975, must be attributed not to the lack of sufficient power sharing but to constitution writers' choice of unsatisfactory rules and institutions.

These failures highlight the way in which scholarly experts can help constitution writers by developing recommendations regarding power sharing rules and institutions. In this sense, Horowitz's "one size fits all" charge should serve as an inspiration to try to specify the optimal form of power sharing. While the power sharing model should be adapted according to the particular features of the country at hand, it is not true that *everything* depends on these individual characteristics. In the following sections I outline nine areas of constitutional choice and provide my recommendations in each area. These constitute a "one size" power sharing model that offers the best fit for most divided societies regardless of their individual circumstances and characteristics.

The legislative electoral system

The most important choice facing constitution writers is that of a legislative electoral system, for which the three broad categories are proportional representation (PR), majoritarian systems, and intermediate systems. For divided societies, ensuring the election of a broadly representative legislature should be the crucial consideration, and PR is undoubtedly the optimal way of doing so.

Within the category of majoritarian systems, a good case could be made for Horowitz's alternative-vote proposal, which I agree is superior to both the plurality method and the two-ballot majority runoff.[12] Nevertheless, there is a scholarly consensus against majoritarian systems in divided societies. As Larry Diamond explains:

> If any generalization about institutional design is sustainable ... it is that majoritarian systems are ill-advised for countries with deep ethnic, regional, religious, or other emotional and polarizing divisions. Where cleavage groups are sharply defined and group identities (and intergroup

insecurities and suspicions) deeply felt, the overriding imperative is to avoid broad and indefinite exclusion from power of any significant group.[13]

The intermediate category can be subdivided further into semi-proportional systems, "mixed" systems, and finally, majoritarian systems that offer guaranteed representation to particular minorities. Semi-proportional systems – like the cumulative and limited vote (which have been primarily used at the state and local levels in the United States) and the single nontransferable vote (used in Japan until 1993)[14] – may be able to yield minority representation, but never as accurately and consistently as PR. Unlike these rare semi-proportional systems, mixed systems have become quite popular since the early 1990s.[15] In some of the mixed systems (such as Germany's and New Zealand's) the PR component overrides the plurality component, and these should therefore be regarded not as mixed but as PR systems. To the extent that the PR component is not, or is only partly, compensatory (as in Japan, Hungary, and Italy), the results will necessarily be less than fully proportional – and minority representation less accurate and secure. Plurality combined with guaranteed representation for specified minorities (as in India and Lebanon) necessarily entails the potentially invidious determination of which groups are entitled to guaranteed representation and which are not. In contrast, the beauty of PR is that in addition to producing proportionality and minority representation, it treats all groups – ethnic, racial, religious, or even noncommunal groups – in a completely equal and even-handed fashion. Why deviate from full PR at all?

Guidelines within PR

Once the choice is narrowed down to PR, constitution writers need to settle on a particular type within that system. PR is still a very broad category, which spans a vast spectrum of complex possibilities and alternatives. How can the options be narrowed further? I recommend that highest priority be given to the selection of a PR system that is simple to understand and operate – a criterion that is especially important for new democracies. From that simplicity criterion, several desiderata can be derived: a high, but not necessarily perfect, degree of proportionality; multi-member districts that are not too large, in order to avoid creating too much distance between voters and their representatives; list PR, in which parties present lists of candidates to the voters, instead of the rarely used single transferable vote, in which voters have to rank order individual candidates; and closed or almost closed lists, in which voters mainly choose parties instead of individual candidates within the list. List PR with closed lists can encourage the formation and maintenance of strong and cohesive political parties.

One attractive model along these lines is the list-PR system used in Denmark, which has seventeen districts that elect an average of eight representatives each from partly open lists. The districts are small enough for minority parties with more than 8 percent of the vote to stand a good chance of being elected.[16] In addition to the 135 representatives elected in these districts, there are forty national compensatory seats that are apportioned to parties (with a minimum of 2 percent of the national vote) in a way that aims to maximize overall national proportionality.[17] The Danish model is advantageous for divided societies, because the compensatory seats plus the low 2 percent threshold give small minorities that are not geographically concentrated a reasonable chance to be represented in the national legislature. While I favor the idea of maximizing proportionality, however, this system does to some extent detract from the goal of keeping the electoral system as simple and transparent as possible. Moreover, national compensatory seats obviously make little sense in those divided societies where nationwide parties have not yet developed.

Parliamentary or presidential government

The next important decision facing constitution writers is whether to set up a parliamentary, presidential, or semi-presidential form of government. In countries with deep ethnic and other cleavages, the choice should be based on the different systems' relative potential for power sharing in the executive. As the cabinet in a parliamentary system is a collegial decision-making body – as opposed to the presidential one-person executive with a purely advisory cabinet – it offers the optimal setting for forming a broad power sharing executive. A second advantage of parliamentary systems is that there is no need for presidential elections, which are necessarily majoritarian in nature. As Juan Linz states in his well known critique of presidential government, "perhaps the most important implication of presidentialism is that it introduces a strong element of zero-sum game into democratic politics with rules that tend toward a 'winner-take-all' outcome."[18] Presidential election campaigns also encourage the politics of personality and overshadow the politics of competing parties and party programs. In representative democracy, parties provide the vital link between voters and the government, and in divided societies they are crucial in voicing the interests of communal groups. Seymour Martin Lipset has recently emphasized this point again by calling political parties "indispensable" in democracies and by recalling E. E. Schattschneider's famous pronouncement that "modern democracy is unthinkable save in terms of parties."[19]

Two further problems of presidentialism emphasized by Linz are frequent executive-legislative stalemates and the rigidity of presidential terms of office. Stalemates are likely to occur because president and legislature can both claim the democratic legitimacy of being popularly elected, but the president and the majority of the legislature may belong to different parties or may have divergent preferences even if they belong to the same party. The rigidity inherent in presidentialism is that presidents are elected for fixed periods that often cannot be extended because of term limits, and that cannot easily be shortened even if the president proves to be incompetent, becomes seriously ill, or is beset by scandals of various kinds. Parliamentary systems, with their provisions for votes of confidence, snap elections, and so on, do not suffer from this problem.

Semi-presidential systems represent only a slight improvement over pure presidentialism. Although there can be considerable power sharing among president, prime minister, and cabinet, the zero-sum nature of presidential elections remains. Semi-presidential systems actually make it possible for the president to be even more powerful than in most pure presidential systems. In France, the best known example of semi-presidentialism, the president usually exercises predominant power; the 1962–74 and 1981–86 periods have even been called "hyperpresidential" phases.[20] The stalemate problem is partly solved in semi-presidential systems by making it possible for the system to shift from a mainly presidential to a mainly parliamentary mode if the president loses the support of his party or governing coalition in the legislature. In the Latin American presidential democracies, constitutional reformers have often advocated semi-presidential instead of parliamentary government, but only for reasons of convenience: A change to parliamentarism seems too big a step in countries with strong presidentialist traditions. While such traditional and sentimental constraints may have to be taken into account in constitutional negotiations, parliamentary government should be the general guideline for constitution writers in divided societies.

There is a strong scholarly consensus in favor of parliamentary government. In the extensive literature on this subject, the relatively few critics have questioned only parts of the pro-parliamentary consensus. Pointing to the case of US presidentialism, for instance, they have noted that the stalemate problem has not been as serious as Linz and others have alleged – without, however, challenging the validity of the other charges against presidential government.[21]

Power sharing in the executive

The collegial cabinets in parliamentary systems facilitate the formation of power sharing executives, but they do not by themselves guarantee that power sharing will be instituted. Belgium and South Africa exemplify the two principal methods of doing so. In Belgium, the constitution stipulates that the cabinet must comprise equal numbers of Dutch-speakers and French-speakers. The disadvantage of this approach is that it requires specifying the groups entitled to a share in power, and hence the same discriminatory choices inherent in electoral systems with guaranteed representation for particular minorities. In South Africa there was so much disagreement and controversy about racial and ethnic classifications that these could not be used as a basis for arranging executive power sharing in the 1994 interim constitution. Instead, power sharing was mandated in terms of political parties: Any party, ethnic or not, with a minimum of 5 percent of the seats in parliament was granted the right to participate in the cabinet on a proportional basis.[22] For similar situations in other countries, the South African solution provides an attractive model. But when there are no fundamental disagreements about specifying the ethnic groups entitled to a share of cabinet power, the Belgian model has two important advantages. First, it allows for power sharing without mandating a grand coalition of all significant parties and therefore without eliminating significant partisan opposition in parliament. Second, it allows for slight deviation from strictly proportional power sharing by giving some overrepresentation to the smaller groups, which may be desirable in countries where an ethnic majority faces one or more ethnic minority groups.

Cabinet stability

Constitution writers may worry about one potential problem of parliamentary systems: The fact that cabinets depend on majority support in parliament and can be dismissed by parliamentary votes of no confidence may lead to cabinet instability – and, as a result, regime instability. The weight of this problem should not be overestimated; the vast majority of stable democracies have parliamentary rather than presidential or semi-presidential forms of government.[23] Moreover, the position of cabinets vis-à-vis legislatures can be strengthened by constitutional provisions designed to this effect. One such provision is the constructive vote of no confidence, adopted in the 1949 constitution of West Germany, which stipulates that the prime minister (chancellor) can be dismissed by parliament only if a new prime minister is elected simultaneously. This eliminates the risk of a cabinet being voted out of office by a "negative" legislative majority that is unable to form an alternative cabinet. Spain and Papua New Guinea have adopted similar requirements for a constructive vote of no confidence. The disadvantage of this provision is that it may create an executive that cannot be dismissed by parliament but does not have a parliamentary majority to pass its legislative program – the same kind of stalemate that plagues presidential systems. A suggested solution to this potential problem was included in the 1958 constitution of the French Fifth Republic in the form of a provision that the cabinet has the right to make its legislative proposals matters of confidence, and these proposals are adopted automatically unless an absolute majority of the legislature votes to dismiss the cabinet. No constitution has yet tried to combine the German and French rules, but such a combination could undoubtedly give strong protection to cabinets and their legislative effectiveness – without depriving the parliamentary majority of its fundamental right to dismiss the cabinet and replace it with a new one in which parliament has greater confidence.

Selecting the head of state

In parliamentary systems, the prime minister usually serves only as head of government, while a constitutional monarch or a mainly ceremonial president occupies the position of head of state. Assuming that no monarch is available, constitution writers need to decide how the president should be chosen. My advice is twofold: to make sure that the presidency will be a primarily ceremonial office with very limited political power, and not to elect the president by popular vote. Popular election provides democratic legitimacy and, especially in combination with more than minimal powers specified in the constitution, can tempt presidents to become active political participants – potentially transforming the parliamentary system into a semi-presidential one. The preferable alternative is election by parliament.

A particularly attractive model was the constitutional amendment proposed as part of changing the Australian parliamentary system from a monarchy to a republic, which specified that the new president would be appointed on the joint nomination of the prime minister and the leader of the opposition, and confirmed by a two-thirds majority of a joint session of the two houses of parliament. The idea behind the two-thirds rule was to encourage the selection of a president who would be nonpartisan and non-political. (Australian voters defeated the entire proposal in a 1999 referendum mainly because a majority of the pro-republicans strongly – and unwisely – preferred the popular election of the president.) In my opinion, the best solution is the South African system of not having a separate head of state at all: There the president is in fact mainly a prime minister, subject to parliamentary confidence, who simultaneously serves as head of state.

Federalism and decentralization

For divided societies with geographically concentrated communal groups, a federal system is undoubtedly an excellent way to provide autonomy for these groups. My specific recommendation regards the second (federal) legislative chamber that is usually provided for in federal systems. This is often a politically powerful chamber in which less populous units of the federation are overrepresented (consider, for example, the United States Senate, which gives two seats to tiny Wyoming as well as gigantic California). For parliamentary systems, two legislative chambers with equal, or substantially equal, powers and different compositions is not a workable arrangement: It makes too difficult the forming of cabinets that have the confidence of both chambers, as the 1975 Australian constitutional crisis showed: The opposition-controlled Senate refused to pass the budget in an attempt to force the cabinet's resignation, although the cabinet continued to have the solid backing of the House of Representatives. Moreover, a high degree of smaller-unit overrepresentation in the federal chamber violates the democratic principle of "one person, one vote." In this respect, the German and Indian federal models are more attractive than the American, Swiss, and Australian ones.

Generally, it is advisable that the federation be relatively decentralized and that its component units (states or provinces) be relatively small – both to increase the prospects that each unit will be relatively homogeneous and to avoid dominance by large states on the federal level. Beyond this, a great many decisions need to be made regarding details that will vary from country to country (such as exactly where the state boundaries should be drawn). Experts have no clear advice to offer on how much decentralization is desirable within the federation, and there is no consensus among them as to whether the American, Canadian, Indian, Australian, German, Swiss, or Austrian model is most worthy of being emulated.

Nonterritorial autonomy

In divided societies where the communal groups are not geographically concentrated, autonomy can also be arranged on a nonterritorial basis. Where there are significant religious divisions, for example, the different religious groups are often intent on maintaining control of their own schools. A solution that has worked well in India, Belgium, and the Netherlands is to provide educational autonomy by giving equal state financial support to all schools, public and private, as long as basic educational standards are met. While this goes against the principle of separating church and state, it allows for the state to be completely neutral in matters of education.

Power sharing beyond the cabinet and parliament

In divided societies, broad representation of all communal groups is essential not only in cabinets and parliaments, but also in the civil service, judiciary, police, and military. This aim can be achieved by instituting ethnic or religious quotas, but these do not necessarily have to be rigid. For example, instead of mandating that a particular group be given exactly 20 percent representation, a more flexible rule could specify a target of 15 to 25 percent. I have found, however, that such quotas are often unnecessary; it is sufficient to have an explicit constitutional provision in favor of the general objective of broad representation and to rely on the power sharing cabinet and the proportionally constituted parliament for the practical implementation of this goal.

Other issues

As far as several other potentially contentious issues are concerned, my advice would be to start out with the modal patterns found in the world's established democracies, such as a two-thirds majority requirement for amending the constitution (with possibly a higher threshold for amending minority rights and autonomy), a size of the lower house of the legislature that is approximately the cube root of the country's population size[24] (which means that a country with about 25 million inhabitants, such as Iraq, "should" have a lower house of about 140 representatives), and legislative terms of four years.

While approval by referendum can provide the necessary democratic legitimacy for a newly drafted constitution, I recommend a constitutional provision to limit the number of referenda. One main form of referendum entails the right to draft legislation and constitutional amendments by popular initiative and to force a direct popular vote on such propositions. This is a blunt majoritarian instrument that may well be used against minorities. On the other hand, the Swiss example has shown that a referendum called by a small minority of voters to challenge a law passed by the majority of the elected representatives may have the desirable effect of boosting power sharing. Even if the effort fails, it forces the majority to pay the cost of a referendum campaign; hence the potential calling of a referendum by a minority is a strong stimulus for the majority to be heedful of minority views. Nevertheless, my recommendation is for extreme caution with regard to referenda, and the fact that frequent referenda occur in only three democracies – the United States, Switzerland, and, especially since about 1980, Italy – underscores this guideline.

Constitution writers will have to resolve many other issues that I have not mentioned, and on which I do not have specific recommendations: for example, the protection of civil rights, whether to set up a special constitutional court, and how to make a constitutional or supreme court a forceful protector of the constitution and of civil rights without making it too interventionist and intrusive. And as constitution writers face the difficult and time-consuming task of resolving these issues, it is all the more important that experts not burden or distract them with lengthy discussions on the relative advantages and disadvantages of flawed alternatives like presidentialism and non-PR systems.

I am not arguing that constitution writers should adopt all my recommendations without *any* examination of various alternatives. I recognize that the interests and agendas of particular parties and politicians may make them consider other alternatives, that a country's history and traditions will influence those who must draft its basic law, and that professional advice is almost always – and very wisely – sought from more than one constitutional expert. Even so, I would contend that my recommendations are not merely based on my own preferences, but on a strong scholarly consensus and solid empirical evidence, and that at the very least they should form a starting point in constitutional negotiations.

Acknowledgments

I am grateful to the Bellagio Study and Conference Center of the Rockefeller Foundation for offering me the opportunity to work on this project while I was a resident of the Center in May-June 2003, and to Roberto Belloni, Torbjörn Bergman, Joseph H. Brooks, Florian Bieber, Jørgen Elklit, Svante Ersson, John McGarry, Brendan O'Leary, Mogens N. Pedersen, Hugh B. Price, and Timothy D. Sisk for their valuable advice. Some of the ideas presented in this article were first published in my chapter "The Wave of Power-Sharing Democracy," in Andrew Reynolds, ed., *The Architecture of Democracy: Constitutional Design, Conflict Management, and Democracy* (Oxford: Oxford University Press, 2002), 37–54; and in *Democracy in the Twenty-First Century: Can We Be Optimistic?*, Uhlenbeck Lecture no. 18 (Wassenaar: Netherlands Institute for Advanced Study, 2000).

Notes

1 This paper was first published in the *Journal of Democracy*, vol. 15, no. 2, April 2004.
2 The secondary characteristics are proportionality, especially in legislative elections (in order to ensure a broadly representative legislature – similar to the aim of effecting a broadly constituted executive) and a minority veto on the most vital issues that affect the rights and autonomy of minorities.
3 Some of these scholars are Dirk Berg-Schlosser, William T. Bluhm, Laurence J. Boulle, Hans Daalder, Edward Dew, Robert H. Dix, Alan Dowty, Jonathan Fraenkel, Hermann Giliomee, Theodor Hanf, Jonathan Hartlyn, Martin O. Heisler, Luc Huyse, Thomas A. Koelble, Gerhard Lehmbruch, Franz Lehner, W. Arthur Lewis, Val R. Lorwin, Diane K. Mauzy, John McGarry, Kenneth D. McRae, Antoine N. Messarra, R. S. Milne, S. J. R. Noel, Eric A. Nordlinger, Brendan O'Leary, G. Bingham Powell, Jr., Andrew Reynolds, F. van Zyl Slabbert, Jürg Steiner, Albert J. Venter, Karl von Vorys, David Welsh, and Steven B. Wolinetz. Their most important writings on the subject (if published before the mid-1980s) can be found in the bibliography of Arend Lijphart, *Power-Sharing in South Africa* (Berkeley CA: Institute of International Studies, University of California, 1985), 137–71.
4 Ted Robert Gurr, *Minorities at Risk: A Global View of Ethnopolitical Conflicts* (Washington DC: US Institute of Peace Press, 1993), 292, italics added.
5 I have responded to these criticisms at length elsewhere. See especially Lijphart, "The Wave of Power-Sharing Democracy," in Andrew Reynolds, ed., *The Architecture of Democracy: Constitutional Design, Conflict Management, and Democracy* (Oxford: Oxford University Press, 2002), 40–47; and Lijphart, *Power-Sharing in South Africa*, 83–117.
6 Brian Barry, "The Consociational Model and Its Dangers," *European Journal of Political Research* 3 (December 1975): 406.
7 Donald L. Horowitz, *A Democratic South Africa? Constitutional Engineering in a Divided Society* (Berkeley CA: University of California Press, 1991), 188–203; and "Electoral Systems: A Primer for Decision Makers," *Journal of Democracy* 14 (October 2003): 122–23. In alternative-vote systems, voters are asked to rank order the candidates. If a candidate receives an absolute majority of first preferences, he or she is elected; if not, the weakest candidate is eliminated, and the ballots are redistributed according to second preferences. This process continues until one of the candidates receives a majority of the votes.

8 For a detailed critique, see Lijphart, "The Alternative Vote: A Realistic Alternative for South Africa?" *Politikon* 18 (June 1991): 9–101; and Lijphart, "Multiethnic Democracy," in Seymour Martin Lipset, ed., *The Encyclopedia of Democracy* (Washington, DC: Congressional Quarterly, 1995), 863–64.

9 The alternative vote was also used for the 1982 and 1988 presidential elections in Sri Lanka and for the 2000 presidential elections in the Republika Srpska in Bosnia. Nigeria has used a similar system favored by Horowitz (requiring a plurality plus at least 25 percent of the votes in at least two thirds of the states for victory) for its presidential elections. The third and sixth guidelines that I describe in the present essay recommend a parliamentary system without a popularly elected president – and therefore no direct presidential elections at all.

10 Benjamin Reilly has come to Horowitz's defense, but only with significant qualifications; for instance, Reilly dissents from Horowitz's advocacy of the alternative vote for the key case of South Africa. See Reilly, *Democracy in Divided Societies: Electoral Engineering for Conflict Management* (Cambridge: Cambridge University Press, 2001). Andreas Wimmer advocates the alternative vote for Iraq in "Democracy and Ethno-Religious Conflict in Iraq," *Survival* 45 (winter 2003–4): 111–34.

11 Donald L. Horowitz, "Constitutional Design: Proposals versus Processes," in Andrew Reynolds, ed., *The Architecture of Democracy*, 25.

12 In contrast with plurality, the alternative vote (instant runoff) ensures that the winning candidate has been elected by a majority of the voters, and it does so more accurately than the majority-runoff method and without the need for two rounds of voting.

13 Larry Diamond, *Developing Democracy: Toward Consolidation* (Baltimore MD: Johns Hopkins University Press, 1999), 104.

14 All three of these systems use multi-member election districts. The cumulative vote resembles multi-member district plurality in which each voter has as many votes as there are seats in a district, but, unlike plurality, the voter is allowed to cumulate his or her vote on one or a few of the candidates. In limited-vote systems, voters have fewer votes than the number of district seats. The single nontransferable vote is a special case of the limited vote in which the number of votes cast by each voter is reduced to one.

15 See Matthew Soberg Shugart and Martin P. Wattenberg, eds, *Mixed-Member Electoral Systems: The Best of Both Worlds?* (Oxford: Oxford University Press, 2001).

16 This estimate is based on the $T = 75\% /(M+1)$ equation – in which T is the effective threshold and M the number of representatives elected in a district – suggested by Rein Taagepera; see Arend Lijphart, "Electoral Systems," in Seymour Martin Lipset, ed., *Encyclopedia of Democracy*, 417. There is considerable variation around the average of eight representatives per district, but 9 of the 17 districts are very close to this average, with between 6 and 9 seats. The open-list rules are very complex and, in my opinion, make the lists too open. In addition to the 175 seats described here, Greenland and the Faeroe Islands elect two representatives each. I should also point out that my recommendation of the Danish model entails a bit of a paradox: It is a system that is very suitable for ethnically and religiously divided countries, although Denmark itself happens to be one of the most homogeneous countries in the world.

17 Parties below the 2 percent threshold may still benefit from the compensatory seats if certain other requirements are met, such as winning at least one district seat.

18 Juan J. Linz, "Presidential or Parliamentary Democracy: Does It Make a Difference?" in Juan J. Linz and Arturo Valenzuela, eds, *The Failure of Presidential Democracy* (Baltimore MD: Johns Hopkins University Press, 1994), 18.

19 Seymour Martin Lipset, "The Indispensability of Political Parties," *Journal of Democracy* 11 (January 2000): 48–55; E. E. Schattschneider, *Party Government* (New York: Rinehart, 1942), 1.

20 John T. S. Keeler and Martin A. Schain, "Institutions, Political Poker, and Regime Evolution in France," in Kurt von Mettenheim, ed., *Presidential Institutions and Democratic Politics: Comparing Regional and National Contexts* (Baltimore MD: Johns Hopkins University Press, 1997), 95–97. Horowitz favors a president elected by the alternative vote or a similar vote-pooling method, but in other respects his president does not differ from presidents in pure presidential systems; see his *A Democratic South Africa?*, 205–14.

21 Scholars have also indicated methods to minimize the problem of presidential-legislative deadlock – for instance, by holding presidential and legislative elections concurrently and electing the president by plurality instead of the more usual majority-runoff method. Such measures may indeed be able to ameliorate the problem to some extent, but cannot solve it entirely. See Matthew Soberg Shugart and John M. Carey, *Presidents and Assemblies: Constitutional Design and Electoral Dynamics* (Cambridge: Cambridge University Press, 1992); and Mark P. Jones, *Electoral Laws and the Survival of Presidential Democracies* (Notre Dame IN: University of Notre Dame Press, 1995).

22 The 1998 Good Friday Agreement provides for a similar power sharing executive for Northern Ireland.

23 In my comparative study of the world's stable democracies, defined as countries that were continuously democratic from 1977 to 1996 (and had populations greater than 250,000), 30 of the 36 stable democracies had parliamentary systems. See Lijphart, *Patterns of Democracy: Government Forms and Performance in Thirty-Six Countries* (New Haven CT: Yale University Press, 1999).

24 This pattern was discovered by Rein Taagepera; see his "The Size of National Assemblies," *Social Science Research* 1 (December 1972): 385–401.

6 The quality of democracy
Consensus democracy makes a difference

The conventional wisdom, cited in the previous chapter, argues – erroneously, as I have shown – that majoritarian democracy is better at governing, but admits that consensus democracy is better at representing – in particular, representing minority groups and minority interests, representing everyone more accurately, and representing people and their interests more inclusively. In the first part of this chapter I examine several measures of the quality of democracy and democratic representation and the extent to which consensus democracies perform better than majoritarian democracies according to these measures. In the second part of the chapter I discuss differences between the two types of democracy in broad policy orientations. Here I show that consensus democracy tends to be the "kinder, gentler" form of democracy. I borrow these terms from President George Bush's acceptance speech at the Republican presidential nominating convention in August 1988, in which he asserted: "I want a kinder, and gentler nation" (*New York Times*, 19 August 1988, A14). Consensus democracies demonstrate these kinder and gentler qualities in the following ways: they are more likely to be welfare states; they have a better record with regard to the protection of the environment; they put fewer people in prison and are less likely to use the death penalty; and the consensus democracies in the developed world are more generous with their economic assistance to the developing nations.

Consensus democracy and democratic quality

Table 6.1 presents the results of bivariate regression analyses of the effect of consensus democracy on eight sets of indicators of the quality of democracy. The independent variable is the degree of consensus democracy on the executives-parties dimension, generally in the period 1971–96 (unless indicated otherwise). The first two indicators are general indicators of democratic quality. Many studies have attempted to distinguish between democracy and nondemocratic forms of government not in terms of a dichotomy but in terms of a scale with degrees of democracy from perfect democracy to the complete absence of democracy. These degrees of democracy can also be interpreted as degrees of the quality of democracy: how democratic a country is reflects the degree to which it approximates perfect democracy. Unfortunately, most of these indexes cannot be used to measure different degrees of democratic quality among our thirty-six democracies because there is insufficient variation: all or most of our democracies are given the highest ratings. For instance, both the ratings of the Freedom House Survey Team (1996) and those by Keith Jaggers and Ted Robert Gurr (1995), which I have used to defend the selection of the thirty-six democracies for the analysis in this book, place almost all of these countries in their highest category.

There are two exceptions. One is Robert A. Dahl's (1971, 231–45) *Polyarchy*, in which 114 countries are placed in thirty-one scale types from the highest type of democracy to the lowest type of nondemocracy as of approximately 1969. All of our democracies that were independent and democratic at that time, except Barbados, Botswana, and Malta, were rated by Dahl – a total of twenty-six of our thirty-six democracies – and their ratings span nine scale types. To give a few examples, the highest summary ranking goes to Belgium, Denmark, and Finland; Austria and Germany are in the middle; and Colombia and Venezuela at the bottom. Table 6.1 shows that consensus democracy is strongly and significantly correlated (at the 1 percent level) with the Dahl rating of democratic quality.[1] The difference between consensus and majoritarian democracy is more than three points (twice the estimated regression coefficient) on the nine-point scale. Dahl's rating contains a slight bias in favor of consensus democracy because it is partly based on a higher ranking of multiparty compared with two-party systems. However, this difference represents only a third of the variation on one of ten components on which the rating is based; if it could somehow be discounted, the very strong correlation between consensus democracy and the rating of democratic quality would only be reduced marginally. A more serious potential source of bias is that the Third World democracies are all placed in the lowest three categories. However, when the level of development is used as a control variable, the estimated regression coefficient goes down only slightly (to 1.28 points) and the correlation remains statistically significant at the 1 percent level.

The second rating of democratic quality is the average of Tatu Vanhanen's (1990, 17–31) indexes of democratization for each year from 1980 to 1988 for almost all of the countries in the world, including all thirty-six of our democracies. Vanhanen bases his index on two elements: the degree of competition, defined as the share of the vote received by all parties except the largest party, and participation, defined as the percentage of the total population that voted in the most recent election; these two numbers are multiplied to arrive at the overall index. The values of the index range from a high of 43.2, for Belgium, to a low of zero; for our thirty-six countries the lowest value is 5.7 for Botswana. The first element effectively distinguishes one-party rule from democratic electoral contestation, but it

Table 6.1 Bivariate regression analyses of the effect of consensus democracy (executives-parties dimension) on seventeen indicators of the quality of democracy

	Estimated regression coefficient	Standardized regression coefficient	Absolute t-value	Countries (N)
Dahl rating (1969)	1.57***	0.58	3.44	26
Vanhanen rating (1980–88)	4.89***	0.54	3.75	36
Women's parliamentary representation (1971–95)	3.33***	0.46	3.06	36
Women's cabinet representation (1993–95)	3.36**	0.33	2.06	36
Family policy (1976–82)	1.10*	0.33	1.41	18
Rich-poor ratio (1981–93)	−1.41**	−0.47	2.50	24
Decile ratio (c.1986)	−0.38**	−0.49	2.20	17
Index of power resources (c.1990)	3.78*	0.26	1.57	36
Voter turnout (1971–96)	3.07*	0.24	1.46	36
Voter turnout (1960–78)	3.31*	0.30	1.49	24
Satisfaction with democracy (1995–96)	8.42*	0.36	1.55	18
Differential satisfaction (1990)	−8.11***	−0.83	4.51	11
Government distance (1978–85)	−0.34**	−0.62	2.51	12
Voter distance (1978–85)	−5.25**	−0.64	2.63	12
Corruption index (1997)	−0.32	−0.14	0.71	27
Popular cabinet support (1945–96)	1.90*	0.22	1.32	35
J. S. Mill criterion (1945–96)	2.51	0.07	0.42	35

Notes: *Statistically significant at the 10 percent level (one-tailed test)
**Statistically significant at the 5 percent level (one-tailed test)
***Statistically significant at the 1 percent level (one-tailed test)
Source: Based on data in Dahl 1971, 232; Vanhanen 1990, 27–28; Inter-Parliamentary Union 1995; Banks 1993; Banks *et al.* 1996; Wilensky 1990, 2; and additional data provided by Harold L. Wilensky; United Nations Development Programme 1996, 170–71, 198; Atkinson *et al.* 1995, 40; Vanhanen 1997, 86–89; International IDEA 1997, 51–95; Powell 1980, 6; Klingemann 1999; Anderson and Guillory 1997, and additional data provided by Christopher J. Anderson; Huber and Powell 1994, and additional data provided by John D. Huber; Transparency International 1997.

also necessarily suffers from the bias that two-party systems tend to get lower scores than multiparty systems. Moreover, this bias affects one of the two components of Vanhanen's index and therefore has a much greater impact than the slight bias in Dahl's index. Because the Vanhanen index is widely used and because it is available for all of our democracies, I report the result of its regression on consensus democracy in Table 6.1 anyway. The correlation is impressively strong and remains strong at the same level of significance when the level of development is controlled for and when Botswana, which is somewhat of an outlier, is removed from the analysis. However, its sizable bias in favor of multiparty systems makes the Vanhanen index a less credible index of democratic quality than the Dahl index.

Women's representation

The next three indicators in Table 6.1 measure women's political representation and the protection of women's interests. These are important measures of the quality of democratic representation in their own right, and they can also serve as indirect proxies of how well minorities are represented generally. That there are so many kinds of ethnic and religious minorities in different countries makes comparisons extremely difficult, and it therefore makes sense to focus on the "minority" of women – a political rather than a numerical minority – that is found everywhere and that can be compared systematically across countries. As Rein Taagepera (1994, 244) states, "What we know about women's representation should [also] be applicable to ethnoracial minorities."

The average percentage of women elected to the lower or only houses of parliament in all elections from 1971 to 1995 in our thirty-six democracies ranges from a high of 30.4 percent in Sweden to a low of 0.9 percent in Papua New Guinea. These differences are strongly and significantly related to the degree of consensus democracy. The percentage of women's parliamentary representation is 6.7 percentage points higher (again, twice the estimated regression coefficient) in consensus democracies than in majoritarian systems. Women tend to be better represented in developed than in developing countries, but when the level of development is controlled for, the relationship between consensus democracy and women's legislative representation weakens only slightly and is still significant at the 1 percent level. It can be argued that in presidential systems the percentage of women's representation should not be based only on women's election to the legislature but also, perhaps equally, on their election to the presidency. If this were done, the relationship between consensus democracy and women's political representation would be reinforced because not a single woman president was elected in Colombia, Costa Rica, France, the United States, and Venezuela in the entire period under consideration and because all five presidential democracies are on the majoritarian side of the spectrum (see figures 14.1 and 14.2 in Lijphart 1999).

The pattern is similar for the representation of women in cabinets in two recent years – 1993 and 1995 – although the correlation is significant only at the 5 percent level.[2] The percentages range from 42.1 percent in Norway to 0 percent in Papua New Guinea. Here again, the level of development is also a strong explanatory variable, but controlling for it does not affect the correlation between consensus democracy and women's cabinet representation.

As a measure of the protection and promotion of women's interests, I examined Harold L. Wilensky's (1990) rating of the industrialized democracies with regard to the innovativeness and expansiveness of their family policies – a matter of special concern to women. On Wilensky's thirteen-point scale, from a maximum of twelve to a minimum of zero, France and Sweden have the highest score of eleven points and Australia and Ireland the lowest score of one point.[3] Consensus democracies score more than two points higher on the scale, and the correlation is significant at the 10 percent level and unaffected by level of development. France is an unusual deviant case: it is a mainly majoritarian system but receives one of the highest family-policy scores. When it is removed from the analysis, the correlation becomes stronger and is statistically significant at the 5 percent level.

Political equality

Political equality is a basic goal of democracy, and the degree of political equality is therefore an important indicator of democratic quality. Political equality is difficult to measure directly, but economic equality can serve as a valid proxy, since political equality is more likely to prevail in the absence of great economic inequalities: "Many resources that flow directly or indirectly from one's position in the economic order can be converted into political resources" (Dahl 1996, 645). The rich-poor ratio is the ratio of the income share of the highest 20 percent to that of the lowest 20 percent of households. The United Nations Development Programme (1996) has collected the relevant statistics for twenty-four of our democracies, including six of the developing countries: Botswana, Colombia, Costa Rica, India, Jamaica, and Venezuela. The ratio varies between 16.4 in highly inegalitarian Botswana and 4.3 in egalitarian Japan. Consensus democracy and inequality as measured by the rich-poor ratio are negatively and very strongly related (statistically significant at the 5 percent level and almost at the 1 percent level). The difference between the average consensus democracy and the average majoritarian democracy is about 2.8. The more developed countries have less inequality than the developing countries; when the level of development is controlled for, the correlation between consensus democracy and equality weakens only slightly and is still significant at the 5 percent level. When, in addition, the most extreme case of Botswana is removed from the analysis, the relationship remains significant at the same level.

The decile ratio is a similar ratio of income differences: the income ratio of the top to the bottom decile. It is available for most of the OECD countries, based on the most painstaking comparative study of income differences that has been done so far (Atkinson *et al.* 1995). Consensus democracies are again the more egalitarian; the correlation is significant at the 5 percent level and is not affected when level of development is controlled for. Finland has the lowest decile ratio, 2.59, and the United States has the highest, 5.94. The United States is an extreme case: the midpoint between its ratio and that of Finland is 4.26, and the sixteen other democracies are all below this midpoint; the country with the next highest decile ratio after the United States is Ireland with a ratio of 4.23. When the United States is removed from the analysis, the correlation between consensus democracy and income equality becomes even stronger, although not enough to become significant at the higher level.

Vanhanen's (1997, 43, 46) Index of Power Resources is an indicator of equality based on several indirect measures such as the degree of literacy ("the higher the percentage of literate population, the more widely basic intellectual resources are distributed") and the percentage of urban population ("the higher [this] percentage . . . the more diversified economic activities and economic interest groups there are and, consequently, the more economic power resources are distributed among various groups"). Although Vanhanen's index is an indirect and obviously rough measure, it has the great advantage that it can be calculated for many countries, including all of our thirty-six democracies. The highest value, 53.5 points, is found in the Netherlands, and the lowest, 3.3 points, in Papua New Guinea. Consensus democracy is positively correlated with the Index of Power Resources but only at the 10 percent level of significance. However, when level of development, which is also strongly correlated with Vanhanen's index, is controlled for, the relationship becomes stronger and is significant at the 5 percent level.

Electoral participation

Voter turnout is an excellent indicator of democratic quality for two reasons. First, it shows the extent to which citizens are actually interested in being represented. Second, turnout is strongly correlated with socio-economic status and can therefore also serve as an indirect indicator of political equality: high turnout means more equal participation and hence greater political equality; low turnout spells unequal participation and hence more inequality (Lijphart 1997b). Table 6.1 uses the turnout percentages in national elections that attract the largest numbers of voters: legislative elections in parliamentary systems and, in presidential systems, whichever elections had the highest turnout – generally the presidential rather than the legislative elections and, where presidents are chosen by majority-runoff, generally the runoff instead of the first-ballot elections. The basic measure is the number of voters as a percentage of voting-age population.[4]

In the period 1971–96, Italy had the highest average turnout, 92.4 percent, and Switzerland the lowest, 40.9 percent. Consensus democracy and voter turnout are positively correlated, but the correlation is significant only at the 10 percent level. However, several controls need to be introduced. First of all, compulsory voting, which is somewhat more common in consensus than in majoritarian democracies, strongly stimulates turnout.[5] Second, turnout is severely depressed by the high frequency and the multitude of electoral choices to be made both in consensual Switzerland and the majoritarian United States. Third, turnout tends to be higher in more developed countries. When compulsory voting and the frequency of elections (both in the form of dummy variables) as well as the level of development are controlled for, the effect of consensus democracy on voter turnout becomes much stronger and is now significant at the 1 percent level.

With these controls in place, consensus democracies have approximately 7.5 percentage points higher turnout than majoritarian democracies.

The regression analysis was repeated with the average turnout figures collected by G. Bingham Powell (1980) for an earlier period, 1960–78.[6] Both the bivariate and multivariate relationships are very similar to the pattern reported in the previous paragraph. The bivariate correlation is significant at the 10 percent level, but when the three control variables are added, the correlation between consensus democracy and turnout becomes strong and significant at the 1 percent level. The difference in turnout between consensus and majoritarian democracies is about 7.3 percentage points – very close to the 7.5 percent difference in the period 1971–96.[7]

Satisfaction with democracy

Does the type of democracy affect citizens' satisfaction with democracy? Hans-Dieter Klingemann (1999) reports the responses to the following survey question asked in many countries, including eighteen of our democracies, in 1995 and 1996: "On the whole, are you very satisfied, fairly satisfied, not very satisfied, or not at all satisfied with the way democracy works in (your country)?" The Danes and Norwegians expressed the highest percentage of satisfaction with democracy: 83 and 82 percent, respectively, said that they were "very" or "fairly" satisfied. The Italians and Colombians were the least satisfied: only 19 and 16 percent, respectively, expressed satisfaction. Generally, as Table 6.1 shows, citizens in consensus democracies are significantly more satisfied with democratic performance in their countries than citizens of majoritarian democracies; the difference is approximately 17 percentage points.

In an earlier study of eleven European democracies, Christopher J. Anderson and Christine A. Guillory (1997) found that, in each of these countries, respondents who had voted for the winning party or parties were more likely to be satisfied with how well democracy worked in their country than respondents who had voted for the losing party or parties. Because it is easy to be satisfied when one is on the winning side, the degree to which winners and losers have similar responses can be regarded as a more sensitive measure of the *breadth* of satisfaction than simply the number of people who say they are very or fairly satisfied. The largest difference, 37.5 percentage points, was in Greece, where 70.3 percent of the respondents on the winning side expressed satisfaction compared with only 32.8 percent of the losers; the smallest difference occurred in Belgium, where 61.5 percent of the winners were satisfied compared with 56.8 percent of the losers – a difference of only 4.7 percentage points. The general pattern discovered by Anderson and Guillory was that in consensus democracies the differences between winners and losers were significantly smaller than in majoritarian democracies. My replication of Anderson and Guillory's analysis, using the degree of consensus democracy on the executives-parties dimension in the period 1971–96, strongly confirms their conclusion. As Table 6.1 shows, the difference in satisfaction is more than 16 percentage points smaller in the typical consensus than in the typical majoritarian democracy. The correlation is highly significant (at the 1 percent level).[8]

Government-voter proximity

The next two variables can be used to test the following key claim that is often made on behalf of majoritarian democracy: because in the typical two-party system the two major parties are both likely to be moderate, the government's policy position is likely to be close to that of the bulk of the voters. John D. Huber and G. Bingham Powell (1994) compared the government's position on a ten-point left-right scale with the voters' positions on the same scale in twelve Western democracies in the period 1978–85. One measure of the distance between government and voters is simply the distance between the government's position on the left-right scale and the position of the median voter; this measure is called "government distance" in Table 6.1. The other measure is the percentage of voters between the government and the median citizen, called "voter distance" in the table. The smaller these two distances are, the more representative the government is of the citizens' policy preferences.

Government distance ranges from a high of 2.39 points on the ten-point scale in the United Kingdom to a low of 0.47 in Ireland. Voter distance is the greatest in Australia, 37 percent, and the smallest in Ireland, 11 percent. Contrary to the majoritarian claim, both distances are actually smaller in consensus than in majoritarian democracies: the differences in the respective distances are about two thirds of a point on the ten-point scale and more than 10 percent of the citizens. Both correlations are significant at the 5 percent level.

Accountability and corruption

Another important claim in favor of majoritarian democracy is that its typically one-party majority governments offer clearer responsibility for policy-making and hence better accountability of the government to the citizens – who can use elections either to "renew the term of the incumbent government" or to "throw the rascals out" (Powell 1989, 119). The claim is undoubtedly valid for majoritarian systems with pure two-party competition. However, in two-party systems with significant third parties, "rascals" may be repeatedly returned to office in spite of clear majorities of the voters voting for other parties and hence against the incumbent government; all reelected British cabinets since 1945 fit this description. Moreover, it is actually easier to change governments in consensus democracies than in majoritarian democracies, as shown by the shorter duration of cabinets in consensus systems (see the first two columns of Table 7.1 in Lijphart 1999). Admittedly, of course, changes in consensus democracies tend to be partial changes in the composition of cabinets, in contrast with the more frequent complete turnovers in majoritarian democracies.

A related measure is the incidence of corruption. It may be hypothesized that the greater clarity of responsibility in majoritarian democracies inhibits corruption and that the consensus systems' tendency to compromise and "deal-making" fosters corrupt practices. The indexes of perceived corruption in a large number of countries, including twenty-seven of our democracies, by Transparency International (1997) can be used to test this hypothesis. An index of 10 means "totally corrupt" and 0 means "totally clean."[9] Among our democracies, India and Colombia are the most corrupt, with scores between 7 and 8; at the other end of the scale, six countries are close to "totally clean" with scores between 0 and 1: Denmark, Finland, Sweden, New Zealand, Canada, and the Netherlands. Contrary to the hypothesis, there is no significant relationship between consensus democracy and corruption. Moreover, the weak relationship that does appear is actually negative: consensus democracies are slightly *less* likely to be corrupt than majoritarian systems (by about two thirds of a point on the index). This relationship becomes a bit stronger, but is still not statistically significant, when the level of development, which is strongly and negatively correlated with the level of corruption, is controlled for.

John Stuart Mill's hypotheses

The final two variables that measure the quality of democracy are inspired by John Stuart Mill's (1861, 134) argument that majority rule is the most fundamental requirement of democracy and that the combination of plurality or majority elections and parliamentary government may lead to minority rule. He proves his point by examining the most extreme case:

> Suppose ... that, in a country governed by equal and universal suffrage, there is a contested election in every constituency, and every election is carried by a small majority. The Parliament thus brought together represents little more than a bare majority of the people. This Parliament proceeds to legislate, and adopts important measures by a bare majority of itself.

Although Mill does not state so explicitly, the most important of these "important measures" is the formation of a cabinet supported by a majority of the legislators. Mill continues: "It is possible, therefore, and even probable" that this two-stage majoritarian system delivers power "not to a majority but to a minority." Mill's point is well illustrated by the fact that, as I showed in Chapter 2 (in Lijphart 1999), the United Kingdom and New Zealand have tended to be *pluralitarian* instead of majoritarian democracies since 1945 because their parliamentary majorities and the one-party cabinets based on them have usually been supported by only a plurality – the largest minority – of the voters.

Mill argues that the best solution is to use PR for the election of the legislature, and he is obviously right that under a perfectly proportional system the problem of minority control cannot occur. His argument further means that consensus democracies, which frequently use PR and which in addition tend to have more inclusive coalition cabinets, are more likely to practice true majority rule than majoritarian democracies. Two measures can be used to test this hypothesis derived from Mill. One is popular cabinet support: the average percentage of the voters who gave their votes to the party or parties that formed the cabinet, or, in presidential systems, the percentage of the voters who voted for the winning presidential candidate, weighted by the time that each cabinet or president was in office. The second measure may be called the John Stuart Mill Criterion: the percentage of time that the majority-rule requirement – the requirement that the cabinet or president be supported by popular majorities – is fulfilled. Both measures can be calculated for the entire period 1945–96 for all democracies except Papua New Guinea due to the large number of independents elected to its legislature and frequently participating in its cabinets.[10]

The highest average popular cabinet support occurred in Switzerland (76.6 percent), Botswana (71.2 percent), and Austria (70.7 percent), and the lowest in Denmark (40.3 percent) and Spain (40.7 percent). The John Stuart Mill Criterion was always satisfied – 100 percent of the time – in the Bahamas, Botswana, Jamaica, Luxembourg, and Switzerland, and never – 0 percent of the time – in Norway, Spain, and the United Kingdom. These examples already make clear that the best and the poorest performers on these measures include both consensus and majoritarian democracies. We should therefore not expect strong statistical correlations between consensus democracy and either measure. Table 6.1 shows that, though both correlations are positive, they are fairly weak and only one is statistically significant. Popular cabinet support is only about 3.8 percent greater in consensus than in majoritarian democracies.

The evidence does not lend stronger support to Mill's line of thinking for three reasons. One is that the smallest majoritarian democracies – Botswana, the Bahamas, Jamaica, Trinidad, and Barbados – have high popular cabinet support as a result of their almost pure two-party systems in which the winning party usually also wins a popular majority or at least a strong popular plurality. This finding is in line with Robert A. Dahl and Edward R. Tufte's (1973, 98–108) conclusion that smaller units have fewer political parties even when they use PR. Dag Anckar (1993) argues that, in addition to size, insularity plays a role in reducing the number of parties. The case of the small island state of Malta, with PR elections but virtually pure two-party competition, bears out both arguments. When population size is controlled for, the correlation between consensus democracy and popular cabinet support becomes statistically significant at the 5 percent level. Controlling for population has an even more dramatic effect on the correlation between consensus democracy and the John Stuart Mill Criterion: it is now both strong and highly significant (at the 1 percent level).

The second explanation is that the presidential systems are on the majoritarian half of the spectrum but that they tend to do well in securing popular support for the executive: competition tends to be between two strong presidential candidates, and majority support is guaranteed – or, perhaps more realistically speaking, contrived – when the majority-runoff method is used.

Third, consensus democracies with frequent minority cabinets, especially the Scandinavian countries, have relatively low popular cabinet support. There is still a big difference, of course, between cabinets with only minority popular support but also minority status in the legislature, as in Scandinavia, and cabinets with minority popular support but with majority support in parliament, as in Britain and New Zealand; the lack of popular support is clearly more serious in the latter case. Moreover, popular cabinet support is based on actual votes cast and does not take into account strategic voting, that is, the tendency – which is especially strong in plurality elections – to vote for a party not because it is the voters' real preference but because it appears to have a chance to win. Hence, if popular cabinet support could be calculated on the basis of the voters' sincere preferences instead of their actual votes, the consensus democracies would do much better on this indicator of democratic quality.

The general conclusion is that consensus democracies have a better record than majoritarian democracy on all of the measures of democratic quality in Table 6.1, that all except two correlations are statistically significant, and that most of the correlations are significant at the 1 or 5 percent level. For reasons of space, I am not presenting a table, similar to Table 6.1, with the bivariate correlations between consensus democracy on the federal-unitary dimension and the seventeen indicators of democratic quality. The reason is that there are no interesting results to report: the only strongly significant bivariate relationship (at the 5 percent level) is a negative correlation between consensus democracy and voter turnout in the period 1971–96. However, when compulsory voting, the frequency of elections, and level of development are controlled for, the correlation becomes very weak and is no longer significant.

Consensus democracy and its kinder, gentler qualities

The democratic qualities discussed so far in this chapter should appeal to all democrats: it is hard to find fault with better women's representation, greater political equality, higher participation in elections, closer proximity between government policy and voters' preferences, and more faithful adherence to John Stuart Mill's majority principle. In addition, consensus democracy (on the executives-parties dimension) is associated with some other attributes that I believe most, though not necessarily all, democrats will also find attractive: a strong community orientation and social consciousness – the kinder, gentler qualities mentioned in the beginning of this chapter. These characteristics are also consonant with feminist conceptions of democracy that emphasize, in Jane Mansbridge's (1996, 123) words, "connectedness" and "mutual persuasion" instead of self-interest and power politics: "The processes of persuasion may be related to a more consultative, participatory style that seems to characterize women more than men." Mansbridge further relates these differences to her distinction between "adversary" and "unitary" democracy, which is similar to the majoritarian-consensus contrast. Accordingly, consensus democracy may also be thought of as the more feminine model and majoritarian democracy as the more masculine model of democracy.

There are four areas of government activity in which the kinder and gentler qualities of consensus democracy are likely to manifest themselves: social welfare, the protection of the environment, criminal justice, and foreign aid. My hypothesis is that consensus democracy will be associated with kinder, gentler, and more generous policies. Table 6.2 presents the results of the bivariate regression analyses of the effect of consensus democracy on ten indicators of the policy orientations in these four areas. The independent variable in all cases is the degree of consensus democracy on the executives-parties dimension in the period 1971–96.

The first indicator of the degree to which democracies are welfare states is Gösta Esping-Andersen's (1990) comprehensive measure of "decommodification" – that is, the degree to which welfare policies with regard to unemployment, disability, illness, and old age permit people to maintain decent living standards independent of pure market forces. Among the eighteen OECD countries surveyed by Esping-Andersen in 1980, Sweden has the highest score of 39.1 points and Australia and the United States the lowest – 13.0 and 13.8 points, respectively. Consensus democracy has a strong positive correlation with these welfare scores. The difference between the average consensus democracy and the average majoritarian democracy is almost ten points. Wealthy countries can afford to be more generous with welfare than less wealthy countries, but when the level of development is controlled for, the correlation between consensus democracy and welfare becomes even a bit stronger.

Esping-Andersen's measure has been severely criticized for understating the degree to which Australia, New Zealand, and the United Kingdom are welfare states (Castles and Mitchell 1993). Because these three countries are, or were, also mainly majoritarian systems, this criticism throws doubt on the link between consensus democracy and welfare statism. In order to test whether the original finding was entirely driven by Esping-Andersen's classification of Australia, New Zealand, and the United Kingdom, I re-ran the regression without these three disputed cases. The result is reported in the second row of Table 6.2. The relationship between consensus democracy and the welfare state is weakened only slightly, and it is still statistically significant at the 5 percent level.

Another indicator of welfare statism is social expenditure as a percentage of gross domestic product in the same eighteen OECD countries in 1992, analyzed by Manfred G. Schmidt (1997). Sweden is again the most welfare-oriented democracy with 37.1 percent social expenditure, but Japan now has the lowest percentage, 12.4 percent, followed by the United States with 15.6 percent. The correlation with consensus democracy is again strong and significant, and it is not affected when level of development is controlled for. Consensus democracies differ from majoritarian democracies in that they spend an additional 5.3 percent of their gross domestic product on welfare.

Environmental performance can be measured by means of two indicators that are available for all or almost all of our thirty-six democracies. The first is Monte Palmer's (1997) composite index of concern for the environment, based mainly on carbon dioxide emissions, fertilizer consumption, and deforestation. This index ranges from a theoretical high of 100 points, indicating the best environmental performance to a low of zero points for

Table 6.2 Bivariate regression analyses of the effect of consensus democracy (executives-parties dimension) on ten indicators of welfare statism, environmental performance, criminal justice, and foreign aid

	Estimated regression coefficient	*Standardized regression coefficient*	*Absolute t-value*	*Countries (N)*
Welfare state index (1980)	4.90***	0.68	3.70	18
Adjusted welfare index (1980)	4.29**	0.58	2.60	15
Social expenditure (1992)	2.66**	0.44	1.94	18
Palmer index (c.1990)	4.99*	0.30	1.67	31
Energy efficiency (1990–94)	0.93***	0.51	3.50	36
Incarceration rate (1992–95)	−32.12*	−0.30	1.39	22
Death penalty (1996)	−0.35***	−0.44	2.86	36
Foreign aid (1982–85)	0.09*	0.30	1.38	21
Foreign aid (1992–95)	0.10**	0.39	1.86	21
Aid versus defense (1992–95)	5.94***	0.51	2.58	21

Notes: *Statistically significant at the 10 percent level (one-tailed test)
**Statistically significant at the 5 percent level (one-tailed test)
***Statistically significant at the 1 percent level (one-tailed test)
Source: Based on data in Esping-Andersen 1990, 52; Schmidt 1997, 155; Palmer 1997, 16–20; World Bank 1992, 26–27; World Bank 1993, 26–27; World Bank 1994, 26–27; World Bank 1995, 26–27; World Bank 1997, 26–27; Mauer 1994, 3; Mauer 1997, 4; Bedau 1997, 78–82; United Nations Development Programme 1994, 197; United Nations Development Programme 1995, 204, 206; United Nations Development Programme 1996, 199, 201; United Nations Development Programme 1997, 214–15.

the worst performance. The highest score among our democracies is for the Netherlands, seventy-seven points, and the lowest score is Botswana's, zero points.[11] Consensus democracies score almost ten points higher than majoritarian democracies; the correlation is statistically significant at the 10 percent level and is not affected when level of development is controlled for.

An even better overall measure of environmental responsibility is energy efficiency. Table 6.2 uses the World Bank's figures for the gross domestic product divided by total energy consumption for the years from 1990 to 1994. The most environmentally responsible countries produce goods and services with the lowest relative consumption of energy; the least responsible countries waste a great deal of energy. Among our thirty-six democracies, Switzerland has the highest value, an annual average of $8.70, and Trinidad the lowest, $0.80. The correlation between consensus democracy and energy efficiency is extremely strong (significant at the 1 percent level) and unaffected by the introduction of level of development as a control variable.

One would also expect the qualities of kindness and gentleness in consensus democracies to show up in criminal justice systems that are less punitive than those of majoritarian democracies, with fewer people in prison and with less or no use of capital punishment. To test the hypothesis with regard to incarceration rates, I used the average rates in 1992–93 and 1995 collected by the Sentencing Project (Mauer 1994, 1997). These rates represent the number of inmates per 100,000 population. The highest and lowest rates are those for the United States and India: 560 and 24 inmates per 100,000 population, respectively. Consensus democracy is negatively correlated with incarceration, but only at the modest 10 percent level of significance. However, this result is strongly affected by the extreme case of the United States: its 560 prisoners per 100,000 people is more than four times as many as the 131 inmates in the next most punitive country, New Zealand. When the United States is removed from the analysis, the negative correlation between consensus democracy and the incarceration rate is significant at the 5 percent level; when in addition the level of development is controlled for, the correlation becomes significant at the 1 percent level. The remaining twenty-one countries range from 24 to 131 inmates per 100,000 population; with level of development controlled, the consensus democracies put about 26 fewer people per 100,000 population in prison than the majoritarian democracies.

As of 1996, eight of our thirty-six democracies retained and used the death penalty for ordinary crimes: the Bahamas, Barbados, Botswana, India, Jamaica, Japan, Trinidad, and the United States. The laws of twenty-two countries did not provide for the death penalty for any crime. The remaining six countries were in intermediate positions: four still had the death penalty but only for exceptional crimes such as wartime crimes – Canada, Israel, Malta, and the United Kingdom – and two retained the death penalty but had not used it for at least ten years – Belgium and Papua New Guinea (Bedau 1997, 78–82). On the basis of these differences, I constructed a three-point scale with a score of two for the active use of the death penalty, zero for the absence of the death penalty, and one for the intermediate cases. The negative correlation between consensus democracy and the death penalty is strong and highly significant (at the 1 percent level), and is not affected by controlling for level of development.

In the field of foreign policy, one might plausibly expect the kind and gentle characteristics of consensus democracy to be manifested by generosity with foreign aid and a reluctance to rely on military power.[12] Table 6.2 uses three indicators for twenty-one OECD countries: average annual foreign aid – that is, economic development assistance, not military aid – as a percentage of gross national product in the period 1982–85 before the end of the Cold War; average foreign aid levels in the post-Cold War years from 1992 to 1995; and foreign aid in the latter period as a percent of defense expenditures. In the period 1982–85, foreign aid ranged from a high of 1.04 percent of gross national product (Norway) to a low of 0.04 percent (Portugal); in the period 1992–95, the highest percentage was 1.01 percent (Denmark and Norway) and the lowest 0.14 percent (the United States). The highest foreign aid as a percent of defense expenditure was Denmark's 51 percent, and the lowest that of the United States, 4 percent.

In the bivariate regression analysis, consensus democracy is significantly correlated with all three indicators, albeit at different levels. However, two important controls need to be introduced. First, because wealthier countries can better afford to give foreign aid than less wealthy countries, the level of development should be controlled for. Second, because large countries tend to assume greater military responsibilities and hence tend to have larger defense expenditures, which can be expected to limit their ability and willingness to provide foreign aid, population size should be used as a control variable; Dahl and Tufte (1973, 122–23) found a strong link between population and defense spending. When these two controls are introduced, the correlations between consensus democracy and the three measures of foreign aid remain significant, all at the 5 percent level. With the controls in place, the typical consensus democracy gave about 0.20 percent more of its gross national product in foreign aid than the typical majoritarian democracy in both the Cold War and post-Cold War periods, and its aid as a percent of defense spending was about 9.5 percentage points higher.

Similar regression analyses can be performed to test the effect of the other (federal-unitary) dimension of consensus democracy on the above ten indicators, but few interesting results appear. The only two significant bivariate correlations are between consensus democracy on one hand and the incarceration rate and social expenditure on the other, both at the 5 percent level. The negative correlation with social expenditure is not affected when the level of development is controlled for; the explanation is that three federal systems – Australia, Canada, and the United States – are among the only four countries with social spending below 20 percent of gross domestic product. The positive correlation with the rate of incarceration is entirely driven by the extreme case of the United States; when the United States is removed from the analysis, the relationship disappears.

As the subtitle of this chapter states, consensus democracy makes a difference. Indeed, consensus democracy – on the executives–parties dimension – makes a big difference with regard to almost all of the indicators of democratic quality and with regard to all of the kinder and gentler qualities. Furthermore, when the appropriate controls are introduced, the positive difference that consensus democracy makes generally tends to become even more impressive.

Notes

1 The independent variable is consensus democracy in the 1945–70 period. On Dahl's scale, 1 is the highest and 9 the lowest point; I reversed the sign in order to make the higher values represent higher degrees of democratic quality.

2 The percentages are based on data in the *Political Handbook of the World* (Banks 1993; Banks *et al.* 1996); 1993 is the first year for which the *Political Handbook* reports the gender of cabinet members.

3 Wilensky's (1990, 2) ratings are based on a five-point scale, from four to zero,

> for each of three policy clusters: existence and length of maternity and parental leave, paid and unpaid; availability and accessibility of public daycare programs and government effort to expand daycare; and flexibility of retirement systems. They measure government action to assure care of children and maximize choices in balancing work and family demands for everyone.

4 This is a more accurate measure of turnout than actual voters as a percent of registered voters, because voter registration procedures and reliability differ greatly from country to country. The only problem with the voting-age measure is that it includes noncitizens and hence tends to depress the turnout percentages of countries with large noncitizen populations. Because this problem assumes extreme proportions in Luxembourg with its small citizen and relatively very large noncitizen population, I made an exception in this case and used the turnout percentage based on registered voters.

5 The democracies with compulsory voting in the 1971–96 period are Australia, Belgium, Costa Rica, Greece, Italy, Luxembourg, and Venezuela. Compulsory voting was abolished in the Netherlands in 1970. For the regression analysis with the 1960–78 Powell data, reported below, the Netherlands is counted as having compulsory voting, and the average Dutch turnout percentage is only for the elections in which voting was still compulsory.

6 The independent variable here is the degree of consensus democracy for the entire 1945–96 period.

7 PR is probably the most important institutional element responsible for the strong relationships between consensus democracy on the one hand and voter turnout and women's representation on the other; PR is the usual electoral system in consensus democracies, and it has been found to be a strong stimulant to both voter participation and women's representation (Blais and Carty 1990, Rule and Zimmerman 1994).

8 In Anderson and Guillory's eleven countries, there was also a positive, but not statistically significant, relationship between consensus democracy and the

percentage of respondents expressing satisfaction with democracy. However, Italy is an extreme outlier, with only 21.7 percent of the respondents expressing satisfaction; the percentages in the other countries range from 83.8 percent in Germany to 44.7 percent in Greece. When the Italian case is removed from the analysis, the correlation becomes significant at the 5 percent level.

9 Transparency International's highest scores are for the "cleanest" and the lowest scores for the most "corrupt" countries. I changed this 10–0 scale to a 0–10 scale so that higher values would indicate more corruption.

10 In a few other countries, relatively short periods had to be excluded: for instance, the period 1958–65 in France because the president was not popularly elected, and the periods 1979–80 and 1984–86 in India and Mauritius, respectively, because the cabinets contained fragments of parties that had split after the most recent elections. Moreover, nonpartisan cabinets and cabinets formed after boycotted elections were excluded.

11 Palmer (1997, 16) gives the highest scores to "the most environmentally troubled nations." I changed his 0–100 scale to a 100–0 scale so that higher scores would indicate better environmental performance.

12 This hypothesis can also be derived from the "democratic peace" literature (Ray 1997). The fact that democracies are more peaceful, especially in their relationships with each other, than nondemocracies is often attributed to their stronger compromise-oriented political cultures and their institutional checks and balances. If this explanation is correct, one should expect consensus democracies to be even more peace-loving than majoritarian democracies.

References

Anckar, Dag. 1993. "Notes on the Party Systems of Small Island States." In Tom Bryder (ed.) *Party Systems, Party Behaviour and Democracy*, pp. 153–68. Copenhagen: Copenhagen Political Studies Press.

Anderson, Christopher J., and Christine A. Guillory. 1997. "Political Institutions and Satisfaction with Democracy: A Cross-National Analysis of Consensus and Majoritarian Systems." *American Political Science Review*, vol. 91, no. 1 (March): 66–81.

Atkinson, Anthony B., Lee Rainwater, and Timothy M. Smeeding. 1995. *Income Distribution in OECD Countries: Evidence from the Luxembourg Income Study*. Paris: Organisation for Economic Co-operation and Development.

Banks, Arthur S. 1993. *Political Handbook of the World: 1993*. Binghamton NY: CSA Publications.

Banks, Arthur S., Alan J. Day, and Thomas C. Muller. 1996. *Political Handbook of the World: 1995–1996*. Binghamton NY: CSA Publications.

Bedau, Hugh Adam (ed.) 1997. *The Death Penalty in America: Current Controversies*. New York: Oxford University Press.

Blais, André, and R. K. Carty. 1990. "Does Proportional Representation Foster Voter Turnout?" *European Journal of Political Research*, vol. 18, no. 2 (March): 167–81.

Castles, Francis G., and Deborah Mitchell. 1993. "Worlds of Welfare and Families of Nations." In Francis G. Castles (ed.) *Families of Nations: Patterns of Public Policy in Western Democracies*, pp. 93–128. Aldershot: Dartmouth.

Dahl, Robert A. 1971. *Polyarchy: Participation and Opposition*. New Haven CT: Yale University Press.

——1996. "Equality versus Inequality." *PS: Political Science & Politics*, vol. 29, no. 4 (December): 639–48.

Dahl, Robert A., and Edward R. Tufte. 1973. *Size and Democracy.* Stanford CA: Stanford University Press.

Esping-Andersen, Gösta. 1990. *The Three Worlds of Welfare Capitalism.* Princeton NJ: Princeton University Press.

Freedom House Survey Team. 1996. *Freedom in the World: The Annual Survey of Political Rights and Civil Liberties, 1995–1996.* New York: Freedom House.

Huber, John D., and G. Bingham Powell, Jr. 1994. "Congruence Between Citizens and Policymakers in Two Visions of Liberal Democracy." *World Politics*, vol. 46, no. 3 (April): 291–326.

International IDEA. 1997. *Voter Turnout from 1945 to 1997: A Global Report on Political Participation.* Stockholm: International Institute for Democracy and Electoral Assistance.

Inter-Parliamentary Union. 1995. *Women in Parliaments, 1945–1995: A World Statistical Survey.* Geneva: Inter-Parliamentary Union.

Jaggers, Keith, and Ted Robert Gurr. 1995. *Polity III: Regime Change and Political Authority, 1800–1994* (computer file). Ann Arbor MI: Inter-University Consortium for Political and Social Research.

Klingemann, Hans-Dieter. 1999. "Mapping Political Support in the 1990s: A Global Analysis." In Pippa Norris (ed.) *Critical Citizens: Global Support for Democratic Government.* Oxford: Oxford University Press.

Lijphart, Arend. 1997b. "Unequal Participation: Democracy's Unresolved Dilemma." *American Political Science Review*, vol. 91, no. 1 (March): 1–14.

——1999. *Patterns of Democracy: Government Forms and Performance in Thirty-six Countries,* New Haven CT: Yale University Press.

Mansbridge, Jane. 1996. "Reconstructing Democracy." In Nancy J. Hirschmann and Christine Di Stefano (eds) *Revisioning the Political: Feminist Reconstructions of Traditional Concepts in Western Political Theory,* pp. 117–38. Boulder CO: Westview Press.

Mauer, Marc. 1994. *Americans Behind Bars: The International Use of Incarceration, 1992–1993.* Washington DC: Sentencing Project.

—— 1997. *Americans Behind Bars: U.S. and International Use of Incarceration, 1995.* Washington DC: Sentencing Project.

Mill, John Stuart. 1861. *Considerations on Representative Government.* London: Parker, Son, and Bourn.

Palmer, Monte. 1997. *Political Development: Dilemmas and Challenges.* Itasca IL: Peacock.

Powell, G. Bingham, Jr. 1980. "Voting Turnout in Thirty Democracies: Partisan, Legal, and Socio-Economic Influences." In Richard Rose (ed.) *Electoral Participation: A Comparative Analysis,* pp. 5–34. Beverly Hills CA: Sage.

——1989. "Constitutional Design and Citizen Electoral Control." *Journal of Theoretical Politics*, vol. 1, no. 2 (April): 107–30.

Ray, James Lee. 1997. "The Democratic Path to Peace." *Journal of Democracy*, vol. 8, no. 2 (April): 49–64.

Rule, Wilma, and Joseph F. Zimmerman (eds) 1994. *Electoral Systems in Comparative Perspective: Their Impact on Women and Minorities.* Westport CT: Greenwood Press.

Schmidt, Manfred G. 1997. "Determinants of Social Expenditure in Liberal Democracies: The Post World War II Experience." *Acta Politica*, vol. 32, no. 3 (summer): 153–73.

Taagepera, Rein. 1994. "Beating the Law of Minority Attrition." In Wilma Rule and Joseph F. Zimmerman (eds) *Electoral Systems in Comparative Perspective: Their Impact on Women and Minorities*, pp. 236–45. Westport CT: Greenwood Press.

Transparency International. 1997. *Corruption Perception Index*. Berlin: http://gwdu19.gwdg.de/~uwvw/rank-97.htm

United Nations Development Programme. 1994. *Human Development Report 1994*. New York: Oxford University Press.

——1995. *Human Development Report 1995*. New York: Oxford University Press.

——1996. *Human Development Report 1996*. New York: Oxford University Press.

——1997. *Human Development Report 1997*. New York: Oxford University Press.

Vanhanen, Tatu. 1990. *The Process of Democratization: A Comparative Study of 147 States, 1980–88*. New York: Crane Russak.

——1997. *Prospects of Democracy: A Study of 172 Countries*. London: Routledge.

Wilensky, Harold L. 1990. "Common Problems, Divergent Policies: An 18-Nation Study of Family Policy." *Public Affairs Report*, vol. 31, no. 3 (May): 1–3.

World Bank. 1992. *The World Bank Atlas: 25th Anniversary Edition*. Washington DC: International Bank for Reconstruction and Development.

——1993. *The World Bank Atlas 1994*. Washington DC: International Bank for Reconstruction and Development.

——1994. *The World Bank Atlas 1995*. Washington DC: International Bank for Reconstruction and Development.

——1995. *The World Bank Atlas 1996*. Washington DC: International Bank for Reconstruction and Development.

——1997. *1997 World Bank Atlas*. Washington DC: International Bank for Reconstruction and Development.

Part III
Majority rule

7 Majority rule in theory and practice
The tenacity of a flawed paradigm[1]

Introduction

The 1990s are likely to become the "decade of democracy": more and more nations are contemplating the establishment of democratic systems, actually instituting democracy, or consolidating existing systems of democratic rule. This trend encourages us to reflect on the meaning of democracy and its various forms. I shall argue in this article that two basic models of democracy should be distinguished – majoritarian democracy and consensus democracy – but that there is a strong and dangerous tendency to define democracy almost exclusively in terms of the former. Majority rule suffers from a serious contradiction between its theory and its practice. In theory, majority rule tends to be regarded as the crucial decision rule – and hence as the defining criterion – of democracy. In practice, however, strict application of majority rule is extremely rare. Especially with regard to the most important decisions and to issues that cause deep splits in societies, democracies almost uniformly deviate from majoritarian decision-making rules, to adopt mechanisms more likely to rally a broad consensus.

The existence of this gap between the theory and practice of majority rule is important for two reasons. One is that most of the democratizing and newly democratic countries need consensus democracy even more than the stable and mature democracies that have been in existence for a long time, because they tend to suffer from more serious internal cleavages and face more sensitive and divisive issues. The second reason is that the view equating democracy with majority rule is so strong and widespread as to constitute a major obstacle to any serious consideration of the consensus model. Democratization means the drafting of democratic constitutions, and the careful drafting of a new or improved constitution starts badly if it takes the majoritarian definition of democracy as its only point of departure.

Let us begin with a brief and preliminary description of the differences between the two conceptions of democracy, both based on the standard definition of "government by and for the people." They differ radically with regard to a fundamental question raised by this definition: who is to do the governing and to whose interests should a government be responsive when the people are in disagreement and express divergent preferences? One answer is: the majority of the people. The alternative is: as many people as possible. Accordingly, the majoritarian model of democracy concentrates political power in the hands of the majority, whereas the consensus model tries to share, disperse, restrain, and limit power in a variety of ways.

My argument will proceed in four steps. First I shall discuss the extent to which democracy tends to be conceived in purely majoritarian terms. Second, I shall follow the logic of the principle of majority rule, and define what a purely majoritarian democracy looks like. Third, I shall demonstrate that this pure model of majoritarian democracy is completely at variance with actually functioning democracies and democratic traditions in all parts of the world. Finally, I shall speculate on the reasons why the majority-rule paradigm continues to dominate, despite its being so completely out of touch with the reality of democratic practice.

The democracy = majority rule equation

Pennock begins his discussion of majority rule with the following statement: "We must note at once that rule by the majority is often alleged to be the very essence of democracy."[2] Recent pronouncements by spokesmen at the two extreme ends of the political spectrum – the American conservative columnist William Safire, and the South African communist leader Joe Slovo – illustrate Pennock's assertion very nicely. In a commentary about developments in South Africa, Safire argued that democracy means real political equality and "one person, one vote," to conclude "that means majority rule." And to make his point unmistakably clear, he added that "no democrat can oppose the idea of majority rule."[3] Slovo was quoted as saying "We should stop playing with words. We know only one kind of democracy and that is majority rule."[4]

Two explanations for these remarkably apodictic statements may be advanced. One is that the term "majority" is very flexible and ambiguous, consequently, "majority rule" does not necessarily mean rule by a bare majority (50 percent plus one). As Sartori points out,

> there are at least three magnitudes subsumed, often confusedly, under the majority rule heading: (a) qualified majorities (often a two-thirds majority); (b) simple or absolute majority (50.01 per cent); (c) relative majority, or plurality, that is, the major minority (a less than 50 per cent majority).[5]

Sartori is undoubtedly right but if majority rule can mean rule by groups ranging from mere plurality to complete unanimity, it becomes so broad as to be meaningless. Moreover, it seems quite clear to me that the likes of Safire and Slovo do not have such a broad definition in mind when they equate democracy with majority rule: they mean a bare but absolute "50 percent plus one" majority.

The second explanation has greater merit. It may well be argued that statements like those of Safire and Slovo should not be taken literally and do not mean absolute and unrestrained majority rule. Even when they do not explicitly add that majority rule must be limited by minority rights, they implicitly mean to make this reservation. For instance, Dahl argues that

> no one has ever advocated, and no one except its enemies has ever defined democracy to mean that a majority would or should do anything it felt an impulse to do. Every advocate of democracy ... and every friendly definition of it, includes the idea of restraints on majorities.[6]

As an illustration, Dahl quotes from Abraham Lincoln's First Inaugural Address: "Unanimity is impossible; the rule of a minority, as a permanent arrangement, is wholly inadmissible; so that, rejecting the majority principle, anarchy or despotism in some form is all that is left." As Dahl points out, Lincoln certainly did not mean to quarrel with the many limits on majority rule in the United States Constitution. Neither did Alexis de Tocqueville, who nevertheless made the following very strong majority-rule statement: "The very essence of democratic government consists in the absolute sovereignty of the majority; for there is nothing in democratic states which is capable of resisting it."[7] I shall return to Lincoln's and de Tocqueville's statements later.

Even if we concede the point that restraints on majorities are usually assumed when majority rule is used as the defining criterion of democracy, Dahl points out that this still leaves the issue of what form these restraints take or should take: (1) ethical and cultural restraints, primarily operative at the level of individual consciences, (2) social checks and balances, or (3) legal and constitutional restraints?[8] The first type consists of informal limits, the third of formal restraints, and the second a combination of the two. For instance, a flexible multiparty system can operate as an informal social mechanism checking straight majority rule, but the emergence and maintenance of such a party system can be encouraged by the formal-legal framework of the electoral system used in a country.

Yet informal restraints on majority rule only barely modify absolute majority rule. One may hope and trust that majorities will act with prudence and restraint, but any limits the majority imposes upon itself can also be removed by it. As Spitz points out, such

> self-denying and self-controlled limits should not blind us to the actual ability of majorities to control all of government – legislative, executive, and, if they have a mind to, judicial – and thus to control everything politics can touch. Nothing clarifies the total sway of majorities more than their ability to alter and adjust the standard of legitimacy.

And she adds, revealing herself to be a committed majoritarian: "In democratic theory it is hard to imagine who else might make such decisions."[9] Kendall reached the same conclusion about John Locke's position with regard to majority rule. Despite Locke's strong concern for and commitment to individual rights, his preferred political system relied exclusively on informal restraints on the majority – which means that, in the final analysis, Locke can be regarded as a majority-rule democrat.[10]

The situation is quite different when the restraints are of a formal-legal or formal-constitutional nature which cannot be changed by bare majorities. But it is absurd to qualify such a dispensation as majority rule without adding the proviso that it is not unlimited. Sartori argues that majority rule used to be "only a shorthand formula for *limited* majority rule, for a restrained majority rule that respects minority rights. Until a few decades ago this was well understood. I doubt that this is still the case today."[11] Perhaps it has "gone without saying" for so long that majority rule does not mean absolute majority rule that we have started to forget this crucial proviso. I am not arguing here that there is not a good case to be made for majority rule on logical and theoretical grounds – a case that is made both by Spitz and, reluctantly, by Locke. But it is both wrong and dangerous to argue, explicitly or implicitly, that majority rule is the only or the only legitimate form of democracy.

Majority rule in practice

So far I have discussed majority rule merely as an abstract principle. Let me now bring this discussion down to the empirical earth by asking: what would a democratic government based squarely on majoritarian principles actually look like? In answer, I shall make three simplifying assumptions. One is that the government we have in mind is a representative rather than a direct democracy. Given the large populations of most countries, direct democracy is exceedingly rare, so this assumption hardly requires an apology. My second assumption is that representation takes place primarily via political parties, which entails somewhat greater simplification but is still quite realistic and reasonable. The third assumption is somewhat more far-reaching: I shall assume a parliamentary form of government rather than a presidential form or some hybrid of the two. Later, I shall discuss the complications added by presidentialism.

Since majority rule means that political power is, or should be, concentrated in the hands of the majority, my question can be phrased as: which political forms, institutions, and practices are optimal for concentrating power in the majority's hands? Majority rule is maximized, first of all, if one political party, supported by a majority in the legislature, controls the cabinet. Second, this one-party majority cabinet should predominate over the legislature, in which one or more other parties will also be represented. Third, the legislature should obviously be unicameral in order to ensure that there is only one clear majority, that is, in order to avoid the possibility of competing majorities that may occur when there are two chambers. Fourth, the governmental system should be unitary and centralized in order to ensure that there are no clearly designated geographical and/or functional areas which the cabinet and the parliamentary majority fail to control. Fifth, the cabinet and the parliamentary majority should not be constrained by constitutional limitations; this means that there should not be any constitution at all, or merely an "unwritten" constitution, or a written constitution that can be amended by simple majority vote. Sixth, the courts should not have the power to limit the majority's power by exercising judicial review, though if the constitution can be amended by majority vote (according to the previous characteristic), the impact of judicial review would be minimal anyway because it can easily be overridden by the majority.

These six characteristics of majoritarian democracy are all logically derived from the principle of concentrating power in the hands of the majority. Three further characteristics can be added, not on logical grounds but because empirical analysis has shown that they increase the chances that one-party dominance will in fact occur. The first is a two-party system: when two major parties dominate the party system, it is highly likely that one of them will emerge as the winning or majority party in every election. In turn, a two-party system is enhanced by a plurality form of elections (according to "Duverger's Law," to which only minor exceptions have been discovered)[12] and to the extent that there is only one dominant cleavage, typically the socio-economic or left-right division, in a country and its party system.[13]

The nine contrasting characteristics of consensus democracy – or non-majoritarian democracy – can be formulated by logical derivation from the nine characteristics of majoritarian democracy, that is, by taking the opposites of each: (1) broad coalition cabinets instead of one-party bare-majority cabinets; (2) a balanced power relationship between the cabinet and the legislature instead of cabinet predominance; (3) a bicameral legislature, particularly one in which the two chambers have roughly equal powers and are differently constituted, instead of unicameralism; (4) a federal and decentralized structure instead of unitary and centralized government; (5) a "rigid" constitution that can only be amended by extraordinary majorities, instead of a "flexible" written or unwritten constitution; (6) judicial review of the constitutionality of legislation; (7) a multiparty instead of a two-party system; (8) a multidimensional party system, in which the parties differ from each other on one or more issue dimensions in addition to socio-economic issues, for instance, along religious, cultural-ethnic, urban-rural, or foreign policy dimensions; and (9) elections by proportional representation instead of by plurality.[14]

I borrowed the terms "majoritarian" and "consensus" democracy from Robert G. Dixon, Jr., and my lists of contrasting characteristics are similar, though not identical, to his.[15] Other scholars have made similar distinctions between the two basic types of democracy. What I call majoritarian democracy is called "populistic" democracy by both Dahl and Riker; and what I call consensus democracy corresponds roughly to Riker's "liberal" democracy and to a combination of Dahl's "Madisonian" and "polyarchal" democracy.[16]

The rarity of majority rule in contemporary democracies

Even a very casual application of the above lists of contrasting character-istics to contemporary democracies reveals the numerous exceptions to majority rule: for instance, coalition cabinets, multiparty systems, propor-tional representation, bicameral legislatures, judicial review, and federalism are all common democratic patterns. Moreover, a more systematic mapping of contemporary democracies according to these criteria shows that major-itarian democracy is very much the exception rather than the rule. I have made such an effort in *Democracies* for the twenty-one countries that have been democratic without major interruptions from approximately the end of the Second World War until 1980: fifteen West European democracies plus the United States, Canada, Israel, Japan, Australia, and New Zealand.[17] (Because French democracy underwent major changes in the transition from the Fourth to the Fifth Republic, I treated the two Republics as separate cases.) In a subsequent co-authored analysis, the cases of the three newly democratic Southern European countries were added: Spain, Portu-gal, and Greece (based on their democratic experience from the mid-1970s to the mid-1980s).[18]

The positions between majoritarianism and consensus occupied by these twenty-five democracies are shown in Figure 7.1. Empirical analysis demonstrates that the several traits distinguishing the two basic forms of democracy cluster along two principal dimensions, on which the figure is based. The first may be called the executives-parties dimension since it groups the closely related variables of the type of cabinet, cabinet power, the party system, and the electoral system. The second dimension consists of the closely related variables of degree of centralization, type of legislature, and degree of constitutional flexibility. Since, in classical federal theory, these are also the characteristics distinguishing federalism from unitary government, this second dimension may also be called the federal-unitary one.[19] In order to calculate the scores for each country along the two dimensions, the indi-vidual variables were operationalized and, since they were measured on different scales, their values were standardized (so as to obtain a mean of 0 and a standard deviation of 1). The values along the two dimensions are the averages (again standardized) of the variables included in them. Positive values in Figure 7.1 indicate majoritarianism, negative values consensus.

Figure 7.1 shows that only two countries can unambiguously be labeled majority-rule democracies: New Zealand and, to a lesser extent, the United

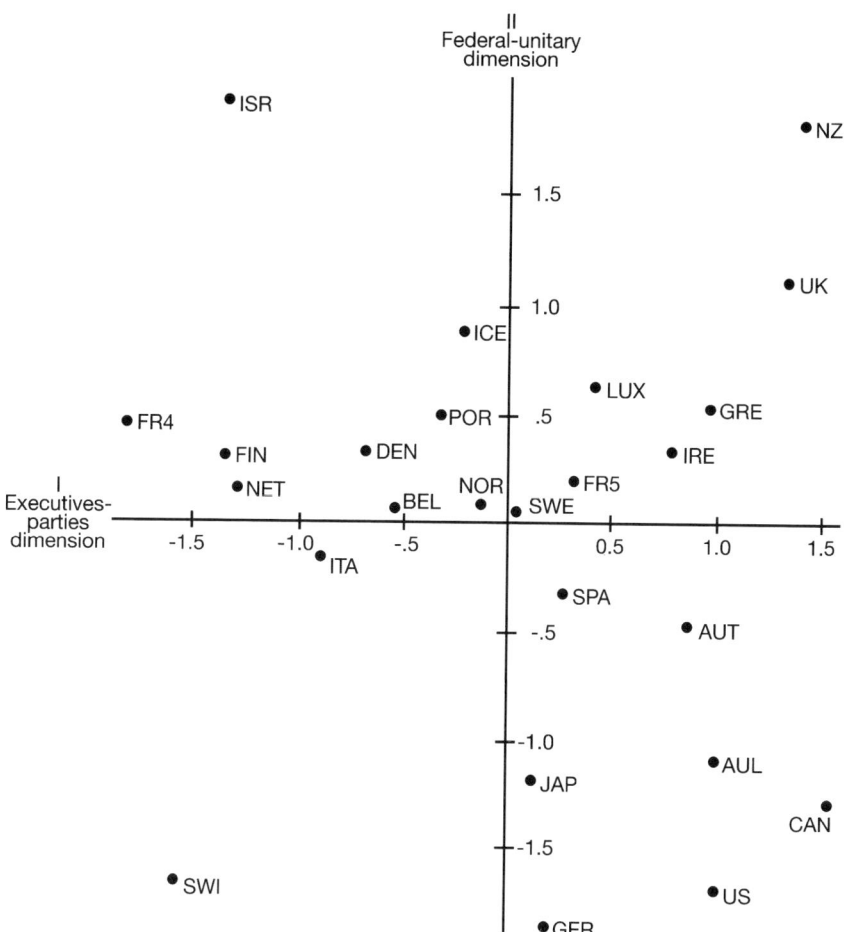

Figure 7.1 Twenty-five democratic regimes plotted on the two majoritarian-consensual dimensions

Note: AUL stands for Australia. AUT Austria, FR4 the Fourth French Republic and FR5 the Fifth French Republic.

Source: Arend Lijphart, Thomas C. Bruneau, P. Nikiforos Diamandouros and Richard Gunther, A Mediterranean Model of Democracy? The Southern European Democracies in Comparative Perspective. *West European Politics*, vol. 11, no. 1, 1988, p. 12.

Kingdom. All other democracies diverge considerably from the majoritarian model.[20] Moreover, a closer inspection of the British and New Zealand cases reveals that they may be regarded as mainly but not purely majoritarian, and that, significantly, their deviations from pure majority rule have to do with the management of serious societal cleavages. New Zealand uses an adjusted system of plurality elections in which several districts are reserved for the Maori minority so as to guarantee Maori representation in parliament – which would be much less likely if pure plurality were used. In the United Kingdom, government policy toward deeply divided Northern Ireland has evolved in a clearly consensual direction: the British have instituted proportional representation in this province for all elections except those to the House of Commons, the aim being to establish a broad coalition government including both the Protestant majority and the Catholic minority. Of course, the British bicameral legislature is also a deviation from pure majoritarianism but, since the power of the House of Lords is extremely limited, this represents only a slight exception.

The remaining twenty-three democracies deviate even more clearly from pure majority rule, although only one – Switzerland – is a virtually pure consensus democracy. Most countries are located somewhere between the extremes of majority rule and consensus. Moreover, the picture presented by Figure 7.1 still exaggerates majoritarian tendencies because computation of the majoritarianism-consensus scores, as explained above, based on the relative positions of countries between majoritarianism and consensus virtually guarantees that equal (or almost equal) numbers of countries will be located to the right and to the left of the vertical axis, and above and below the horizontal axis. If we were to use absolute values, there would be a general shift toward the left and the bottom of Figure 7.1 – that is, in the direction of consensus democracy – because for almost all differences between majority rule and consensus, the consensus characteristics are much more common.[21]

In the twenty-five democracies in Figure 7.1, coalition governments occur much more frequently than one-party cabinets; legislatures tend to be considerably more influential than the docile House of Commons in London; fifteen countries have bicameral legislatures; twenty-one have written constitutions protected by a qualified-majority amendment procedure and/or judicial review; nineteen countries use proportional or semi-proportional representation; and multiparty and multidimensional party systems are much more common than two-party and one-dimensional party systems. The only characteristic on which majority rule appears to be the winner is unitary government: only six of the twenty-five democracies are formally federal: the United States, Canada, the Federal Republic of Germany, Switzerland, Austria, and Australia. On the other hand, two (Belgium and Spain) should be regarded as at least semi-federal, and several of the formally unitary states (notably the Scandinavian countries and Japan) are in fact quite decentralized – comparable to federal Australia and Austria.[22] This single exception does not affect the overall pattern, which is much closer to the consensus than to the majoritarian model of democracy.

An additional remarkable, but often overlooked, fact is that in the two mainly majority-rule democracies, New Zealand and the United Kingdom, the majorities that rule are usually artificial ones in the legislature, and are not based on popular majorities. "Winning" parties in Britain since 1945 and in New Zealand since 1954 have never won majorities of the total vote. In this important respect, even these two countries cannot really be regarded as good examples of majority rule.

One possible objection to the above arguments is that it is based on only twenty-five cases which are not a representative sample of the world's democracies: they are mainly West European and all belong to the industrialized world. If we were to cast our net more widely, we should also include some of the more recently independent countries with a British political heritage, such as Jamaica, and Trinidad and Tobago, which practice democracy roughly along British lines. On the other hand, we should then also include federal India, federal and strongly coalitional Malaysia, and the Latin American democracies, virtually all of which use proportional representation. My estimate is that the overall pattern would not change appreciably if we extended our sample from the original twenty-five to, say, the roughly fifty contemporary democracies.

A further counter-argument is that majoritarian traditions in the non-Western world are stronger than in the twenty-four Western countries (Japan being the only non-Western country in the set of twenty-five in Figure 7.1). This point is made forcefully by the Philippine statesman and scholar Raul S. Manglapus in his recent book *Will of the People*, significantly subtitled *Original Democracy in Non-Western Societies*, the main aim of which is to disprove "the notion that despotism is the natural non-Western way of life" – a notion expressed by Clare Boothe Luce, whom he quotes, to the effect that "three quarters of the nations of the world [that is, the non-Western world] are not culturally adapted to democracy."[23] He presents massive evidence of democratic traditions and practices in all parts of the non-Western world, and particularly important for our purposes – almost all his examples show that the non-Western democratic tradition is much more consensual than majoritarian. In his own words, "the common characteristic" is "the element of consensus as opposed to adversarial [majoritarian] decisions,"[24] and he repeatedly describes the non-Western democratic process as a "consensual process" based on a strong "concern for harmony."[25]

Earlier writers had reached the same conclusion. For instance, Rupert Emerson is in error when he identifies the "assumption of the majority's right to overrule a dissident minority after a period of debate" as a "Western assumption" – this being specifically British – but he is undoubtedly right when he argues that this assumption "does violence to conceptions basic to non-Western peoples." Although there are important differences among the traditions of Asian and African societies, "their native inclination is generally toward extensive and unhurried deliberation aimed at ultimate consensus. The gradual discovery of areas of agreement is the significant feature and not the ability to come to a speedy resolution of issues by counting heads."[26] Similarly, Michael Haas argues that there is a typical "Asian way" of decision-making based on such ideas as *mufakat*, a

Malay term for the "principle of unanimity built through discussion rather than voting," and *mushawarah*, the "traditional Indonesian method of coming to agreement not through majority decision but by a search for something like the Quaker "sense of the meeting."[27] And in his famous study of West African politics, Sir Arthur Lewis emphasizes the strong consensual democratic traditions in this area: "The tribe has made its decision by discussion, in much the way that coalitions function; this kind of democratic procedure is at the heart of the original institutions of the people."[28]

The evidence is overwhelming that majoritarian democracy is the exception rather than the rule in actual practices and traditions in all parts of the world. In fact, it is highly exceptional, limited to very few countries – mainly the United Kingdom and countries heavily influenced by the British political tradition.

Majority rule as a Kuhnian paradigm

How can this striking discrepancy between the theoretical prominence and the empirical rarity of majority rule be explained? The answer, it seems to me, is that majority rule is a "paradigm" as defined by Thomas S. Kuhn: a basic concept, model, or approach, that is widely accepted – and rarely seriously examined – in a particular field of study. It is a typical feature of such a paradigm that discrepancies between facts and theory are not sufficient to lead to its abandonment: "There are always difficulties somewhere in the paradigm-nature fit," but these tend to be either disregarded or viewed as remediable by means of small adjustments.[29] In the case of the majority rule paradigm, discrepancies are generally explained away by saying that they are just slight exceptions to an interpretation of democracy that remains basically valid. Its tenacity can also be partly explained in terms of its beautiful, and hence seductive, simplicity – much simpler and more attractive than the notion (stated, for instance, by Jean-Jacques Rousseau), that the democratic decision-making rule may range from majority to unanimity, depending on the importance and urgency of the issues involved.[30]

Kuhn also argues, however, that when a discrepancy becomes a major anomaly, it is no longer possible to ignore it or to explain it away, and the flawed paradigm is toppled in a "scientific revolution."[31] It is hard to regard the discrepancy between the theory and practice of majority rule as anything less than a striking anomaly. We therefore need further explanations why the expected scientific revolution has failed to occur. Let me advance, somewhat tentatively and speculatively, four such explanations.

One explanation is that while political science is practiced world-wide, it is especially strong in – some would say dominated by – the Anglo-American countries. And in this area, the weight of British practices and traditions is proportionally much greater than in the world as a whole. However, this argument begs the question of why the non-majoritarian features of the

United States political system have not been able to serve as a sufficient counterweight to British majoritarianism. The US Constitution is based on such Madisonian principles as separation and division of powers, checks and balances, minority protection, extraordinary majorities, and so on – the very opposites of simple majoritarianism. Dahl, for instance, describes Madisonian democracy and populistic (majoritarian) democracy as the two principal contrasting conceptions.[32] The additional explanation is that many American political scientists, from Woodrow Wilson to the Committee on Political Parties of the American Political Science Association, have tended to be Anglophiles, strong admirers of British politics, and interested in reforming US politics along British majoritarian lines.[33]

A different explanation – my third – is that, if the essence of Madisonianism is the restraint of the majority's power, the US political system has some striking un-Madisonian characteristics. The most important of these are the concentration of executive power in the hands of one individual, the election of the president by a majoritarian method, the one-party composition of the cabinet, the predominance of the plurality method in legislative elections at all levels, and the two-party system. For all of these reasons, the United States is classified as mainly majoritarian on one of the dimensions – the executives-parties dimension – in Figure 7.1. Only with regard to the federal-unitary dimension is the United States strongly consensual. In the light of these majoritarian characteristics, the statements by Lincoln and de Tocqueville, cited earlier, become more understandable. It is also important to realize that presidential government has ambivalent consequences for the degree of majoritarian or consensus government: on the one hand, it means separation of powers – a consensual characteristic – but on the other hand it means highly concentrated executive power and, since for the election of a single official proportional representation cannot be used, necessarily entails the application of plurality or a similar majoritarian electoral method.

A fourth explanation is suggested by Dogan and Pahre, who argue that scientific innovation is more likely to occur at the margins than in the core of fields and disciplines.[34] The study of democracy, dominated by political scientists, has been at the very core of political science, which may have been an obstacle to innovative and original thinking. Prominent mainstream political scientists – like Dahl and Sartori whom I have quoted frequently – have made a major contribution to the better understanding of majority rule by pointing out that it is not the only form of democracy. But it seems significant that the most important frontal assault on majority rule (by a convinced democrat) was launched by a political scientist working in the new public choice tradition – Riker, arguing the logical flaws and inconsistencies of majority rule and the superiority of liberal democracy[35] – and that the first modern consensus theorist was Sir Arthur Lewis, an economist rather than a political scientist. It is worth presenting the essence of Lewis' position in his own wise words:

The word "democracy" has two meanings. Its primary meaning is that all who are affected by a decision should have the chance to participate in making that decision, either directly or through chosen representatives. Its secondary meaning is that the will of the majority shall prevail.

The second meaning, Lewis writes, violates the primary rule if representatives are grouped into a government and an opposition, as in Britain, because it excludes the minority from decision-making for an extended period. Majority rule can still be acceptable in homogeneous societies, but in countries with deep societal divisions, "it is totally immoral, inconsistent with the primary meaning of democracy, and destructive of any prospect of building a nation in which different peoples might live together in harmony."[36]

These four explanations of why no revolution against the paradigm of majority rule has taken place should obviously not be read as justifications for the absence of such a revolution. To restate my argument at the beginning of this article, I believe that the narrow and unrealistic equation of democracy with majority rule is not only theoretically untenable but also misleading and hence practically very dangerous when used as a guideline for writing new democratic constitutions. In my opinion, we should revolt against majority rule as the sole criterion of democracy, replace it with the broader conception of democracy that also includes consensus democracy, accept that, in practice, the world's democracies and democratic traditions are much closer to the consensus model than to the majoritarian model, and take the consensus model as our point of departure – particularly, as urged by Lewis, in designing democratic constitutions for the many divided societies in today's world.

Notes

1 This paper first appeared in *International Social Science Journal*, no. 129 (August 1991), pp. 483–93.
2 J. Roland Pennock, *Democratic Political Theory*. Princeton NJ: Princeton University Press, 1979, p. 370.
3 William Safire, "The Suzman Plan," *New York Times*, 7 August 1986.
4 *San Diego Union*, 7 May 1990, based on a report from the New York Times News Service.
5 Giovanni Sartori, *The Theory of Democracy Revisited*. Chatham NJ: Chatham House Publishers, 1987, p. 221.
6 Robert A. Dahl, *A Preface to Democratic Theory*. Chicago IL: University of Chicago Press, 1956, p. 36.
7 Abraham Lincoln, *First Inaugural Address*, and Alexis de Tocqueville, *Democracy in America*, cited in Dahl, *A Preface to Democratic Theory*, p. 35. Let me add a contemporary example of a statement by a practicing politician, President Jimmy Carter. In his 1978 address to the United States Naval Academy, he proclaimed that his government was strongly committed to democracy and "particularly dedicated to genuine self-determination and majority rule in those areas of the world where these goals have not yet been attained." In a later part of his speech, he described American democracy in quite different – consensual instead

of majoritarian – terms: "We are … strong because of what we stand for as a nation [including] the right of every individual to speak out, to participate fully in government and to share political power." "Speech of the President on Soviet-American Relations at the US Naval Academy." *New York Times*, 8 June 1978.

8 Dahl, op. cit., p. 36.

9 Elaine Spitz, *Majority Rule*. Chatham NJ: Chatham House Publishers, 1984, p. 203.

10 Willmoore Kendall, *John Locke and the Doctrine of Majority Rule*. Urbana IL: University of Illinois Press, 1941.

11 Sartori, op. cit., p. 31.

12 See William H. Riker, "Duverger's Law Revisited," and Maurice Duverger, "Duverger's Law: Forty Years Later," in Bernard Grofman and Arend Lijphart (eds) *Electoral Laws and Their Political Consequences*. New York: Agathon Press, 1986, pp. 19–42, 69–84.

13 See Rein Taagepera and Bernard Grofman, "Rethinking Duverger's Law: Predicting the Effective Number of Parties in Plurality and PR Systems – Parties Minus Issues Equals One." *European Journal of Political Research*, vol. 13, no. 4, December 1985, pp. 341–52.

14 See Arend Lijphart, *Democracies: Patterns of Majoritarian and Consensus Government in Twenty-One Countries*. New Haven CT: Yale University Press, 1984, pp. 1–36.

15 Robert G. Dixon, Jr., *Democratic Representation: Reapportionment in Law and Politics*. New York: Oxford University Press, 1968.

16 Dahl, op. cit., esp. pp. 1–89; William H. Riker, *Liberalism Against Populism: A Confrontation Between the Theory of Democracy and the Theory of Social Choice*. San Francisco CA: W. H. Freeman, 1982.

17 Lijphart, op. cit., esp. pp. 211–22.

18 Arend Lijphart, Thomas C. Bruneau, P. Nikiforos Diamandouros and Richard Gunther, "A Mediterranean Model of Democracy? The Southern European Democracies in Comparative Perspective." *West European Politics*, vol. 11, no. 1, January 1988, pp. 7–25.

19 See, for instance, K. C. Wheare, *Federal Government*. Oxford: Oxford University Press, 1946; Daniel J. Elazar, "Federalism," in David L. Sills (ed.) *International Encyclopedia of the Social Sciences*, vol. 5. New York: Macmillan and Free Press, 1968; Carl J. Friedrich, *Limited Government: A Comparison*. Englewood Cliffs NJ: Prentice-Hall, 1974; Ivo D. Duchacek, *Comparative Federalism: The Territorial Dimension of Politics*. New York: Holt, Rinehart & Winston, 1970.

20 See Robert W. Jackman, "Elections and the Democratic Class Struggle," *World Politics*, vol. 39, no. 1, October 1986, pp. 132–35; Anthony Downs, "The Evolution of Democracy: How Its Axioms and Institutional Forms Have Been Adapted to Changing Social Forces," *Daedalus*, vol. 116, no. 3, summer 1987, pp. 129–34.

21 This point is made with special force by Robert A. Dahl, *Democracy and Its Critics*. New Haven CT: Yale University Press, 1989, pp. 156–60.

22 For the decentralization scores, see Lijphart, op. cit., p. 178.

23 Raul S. Manglapus, *Will of the People: Original Democracy in Non-Western Societies*. New York: Greenwood Press, 1987, pp. 5, 10.

24 Manglapus, op. cit., p. 69.

25 For instance, Manglapus, op. cit., pp. 78, 82, 103, 107, 123, 129.

26 Rupert Emerson, *From Empire to Nation: The Rise of Self-Assertion of Asian and African People*. Cambridge MA: Harvard University Press, 1960, p. 284.

27 Michael Haas, "The 'Asian Way' to Peace," *Pacific Community*, vol. 4, no. 4, July 1973, pp. 503–5. The definition of *mushawarah* is from Herbert Feith, "Indonesia," in George McT. Kahin (ed.) *Governments and Politics of Southeast Asia*. Ithaca NY: Cornell University Press, 1959, p. 192.

28 W. Arthur Lewis, *Politics in West Africa*. London: Allen & Unwin, 1965, p. 86.
29 Thomas S. Kuhn, *The Structure of Scientific Revolutions*. Chicago IL: University of Chicago Press, 1970.
30 Rousseau speaks of a range of qualified majorities between a simple majority and unanimity, and argues that two maxims should determine the proper position on this range:

>One, that the more important and serious the deliberations, the closer the winning opinion should be to unanimity. The other, that the more speed the business at hand requires, the smaller the prescribed difference in the division of opinions should be. In deliberations that must be finished on the spot, a majority of a single vote should suffice. The first of these maxims appears more suited to laws; the second, to business matters. However, that may be, it is a combination of the two that establishes the proper ratio of the deciding majority.
>(*Social Contract*, book 4, chapter 2, cited in Dahl, 1989, op. cit., p. 355)

31 Kuhn, op. cit., pp. 82–90.
32 Dahl, 1956, op. cit., pp. 4–62.
33 See especially Woodrow Wilson, "Cabinet Government in the United States" and "Committee or Cabinet Government?" in Ray Stannard Baker and William E. Dodd (eds) *College and State: Educational, Literary and Political, Papers (1875–1913) by Woodrow Wilson*. New York: Harper, 1925, vol. 1, pp. 19–42, 95–129; and Committee on Political Parties, American Political Science Association, *Toward a More Responsible Two-Party System*. New York: Rinehart & Company, 1950.
34 Mattei Dogan and Robert Pahre, *Creative Marginality: Innovation at the Intersections of Social Sciences*. Boulder CO: Westview Press, 1990.
35 Riker, op. cit.
36 Lewis, op. cit., pp. 64–66.

8 Back to democratic basics

Who really practices majority rule?

Democracy's victory in the 1990s, while a major development in world history, is only a partial victory. It represents the defeat of communism, fascism, and other ideological anti-democratic forces, but democracy continues to face enemies of a different nature: in particular, the deep ethnic-communal divisions within countries, often aggravated by great socioeconomic inequalities, which pose a grave threat to the viability and consolidation of democracy in the many newly democratic countries.

The leitmotiv of much of my previous work has been that the challenge of deep cleavages does not represent an insuperable problem. Democracy of the "consociational" or "consensus" type – similar concepts, although I have defined them in slightly different terms (Lijphart 1977, 1984) – provides formal and informal constitutional rules that can facilitate interethnic and intercommunal accommodation. The two most important elements are broad participation in decision-making by the representatives of the different ethnic-communal groups and cultural autonomy for those groups that wish to have it. The empirical evidence for this proposition is very strong. For instance, Ted Robert Gurr's recent *Minorities at Risk* (1993: esp. 290–313), a massive study of all of the world's minorities in the post-World War II era, concludes that, first of all, intercommunal conflict is by no means intractable; that, second, partition and secession do not work well, mainly because it is in practice very difficult to draw boundaries in such a clean and neat way that homogeneous countries are created; but that, third, there are methods that do work, namely broad power sharing and group autonomy.[1]

This chapter explores one aspect of the question of how broadly representative democratic governments are: to what extent do democratic governments – in the narrow sense of "governments," that is, democratic *executives* – enjoy the support of the voters and citizens in their countries? In particular, do democratic executives have sufficiently broad support to satisfy the principle of majority rule? These questions affect both the quality and stability of democracy. As John Stuart Mill forcefully argues in his famous *Considerations on Representative Government* (1861), majority rule is a basic qualitative requirement of democracy. He worries that when democratic majority rule is used twice – first, in the conversion of popular votes to legislative seats, and, second, as a decision rule in the legislature – it runs the risk of turning into undemocratic minority rule.

In ethnically and communally divided countries – that is, in most of the countries of the world – the breadth of representation is also important for the viability of democracy. In fact, as stated with exceptional clarity by Sir Arthur Lewis in his classic *Politics in West Africa* (1965: 66), majority rule – if it means bare-majority rule – is dysfunctional for such plural societies. The most important requirement of democracy is that citizens have the opportunity to participate, directly or indirectly, in decision-making. This meaning of democracy is violated if significant minorities are excluded from the decision-making process for extended periods of time. Under such circumstances, narrow majority rule is "totally immoral, inconsistent with the primary meaning of democracy, and *destructive of any prospect of building a nation in which different peoples might live together in harmony*" (emphasis added). Lewis would therefore certainly agree with Mill that minority government is unacceptably undemocratic. And he would add that minority rule is even more dangerous than narrow majority rule for the chances that democracies will be stable and peaceful.

After discussing Mill's arguments in greater detail below, I shall explore the influence on the breadth of representation by two basic institutional features of democratic systems: the contrast between plurality and majority election systems on the one hand and proportional representation on the other, and the contrast between majoritarian and consensus institutions. [...]

My universe consists of the twenty-one advanced industrial democracies that have been continuously democratic since approximately the end of World War II: fifteen West European democracies plus the United States, Canada, Japan, Israel, Australia, and New Zealand.[2] These are the twenty-one countries analyzed in my book *Democracies* (Lijphart 1984), which covers the 1945–80 period. Here I extend the coverage by ten years to 1945–90. The one exception is France which drastically changed its constitutional system in 1958: I shall focus exclusively on the Fifth Republic, because the Fourth Republic (1946–58), as it recedes into the past, looks more and more like a brief and fairly insignificant interlude in French political history.

John Stuart Mill's majority-rule criterion

Majoritarians and consensualists disagree on the basic goal of democracy: the former seek to concentrate power as much as possible in the hands of the majority, whereas the latter try to include as many citizens as possible in the sharing of power. Consensualists can argue that they are not against majority rule as such but that they favor broad instead of narrow majority rule. The majoritarians counter that insistence on extraordinary majorities leads to too much minority power and/or political stalemate. In *Federalist Paper* Number 22, Alexander Hamilton (1788) presents the majoritarian argument in the following words:

What at first sight may seem a remedy, is, in reality, a poison. To give a minority a negative upon the majority (which is always the case where more than a majority is requisite to a decision), is, in its tendency, to subject the sense of the greater number to that of the lesser. ... Hence, tedious delays; continual negotiation and intrigue; contemptible compromises of the public good.

Hamilton's principal worry here is minority *veto* power or what may be called *negative* minority power. Neither Hamilton and other majoritarians nor the consensualists favor *positive* minority rule, that is, the power of minorities to make decisions against the wishes of majorities. In other words, they agree on majority rule as a *minimum* requirement of democracy.

The criterion of majority rule in this sense was first clearly formulated as the most fundamental requirement of democracy by John Stuart Mill in his *Considerations on Representative Government* (1861; see also Spafford 1985). I shall henceforth refer to it as the John Stuart Mill criterion. The further innovation proposed by Mill is that proportional representation must be used to satisfy the basic majority-rule criterion – a rather surprising proposition because proportional representation is the consensualists', instead of the majoritarians', preferred electoral system.

Mill's (1861: chapter 7) argument proceeds as follows. First, he defines the objective of democracy as "giving the powers of government in all cases to the numerical majority." He then states that his objective is violated in representative democracy if a majoritarian method for electing representatives is used: this gives governmental power "to a majority of the majority, who may be, and often are, but a minority of the whole."

Next he proves this point by examining the logic of the most extreme case:

Suppose ... that, in a country governed by equal and universal suffrage, there is a contested election in every constituency, and every election is carried by a small majority. The Parliament thus brought together represents little more than a bare majority of the people. This Parliament proceeds to legislate and adopts important measures by a bare majority of itself.

Although Mill does not state so explicitly himself, one of these "important measures" would be the formation of a cabinet supported by a majority of the legislators. Mill continues:

What guarantee is there that these measures accord with the wishes of a majority of the people? Nearly half the electors, having been outvoted at the hustings, have had no influence at all in the decision; and the whole of these may be, a majority of them probably are, hostile to the measures, having voted against those by whom they have been carried.

Of the remaining electors, nearly half have chosen representatives who, by supposition, have voted against the measures. It is possible, therefore, and not at all improbable, that the opinion which has prevailed was agreeable only to a minority of the nation, through a majority of that portion of it whom the institutions of the country have erected into a ruling class.

Mill's final conclusion is that proportional representation is necessary in order to avoid giving the powers of government to such a minority "ruling class":

If democracy means the certain ascendancy of the majority, there are no means of insuring that but by allowing every individual figure to tell equally in the summing up. Any minority left out, either purposely or by the play of the [two-stage majoritarian] machinery, gives the power not to the majority but to a minority.

Mill's logical argument clearly proves that it is possible that plurality and other majoritarian electoral systems may lead to a violation of the John Stuart Mill criterion. But, in the passage quoted above, he also argues that this situation is not just possible but also probable or "not at all improbable." As far as proportional representation is concerned, he proves that perfect proportionality will satisfy the John Stuart Mill criterion. He does not consider less than perfectly proportional methods, but presumably even such methods are more likely to satisfy the criterion than majoritarian election systems. We can therefore also read his argument as an empirical hypothesis: democracies that use proportional representation are more likely to satisfy the John Stuart Mill criterion, that is, they are more likely to have true majority rule than democracies that use plurality or other majoritarian election systems. A related, more general, hypothesis is that consensus democracies are more likely to pass the minimum requirement of majority rule than "majoritarian" democracies – which are more likely to be pluralitarian or minoritarian instead of truly majoritarian.

Measuring breadth of representation

In *Democracies,* I define the contrast between majoritarian and consensus forms of democratic governments in terms of two dimensions and eight characteristics (Lijphart 1984). I shall focus here on the first dimension consisting of five closely related characteristics of executives, parties, and elections: bare-majority versus power sharing executives, dominant executives versus executive-legislative balance of power, two-party versus multiparty systems, party systems in which the main parties differ primarily on socioeconomic issues versus systems in which the parties also differ on religious, ethnic, urban-rural, foreign policy, or other dimensions, and majoritarian and disproportional versus more proportional electoral systems.[3]

Of these five characteristics, the contrast between bare-majority and power sharing cabinets is the most important because it appears to capture the essence of the conceptual distinction between majoritarian and consensus democracy particularly well. My operational measure was the percentage of time each of my countries was ruled by minimal winning cabinets instead of oversized cabinets – a dichotomous classification that has become standard, and that has proved to be very fruitful, in the analyses of coalition theorists from the early work of William H. Riker (1962) on.

My one practical problem was the question of how to fit minority cabinets into this dichotomy. Minority cabinets may be near-majority cabinets which govern with the steady support of one other party that gives them a parliamentary majority. But they may also be either near-majority or much smaller cabinets that govern with the support of shifting parliamentary coalitions. The former resemble minimal winning cabinets, and the latter oversized cabinets. My solution was to apportion periods of minority cabinet rule equally to the periods under minimal winning cabinets and under oversized cabinets (Lijphart 1984: 61–62).

Although this solution has not, to my knowledge, been criticized by other scholars, I am no longer fully satisfied with it, and I have also become dissatisfied with two other aspects of the measurement in terms of minimal winning versus oversized cabinets. One is that minimal winning cabinets can, in fact, be very broadly based cabinets. For instance, the Christian Democratic-Socialist *Grosse Koalition* cabinets in Austria from 1949 to 1966 and in Germany from 1966 to 1969 were technically minimal winning cabinets, because both parties were necessary to give the coalitions majority support in parliament, and the withdrawal of either party would have turned the cabinets into minority cabinets. Yet, all of these cabinets had the support of about 90 percent of their legislatures. On the other hand, oversized cabinets may not have a very broad base of parliamentary support. For example, most oversized cabinets in Israel, with the exception of the 1967–70 and 1984–90 "national unity" governments, have included one or a few quite small surplus parties and have had the support of only 55 to 60 percent of the members of parliament. The solution to this problem could be to use the percentage of a cabinet's parliamentary support as an alternative or additional measure of the degree of power sharing.

The second problem is that the general category of minimal winning cabinets includes both one-party cabinets and minimal winning coalitions of two or more parties, but that the bargaining style of coalitions, even when these are merely minimal winning, makes them at least a bit less majoritarian in orientation than one-party, non-coalition cabinets. For instance, most German cabinets have been minimal winning cabinets with a relatively narrow support base in the Bundestag, but they have been considerably more consensual, centrist, and compromise-oriented than British bare-majority, single-party cabinets – a difference that has loomed large for British critics of their country's adversarial style of politics and that has made them advocate German-style electoral reform (see Finer 1975). This problem could be solved by including either the one-party versus coalition distinction or the number of cabinet parties in the measure of the degree of power sharing in addition to one or both of the two measures discussed above. A further variant would be to count not the raw number of cabinet parties but their effective number so as to give greater weight to larger than to smaller parties in the cabinet – similar to the measure of the effective number of parties in the legislature (Taagepera and Shugart 1989: 77–81).

Yet another possibility is suggested by John Stuart Mill's view of the essence of democratic government: the percentage of popular or voter support on which a cabinet is based. This measure has the potential advantage of being very directly and closely linked to the basic conceptual distinction between narrow majority rule and power sharing, and may thus have greater validity than the other measures. It is also a simple and straightforward measure. [...]

Measurement problems

Measuring the degree of popular support for cabinets does not present many serious problems in most parliamentary democracies. It is simply the total percentage of the vote in the most recent parliamentary election received by the parties included in a particular cabinet. The data are also readily available: I used the 1945–90 cabinet data collected by Jaap Woldendorp *et al.* (1993) – with a few adjustments suggested in the work of Jean-Claude Colliard (1978: 311–54), Heikki Paloheimo (1984), and Kaare Strom (1990: 245–69) – and Thomas T. Mackie and Richard Rose's (1991) election data. Nevertheless, there are a number of issues with regard to operationalization and measurement that must be addressed.

1   First of all, parties that actually participate in cabinets should clearly be counted as cabinet parties, but what about parties that support a cabinet without being represented in it? Coalition experts have tended to disagree on this issue: most have counted actual participants in cabinets only, but a few have also included so-called support parties (e.g. De Swaan 1973: 143–44). In *Democracies*, I followed the majority practice of ignoring any support parties. On second thought, however, it seems to me that a better solution – instead of either completely including or completely excluding support parties – is the compromise solution of regarding them as half in and half out of the cabinet. After all, support parties are in a kind of half-way position between the governing parties that are actually in the cabinet on the one hand and opposition parties on the other. In accordance with this reasoning, I counted half of the votes for support parties toward the total popular support for a cabinet. For instance, I credited Denmark's 1955–57 Social Democratic cabinet, which enjoyed Radical Party support, with the popular votes cast in the

previous election for the Social Democrats, 41.3 percent, plus half of the 7.8 percent of the votes cast for the Radicals, for a total of 45.2 percent popular cabinet support.[4]

2 A related problem is the treatment of minority cabinets. In parliamentary systems, they can survive only if they are supported – or merely tolerated – by half of the legislators, and, in countries in which their installation requires a formal vote of investiture, slightly more than 50 percent support is needed. This problem can be solved analogously to the solution of counting support parties. Minority cabinets have the implicit support of enough legislators to bridge the gap between the number of legislators belonging to the cabinet parties and half of the membership of the legislature. These bridging legislators can be regarded as an implicit support party. The only practical problem that remains is that we do not know who exactly these legislators are, and hence that we do not know what their popular support is. My solution is to simply count this implicit support in terms of seats – and to assume that there is not too much of a discrepancy between seats and votes. To give one specific example, Canada's 1962–63 Conservative minority cabinet was formed after the Conservatives won 37.3 percent of the votes and 43.8 percent of the seats; popular cabinet support was 37.3 percent plus half of the difference between 50 percent and 43.8 percent (3.1 percent): a total of 40.4 percent.

3 Three of our parliamentary or semi-parliamentary democracies have bicameral legislatures in which the two houses have equal powers and are both popularly elected: Belgium, Italy, and Switzerland.[5] Belgian and Italian cabinets are responsible to both chambers, and the Swiss executive (Federal Council) is elected by a joint session of the two chambers. On which of the two parliamentary elections should the measure of popular cabinet support be based? Partly for pragmatic reasons – the easier availability of the necessary election data – my decision was to use the lower house elections. This choice can also be defended on substantive grounds: the similarity of the electoral systems (proportional representation) used for the simultaneous election of the two chambers in Belgium and Italy, and the fact that in joint sessions of the Swiss legislature the lower chamber outweighs the much smaller upper chamber by about four to one.

4 How should popular cabinet support be measured in systems with powerful and directly elected presidents? In the case of the United States, I used the votes cast for the winning presidential candidate. In semi-presidential France and Finland, cabinets require the confidence of the legislature; hence they can be treated like the cabinets in fully parliamentary systems. The only nettlesome problem concerns the 1986–88 French cabinet mainly consisting of Gaullists and Republicans but chaired by Socialist president François Mitterrand; were the Socialists part of this cabinet? My solution was to split the difference again and to count half

of the Socialist vote in the 1986 election toward the popular support of this cabinet.

5 A much more serious problem is that of insincere voting (often also referred to as tactical, strategic, or sophisticated voting). When we compare the raw percentages of popular cabinet support in plurality systems – Canada, New Zealand, the United Kingdom, and the United States – with that in proportional representation systems, the former are deceptively high because some of the votes cast for the winning parties are votes that, in the latter, would have been cast for small parties. Some adjustment is also clearly required in order to do justice to the majoritarian systems of Australia and France where the popular support percentages are based on, respectively, the first-preference and first-ballot votes, which are influenced only marginally by insincere voting. The big difficulty is to estimate the percentage of insincere voters among those who voted for the cabinet parties. My initial rough estimate is that this percentage is somewhere between 10 and 30 percent.

There are two additional problems. One is that insincere voters may support a small party because of, rather than in spite of, its small size and low probability of entering the government, in order to "send a message" to the major well established parties – like some of the Ross Perot supporters in the 1992 American presidential election. This difference corresponds with the distinction that Mark Franklin *et al.* (1994: 552) make between the "instrumental" form of insincere voting, based on the voters' calculation that they do not want to waste their votes on weak parties and candidates, and the "expressive" form of insincere voting based on various other considerations. They also suggest, however, that the latter occurs much more rarely than the former. The other problem is that a certain amount of insincere voting can also occur under proportional systems, especially those that use low-magnitude districts or high thresholds (Sartori 1986; Cox and Shugart 1994).

The major contrast, however, is between the different systems of proportional representation on the one hand and plurality on the other. In order to take these two problems into consideration, the adjustment percentage should be on the low end of my initial estimate of 10 to 30 percent. I opted for the lowest estimate in this range: 10 percent insincere voting – which I believe is an extremely conservative estimate. One example: the country with the lowest average popular cabinet support in the 1945–90 period is Canada; its adjusted percentage is 41.2 percent, that is, 90 percent of its unadjusted 45.8 percent. In a further effort not to "penalize" plurality systems unduly, I used the adjusted figures only to calculate average popular cabinet support and not in the determination of the extent to which the different democracies fulfill the John Stuart Mill criterion.

6 Democratic purists might argue that popular cabinet support should be based on the votes cast for cabinet parties as a percentage not of all

voters (casting valid votes), but of all adult *citizens* (eligible voters). For instance, when we compare the two highest average percentages of popular cabinet support, 77.7 percent in Switzerland and 70.6 percent in Austria, the latter is especially impressive because Austrian turnout rates have generally been above 90 percent, whereas Swiss turnout decreased gradually from just above 70 percent to below 50 percent. An adjustment for low turnout seems particularly justified in the other low-turnout country, the United States, where onerous registration requirements represent a deliberate attempt to depress voter participation.

The big difficulty is to find the appropriate adjustment. First of all, using 100 percent voter turnout as the basic yardstick is patently unrealistic. But which turnout level *is* an expectation that can realistically be attained: 90 percent, 85 percent, 80 percent? Second, does not any adjustment of this kind unfairly "advantage" countries with compulsory voting? Third, for many countries it is by no means easy to find accurate figures for the total number of eligible voters (Powell 1986; Jackman 1987). Faced with these dilemmas, my final operational decision was not to make any adjustments for different turnout levels – but without full confidence that this is the optimal decision.[6]

John Stuart Mill's hypotheses

The first two columns of Table 8.1 show average popular cabinet support, in descending order of magnitude, as well as the percentage of time that John Stuart Mill's majority-rule criterion was fulfilled for the twenty-one democracies. For each country, the period covered is from the first to the last parliamentary election between 1945 and 1990. Both sets of percentages are averages for these periods, weighted according to the length of time (number of days) that each cabinet was in office.

Average cabinet support has a very wide range: from a low of 41.2 percent in Canada to a high of 77.7 percent – almost twice as high – in Switzerland. The range was considerably smaller within most countries. The Finnish case, with a high of more than 83 percent popular support (the first postwar cabinet) and a low of about 25 percent (several non-party cabinets relying solely on support parties and implicit parliamentary support), is exceptional. The range is similarly wide as far as the fulfillment of the John Stuart Mill criterion is concerned: two countries (Switzerland and Luxembourg) *always* and two countries (the United Kingdom and Norway) *never* satisfied it. Approximately half of the countries have an average popular cabinet support above 50 percent, and about half below 50 percent. And about half of the countries satisfied the Mill criterion more than 50 percent of the time; the other half less than 50 percent of the time. The two variables are highly correlated ($r = 0.87$).

Mill predicts that majoritarian countries are likely to fail his majority rule criterion but that proportional representation countries are more likely to

Table 8.1 Popular cabinet support, John Stuart Mill criterion, disproportionality, consensus democracy, and minimal winning coalitions in twenty-one democracies, 1945–1990

	Popular cabinet support (%)	J. S. Mill criterion (%)	Index of disproportionality (%)	Majority/ consensus democracy (factor scores)	Minimal winning cabinets (%)
Switzerland	77.7	100.0	2.4	−1.65	4.9
Austria	70.6	87.7	2.7	1.50	89.7
Luxembourg	64.0	100.0	3.1	0.08	91.7
Israel	62.6	85.2	1.7	−1.07	20.3
Netherlands	61.6	87.9	1.3	−1.69	44.7
Iceland	60.6	97.0	4.5	−0.06	82.7
Belgium	59.3	80.3	3.2	−0.55	71.3
Germany	55.9	82.1	2.3	0.68	75.3
Finland	55.3	59.9	2.9	−1.49	25.8
Italy	51.8	53.2	2.8	−0.10	30.8
Japan	50.4	32.6	5.7	0.12	86.7
Sweden	48.3	25.3	2.1	0.48	64.7
United States	48.3	70.0	5.4	1.11	100.0
Ireland	47.9	17.6	3.5	0.61	81.1
Australia	47.8	15.0	8.9	0.67	88.7
France	47.7	49.4	13.1	−0.18	44.7
Denmark	45.1	15.9	1.8	−0.78	61.1
Norway	45.0	0.0	5.0	0.42	77.0
New Zealand	41.9	18.1	10.7	1.42	100.0
United Kingdom	41.4	0.0	10.5	1.16	97.4
Canada	41.2	20.1	11.3	0.81	89.5

Source: based on data in Woldendorp *et al.* (1993) (columns 1, 2, and 5); Lijphart (1994: 160–62) (column 3); and Lijphart (1984: 216) (column 4).

satisfy it. This prediction is largely borne out. Of the six democracies with majoritarian election systems (Australia, Canada, France, New Zealand, the United Kingdom, and the United States), only the United States satisfies Mill's criterion more than half of the time. Of the fourteen proportional systems (the remaining countries except semiproportional Japan), only four – Denmark, Norway, Sweden, and Ireland – fail Mill's criterion.

A more sensitive test regresses the percentage of time that the Mill criterion is fulfilled on the exact degree of disproportionality, using the least-squares index designed by Michael Gallagher (1991: 38–40; Lijphart 1994: 60–61, 160–62). The values of this index are shown in the third column of Table 8.1. The correlation coefficient is −0.51, significant at the 1 percent level.[7] The regression line in Figure 8.1 shows that for each percentage increase in electoral disproportionality there is an almost 5 percent decrease in the time that Mill's majority-rule criterion is satisfied. The principal deviant cases are the four countries that are located far above the regression

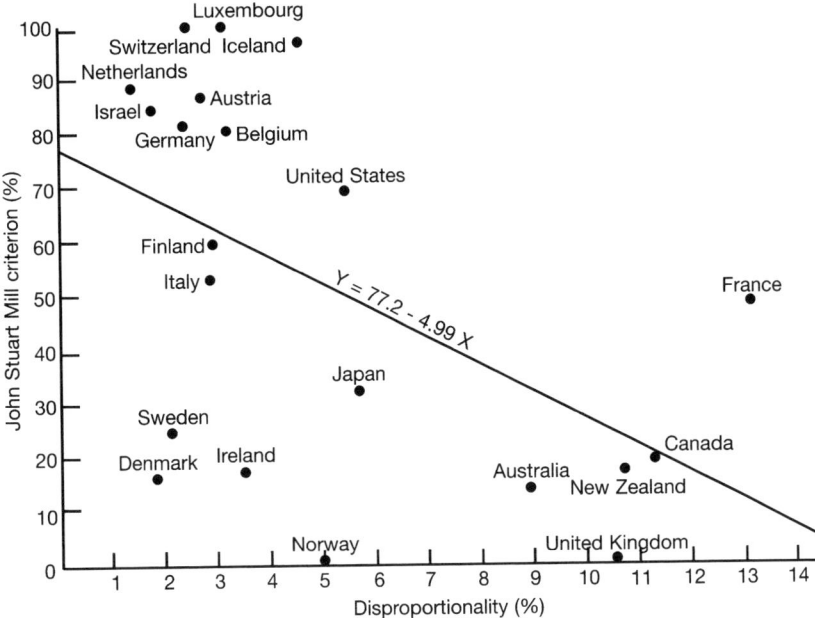

Figure 8.1 Disproportionality and John Stuart Mill criterion in twenty-one countries, 1945–90

line (Switzerland, Luxembourg, Iceland, and France) and four countries at a considerable distance below the regression line (the three Scandinavian countries and Ireland). The latter satisfy the Mill criterion less often than expected on the basis of their relatively low levels of electoral disproportionality; the former fulfill the Mill criterion more often than expected.

The main explanation of the deviant position of Denmark, Sweden, Norway, and Ireland is their frequent minority cabinets which almost inevitably have less than 50 percent popular support; minority cabinets were in office in these four countries during respectively 77.8 percent, 70.7 percent, 46.0 percent, and 37.9 percent of the period. Of the other four countries, Switzerland's 100 percent performance can be explained in terms of its almost permanent grand coalition, while Luxembourg and Iceland had mainly minimal winning cabinets which still had ample parliamentary support. The French outlying position is partly an artifact of the way disproportionality is calculated in two-ballot systems, which tends to exaggerate the "true" degree of disproportionality. Disproportionality is also significantly correlated at the 1 percent level – in fact, somewhat more strongly correlated – with average popular cabinet support ($r = -0.60$).

Moreover, the more general hypothesis that I derived from Mill concerning the relationship between majoritarian versus consensus democracy on the one hand and both popular cabinet support and the Mill criterion on the other is also significantly supported, albeit less strongly and only at the 5 percent level: the correlation coefficients are -0.48 and -0.43 respectively. To sum up, as Mill suggests, consensus and proportional democracies are indeed more likely to be truly majority-rule systems, and supposedly "majoritarian" democracies and electoral systems are indeed more likely to be pluralitarian and minoritarian instead of genuinely majoritarian.

Notes

1 The only minor exceptions to Gurr's broad coverage is that he excludes countries with less than 1 million inhabitants and groups with less than 100,000 members or 1 percent of a country's population.
2 According to my definition of long-term democracy, India and Costa Rica should have been included in *Democracies*, too. I again exclude these two countries here, but purely on practical grounds: their cabinet data are not in the Woldendorp *et al.* (1993) data set on which I relied. My definition of democracy is not a very demanding one: I follow the basic criterion of "one person, one vote," but I obviously do not apply this standard very strictly when I include pre-1971 Switzerland, in which women did not yet have the right to vote, and the United States before the 1965 Voting Rights Act, which finally introduced universal suffrage. I also ignore the arguably just as serious violations of "one person, one vote" represented by colonial control and lengthy occupation of territories conquered by military action: the cases in point are the United Kingdom, France, the Netherlands, Belgium, the United States, and Israel.
3 The second dimension, which I shall not discuss further, may be called the federal-unitary dimension and consists of the three related characteristics of centralization-decentralization, unicameralism-bicameralism, and flexible versus rigid constitutions.
4 This solution obviously does not solve the problem that it is often difficult to determine which parties should be counted as support parties. I simply accepted the judgments of Woldendorp *et al.* (1993).
5 In Belgium and Switzerland, not all, but a large majority of the second chamber legislators are popularly elected.
6 In addition, there were a number of minor methodological problems to be resolved, in particular, the question of how to apportion votes received by joint party lists to the separate parties; on this matter, I used the procedures outlined in my book on electoral systems (Lijphart 1994: 163–77).
7 All of my tests of significance are one-tailed.

References

Colliard, Jean-Claude. 1978. *Les régimes parlementaires contemporains.* Paris: Presses de la Fondation Nationale des Sciences Politiques.

Cox, Gary W., and Matthew Soberg Shugart. 1994. "Strategic Voting under Proportional Representation." Unpublished paper.

De Swaan, Abram. 1973. *Coalition Theories and Cabinet Formations: A Study of Formal Theories of Coalition Formation Applied to Nine European Parliaments after 1918.* Amsterdam: Elsevier.

Finer, S. E. 1975. *Adversary Politics and Electoral Reform.* London: Anthony Wigram.

Franklin, Mark, Richard Niemi, and Guy Whitten (1994). "The Two Faces of Tactical Voting," *British Journal of Political Science* 24 no. 4: 549–57.

Gallagher, Michael. 1991. "Proportionality, Disproportionality and Electoral Systems," *Electoral Studies* 10 no. 1: 33–51.

Gurr, Ted Robert. 1993. *Minorities at Risk: A Global View of Ethnopolitical Conflicts*. Washington DC: United States Institute of Peace Press.

Hamilton, Alexander, James Madison, and John Jay. 1788. *Federalist Papers*. New York: McLean.

Jackman, Robert W. 1987. "Political Institutions and Voter Turnout in the Industrial Democracies," *American Political Science Review* 81 no. 2: 405–23.

Lewis, W. Arthur. 1965. *Politics in West Africa*. London: George Allen and Unwin.

Lijphart, Arend. 1977. *Democracy in Plural Societies: A Comparative Exploration*. New Haven CT: Yale University Press.

——1984. *Democracies: Patterns of Majoritarian and Consensus Government in Twenty-One Democracies*. New Haven CT: Yale University Press.

—— 1994. *Electoral Systems and Party Systems: A Study of Twenty-Seven Democracies, 1945–1990*. Oxford: Oxford University Press.

Mackie, Thomas T., and Richard Rose. 1991. *The International Almanac of Electoral History*. 3rd edn. London: Macmillan.

Mill, John Stuart. 1861. *Considerations on Representative Government*. London: Parker and Bourn.

Paloheimo, Heikki. 1984. *Governments in Democratic Capitalist States, 1950–1983: A Data Handbook*. Turku: University of Turku, Department of Sociology and Political Science.

Powell, G. Bingham, Jr. 1986. "American Voter Turnout in Comparative Perspective," *American Political Science Review* 80 no. 1: 17–43.

Riker, William H. 1962. *The Theory of Political Coalitions*. New Haven CT: Yale University Press.

Sartori, Giovanni. 1986. "The Influence of Electoral Systems: Faulty Laws or Faulty Method?" in Bernard Grofman and Arend Lijphart (eds) *Electoral Laws and their Political Consequences*. New York: Agathon Press.

Spafford, Duff. 1985. "Mill's Majority Principle," *Canadian Journal of Political Science* 18 no. 3: 599–608.

Strom, Kaare. 1990. *Minority Government and Majority Rule*. Cambridge: Cambridge University Press.

Taagepera, Rein, and Matthew Soberg Shugart. 1989. *Seats and Votes: The Effects and Determinants of Electoral Systems*. New Haven CT: Yale University Press.

Woldendorp, Jaap, Hans Keman, and Ian Budge. 1993. "Political Data 1945–90: Party Government in 20 Democracies," *European Journal of Political Research* 24 no. 1: 1–119.

Part IV

Presidential versus parliamentary government

9 Presidentialism and majoritarian democracy

Theoretical observations[1]

The purpose of this chapter is to establish the theoretical link between two sets of contrasting types of democracy: presidential versus parliamentary democracy on the one hand, and majoritarian versus consensus democracy on the other. In my book *Democracies* (1984), a comparative study of the twenty-one countries that have had uninterrupted democratic government since approximately the end of the Second World War,[2] I dealt with both, but my main focus was on the contrast between the majoritarian and consensus models of democracy. Moreover, my discussion of the presidential-parliamentary contrast was not sufficiently integrated with my comparison of majoritarian and consensus democracy.[3] In particular, I defined presidentialism and parliamentarism in terms of two contrasting characteristics, ignoring a crucial third distinction, and I linked the presidential-parliamentary contrast to only one of the differences between majoritarian and consensus democracy, ignoring its impact on several other relevant distinctions This chapter offers me a welcome opportunity to correct these deficiencies and to establish the overall connection between the presidential-parliamentary and majoritarian-consensus contrasts.[4]

My analysis entails a critique of presidential government but on different grounds than Juan J. Linz, Arturo Valenzuela, and others in this volume. I especially do not address the rigidity and immobilism that presidentialism introduces in the political process, although I hasten to say that I am in full agreement that these are its most serious weaknesses. My criticism in this chapter focuses on an additional weakness of the presidential form of government: its strong inclination toward majoritarian democracy, especially in the many countries where, because a natural consensus is lacking a consensual instead of a majoritarian form of democracy is needed. These countries include not only those with deep ethnic, racial, and religious cleavages but also those with intense *political* differences stemming from a recent history of civil war or military dictatorship, huge socioeconomic inequalities, and so on. Moreover, in democratizing and redemocratizing countries undemocratic forces must be reassured and reconciled, and they must be persuaded not only to give up power but also not to insist on "reserved domains" of undemocratic power within the new, otherwise

democratic, regime. Consensus democracy, which is characterized by sharing, limiting, and dispersing power, is much more likely to achieve this
objective than straight majority rule. As Philippe C. Schmitter has suggested, consensus democracy means "defensive" democracy, which is much
less threatening to cultural-ethnic and political minorities than "aggressive"
majority rule.[5]

I deal with my topic in three steps. First, I define presidentialism in terms
of three essential characteristics. Second, I show that, especially as a result
of its third characteristic, presidentialism has a strong tendency to make
democracy majoritarian. Third, I examine the various nonessential characteristics of presidentialism – features that are not distinctive to, although
frequently present in, presidential forms of government – and their impact
on the degree of majoritarianism or consensus.

Presidential democracy: three essential elements

In *Democracies* (Lijphart 1984, 68–69), I define presidential and parliamentary regimes in terms of two crucial differences. First, in parliamentary
democracies, the head of the government – who may have different official
titles such as prime minister, premier, chancellor, minister-president, and (in
Ireland) *taoiseach* – and his or her cabinet are dependent on the legislatures
confidence and can be dismissed from office by a legislative vote of no
confidence or censure. In presidential systems, the head of government –
invariably called president – is elected for a fixed, constitutionally prescribed
term and in normal circumstances cannot be forced by the legislature to
resign (although it may be possible to remove a president by the highly
unusual and exceptional process of impeachment). The second crucial difference is that presidential heads of government are popularly elected, either
directly or via an electoral college, and that prime ministers are selected by
the legislatures. I use the general term "selected" advisedly because the
process of selection can range widely from formal election to informal
interparty bargaining in the legislature.[6]

Several eminent political scientists (Verney 1959, 17–56; Kaltefleiter 1970;
Duchacek 1973, 175–91; Steffani 1979; Powell 1982, 55–57) have argued
that, in addition to the above two crucial differences, there are several other
important distinctions. For instance, presidents cannot simultaneously be
members of the legislature, whereas prime ministers (and the other ministers
in their cabinets) usually are; and presidents are both heads of government
and heads of state, whereas prime ministers are mere heads of government.
There are two problems with these additional distinctions. One is that there
are serious empirical exceptions; for example, Dutch and Norwegian legislators have to resign their legislative seats when they join the cabinet, but
this does not affect the basically parliamentary pattern of government in
these countries in any significant way. Second, even when there are no
exceptions, as in the case of presidents being the heads of both state and

government, this attribute cannot be argued to be logically necessary. This does not mean that these differences are unimportant. I try to show later on that they affect the balance of power between the executive and the legislature – and hence the degree of majoritarianism or consensus – but, in my view, they cannot be regarded as criteria for *defining* presidentialism and parliamentarism.

I have come to the conclusion, however, that a third essential difference must be stated and that this difference accounts for much of the majoritarian proclivity of presidential democracy: the president is a one-person executive, whereas the prime minister and the cabinet form a collective executive body. Within parliamentary systems, the prime minister's position in the cabinet can vary from preeminence to virtual equality with the other ministers, but there is always a relatively high degree of collegiality in decision-making. In contrast, the members of presidential cabinets are mere advisers and subordinates of the president.

The three dichotomous criteria I use yield not only the pure presidential and parliamentary types but six additional types of democracy, as shown in Figure 9.1. As the typology shows, there are very few democracies that combine presidential and parliamentary characteristics, and three of the potential "mixed" types have no empirical examples at all. The vast majority of democracies fit the pure parliamentary or presidential types.

It is also worth emphasizing that most empirical cases can be classified in the typology without difficulty or ambiguity, including the cases of Switzerland and Uruguay, which are extremely awkward to classify without using the distinction between one-person and collegial executives. The Swiss Federal Council is a seven-member coequal executive elected by the legislature for a fixed term of office. The Uruguayan *colegiado*, which operated from 1952 to 1967, was a Swiss-inspired, nine-member body, also serving for a fixed term but popularly elected. Cyprus during its first few years of independence was ruled by a directly elected duumvirate (a Greek Cypriot president and a Turkish Cypriot vice president with virtually equal powers) and therefore fits the same type. These characteristics make Switzerland more parliamentary than presidential and Uruguay under the *colegiado* system as well as Cyprus in the early 1960s more presidential than parliamentary, although none of these three cases conform to the pure parliamentary or presidential type.

The cell in the top righthand corner has only a single occupant: Lebanon has a "presidential" system except that the president is elected by parliament instead of the voters.[7] A nondemocratic example of this form of government is South Africa under its 1983 constitution: the president is elected by an electoral college that is in turn elected by the three houses of parliament. I do *not* include in this category presidential systems like the United States and Chile, where the legislature has a role in the election of the president if the popular (or electoral college) vote fails to yield a majority winner. The strong Chilean tradition is that the legislature simply ratifies

	Collegial executive		One-person executive	
	Dependent on legislative confidence	Not dependent on legislative confidence	Dependent on legislative confidence	Not dependent on legislative confidence
Executive selected legislature	*Pure Parliamentarism:* Most West European democracies Australia Canada France (1986-88) India Isreal Jamaca Japan Malaysia New Zealand Turkey Nigeria (1960-66)	Switzerland	No empirical examples A	Lebenon
Executive selected by voters	No empirical examples B	Cyprus (1960-63) Uruguay (1952-67)	No empirical examples C	*Pure Presidentialism:* Most Latin American democracies Cyprus France (5th Republic except 1986-88) Nigeria (1979-83) Philippines South Korea United States

Figure 9.1 A typology of parliamentary, presidential, and mixed forms of democracy, with some empirical examples

the plurality winner, and in the United States there is almost always a majority winner. The Bolivian case is more problematic; the legislature awarded the presidency to the runner-up instead of the plurality winner in 1985 and to the third-place finisher in 1989. Even here, however, the legislature's powers of selection are severely constrained by the preceding direct popular election.

That three of the types are empty cells in Figure 9.1 is not surprising because the logic of the system of legislative confidence militates against them. Type A would be a strong form of *Kanzlerdemokratie:* a parliamentary system except that the prime minister's relationship to the cabinet resembles that of a president and his or her cabinet. On paper, the West German constitution appears to call for such a system, but since the chancellor needs the Bundestag's continuing confidence, the negotiation of a collegial coalition cabinet takes place prior to the formal election of the chancellor by the Bundestag. Types B and C are problematic because a legislative vote of no confidence in a popularly elected executive would be seen as defiance of the popular will and of democratic legitimacy. The only democratically acceptable form of types B and C would be one in which a legislative vote of no confidence in the executive would be matched by the executive's right to dissolve the legislature, and where either action would trigger new elections of both legislature and executive. The C form of such a system resembles Lloyd N. Cutler's (1980) well known proposal.

The only empirical cases that appear to be difficult to classify are those with both a popularly elected president and a parliamentary prime minister. Here the key question is: who is the *real* head of government – president or prime minister? And this question is usually not hard to answer. In Austria, Iceland, and Ireland, the presidents are weak in spite of their popular election; these systems are unambiguously parliamentary. But what about the so-called semipresidential (or semiparliamentary) Fifth Republic? Raymond Aron wrote in 1981 (p. 8):

> The President of the Republic is the supreme authority [that is, the true head of government] as long as he has a majority in the National Assembly; but he must abandon the reality of power to the prime minister if ever a party other than his own has a majority in the Assembly.

This is exactly what happened in 1986: premier Jacques Chirac became the head of government and President François Mitterrand was reduced to merely a special role in foreign policy. The Finnish and post-1982 Portuguese systems resemble the 1986–88 pattern in France and should therefore also be classified as parliamentary.

It may be possible to design a true half-presidential and half-parliamentary system – perhaps by specifying in the constitution that the president and prime minister jointly head the government – but there are no actual examples of such intermediate regimes. In particular, the Fifth Republic is, instead of semipresidential, usually presidential and only occasionally parliamentary. Maurice Duverger (1980, 186) correctly anticipating the shift to parliamentarism in 1986 and back to presidentialism in 1988 – as prescient as Aron – concludes that the Fifth Republic is not "a *synthesis* of the parliamentary and presidential system" but an "*alternation* between presidential and parliamentary phases" (emphasis in original).[8]

Presidentialism between majoritarian and consensus democracy

In *Democracies*, I fail to resolve the question of whether presidentialism is conducive to majoritarianism or consensus. On the one hand, I argue that the formal *separation* of powers between the executive and the legislature in presidential regimes contributes to a *balance* of power between these branches of government – one of the characteristics of consensus democracy. But later on, I characterize the presidential French Fifth Republic as having a "high degree of executive dominance" (Lijphart 1984, 24–25, 33–34, 82–83, 212). The main problem is that I focus on the impact of presidentialism on only one of the eight traits that distinguish majoritarian from consensus democracy. These traits, which cluster along two dimensions, are:

Executives-parties dimension

1   One-party cabinets versus broad coalitions
2   Executive dominance versus executive-legislative balance
3   Two-party versus multiparty systems
4   Unidimensional versus multidimensional party systems
5   Plurality elections versus proportional representation.

Federal-unitary dimension

6   Unitary and centralized versus federal and decentralized government
7   Unicameral legislatures versus strong bicameralism
8   Unwritten versus written and rigid constitutions.

For each trait in the list, the majoritarian characteristic (e.g. one-party cabinets) is listed first and the corresponding consensual characteristic (e.g. broad coalitions) second. I argue that the five characteristics of the first dimension, having to do with executive power and political parties, are affected by presidentialism – mainly in the direction of promoting majoritarian rule. (On the other hand, presidentialism does not appear to have significant consequences for the characteristics of the second, federal-unitary, dimension, and I therefore do not discuss these differences between the majoritarian and consensus models.)

I still believe that separating the executive from the legislative power helps to balance these powers. This is the result of the paradox of the requirement of parliamentary confidence. In theory, it makes the executive subservient to the legislature, but in practice it means that, on every important vote, legislators must cast their votes not only on the merits of the particular issue but also on keeping the cabinet in office: the fact that most legislators do not want to upset the cabinet too frequently gives the cabinet very strong leverage over the process of legislation. In presidential systems, the legislature can deal with bills on their merits without the fear of causing a cabinet crisis – and hence also without being "blackmailed" by the executive into accepting its proposals. Consequently, in a hypothetical ceteris paribus situation, separation of power entails greater legislative independence and a more balanced executive-legislative relationship.

But all other factors are by no means equal, and they can easily negate the effect of separation of power. In France, for instance, the president's power to dissolve the National Assembly and the many constitutional provisions curtailing the legislature's prerogatives produce executive dominance in spite of the separation of power. Similarly, Latin American presidents are usually regarded as dominant, although as Scott Mainwaring (1990) has forcefully argued, this appraisal is exaggerated and it applies only to some of the presidential systems in Latin America. I return to some of the "other factors" in the next section.

When we look at the other characteristics of the executive and of the party and electoral systems on which majoritarian and consensus systems differ – those numbered 1, 3, 4, and 5 in the list – presidentialism invariably entails greater majoritarianism and fewer chances for consensual politics. The first characteristic concerns the concentration of executive power, and it ranges from one-party majority governments to grand coalitions of all significant parties; intermediate forms are minimal winning coalitions (that is, coalitions of two or more parties that together have majority support) and oversized (larger than minimal winning) coalitions that do not include all major parties. Presidentialism entails the concentration of executive power at the extreme majoritarian end of the range: power is concentrated not just in one *party* but in one *person*.

For this reason, it is extremely difficult to introduce executive power sharing in presidential systems. In my book *Democracy in Plural Societies*, I concluded that "while consociational democracy is not incompatible with presidentialism ... a better institutional framework is offered by ... parliamentary systems" (Lijphart 1977, 224). This could be stated more strongly: presidentialism is inimical to the kind of consociational compromises and pacts that may be necessary in the process of democratization and during periods of crisis, whereas the collegial nature of parliamentary executives makes them conducive to such pacts. Moreover, as Linz (1987, 34; see also Hartlyn 1988) points out, when consociational arrangements are squeezed into a presidential system – for instance, by the pact that included, *inter alia*, equal legislative representation and alternation in the presidency by the two major parties in Colombia from 1958 to 1974 – the voters' freedom of choice is constrained to a much greater extent than by consociational methods in parliamentary systems.

As far as the party system is concerned, the fact that the presidency is the biggest political prize to be won and that only the largest parties have a chance to win it represents an impulse away from multipartism and in the direction of a two-party system. One generally accepted explanation of the American two-party system – which, with virtually no third parties at all, is the world's most exclusive two-party system – is the winner-take-all nature of presidential elections. In Latin America, the same mechanism appears to operate even when legislative elections are conducted under proportional representation. As Matthew S. Shugart (1988; see also Nilson 1983) has pointed out, this is especially the case when the presidential election is decided by plurality rather than by majority (which may require a runoff election) and, more importantly, when the legislative election is held at the same time or shortly after the presidential election. In France, under a two-ballot majority system for both presidential and legislative elections, the multi-party system has been maintained but in a two-bloc or bipolar format and with considerably fewer parties than in the parliamentary Third Republic, which used the same electoral system. Duverger (1986, 81–82) asks "why the same electoral system coincided with a dozen parties in the Third Republic but ended up with only four [parties in a two-bloc format] in the Fifth Republic." His main explanation is "the direct popular election of the president, which has transformed the political regime."

There is one important countervailing factor. While presidential systems discourage multipartism, they also discourage cohesive parties. In parliamentary systems, reasonably disciplined and cohesive parties are required because they have to support cabinets in office; in presidential systems, this requirement does not apply, and parties can afford to be much laxer with regard to internal party unity. This means that, ceteris paribus, a party system with, say, two or three parties in a presidential democracy would have to be considered less majoritarian than a parliamentary party system with the same number of parties.

The number of parties is closely related to the dimensionality of the party system, that is, the number of issue dimensions that are salient in the party system (Taagepera and Grofman 1985). In two-party systems, only one issue dimension – usually the socioeconomic or left-right dimension – tends to dominate. In multi-party systems, one or more additional dimensions – religious, cultural-ethnic, urban-rural, foreign policy, and so on – is probably present. Consequently, the pressures toward a two-party system exerted by presidentialism are also likely to make the left-right dimension dominant and to squeeze out all other issue dimensions – which may be quite important to political and other minorities.

Finally, presidentialism has a strong effect on the proportionality of the electoral outcome. The fact that a presidential election involves the election of one person means that proportional representation cannot be used; the only possibilities are the plurality and majority methods. And plurality-majority methods (applied in single-member districts) yield increasingly disproportional results as the size of the body to be elected decreases – reaching a peak of disproportionality in the case of the election of one person. The most widely used measure of disproportionality is John Loosemore and Victor J. Hanby's (1971): the percentage by which the overrepresented party or parties are overrepresented (which is, of course, the same as the total percentage of underrepresentation). In proportional representation systems, the Loosemore-Hanby index averages about 5 percent and rarely exceeds 10 percent. It tends to be considerably higher in legislative elections by plurality or majority: between 10 and 20 percent. In Western countries during the 1945–85 period, I found the highest average disproportionality in the French Fifth Republic: almost 21 percent (Lijphart 1988b). The all-or-nothing nature of presidential elections raises the disproportionality to much higher levels: about 46 percent in the 1988 French and American presidential elections, about 59 percent in the Dominican Republic in 1986, and about 63 percent in the 1970 Chilean election won by Salvador Allende.

The argument in this section can be summarized as follows: while the separation of power exerts some pressure toward consensus democracy, the popular election of the president and the concentration of executive power in one person are strong influences in the direction of majoritarianism. The corollary of separation of power – the fixed presidential term of office – does not affect the majoritarian or consensual character of democracy, except that one could argue that unusually long terms of office, such as the six-year and seven-year terms in Argentina and France respectively, accentuate the power concentration and disproportionality features of presidentialism.

Nonessential but frequent attributes of presidentialism and their consequences

So far, I have examined the effects of presidentialism on majoritarianism exclusively in terms of the three essential characteristics of presidentialism. Let me now turn to the additional characteristics of presidentialism formulated by other scholars. I do not regard these as essential, but they are frequent attributes of presidentialism, and they may have important effects on the majoritarian or consensual nature of the system. These attributes of presidentialism are often primarily based on the American example (and on its contrast with the British example of parliamentary government). The American case is just one example of presidentialism, but it has had considerable influence abroad, especially in Latin America (Friedrich 1967; Von Beyme 1987). For this reason, the following six characteristics of presidentialism are based on the American model, but I also use the French Fifth Republic and two Latin American countries with long democratic records – Costa Rica and Venezuela – as examples:

1 *The president does not have the power to dissolve the legislature.*[9] This common characteristic of presidentialism reduces the power of the president and increases that of the legislature – making for a more balanced relationship between the two and hence for a more consensus-oriented system. When, exceptionally, the president does have the right of dissolution, as in France, presidential power is greatly enhanced and the regime becomes much more majoritarian.

2 *The president has a veto power over legislation, and the presidential veto can be overridden only by extraordinary legislative majorities.* This kind of veto strengthens presidential power a great deal. Unless the legislature contains large antipresidential majorities, the veto makes the president the equivalent of a third chamber of the legislature. This is what William H. Riker (1984, 109) means when he speaks of "the tricameral legislature

found in the United States." Not all presidents have veto powers that can only be negated by extraordinary majorities. The Venezuelan president's veto, for instance, can in the final analysis be overridden by a simple majority (unless the Supreme Court agrees with the president that the bill is unconstitutional). The French president, who is very strong in other respects, also appears to be weak in this regard; however, the veto is irrelevant in the French case because France operates as a presidential system only when the president has majority support in the legislature.

3   *The president can appoint the members of the cabinet without legislative interference.* In spite of the "advice and consent" provision in the United States Constitution, the president has virtually complete control over the composition of his or her cabinet. The same is true in France and, with slight qualifications, in most Latin American countries; in Costa Rica and Venezuela, cabinet ministers can be censured and thereby removed by congressional action, but two-thirds majorities are required.

4   *The president is not only the head of government but also the head of state.* It is conceivable that a presidential head of government would *not* simultaneously be the head of state: such a system has been proposed in the Netherlands, where the monarch would continue to be the head of state, and in Israel, where a separate ceremonial head of state would be maintained. But in practice, there are no exceptions to the rule that in presidential systems the two functions are combined in one person. It obviously enhances the president's stature very considerably.

5   *The president can serve no more than two elected terms of office.* This provision, which clearly decreases presidential power, is absent from the French constitution, but more stringent provisions apply in Costa Rica, where reelection is completely prohibited, and in Venezuela, where presidents cannot serve two terms in immediate succession; in these two countries, presidents become "lame ducks" immediately after being elected. While this kind of rule is important as a limit on the president's power, it is even more important as a symptom of the widely perceived danger of too much, even dictatorial, presidential power. It is significant that, while such limitations are common in presidential systems, there is not a single example of a similar limit on a prime minister's tenure in parliamentary systems. Moreover, as Harry Kantor (1977, 23–24) points out, limits on reelection "are infractions upon true democracy, which demands that voters be allowed to vote for whomever they choose." I would add that they also conflict with the democratic assumption that the opportunity to be reelected is a strong incentive for elected officials to remain responsive to the voters' wishes.

6   *The president cannot simultaneously be a member of the legislature.* This contrasts with parliamentary systems, where the prime minister and the other ministers are usually, but not always, members of parliament. However, when ministers are not members of the legislature, as in the Netherlands and Norway, they can still participate in parliamentary

debates and still have to submit to questions and interpellations. The physical distance between president and legislature, combined with the president's dignity as head of state and his or her usual residence in a presidential palace, adds to the "imperial" atmosphere of the presidency and hence to majoritarianism.

When we add up the tendencies of these six features for the American case, we find four that tend toward majoritarianism and only two that tend in a consensual direction. Compared with this 4–2 score, the score for France is 5–0, with one non-applicable item (as explained above, the question of the veto is irrelevant in the French case). Like the United States, Costa Rica also has a 4–2 overall score favoring majoritarianism. Venezuela is the only case with an even 3–3 score. But this unweighted addition makes little sense; for instance, the power to dissolve the legislature is obviously much more important than the incompatibility of executive and legislative offices. Moreover, the above six characteristics do not exhaust a president's potential powers vis-à-vis the legislature; in particular, emergency powers and powers of appointment (of provincial or state governors, supreme court justices, and other officials) would have to be considered in order to complete the picture. Nevertheless, the above examples make clear that the nonessential but frequent features of presidentialism lead, on average, in the same direction as its essential attributes: toward majoritarian democracy.

Conclusions: paradoxes of presidential power

My overall conclusion can be summarized in three words: presidentialism spells majoritarianism. But this conclusion raises several difficult and paradoxical questions. First, majoritarianism means the concentration of political power in the hands of the majority, and if the presidency is the repository of this power, it means a very powerful president; in other words, the logic of presidentialism is that it implies very strong, perhaps even overbearing, presidents. This logic conflicts with the empirical reality of presidentialism in the United States and also, as Mainwaring (1990) has pointed out, in most of the *democratic* presidential regimes in Latin America. How can we explain this paradox?

One explanation is that presidentialism spells not only concentration of (especially executive) power but, by definition, also separation of power; if the separate legislative branch is effectively organized, particularly by a specialized and well staffed committee structure, separation of power can mean an approximate balance of power between president and legislature and a presidency that is less than all-powerful. This reasoning applies well to the exceptional American case of presidentialism. Fred W. Riggs (1988, 260–66) calls the committee structure of the US Congress one of the "para-constitutional practices" that accounts for the survival and success of presidential government in the United States; other factors of this kind are the "indiscipline" of the American parties – which, as I have emphasized earlier, is generally a mitigating influence on majoritarianism – and the federal division of power. The second explanation, which applies to most of the Latin American cases, is that the fear of omnipotent presidents has produced strong efforts to limit presidential power, especially the denial of immediate reelection. Kantor (1977, 23) has pointed out that "all of the countries" in Latin America, even those that are not democratic, "have constitutions which prescribe all kinds of limitations upon the powers of the president."

The paradox becomes even more puzzling when we consider that the empirical reality is frequently not just that of merely moderate presidential power but of *too little* presidential power and presidents who feel stalemated, powerless, and as a result, deeply frustrated. This description fits the situations of all too many Latin American presidents. Mainwaring (1990, 162) argues that

> under democratic conditions, most Latin American presidents have had trouble accomplishing their agendas. They have held most of the power to initiate policy, but they have found it hard to get support to implement policy. If my analysis is correct, it points to a significant *weakness* in democratic presidencies.

Deadlock and presidential weakness in the United States are also the chief complaints of the Committee on the Constitutional System (see Robinson 1985). A possible explanation of why American presidents have not felt as frustrated by their lack of power as their Latin American colleagues is that the United States is a major player on the world scene and that foreign policy has provided American presidents with a sufficiently satisfying outlet for their political energies; the general pattern is that, during their terms of office, they tend to direct more and more of their attention and energy toward foreign policy issues.

It is not immediately clear, however, why a situation of balanced presidential and legislative power should produce deadlock and frustration instead of consensus. It seems to me that the problem of what Linz (1987, 26) calls "dual democratic legitimacy" – the fact that both president and legislature can claim democratic legitimation – is only part of the answer. The same problem potentially arises with regard to bicameral systems, consisting of directly elected houses with different partisan compositions, and also with regard to the federal division of powers. Indeed, all of the characteristics of consensus democracy may be seen as attempts to prevent a *single* "democratic legitimacy," which would necessarily be a single concentration of power.

As I see it, the real problem is not so much that both president and legislature can claim democratic legitimacy but that everyone – including the president, the public at large, and even political scientists – feels that the president's claim is much stronger than the legislature's. One indicator of this is that we have great difficulty envisaging a system in which the legislature has the power to dismiss a popularly elected president, but that we can readily conceive of a president's power to dissolve the legislature – in spite of the fact that, after all, the legislature is also popularly elected. President Charles de Gaulle's grandiose statement is an extreme example of the claim of superior democratic legitimacy: "The indivisible authority of the state is entirely given to the president by the people who elected him. There exists no other authority, neither ministerial, nor civil, nor military, nor judicial that is not conferred or maintained by him." A less extreme version of this claim in the United States is the reminder that the president (together with the vice president) is the only official elected by the whole people – a fact that supposedly gives the president a unique democratic legitimacy. Like de Gaulle's claim, this interpretation conveniently forgets that the Congress is also popularly elected and that, *as a collective body*, it is also elected by the whole people – indeed with larger majorities than are usually garnered by successful presidential candidates. Consequently, although a president's lack of decisive power should induce him or her toward seeking consensus and compromise, the feeling of superior democratic legitimacy may make the president righteously unwilling and psychologically unable to compromise.

If this line of reasoning is correct, presidentialism is inferior to parliamentarism regardless of whether the president is strong or weak. In the first instance, the system will tend to be too majoritarian; in the second case, majoritarianism is not replaced by consensus but by conflict, frustration, and stalemate.

Notes

1 This article is a revised version of a paper presented at the research symposium, "Presidential or Parliamentary Democracy: Does It Make a Difference?" Latin American Studies Program, Georgetown University, Washington DC, 14–16 May 1989. I am grateful to John Carey for his research assistance and his many excellent substantive suggestions.

2 Because I treated the French Fourth (parliamentary) and Fifth (presidential) Republics as separate cases, I had twenty-one democratic countries but twenty-two cases of democracy.

3 One reason for the relative neglect of presidentialism in *Democracies* is that my universe of twenty-two democratic regimes contained only one clear case of presidential government (the United States) and two more ambiguous cases (the French Fifth Republic and Finland). In retrospect, I think that I applied my criterion of uninterrupted democratic rule too strictly and that I should also have included India and Costa Rica among my long-term democracies; the latter would have provided a fourth case of presidentialism. G. Bingham Powell's (1982) comparative study of democracies paid more attention to presidentialism at least partly because Powell had seven cases of it in his universe as a result of his less demanding time frame (a minimum of five years of democracy during the

eighteen-year period from 1958 to 1976). Powell's presidential democracies were Venezuela, Chile, Uruguay, and the Philippines, in addition to the United States, France, and Costa Rica. He did not regard Finland as presidential (pp. 60–61); as I discuss later, this is now also my view.

4 Lijphart (1988a) is an earlier, much briefer, attempt to do the same thing.

5 Schmitter, comments at the conference on "Transformation and Transition in Chile, 1982–89," Center for Iberian and Latin American Studies, University of California, San Diego, Diego, 13–14 March 1989.

6 In *Democracies,* I express these differences in terms of characteristics of the respective "chief executives" (Lijphart 1984, 70). I now think the term "head of government" is preferable.

7 Lebanon also has a prime minister with whom the president shares some of his power, but until the 1989 Taif Accord, which increased the prime minister's powers, the president was clearly more powerful and could be regarded as the real head of government. The Lebanese system has, of course, not functioned normally since the outbreak of civil war in 1975.

8 Since the French model cannot be regarded as intermediate between presidentialism and parliamentarism but is instead a model of alternating systems – an alternation based on shifts in the mood of the electorate that have nothing to do with preferences for one system or the other – it appears to be difficult to argue that this model is a good compromise between the two. However, a strong counterargument (suggested to me by John Carey) is that the French system of alternation can be seen as a solution to one of the basic problems of presidentialism: the possibility of a president opposed by a hostile legislative majority, which is likely to lead to immobilism and stalemate. If this problem occurs in France, it is resolved by the simple temporary shift to a parliamentary arrangement. In other words, France can be said to be able to enjoy the advantages of presidentialism most of the time without suffering this one serious disadvantage. In this special sense, the French model can be argued to be not just a reasonable compromise but one that combines the best of both worlds.

9 Prime ministers sometimes do not have this power either (e.g. Norway) or have it only under special circumstances (e.g. West Germany).

References

Aron, Raymond. 1981. "Alternation in Government in the Industrialized Countries." *Government and Opposition* 17, no. 1: 3–21.

Cutler, Lloyd N. 1980. "To Form a Government." *Foreign Affairs* 59, no. 1: 126–43.

Duchacek, Ivo D. 1973. *Power Maps: Comparative Politics of Constitutions.* Santa Barbara CA: ABC-Clio Press.

Duverger, Maurice. 1980. "A New Political System Model: Semi-Presidential Government." *European Journal of Political Research* 8, no. 2: 165–87.

——1986. "Duverger's Law: Forty Years Later." In *Electoral Laws and Their Political Consequences,* eds Bernard Grofman and Arend Lijphart, pp. 69–84. New York: Agathon Press.

Friedrich, Carl J. 1967. *The Impact of American Constitutionalism Abroad.* Boston MA: Boston University Press.

Hartlyn, Jonathan. 1988. *The Politics of Coalition Rule in Colombia.* Cambridge: Cambridge University Press.

Kaltefleiter, Werner. 1970. *Die Funktionen des Staatsoberhauptes in der parlamentarischen Demokratie.* Cologne: Westdeutscher Verlag.

Kantor, Harry. 1977. "Efforts Made by Various Latin American Countries to Limit the Power of the President." In *Presidential Power in Latin American Politics*, ed. Thomas V. DiBacco, pp. 21–32. New York: Praeger.

Lijphart, Arend. 1977. *Democracy in Plural Societies: A Comparative Exploration.* New Haven CT: Yale University Press.

——1984. *Democracies: Patterns of Majoritarian and Consensus Government in Twenty-one Countries.* New Haven CT: Yale University Press.

——1988a. "Democratización y modelos alternativos de democracia." *Opciones*, no. 14: 29–42.

——1988b. "The Political Consequences of Electoral Laws, 1945–85: A Critique, Re-Analysis, and Update of Rae's Classic Study." Paper presented at the World Congress of the International Political Science Association, Washington DC.

Linz, Juan J. 1987. "Democracy, Presidential or Parliamentary: Does It Make a Difference?" Paper presented at the Annual Meeting of the American Political Science Association, Chicago.

Loosemore, John, and Victor J. Hanby. 1971. "The Theoretical Limits of Maximum Distortion: Some Analytic Expressions for Electoral Systems." *British Journal of Political Science* 1, no. 4: 467–77.

Mainwaring, Scott. 1990. "Presidentialism in Latin America." *Latin American Research Review* 25, no. 1: 157–79.

Nilson, Sten Sparre. 1983. "Elections Presidential and Parliamentary: Contrasts and Connections." *West European Politics* 6, no. 1: 111–24.

Powell, G. Bingham, Jr. 1982. *Contemporary Democracies: Participation, Stability, and Violence.* Cambridge MA: Harvard University Press.

Riggs, Fred W. 1988. "The Survival of Presidentialism in America: Para-Constitutional Practices." *International Political Science Review* 9, no. 4: 247–78.

Riker, William H. 1984. "Electoral Systems and Constitutional Restraints." In *Choosing an Electoral System: Issues and Alternatives*, eds Arend Lijphart and Bernard Grofman, pp. 103–10. New York: Praeger.

Robinson, Donald L. (ed.) 1985. *Reforming American Government: The Bicentennial Papers of the Committee on the Constitutional System.* Boulder CO: Westview.

Shugart, Matthew S. 1988. "Duverger's Rule and Presidentialism: The Effects of the Timing of Elections." Paper presented at the Annual Meeting of the American Political Science Association, Washington DC.

Steffani, Winfried. 1979. *Parlamentarische und präsidentielle Demokratie: Strukturelle Aspekte westlicher Demokratien.* Opladen: Westdeutscher Verlag.

Taagepera, Rein, and Bernard Grofman. 1985. "Rethinking Duverger's Law: Predicting the Effective Number of Parties in Plurality and PR Systems – Parties Minus Issues Equals One." *European Journal of Political Research* 13, no. 4: 341–52.

Verney, Douglas V. 1959. *The Analysis of Political Systems.* London: Routledge and Kegan Paul.

Von Beyme, Klaus. 1987. *America as a Model: The Impact of American Democracy in the World.* New York: St. Martin's Press.

10 Europe, the European Union, and democracy

The European Union is a union of democracies. Especially if it becomes, or is evolving toward, a true sovereign state (and then presumably a federal state, a subject to which I shall return below), it should have a democratic government itself – but what kind of democratic government? The lively debate on this question has focused too much, in my opinion, on how the Union should be governed, and not enough on the fact that it is a European political entity for which a suitable form of government must be found. There are important European democratic traditions and, in designing a democratic system of government for the EU, these traditions should be the main constitutional guidelines. In general, traditions should not be discarded without good reasons, and, in this case, I shall argue that there are very good reasons not to discard them.

When we look at democracy in Europe in worldwide comparative perspective, two special characteristics stand out. One is that Europe is the continent with the largest number of stable and successful democracies. Using a simple definition of stable democracy – continuous democratic rule for twenty years, from 1980 to 2000 – I count thirty-four such democracies in the world (excluding mini-states with populations under 250,000), and nineteen of these, a clear majority, are in Western and Southern Europe (Britain, France, Germany, Italy, Spain, the five Nordic countries, the Benelux countries, Switzerland, Austria, Ireland, Portugal, Greece, and Malta). Second, with regard to the two most crucial choices in constitution-making – parliamentary versus presidential government and proportional representation (PR) versus majoritarian methods for electing national legislatures – what unites most European democracies, and what sets them apart from most democracies elsewhere, is their commitment to both parliamentarism and PR. The fifteen non-European democracies (India, Japan, the United States, Canada, Costa Rica, Australia, New Zealand, Israel, Jamaica, Trinidad and Tobago, Barbados, the Bahamas, Papua New Guinea, Botswana, and Mauritius) tend to have presidentialism or (mainly) majoritarian elections, or both. The only exceptions are New Zealand, a long-time parliamentary system, which adopted PR in 1996, and Israel, although it deviated temporarily from parliamentarism by having a popularly elected prime minister from 1996 until the next election currently scheduled for 2003.

There are a few obvious exceptions among the European democracies, too. The most deviant case is France, which has a semi-presidential form of government and which uses the majoritarian two-ballot method for the election of its National Assembly. Switzerland has a hybrid system, which, however, is more parliamentary than presidential. And Britain still uses the majoritarian first-past-the-post method for House of Commons elections. However, especially in the last ten years, there has also been a convergence toward the parliamentary-PR norm. Portugal and Poland started out with French-style semi-presidential government, but have evolved into predominantly parliamentary systems. Even France itself is increasingly experiencing periods of "cohabitation" that are mainly parliamentary in character: 1986–88, 1993–95, and from 1997 on. In the United Kingdom, PR has been used for Northern Ireland elections since the 1970s, and was also instituted more recently, under Tony Blair's Labour government, for the election of the Scottish and Welsh assemblies, the London municipal council, and British representatives to the European Parliament. French representatives to the European Parliament have been elected by PR ever since the first direct election in 1979. Since 1999, the entire European Parliament has been elected by PR.

The key institutional arrangements for the EU, following these European traditions, must therefore be a prime minister and cabinet, who are responsible to and subject to the confidence of a European legislature which is popularly elected by PR (or, to be more precise, the lower house of a bicameral legislature – more about that later, too). Because PR is no longer controversial, the most important step toward this goal would be the transformation of the current European Commission into such a European cabinet. What is definitely not in consonance with prevalent European democratic traditions is the proposal to have a direct popular election of the Commission's president, which implies a presidential form of government: such a president would presumably not only be popularly elected but also elected for a fixed term of office (it is difficult to envisage a popularly elected president who can be removed easily by a parliamentary vote of no-confidence) and who would be the predominant executive leader instead of a *primus inter pares* prime minister.

Parliamentarism and PR also happen to be optimal in terms of democratic constitutional engineering. Comparative politics experts agree that presidentialism has severe institutional deficiencies: the fixed term of office which makes the government very rigid, the tendency to executive-legislative deadlock resulting from the coexistence of two branches that are separately elected and can both claim democratic legitimacy, the winner-take-all nature of presidential elections, and the encouragement of the politics of personality instead of a politics of competing parties and party programs. Both the winner-take-all rule and the fact that executive power is mainly concentrated in one person are serious obstacles to minority representation in multi-ethnic countries – and the EU is clearly multi-national and multi-ethnic. Moreover, in multi-ethnic settings PR works best; I cannot think of even one major comparative politics expert who believes in the superiority of first-past-the-post for ethnically divided countries.

The parliamentary-PR form of democracy would also largely solve the so-called "democratic deficit" in the EU: prime ministers and cabinets would be selected in the same way as in almost all European democracies. Other frequently mentioned aspects of the democratic deficit are the low voter turnouts in European Parliament elections and the absence of truly European political parties. Both conditions are likely to improve when elections determine the composition of a really powerful legislature and executive. Furthermore, comparative research has shown that parliamentary government and PR are more conducive to voter participation and the development of unified parties with broad geographical support than presidentialism and majoritarian elections. But we must be realistic about the prospects of strong system-wide parties in very large democracies: the two major American parties are usually characterized as no more than federations of fifty state parties, and in India the Congress party is the only party that can claim country-wide support. What about the lack of a uniform electoral system in the EU: PR for all European Parliament elections, but in many variants. Greater uniformity would certainly be desirable, but let us not forget that for US House of Representatives elections, too, the rules vary a great deal from state to state, especially as far as the primary elections are concerned.

Finally, as promised, here are a few remarks about federalism and bicameralism. I find it hard to imagine that a European state could be anything else than some kind of federal system with the current EU members becoming the member states of the federation. Here, too, I would recommend that European traditions be followed rather than the American federal model. In particular, the principle of equal state representation in the US Senate has led to gross overrepresentation of the smallest states. In the federal chambers of EU members Germany and Austria (and also in the current European Parliament), small states are over-represented but not to the extent of equal representation. Bicameralism is a standard element of federalism, and a German/Austrian-style upper house together with a lower house (to which the cabinet would be responsible), elected by PR on a one-citizen, one-vote, one-value basis, is the most attractive option for the federal EU.

Part V

Proportional versus majoritarian election systems

11 Constitutional choices for new democracies[1]

Two fundamental choices that confront architects of new democratic constitutions are those between plurality elections and proportional representation (PR) and between parliamentary and presidential forms of government. The merits of presidentialism and parliamentarism were extensively debated by Juan J. Linz, Seymour Martin Lipset, and Donald L. Horowitz in the fall 1990 issue of the *Journal of Democracy*.[2] I strongly concur with Horowitz's contention that the electoral system is an equally vital element in democratic constitutional design, and therefore that it is of crucial importance to evaluate these two sets of choices in relation with each other. Such an analysis, as I will try to show, indicates that the combination of parliamentarism with proportional representation should be an especially attractive one to newly democratic and democratizing countries.

The comparative study of democracies has shown that the type of electoral system is significantly related to the development of a country's party system, its type of executive (one-party vs. coalition cabinets), and the relationship between its executive and legislature. Countries that use the plurality method of election (almost always applied, at the national level, in single-member districts) are likely to have two-party systems, one-party governments, and executives that are dominant in relation to their legislatures. These are the main characteristics of the Westminster or *majoritarian* model of democracy, in which power is concentrated in the hands of the majority party. Conversely, PR is likely to be associated with multiparty systems, coalition governments (including, in many cases, broad and inclusive coalitions), and more equal executive-legislative power relations. These latter characteristics typify the *consensus* model of democracy, which, instead of relying on pure and concentrated majority rule, tries to limit, divide, separate, and share power in a variety of ways.[3]

Three further points should be made about these two sets of related traits. First, the relationships are mutual. For instance, plurality elections favor the maintenance of a two-party system; but an existing two-party system also favors the maintenance of plurality, which gives the two principal parties great advantages that they are unlikely to abandon. Second, if democratic political engineers desire to promote either the majoritarian cluster of characteristics (plurality, a two-party system, and a dominant, one-party cabinet) or the consensus cluster (PR, multipartism, coalition government, and a stronger legislature), the most practical way to do so is by choosing the appropriate electoral system. Giovanni Sartori has aptly called electoral systems "the most specific manipulative instrument of politics."[4] Third, important variations exist among PR systems. Without going into all the technical details, a useful distinction can be made between *extreme* PR, which poses few barriers to small parties, and *moderate* PR. The latter limits the influence of minor parties through such means as applying PR in small districts instead of large districts or nationwide balloting, and requiring parties to receive a minimum percentage of the vote in order to gain representation, such as the 5 percent threshold in Germany. The Dutch, Israeli, and Italian systems exemplify extreme PR and the German and Swedish systems, moderate PR.

The second basic constitutional choice, between parliamentary and presidential forms of government, also affects the majoritarian or consensus character of the political system. Presidentialism yields majoritarian effects on the party system and on the type of executive, but a consensus effect on executive-legislative relations. By formally separating the executive and legislative powers, presidential systems generally promote a rough executive-legislative balance of power. On the other hand, presidentialism tends to foster a two-party system, as the presidency is the biggest political prize to be won, and only the largest parties have a chance to win it. This advantage for the big parties often carries over into legislative elections as well (especially if presidential and legislative elections are held simultaneously), even if the legislative elections are conducted under PR rules. Presidentialism usually produces cabinets composed solely of members of the governing party. In fact, presidential systems concentrate executive power to an even greater degree than does a one-party parliamentary cabinet – not just in a single *party* but in a single *person*.

Explaining past choices

My aim is not simply to describe alternative democratic systems and their majoritarian or consensus characteristics, but also to make some practical recommendations for democratic constitutional engineers. What are the main advantages and disadvantages of plurality and PR and of presidentialism and parliamentarism? One way to approach this question is to investigate why contemporary democracies made the constitutional choices they did.

Figure 11.1 illustrates the four combinations of basic characteristics and the countries and regions where they prevail. The purest examples of the combination of presidentialism and plurality are the United States and democracies heavily influenced by the United States, such as the Philippines and Puerto Rico. Latin American countries have overwhelmingly opted for presidential-PR systems. Parliamentary-plurality systems exist in the United

	Presidential	Parliamentary
Plurality Elections	United States Philippines	United Kingdom Old Commonwealth India Malaysia Jamaica
Proportional Representation	Latin America	Western Europe

Figure 11.1 Four basic types of democracy

Kingdom and many former British colonies, including India, Malaysia, Jamaica, and the countries of the so-called Old Commonwealth (Canada, Australia, and New Zealand). Finally, parliamentary-PR systems are concentrated in Western Europe. Clearly, the overall pattern is to a large extent determined by geographic, cultural, and colonial factors – a point to which I shall return shortly.

Very few contemporary democracies cannot be accommodated by this classification. The major exceptions are democracies that fall in between the pure presidential and pure parliamentary types (France and Switzerland), and those that use electoral methods other than pure PR or plurality (Ireland, Japan, and, again, France).[5]

Two important factors influenced the adoption of PR in continental Europe. One was the problem of ethnic and religious minorities; PR was designed to provide minority representation and thereby to counteract potential threats to national unity and political stability. "It was no accident," Stein Rokkan writes, "that the earliest moves toward proportional representation (PR) came in the ethnically most heterogeneous countries." The second factor was the dynamic of the democratization process. PR was adopted

> through a convergence of pressures from below and from above. The rising working class wanted to lower the thresholds of representation in order to gain access to the legislatures, and the most threatened of the old-established parties demanded PR to protect their position against the new waves of mobilized voters created by universal suffrage.[6]

Both factors are relevant for contemporary constitution making, especially for the many countries where there are deep ethnic cleavages or where new democratic forces need to be reconciled with the old antidemocratic groups.

The process of democratization also originally determined whether parliamentary or presidential institutions were adopted. As Douglas V. Verney has pointed out, there were two basic ways in which monarchical power could be democratized: by taking away most of the monarch's personal political prerogatives and making his cabinet responsible to the popularly elected legislature, thus creating a parliamentary system; or by removing the hereditary monarch and substituting a new, democratically elected "monarch," thus creating a presidential system.[7]

Other historical causes have been voluntary imitations of successful democracies and the dominant influence of colonial powers. As Figure 11.1 shows very clearly, Britain's influence as an imperial power has been enormously important. The US presidential model was widely imitated in Latin America in the nineteenth century. And early in the twentieth century, PR spread quickly in continental Europe and Latin America, not only for reasons of partisan accommodation and minority protection, but also because it was widely perceived to be the most democratic method of election and hence the "wave of the democratic future."

This sentiment in favor of PR raises the controversial question of the *quality* of democracy achieved in the four alternative systems. The term "quality" refers to the degree to which a system meets such democratic norms as representativeness, accountability, equality, and participation. The claims and counterclaims are too well known to require lengthy treatment here, but it is worth emphasizing that the differences between the opposing camps are not as great as is often supposed. First of all, PR and plurality advocates disagree not so much about the respective effects of the two electoral methods as about the weight to be attached to these effects. Both sides agree that PR yields greater proportionality and minority representation and that plurality promotes two-party systems and one-party executives. Partisans disagree on which of these results is preferable, with the plurality side claiming that only in two-party systems can clear accountability for government policy be achieved.

In addition, both sides argue about the *effectiveness* of the two systems. Proportionalists value minority representation not just for its democratic quality but also for its ability to maintain unity and peace in divided societies. Similarly, proponents of plurality favor one-party cabinets not just because of their democratic accountability but also because of the firm leadership and effective policy-making that they allegedly provide. There also appears to be a slight difference in the relative emphasis that the two sides place on quality and effectiveness. Proportionalists tend to attach greater importance to the *representativeness* of government, while plurality advocates view the *capacity to govern* as the more vital consideration.

Finally, while the debate between presidentialists and parliamentarists has not been as fierce, it clearly parallels the debate over electoral systems. Once again, the claims and counterclaims revolve around both quality and effectiveness. Presidentialists regard the direct popular election of the chief executive as a democratic asset, while parliamentarists think of the concentration of executive power in the hands of a single official as less than optimally democratic. But here the question of effectiveness has been the more seriously debated issue, with the president's strong and effective leadership role being emphasized by one side and the danger of executive-legislative conflict and stalemate by the other.

Evaluating democratic performance

How can the actual performance of the different types of democracies be evaluated? It is extremely difficult to find quantifiable measures of democratic performance, and therefore political scientists have rarely attempted a systematic assessment. The major exception is G. Bingham Powell's pioneering study evaluating the capacity of various democracies to maintain public order (as measured by the incidence of riots and deaths from political violence) and their levels of citizen participation (as measured by electoral turnout).[8] Following Powell's example, I will examine these and other aspects of democratic performance, including democratic representation and responsiveness, economic equality, and macroeconomic management.

Due to the difficulty of finding reliable data outside the OECD countries to measure such aspects of performance, I have limited the analysis to the advanced industrial democracies. In any event, the Latin American democracies, given their lower levels of economic development, cannot be considered comparable cases. This means that one of the four basic alternatives – the presidential-PR form of democracy prevalent only in Latin America – must be omitted from our analysis.

Although this limitation is unfortunate, few observers would seriously argue that a strong case can be made for this particular type of democracy. With the clear exception of Costa Rica and the partial exceptions of Venezuela and Colombia, the political stability and economic performance of Latin American democracies have been far from satisfactory. As Juan Linz has argued, Latin American presidential systems have been particularly prone to executive-legislative deadlock and ineffective leadership.[9] Moreover, Scott Mainwaring has shown persuasively that this problem becomes especially serious when presidents do not have majority support in their legislatures.[10] Thus the Latin American model of presidentialism combined with PR legislative elections remains a particularly unattractive option.

The other three alternatives – presidential-plurality, parliamentary-plurality, and parliamentary-PR systems – are all represented among the firmly established Western democracies. I focus on the fourteen cases that unambiguously fit these three categories. The United States is the one example of presidentialism combined with plurality. There are four cases of parliamentarism-plurality (Australia, Canada, New Zealand, and the United Kingdom), and nine democracies of the parliamentary-PR type (Austria, Belgium, Denmark, Finland, Germany, Italy, the Netherlands, Norway, and

Sweden). Seven long-term, stable democracies are excluded from the analysis either because they do not fit comfortably into any one of the three categories (France, Ireland, Japan, and Switzerland), or because they are too vulnerable to external factors (Israel, Iceland, and Luxembourg).

Since a major purpose of PR is to facilitate minority representation, one would expect the PR systems to outperform plurality systems in this respect. There is little doubt that this is indeed the case. For instance, where ethnic minorities have formed ethnic political parties, as in Belgium and Finland, PR has enabled them to gain virtually perfect proportional representation. Because there are so many different kinds of ethnic and religious minorities in the democracies under analysis, it is difficult to measure systematically the *degree* to which PR succeeds in providing more representatives for minorities than does plurality. It is possible, however, to compare the representation of women – a minority in political rather than strictly numerical terms – systematically across countries. The first column of Table 11.1 shows the percentages of female members in the lower (or only) houses of the national legislatures in these fourteen democracies during the early 1980s. The 16.4 percent average for the parliamentary–PR systems is about four times higher than the 4.1 percent for the United States or the 4.0 percent average for the parliamentary-plurality countries. To be sure, the higher social standing of women in the four Nordic countries accounts for part of the difference, but the average of 9.4 percent in the five other parliamentary-PR countries remains more than twice as high as in the plurality countries.

Table 11.1 Women's legislative representation, innovative family policy, voting turnout, income inequality, and the Dahl rating of democratic quality

	Women's Repr. 1980–82	Family Policy 1976–80	Voting Turnout 1971–80	Income Top 20% 1985	Dahl Rating 1969
Pres.-Plurality (N=1)	4.1	3.00	54.2%	39.9%	3.0
Parl.-Plurality (N=4)	4.0	2.50	75.3	42.9	4.8
Parl.-PR (N=9)	16.4	7.89	84.5	39.0	2.2

Note: The one presidential-plurality democracy is the United States; the four parliamentary-plurality democracies are Australia, Canada, New Zealand, and the United Kingdom; and the nine parliamentary-PR democracies are Austria, Belgium, Denmark, Finland, Germany, Italy, the Netherlands, Norway, and Sweden.
Source: Based on Wilma Rule, "Electoral Systems, Contextual Factors and Women's Opportunity for Election to Parliament in Twenty-Three Democracies," *Western Political Quarterly* 40 (September 1987), 483; Harold L. Wilensky, "Common Problems, Divergent Policies: An 18-Nation Study of Family Policy," *Public Affairs Report* 31 (May 1990), 2; personal communication by Harold L. Wilensky to the author, dated 18 October 1990; Robert W. Jackman, "Polilical Institutions and Voter Turnout in the Industrial Democracies," *American Political Science Review* 81 (June 1987), 420; World Bank, *World Development Report 1989* (New York: Oxford University Press, 1989), 223; Robert A. Dahl, *Polyarchy: Participation and Opposition* (New Haven CT: Yale University Press, 1971), 232.

Does higher representation of women result in the advancement of their interests? Harold L. Wilensky's careful rating of democracies with regard to the innovativeness and expansiveness of their family policies – a matter of special concern to women – indicates that it does.[11] On a 13-point scale (from a maximum of 12 to a minimum of 0), the scores of these countries range from 11 to 1. The differences among the three groups (as shown in the second column of Table 11.1) are striking: the PR countries have an average score of 7.89, whereas the parliamentary-plurality countries have an average of just 2.50, and the United States only a slightly higher score of 3.00. Here again, the Nordic countries have the highest scores, but the 6.80 average of the non-Nordic PR countries is still well above that of the plurality countries.

The last three columns of Table 11.1 show indicators of democratic quality. The third column lists the most reliable figures on electoral participation (in the 1970s); countries with compulsory voting (Australia, Belgium, and Italy) are not included in the averages. Compared with the extremely low voter turnout of 54.2 percent in the United States, the parliamentary-plurality systems perform a great deal better (about 75 percent). But the average in the parliamentary–PR systems is still higher, at slightly above 84 percent. Since the maximum turnout that is realistically attainable is around 90 percent (as indicated by the turnouts in countries with compulsory voting), the difference between 75 and 84 percent is particularly striking.

Another democratic goal is political equality, which is more likely to prevail in the absence of great economic inequalities. The fourth column of Table 11.1 presents the World Bank's percentages of total income earned by the top 20 percent of households in the mid-1980s.[12] They show a slightly less unequal distribution of income in the parliamentary-PR than in the parliamentary-plurality systems, with the United States in an intermediate position.

Finally, the fifth column reports Robert A. Dahl's ranking of democracies according to ten indicators of democratic quality, such as freedom of the press, freedom of association, competitive party systems, strong parties and interest groups, and effective legislatures.[13] The stable democracies range from a highest rating of 1 to a low of 6. There is a slight pro-PR bias in Dahl's ranking (he includes a number-of-parties variable that rates multiparty systems somewhat higher than two-party systems), but even when we discount this bias we find striking differences between the parliamentary–PR and parliamentary-plurality countries: six of the former are given the highest score, whereas most of the latter receive the next to lowest score of 5.

No such clear differences are apparent when we examine the effect of the type of democracy on the maintenance of public order and peace. Parliamentary-plurality systems had the lowest incidence of riots during the period 1948–77, but the highest incidence of political deaths; the latter figure, however, derives almost entirely from the high number of political deaths in the United Kingdom, principally as a result of the Northern Ireland problem. A more elaborate statistical analysis shows that societal division is a much more important factor than type of democracy in explaining variation in the incidence of political riots and deaths in the thirteen parliamentary countries.[14]

A major argument in favor of plurality systems has been that they favor "strong" one-party governments that can pursue "effective" public policies. One key area of government activity in which this pattern should manifest itself is the management of the economy. Thus advocates of plurality systems received a rude shock in 1987 when the average per capita GDP in Italy (a PR and multiparty democracy with notoriously uncohesive and unstable governments) surpassed that of the United Kingdom, typically regarded as the very model of strong and effective government. If Italy had discovered large amounts of oil in the Mediterranean, we would undoubtedly explain its superior economic performance in terms of this fortuitous factor. But it was not Italy but Britain that discovered the oil!

Economic success is obviously not solely determined by government policy. When we examine economic performance over a long period of time, however, the effects of external influences are minimized, especially if we focus on countries with similar levels of economic development. Table 11.2 presents OECD figures from the 1960s through the 1980s for the three most important aspects of macroeconomic performance – average annual economic growth, inflation, and unemployment rates.

Although Italy's economic growth has indeed been better than that of Britain, the parliamentary-plurality and parliamentary-PR countries as groups do not differ much from each other or from the United States. The slightly higher growth rates in the parliamentary-PR systems cannot be considered significant. With regard to inflation, the United States has the best record, followed by the parliamentary-PR systems. The most sizable differences appear in unemployment levels; here the parliamentary-PR countries perform significantly better than the plurality countries.[15] Comparing the parliamentary-plurality and parliamentary-PR countries on all three indicators, we find that the performance of the latter is uniformly better.

Table 11.2 Economic growth, inflation, and unemployment (%)

	Economic Growth 1961–88	Inflation 1961–88	Unemployment 1965–88
Presidential-Plurality (N=1)	3.3	5.1	6.1
Parliamentary-Plurality (N=4)	3.4	7.5	6.1
Parlimentary-PR (N = 9)	3.5	6.3	4.4

Source: OECD Economic Outlook, no. 26 (December 1979), 131; no. 30 (December 1981), 131, 140, 142; no. 46 (December 1989), 166, 176, 182.

Lessons for developing countries

Political scientists tend to think that plurality systems such as the United Kingdom and the United States are superior with regard to democratic quality and governmental effectiveness – a tendency best explained by the fact that political science has always been an Anglo-American-oriented discipline. This prevailing opinion is largely contradicted, however, by the empirical evidence presented above. Wherever significant differences appear, the parliamentary-PR systems almost invariably post the best records, particularly with respect to representation, protection of minority interests, voter participation, and control of unemployment.

This finding contains an important lesson for democratic constitutional engineers: the parliamentary-PR option is one that should be given serious consideration. Yet a word of caution is also in order, since parliamentary-PR democracies differ greatly among themselves. Moderate PR and moderate multipartism, as in Germany and Sweden, offer more attractive models than the extreme PR and multiparty systems of Italy and the Netherlands. As previously noted, though, even Italy has a respectable record of democratic performance.

But are these conclusions relevant to newly democratic and democratizing countries in Asia, Africa, Latin America, and Eastern Europe, which are trying to make democracy work in the face of economic underdevelopment and ethnic divisions? Do not these difficult conditions require strong executive leadership in the form of a powerful president or a Westminster-style, dominant one-party cabinet?

With regard to the problem of deep ethnic cleavages, these doubts can be easily laid to rest. Divided societies, both in the West and elsewhere, need peaceful coexistence among the contending ethnic groups. This requires conciliation and compromise, goals that in turn require the greatest possible inclusion of representatives of these groups in the decision-making process. Such power sharing can be arranged much more easily in parliamentary and PR systems than in presidential and plurality systems. A president almost inevitably belongs to one ethnic group, and hence presidential systems are particularly inimical to ethnic power sharing. And while Westminster-style parliamentary systems feature collegial cabinets, these tend not to be ethnically inclusive, particularly when there is a majority ethnic group. It is significant that the British government, in spite of its strong majoritarian traditions, recognized the need for consensus and power sharing in religiously and ethnically divided Northern Ireland. Since 1973, British policy has been to try to solve the Northern Ireland problem by means of PR elections and an inclusive coalition government.

As Horowitz has pointed out, it may be possible to alleviate the problems of presidentialism by requiring that a president be elected with a stated minimum of support from different groups, as in Nigeria.[16] But this is a palliative that cannot compare with the advantages of a truly collective and inclusive executive. Similarly, the example of Malaysia shows that a parliamentary system can have a broad multiparty and multiethnic coalition cabinet in spite of plurality elections, but this requires elaborate pre-election pacts among the parties. These exceptions prove the rule: the ethnic power sharing that has been attainable in Nigeria and Malaysia only on a limited basis and through very special arrangements is a natural and straightforward result of parliamentary-PR forms of democracy.

PR and economic policy making

The question of which form of democracy is most conducive to economic development is more difficult to answer. We simply do not have enough cases of durable Third World democracies representing the different systems (not to mention the lack of reliable economic data) to make an unequivocal evaluation. However, the conventional wisdom that economic development requires the unified and decisive leadership of a strong president or a Westminster-style dominant cabinet is highly suspect. First of all, if an inclusive executive that must do more bargaining and conciliation were less effective at economic policy making than a dominant and exclusive executive, then presumably an authoritarian government free of legislative interference or internal dissent would be optimal. This reasoning – a frequent excuse for the overthrow of democratic governments in the Third World in the 1960s and 1970s – has now been thoroughly discredited. To be sure, we do have a few examples of economic miracles wrought by authoritarian regimes, such as those in South Korea or Taiwan, but these are more than counterbalanced by the sorry economic records of just about all the non-democratic governments in Africa, Latin America, and Eastern Europe.

Second, many British scholars, notably the eminent political scientist S. E. Finer, have come to the conclusion that economic development requires not so much a *strong* hand as a *steady* one. Reflecting on the poor economic performance of post-World War II Britain, they have argued that each of the governing parties indeed provided reasonably strong leadership in economic policy making but that alternations in governments were too "absolute and abrupt," occurring "between two sharply polarized parties each eager to repeal a large amount of its predecessor's legislation." What is needed, they argue, is "greater stability and continuity" and "greater moderation in policy," which could be provided by a shift to PR and to coalition governments much more likely to be centrist in orientation.[17] This argument would appear to be equally applicable both to developed and developing countries.

Third, the case for strong presidential or Westminster-style governments is most compelling where rapid decision making is essential. This means that in foreign and defense policy parliamentary-PR systems may be at a disadvantage. But in economic policy making speed is not particularly important – quick decisions are not necessarily wise ones.

Why then do we persist in distrusting the economic effectiveness of democratic systems that engage in broad consultation and bargaining aimed at a high degree of consensus? One reason is that multiparty and coalition governments *seem* to be messy, quarrelsome, and inefficient in contrast to the clear authority of strong presidents and strong one-party cabinets. But we should not let ourselves be deceived by these superficial appearances. A closer look at presidential systems reveals that the most successful cases – such as the United States, Costa Rica, and pre-1970 Chile – are at least equally quarrelsome and, in fact, are prone to paralysis and deadlock rather than steady and effective economic policy making. In any case, the argument should not be about governmental aesthetics but about actual performance. The undeniable elegance of the Westminster model is not a valid reason for adopting it.

The widespread skepticism about the economic capability of parliamentary-PR systems stems from confusing governmental strength with effectiveness. In the short run, one-party cabinets or presidents may well be able to formulate economic policy with greater ease and speed. In the long run, however, policies supported by a broad consensus are more likely to be successfully carried out and to remain on course than policies imposed by a "strong" government against the wishes of important interest groups.

To sum up, the parliamentary-PR form of democracy is clearly better than the major alternatives in accommodating ethnic differences, and it has a slight edge in economic policy making as well. The argument that considerations of governmental effectiveness mandate the rejection of parliamentary-PR democracy for developing countries is simply not tenable. Constitution makers in new democracies would do themselves and their countries a great disservice by ignoring this attractive democratic model.

Acknowledgments

I gratefully acknowledge the assistance and advice of Robert W. Jackman, G. Bingham Powell, Jr., Harold L. Wilensky, and Kaare Strom, the research assistance of Markus Crepaz, and the financial support of the Committee on Research of the Academic Senate of the University of California at San Diego.

Notes

1 This paper first appeared in the *Journal of Democracy* 2, no. 1 (winter 1991).
2 Donald L. Horowitz, "Comparing Democratic Systems," Seymour Martin Lipset, "The Centrality of Political Culture," and Juan J. Linz, "The Virtues of Parliamentarism," *Journal of Democracy* 1 (fall 1990): 73–91. A third set of important decisions concerns institutional arrangements that are related to the difference between federal and unitary forms of government: the degree of government centralization, unicameralism or bicameralism, rules for constitutional amendment, and judicial review. Empirical analysis shows that these factors tend to be related; federal countries are more likely to be decentralized, to have significant bicameralism, and to have "rigid" constitutions that are difficult to amend and protected by judicial review.

3 For a fuller discussion of the differences between majoritarian and consensus government, see Arend Lijphart, *Democracies: Patterns of Majoritarian and Consensus Government in Twenty-One Countries* (New Haven CT: Yale University Press, 1984).

4 Giovanni Sartori, "Political Development and Political Engineering," in *Public Policy*, vol. 17, eds John D. Montgomery and Alfred O. Hirschman (Cambridge MA: Harvard University Press, 1968), 273.

5 The first scholar to emphasize the close connection between culture and these constitutional arrangements was G. Bingham Powell, Jr. in his *Contemporary Democracies: Participation, Stability, and Violence* (Cambridge MA: Harvard University Press, 1982), 67. In my previous writings, I have sometimes classified Finland as a presidential or semipresidential system, but I now agree with Powell (pp. 56–57) that, although the directly elected Finnish president has special authority in foreign policy, Finland operates like a parliamentary system in most other respects. Among the exceptions, Ireland is a doubtful case; I regard its system of the single transferable vote as mainly a PR method, but other authors have classified it as a plurality system. And I include Australia in the parliamentary-plurality group, because its alternative-vote system, while not identical with plurality, operates in a similar fashion.

6 Stein Rokkan, *Citizens, Elections, Parties: Approaches to the Comparative Study of the Processes of Development* (Oslo: Universitetsforlaget, 1970), 157.

7 Douglas V. Verney, *The Analysis of Political Systems* (London: Routledge and Kegan Paul, 1959), 18–23, 42–43.

8 Powell, op. cit., esp. 12–29 and 111–74.

9 Juan J. Linz, "The Perils of Presidentialism," *Journal of Democracy* 1 (winter 1990): 51–69.

10 Scott Mainwaring, "Presidentialism in Latin America," *Latin American Research Review* 25 (1990): 167–70.

11 Wilensky's ratings are based on a five-point scale (from 4 to 0)

> for each of three policy clusters: existence and length of maternity and parental leave, paid and unpaid; availability and accessibility of public daycare programs and government effort to expand daycare; and flexibility of retirement systems. They measure government action to assure care of children and maximize choices in balancing work and family demands for everyone.
> (See Harold L. Wilensky, "Common Problems, Divergent Policies: An 18-Nation Study of Family Policy," *Public Affairs Report* 31 [May 1990]: 2)

12 Because of missing data, Austria is not included in the parliamentary-PR average.

13 Robert A. Dahl, *Polyarchy: Participation and Opposition* (New Haven CT: Yale University Press, 1971), 231–45.

14 This multiple-correlation analysis shows that societal division, as measured by the degree of organizational exclusiveness of ethnic and religious groups, explains 33 percent of the variance in riots and 25 percent of the variance in political deaths. The additional explanation by type of democracy is only 2 percent for riots (with plurality countries slightly more orderly) and 13 percent for deaths (with the PR countries slightly more peaceful).

15 Comparable unemployment data for Austria, Denmark, and New Zealand are not available, and these countries are therefore not included in the unemployment figures in Table 11.2.

16 Horowitz, op. cit., 76–77.

17 S. E. Finer, "Adversary Politics and Electoral Reform," in *Adversary Politics and Electoral Reform*, ed. S. E. Finer (London: Anthony Wigram, 1975), 30–31.

12 Double-checking the evidence

In my article "Constitutional Choices for New Democracies," I presented systematic empirical evidence concerning the relative performance of various types of democratic systems in an effort to transcend the usual vague and untestable claims and counterclaims that surround this topic. I compared four parliamentary-plurality democracies (the United Kingdom, Canada, Australia, and New Zealand) with nine parliamentary-proportional representation (PR) democracies (Germany, Italy, Austria, the Netherlands, Belgium, and four Nordic countries – Sweden, Denmark, Norway, Finland) with regard to their performance records on minority representation and protection, democratic quality, the maintenance of public order and peace, and the management of the economy. I found that, where differences between the two groups of democracies appeared, the parliamentary-PR systems showed the better performance. There were sizable differences with regard to minority representation (as measured by the representation of women in national parliaments), the protection of minority interests (measured by innovative family policy), democratic quality (measured by voter turnout), and control of unemployment; smaller differences on income inequality and control of inflation; and little or no difference with regard to the maintenance of public order (as measured by riots and deaths from political violence) and economic growth. Since, according to the conventional – but also rather old-fashioned – wisdom, PR may be superior to plurality as far as minority representation is concerned but leads to less effective decision making, even my finding of minor or no differences on some of the performance indicators must be counted in favor of the parliamentary-PR type.

Guy Lardeyret and Quentin L. Quade, both eloquent exponents of this conventional wisdom, raise a series of objections to my analysis and conclusions – very welcome challenges because they present an opportunity to double-check the validity of my evidence. Lardeyret and Quade argue that (1) the differences in governmental performance may be explained by other factors than the type of democracy, and hence that they do not prove any parliamentary-PR superiority; (2) that, when other important effects of the different types of democracy are considered, plurality systems are superior; (3) that some of my findings are the result of incorrect measurement; and (4) that my findings are biased by my choice and classification of the countries included in the analysis. I shall demonstrate, however, that whenever their objections can be tested against the facts, they turn out to be invalid.

Alternative explanations

I agree with Lardeyret's and Quade's argument that economic success is not solely determined by government policy; I said as much in my original article. There are obviously many external and fortuitous factors that influence a country's economic performance. Neither do I disagree with Quade's argument that several special circumstances have had a negative effect on Britain. On the other hand, some of the PR countries suffered similar setbacks: the Netherlands and Belgium also lost sizable colonial empires, the "seismic social-psychological" shock of decolonization suffered by Britain was no greater than the shock of defeat and division suffered by Germany, and ethnic strife has plagued Belgium as well as the Celtic periphery of the United Kingdom. But my comparison was not just between Britain and one or more PR countries; I compared the four parliamentary-plurality democracies as a group with the group of nine parliamentary-PR countries. I assumed that when the economic performance of groups of democracies is examined over a long period of time, and when all of the countries studied have similar levels of economic development, external and fortuitous influences tend to even out. In the absence of any plausible suggestion that, as a group, the parliamentary-PR countries enjoyed unusual economic advantages from the 1960s through the 1980s – and neither Lardeyret nor Quade offers any such suggestion – my assumption and hence my findings concerning differences in economic performance remain valid.

Lardeyret and Quade do mention a few things that might provide a basis for alternative explanations: the special characteristics of the Nordic countries, the advantage of having a constitutional monarchy, the difference between moderate and extreme PR, and the advantage of US military protection. All of these can be tested empirically. Lardeyret claims that unemployment in the Nordic countries is underestimated because of "highly protected jobs" and that income inequality is relatively modest because of unusual handicaps that conservative parties must contend with in these countries. Whether these factors change my findings can be checked easily by excluding the Nordic countries and comparing the non-Nordic parliamentary-PR countries with the parliamentary-plurality countries. Average unemployment in the Nordic countries was indeed lower than in the non-Nordic countries – 2.7 percent compared with 5.7 percent – but the latter percentage is still slightly better than the 6.1 percent for the parliamentary-plurality countries. As far as income inequality is concerned, there is virtually no difference between the Nordic and non-Nordic parliamentary-PR countries – 39.0 and 38.9 percent respectively – both of which score lower than the 42.9 percent in the parliamentary-plurality democracies.

When we compare monarchies with republics, the first point to be made is that, if a constitutional monarchy is an advantage, all of the parliamentary-plurality countries enjoy this advantage, whereas only about half of the parliamentary-PR democracies do. Second, when we compare the monarchical countries (Belgium, the Netherlands, Sweden, Norway, and Denmark) with the republican PR countries (Germany, Italy, Austria, and Finland), their growth rates are virtually identical and their inflation rates exactly the same. Only their unemployment rates differ somewhat: the monarchies have a 4.0 percent average unemployment rate compared with 4.9 percent in the non-monarchical countries; again, the latter percentage is still better than the 6.1-percent average of the parliamentary-plurality countries. On all of the indicators of minority representation and protection and of democratic quality, there are slight differences between the monarchical and non-monarchical groups, but both still clearly outperform the parliamentary-plurality countries.

Is PR's Achilles heel revealed when we focus on the countries that have extreme PR (Italy, the Netherlands, Denmark, and Finland) and contrast these with the more moderate PR systems (Germany, Sweden, Norway, Belgium, and Austria)? The empirical evidence disproves this. The inflation and unemployment rates in the extreme PR group are indeed higher (7.4 and 5.5 versus 5.4 and 3.6 percent) but still at least a bit lower than the 7.5 and 6.1 percent in the parliamentary-plurality systems; their growth rates are virtually identical. On the four indicators of representation and democratic quality, the differences are slight, and both groups of PR countries remain way ahead of the parliamentary-plurality countries. My own firm preference remains for moderate PR, but the dangers of extreme PR must not be exaggerated.

As Quade correctly states, the parliamentary-PR countries have had the advantage of living under "the umbrella of American military protection" – but so have all four of the parliamentary-plurality countries. In fact, the only slight exceptions are in the PR group: Sweden's neutral but strongly armed posture entailed heavy military expenditures, and Finland lived in precarious dependence on Soviet restraint. On the whole, however, American military protection benefited all thirteen parliamentary democracies more or less equally, and therefore cannot explain any differences in their performance records.

Alternative standards and classifications

Partly in addition to and partly instead of the measures that I used to evaluate the performance of different types of democracy, Lardeyret and Quade state that democracies should be judged in terms of factors like accountability, government stability, decision-making capacity, and the ability to avoid "repeated elections." There are several problems with these suggestions. First of all, while accountability is certainly an important aspect of democratic government, it cannot be measured objectively. Second, it is not at all clear that coalition governments are less responsible and accountable than one-party governments. Quade's description of coalition cabinets as governments "cobbled together out of postelection splinters by a secretive process of interparty bartering" may apply to a few exceptional cases like Israel (which combines extreme PR with an evenly split and polarized electorate), but for most PR countries it is a grossly overdrawn caricature. In fact, once they are formed, coalition cabinets tend to be a good deal *less* secretive and more open than one-party cabinets.

Third, government stability can be measured in terms of average cabinet duration. On the basis of previously collected figures, my calculation shows that the average cabinet life in the parliamentary-plurality countries is about twice that in the parliamentary-PR systems.[1] Longer cabinet duration, Lardeyret assumes, means greater decision-making strength because of greater continuity in government personnel. But when coalition cabinets change they usually do not change as much as the radically alternating cabinets in the parliamentary-plurality countries. Lardeyret admits this when he complains about the "long tenures in office for fixed groups of key politicians" in the PR countries. Fourth, if Lardeyret is right about the superior decision-making capacity of parliamentary-plurality governments, the only convincing proof is that their decisions result in more effective policies. This brings us back to the evaluation of government performance in terms of successful macroeconomic policy making and the successful maintenance of public order. As we have already seen, this hard evidence does not show any parliamentary-plurality superiority.

Lardeyret's complaint about unnecessarily frequent elections in the parliamentary-PR systems suggests an additional useful measure of democratic performance – and one that, happily, can be measured and tested easily. In the 29-year period from 1960 to 1988 – the same period for which two of the three OECD economic indicators were collected – the parliamentary-plurality countries conducted an average of 10.0 national legislative elections, compared with an average of 8.8 in the parliamentary-PR countries.[2] The frequency of elections is actually *smaller* in the PR systems, contrary to Lardeyret's assertion, although the difference is slight. However, Lardeyret's hypothesis is clearly disproved by this simple test.

Lardeyret and Quade have only a few disagreements with my measurements. One question that Lardeyret does raise is the measurement of voter turnout: the US voter-turnout figure would be considerably higher if counted as a proportion of registered voters. He is quite right on this point, but all of my turnout figures are percentages of eligible voters – which means that all countries are treated equally. Moreover, if turnout figures are used as a measure of democratic quality, the low figure for the United States accurately reflects not only an unusually high degree of political apathy but also the fact that voting is deliberately discouraged by the government by means of onerous registration procedures.

Quade questions my equation of "the number of women in legislatures with representation of women's interests." But I did not equate the two at all: I used a separate measure (the innovativeness and expansiveness of family policy, which is of special concern to women) to test whether women's interests were actually better taken care of in the PR countries – and I found that this was indeed the case.

Finally, Lardeyret questions my use of Robert Dahl's ratings of democratic quality because of their alleged pro-PR bias. I already admitted a slight bias of this kind in my original article, but I decided to use the Dahl ratings anyway since they are the most careful overall ratings that are available. However, since they are obviously less objective than my other indicators, I shall not insist on their being used as evidence.

Quade criticizes my favorable judgment of the parliamentary-PR combination by pointing out some examples in which PR did not work well, especially the two cases that are often regarded as spectacular failures of democracy: the Weimar Republic and the French Fourth Republic. Nobody can disagree with the assessment that the Weimar Republic was a failure, but it is less clear that PR was the decisive factor or that plurality would have been able to save Weimar democracy. Moreover, Weimar was a semi-presidential rather than a parliamentary system. In France, the Fourth Republic indeed did not work well, but a reasonable argument can be made that relatively small reforms within the parliamentary-PR framework might have cured the problems and that the radical shift to semi-presidentialism and away from PR was not absolutely necessary. And examples of PR failures can be matched by examples of the failure of plurality systems, such as the failed democracies of West Africa. Sir Arthur Lewis, who served as an economic advisor to these governments, became convinced that "the surest way to kill the idea of democracy" in these divided societies "is to adopt the Anglo-American electoral system of first-past-the-post [plurality]."[3]

Lardeyret does not question my focus on stable contemporary democracies, but argues instead that some of these countries should have been classified differently. Although France is neither fully presidential nor fully plurality, I accept his suggestion that it is close enough on both counts to be classified alongside the United States. I agree that Spain and Portugal belong in the parliamentary-PR category, but comparable data are lacking since the two countries were not yet democratic during the full period covered by the empirical evidence. I disagree that Germany lacks PR and should be classified as a plurality system; it is almost entirely PR in terms of how Bundestag seats are allocated to the parties, though its 5 percent threshold makes it a moderate PR system.

But let us concede Germany to the plurality category; my analysis still stands. Lardeyret's counter-hypothesis is that in "the order of rank according to standards of both efficiency and democracy," the two plurality systems (parliamentary and presidential) are ahead of the parliamentary-PR systems. This can be tested by comparing the seven plurality systems (the parliamentary-plurality countries plus the United States, France, and, arguably, Germany) with eight PR systems (all of the parliamentary-PR systems except Germany). Thus reclassified, the PR countries still have the better record with regard to control of unemployment (4.6 percent versus 5.5 percent average unemployment) and do not differ much with regard to growth (3.5 versus 3.4 percent) and inflation (6.6 versus 6.5 percent). On the indicators of minority representation and protection and of democratic quality, the PR countries are still far ahead of the plurality systems: 17.5 versus 4.5 percent women in parliament; a score of 8.0 versus 4.4 on family policy; 84.5 versus 73.5 percent on voter turnout; and 38.9 versus 41.9 percent of total income earned by the top 20 percent of households. The evidence clearly disproves Lardeyret's counter-hypothesis.

Choices and changes

The demonstrable advantages of parliamentarism and PR appear to be appreciated by the citizens and politicians of democratic countries. In many, if not most, presidential countries, there is widespread dissatisfaction with the operation of presidentialism and sizable support for a shift to a parliamentary form of government; the contrary sentiment can be found in hardly any parliamentary democracy. Similarly, there is great unhappiness about how plurality elections work and strong sentiment for a shift to PR in most democracies that use plurality, but few calls for plurality in PR countries. One important reason for this pattern is that the divisive, winner-take-all nature of plurality and presidentialism is widely understood. From the turn of the century on, democracies with ethnic or other deep cleavages have repeatedly turned to PR in order to accommodate such differences. Lardeyret's recommendation of plurality elections for South Africa and other deeply divided countries is therefore particularly dangerous.

Another important reason for PR's popularity is the feeling that disproportional election results are inherently unfair and undemocratic. None of postwar Britain's governing parties was put in power by a majority of the voters; all of these parties gained power in spite of the fact that most of the voters voted against them. Lardeyret's and Quade's opinion that electoral disproportionality is unimportant is simply not shared by most democrats. As a recent editorial in the London *Economist* puts it, "since the perception of fairness is the acid test for a democracy – the very basis of its legitimacy – the unfairness argument overrules all others."[4]

Fundamental constitutional changes are difficult to effect and therefore rare, but the prevailing pattern of democratic sentiment makes shifts from plurality to PR more likely than the other way around. The reason for this is not, as Lardeyret suggests, that "it is almost impossible to get rid of PR, because doing so requires asking independent parties to cooperate in their own liquidation." On the contrary, this is the main reason why the big parties that benefit from the plurality rule will try to keep it. In PR systems, the large parties usually have enough votes to shift to a system that would greatly benefit them, especially because, as Lardeyret correctly observes, the electoral system is "curiously omitted in most [written] constitutions." That they rarely try to do so cannot be explained in terms of narrow partisan self-interest; the feeling that scrapping PR is undemocratic and dangerous plays a major role. Both the empirical evidence and the weight of opinion in existing democracies make a strong case for the proposition that PR and parliamentarism are also the wisest options for new democracies.

Notes

1 Arend Lijphart, *Democracies: Patterns of Majoritarian and Consensus Government in Twenty-One Countries* (New Haven CT: Yale University Press, 1984), 83. A cabinet is defined as the same cabinet if its party composition does not change; on the basis of this definition and for the 1945–80 period, average cabinet life in the four parliamentary-plurality countries was eighty-eight months and in the parliamentary-PR countries, forty-four months.
2 The dates of parliamentary elections for the thirteen countries can be found in the respective country chapters of Thomas T. Mackie and Richard Rose, *The International Almanac of Electoral History*, 3rd edn (London: Macmillan, 1991).
3 W. Arthur Lewis, *Politics in West Africa* (London: Allen and Unwin, 1965), 71.
4 *Economist*, 11 May 1991, 13.

13 The alternative vote

A realistic alternative for South Africa?[1]

AV and basic constitutional choices

In his recently published book *A Democratic South Africa? Constitutional Engineering in a Divided Society*, Donald L. Horowitz (1991, esp. chapter 5) proposes the alternative vote (AV) electoral system for both parliamentary elections and the direct election of a strong executive president.[2] These proposals pertain to the two most fundamental choices of the many that have to be made when new democratic constitutions are drafted (see Lijphart, 1991).

First, the electoral system has long been recognized as probably the most powerful instrument for shaping the political system. Giovanni Sartori (1968: 273) has aptly called electoral systems "the most specific manipulative instrument of politics." And Horowitz correctly points out that this is especially true for divided societies: "The electoral system is by far the most powerful lever of constitutional engineering for accommodation and harmony in severely divided societies, as indeed it is a powerful tool for many other purposes" (1991: p. 163). The two main categories of electoral systems are first-past-the-post (FPTP) and other majoritarian election methods on the one hand, and proportional representation (PR) methods on the other. FPTP – which is also often called the plurality, relative majority, or winner-take-all method – is almost always applied in single-member election districts (constituencies), and it means that the candidate with the largest number of votes wins even if that number is less than an absolute majority. PR exists in many forms, all of which share the principle that political parties win roughly the same percentage of seats as the percentage of the votes they receive.

The second crucial choice for democratic constitutional engineers concerns the relationship between the executive and the legislature as well as the type of executive. Here the main alternatives are presidential government (in which executive power is concentrated in one person who is elected, directly or indirectly, by popular vote for a fixed term of office) and parliamentary government (characterized by a collegial executive, the cabinet, which is selected by and dependent on the confidence of the legislature).[3]

The scholarly consensus is that the world's many divided societies, like South Africa, are best served by PR and parliamentary government rather than FPTP and presidential government. PR makes it possible for minorities to be fairly represented, and it encourages the development of a multiparty system in which coalition governments, based on compromises among the minorities, have to be formed. Parliamentary systems entail collegial cabinets that are the best sites for coalitions of the leaders of the minorities. FPTP, on the other hand, discriminates against minorities, and it tends to produce artificial majorities, two-party systems, and one-party governments. And presidentialism entails a great deal of concentration of power in the hands of one person and is therefore inimical to the formation of coalitions.

Horowitz deviates from this consensus in both respects: he proposes the alternative vote (AV) which is, like FPTP, a majoritarian electoral system, as well as presidential government. AV asks the voters to rank order the candidates; if a candidate receives an absolute majority of first preferences, he or she is elected; if not, the weakest candidate is eliminated and the ballots with that candidate as first preference are redistributed according to second preferences; this process continues until one of the candidates has reached a majority of the votes. A simple example may help to clarify AV's operation: if there are three candidates – A, B, and C – who are supported by 45 percent, 40 percent, and 15 percent of the voters respectively, C will be eliminated and the ballots with C as first preference will be given to A or B according to the second preferences expressed on these ballots; if these ballots divide 10–5 in favor of A, A will be the winner with 55 percent of the vote, but if the ratio is 12–3 in favor of B, B will emerge as the winner with 52 percent of the vote.

The fact that Horowitz's proposal is at odds with the scholarly consensus does not mean that it should not be taken seriously. On the contrary, I believe that it should be given careful consideration for this very reason. The proposal is certainly highly original: to my knowledge, AV has never been advocated as a method especially suited for divided societies before. Moreover, it is used very rarely; Horowitz mentions only the Australian legislative elections at several levels, including the federal House of Representatives, and the presidential elections in Sri Lanka (pp. 188–89, 191–94). A few more cases can be added – for instance, presidential elections and parliamentary by-elections in Ireland – but this does not change the conclusion that AV is a very infrequently used, and hence not well known, electoral system. Another reason for taking Horowitz seriously is that he is one of the world's foremost experts on ethnicity; his 1985 book *Ethnic Groups in Conflict* is one of the best known comparative analyses of the subject. And the dust jacket of his new 1991 book lists a series of strong endorsements of his proposals by major scholars – although, it should be noted, they are not electoral system experts. Giuseppe Di Palma states that Horowitz presents "a compelling case" in a "brilliant book of great importance for scholars and politicians alike"; Peter H. Schuck admires Horowitz's "wise, imaginative constitutional vision"; and William Foltz calls the book a "highly original work of policy science [and] a major work of scholarship."

Above all, Horowitz's proposals deserve a serious appraisal because he is by no means an old-fashioned political scientist for whom the British and American systems of government are necessarily the models that all other countries should emulate. In fact, he approvingly quotes Sir Arthur Lewis' (1965: 71) conclusion that "the surest way to kill the idea of democracy in a plural society is to adopt the Anglo-American electoral system of first-past-the-post" (p. 164). He sympathizes with the PR advocates' fear of "the frequent tendency of plurality [FPTP] systems to underrepresent minorities and to produce legislative majorities from mere pluralities – or even less than pluralities – of voters," and he emphasizes "the tendency of plurality elections and two-party systems to intensify conflict" in divided societies (pp. 164, 202). Compared with FPTP, it is better, in his view, to use PR and to have a multiparty system "which produces the need to form a coalition" (p. 177).

How can Horowitz's condemnation of FPTP and his approval of coalitions be reconciled with his advocacy of the equally majoritarian AV method and of presidential government? The answer lies in his argument that AV is fundamentally different from FPTP in three respects:

1 AV, unlike FPTP, is a preferential method which produces moderation.
2 AV differs from FPTP in that it is much more proportional.
3 A president elected by AV is likely to be much more broadly representative and responsive than a president elected by FPTP.

I shall try to show that Horowitz is wrong on all three counts.

A critique of AV

1 The most central element in Horowitz's reasoning is that, while PR does have the useful tendency to create a multiparty system in which no party has a majority of the parliamentary seats and in which multiparty coalitions have to be formed, "the mere need to form a coalition will not produce compromise. The incentive to compromise, and not merely the incentive to coalesce, is the key to accommodation" (p. 171). Without incentives to compromise, the only coalitions that will be formed are "coalitions of convenience that will dissolve" (p. 175). Coalescence and compromise are indeed analytically distinct, and there are plenty of examples, cited by Horowitz, of coalitions that have been unable to compromise and that, as a result, have fallen apart. But there are also many contrary examples and, logically, the desire to coalesce implies a need to compromise: if parties are interested in gaining power (which is a

basic assumption in political science), they will, in multiparty situations, want to enter and remain in coalition cabinets (a basic assumption underlying coalition theory), and hence their only choice will be to reach compromises with their coalition partners.

2 Although Horowitz underestimates the moderating effect of coalition-building per se, he is surely right that, if additional incentives to compromise can be introduced, this would be very helpful. Here his recommendation of AV enters. In addition to "seat pooling" (forming government coalitions), AV encourages "vote pooling," that is, it encourages parties to appeal across ethnic boundaries. In our above example of candidates A, B, and C, supported by 45 percent, 40 percent and 15 percent of the voters respectively, A and B will have to bid for the second preferences of C's supporters in order to win – which will, according to Horowitz, reward moderation.

At first blush, this argument seems to make good sense. However, the problem is that precisely the same argument can be used, and is frequently used, in favor of FPTP. In the same example but under FPTP rules, many of C's supporters will not want to waste their votes on C's hopeless candidacy, or may not even be able to vote for C at all because C wisely decides not to pursue a hopeless candidacy. Hence here, too, A and B will have to appeal to C's supporters in order to win. In this respect, there is no significant difference between AV and FPTP. Horowitz believes that moderation will result not only from A's and B's incentive to appeal to C's supporters, but also from the resulting incentive to make a deal with C directly. He recounts an imaginary discussion between a major and a minor candidate, say A and C, in which C trades the second preferences of his or her supporters for A's promise to make concessions on issues important to them (p. 193). The same conversation could just as realistically take place prior to an FPTP election except that the votes instead of the second preferences of C's supporters would be traded. AV and FPTP provide exactly the same incentives.

AV resembles the majority-runoff method – also often called the double-ballot or second-ballot system – even more closely. This is the third principal majoritarian electoral method (FPTP and AV being the first two): as in FPTP, the voters cast their ballots for one candidate only; if no candidate wins an absolute majority of the votes, a runoff election will be held between the top two candidates.[4] In the same hypothetical example, C is now eliminated in the first round, and A and B have to compete for the votes of C's supporters in the runoff. AV merely accomplishes in one round of voting what requires two ballots in the majority-runoff system.[5] The incentives for moderation are exactly the same.

Horowitz does not discuss the majority-runoff method; it is rarely used at the national level – the presidential elections in France and in some Latin American countries offer the best examples – but it was commonly used in Western Europe for parliamentary elections until the beginning of the twentieth century. It is important to note that, in most cases, it was replaced with PR, and that the main reason was its unsatisfactory operation in divided societies. "It was no accident," Stein Rokkan (1970: 157) writes,

> that the earliest moves toward proportional representation (PR) came in the ethnically most heterogeneous countries. ... In linguistically and religiously divided societies majority elections could clearly threaten the continued existence of the political system. The introduction of some element of minority representation came to be seen as an essential step in a strategy of territorial consolidation.

Because the majority-runoff system is so similar to AV, this historical evidence throws additional doubt on the value of AV for divided societies.

3   In one type of situation, AV may actually be even worse for minorities than FPTP: when a majority that is not of overwhelming size (say 60 percent) and that is internally divided, faces a relatively large minority (say 40 percent). Under such circumstances there may be two majority candidates, each receiving about 30 percent of the vote and one minority candidate with 40 percent of the vote. Under FPTP, the minority candidate wins, but under AV he or she will in all likelihood be defeated as second preferences will be transferred to the other majority candidate. For similar reasons, representatives of the black minority in the Southern states of the United States often complain about the discriminatory character of the majority-runoff.

4   In addition to his dubious claim that AV induces moderation, Horowitz's second claim in favor of AV is that it is more proportional than FPTP. He states that it is "perhaps better described" as a majority than as a PR system, but then emphasizes that "like PR systems, AV mitigates the winner-take-all aspects of plurality [FPTP] systems and generally achieves better proportionality of seats to votes than plurality systems do," citing the slender evidence of a "rerun of the 1987 British general election under a hypothetical AV system" (p. 166). However, he fails to make the more obvious comparison between the AV system in Australia and the FPTP systems in Canada, New Zealand, the United Kingdom, and the United States. Douglas W. Rae (1967: 108) does make this comparison in his well known systematic analysis of electoral systems, and he concludes that "the Australian system behaves in all its particulars," including its degree of disproportionality, "as if it were a single-member district plurality [FPTP] formula."

5   The next problem, as Horowitz admits, is that according to his own logic AV can only work well if there is a multiparty system without a majority party: "If a party can win on first preferences, second preferences are irrelevant" (p. 194). Because AV's tendency to disproportionality is similar to that of FPTP, his claim that "AV can provide quite enough

proportionality for the requisite party proliferation" (p. 191) is questionable. Horowitz discusses the only two examples of the use of AV in a divided society – in Sri Lanka's 1982 and 1988 presidential elections – both of which yielded victories on the basis of first preferences (p. 192). The Australian evidence, not examined by Horowitz, lends some support to the hypothesis that AV is slightly more conducive to multipartism than FPTP. The Liberal and National Parties, the parties on the right, have long been in a tight alliance, but AV has allowed them to survive as separate parties – something that in all probability would not have been possible under FPTP.

On the other hand, AV's contribution to multipartism cannot realistically be compared to that of PR. Horowitz states correctly that PR "does not *guarantee* party proliferation" (p. 170, emphasis added), but the important point is that there is a very strong empirical relationship between PR and multipartism, just as there is a very strong link between FPTP and two-party systems. This is an especially crucial point because Horowitz himself repeatedly emphasizes that while "the need to form a coalition" is not a *sufficient* condition for intergroup accommodation, it is a *necessary* condition (p. 177).

6 For parliamentary elections, Horowitz tries to solve the problem of encountering majorities in the election districts by making these heterogeneous: "To achieve this, the constituencies may have to be large, and they may therefore need to be multimember constituencies" (p. 195). The danger here is that in PR systems proportionality increases as district magnitude (the number of representatives per district) increases, but that the relationship is just the other way around for majoritarian election systems. AV's disproportionality will rise sharply when it is applied in multimember districts. The only empirical example of multimember AV is the election of the Australian Senate from 1919 to 1946, and it had disastrous results. The winning party usually won extremely lop-sided victories. In 1925, the Labor Party won 45 percent of the vote but no seats; in 1943, it won 55 percent of the vote and all of the seats contested (Wright, 1986: 131–32).

7 Finally, it should be noted that Horowitz's quest for an electoral system that will deliver moderation and compromise forces him to adopt a restricted view of political representation. Unlike PR, AV makes it difficult for a minority to be represented by members of its own group. This does not bother him because he is satisfied with representation "in the *broader* sense of incorporating the concerns and interests of a given ethnic or racial group in the calculations of politicians belonging to a variety of groups" (p. 165, emphasis added). It seems to me more correct to call this a *narrower* meaning of representation. This narrow interpretation makes it possible for him to make the extremely dubious claim that AV "will result in *real participation in power by minorities*" (p. 202, emphasis in the original).

AV and presidential government

Electing both parliament and a powerful executive president by AV not only doubles AV's troubles but also adds some new problems. Horowitz advances two reasons for his advocacy of presidential government. The first is that it makes it "impossible for a single racial or ethnic group to capture the state permanently by merely capturing a majority in parliament" (p. 205). This statement is, of course, logically correct – but also trivial. What is more important is to ask what the chances are that the same large party, which does not need to have the support of an absolute popular majority, will be able to win both the presidency and a legislative majority when both elections are conducted by majoritarian methods. Here the answer has to be that this is by no means certain (as is shown by the American example of majoritarian presidential and congressional elections with frequently "divided government") but that it is at least somewhat more likely than "divided government." It presents a considerable risk, especially when the combination of PR, multipartism, and coalition government offers a more attractive option.

The second reason why Horowitz likes presidentialism is that it provides "another important arena for intergroup conciliation deriving from an electoral formula based on vote pooling" (p. 205). In other words, presidentialism is advocated because of the value of the AV system. Horowitz does not say so explicitly himself, but the fact that a country as a whole is likely to be much more heterogeneous than parliamentary election districts, and hence that the supposedly moderating effect of AV is more likely to operate at the national than the district level, appears to be an important additional consideration. In any case, this argument in favor of presidentialism depends entirely on the argument in favor of AV – on which we have already reached a negative verdict.

Moreover, recent comparative studies of presidentialism have concluded that presidentialism suffers from many other problems. For instance, Juan J. Linz (1990: 54, 64–67) has emphasized the inflexibility of presidential government resulting from the fixed term of office for which he or she is elected; this makes it very difficult, and in practice often impossible, to remove a president who turns out to be completely ineffective, highly unpopular, or severely but not fatally ill. Linz (1990: 56) also points out that presidentialism is "ineluctably problematic because it operates according to the rule of 'winner-take-all' – an arrangement that tends to make democratic politics a zero-sum game, with all the potential for conflict such games portend." It should be noted that the zero-sum nature of presidential elections does not depend on the electoral system that is used, whether it be FPTP, AV, or majority-runoff. For the election of a single official, only majoritarian methods can be used, and PR is logically excluded as an option. Moreover, the presidency is the single most important political prize to be won; only one candidate can win it, and all other candidates are the losers.

Above all, presidential government entails the concentration of power, not just in one party as is the case in majoritarian parliamentary systems like the United Kingdom, but in one individual. And even when the legislature succeeds in retaining a significant share of power, presidentialism still means that *executive* power is extraordinarily concentrated. Especially because Horowitz repeatedly stresses the need, although not the sufficiency, of coalitions for intergroup accommodation, it is difficult to understand that he is willing to sacrifice this benefit for the highly doubtful advantages that presidential government can bring.

Alternatives to AV?

AV is the centerpiece of Horowitz's proposals and, as shown above, his recommendation of presidential government is closely linked with AV as the electoral system to be used for presidential elections.[6] He also examines several other electoral systems with similar moderation-inducing features – the Nigerian presidential election system with a "geographic distribution" requirement; the Lebanese formula of "ethnically mixed slates"; and the single transferable vote – but he concludes that AV is superior to all of these alternatives (pp. 184–91, 195–96). The Nigerian system, used in the 1979 and 1983 elections, requires the winning candidate to obtain the largest number of votes nationwide plus at least 25 percent of the vote in no less than two-thirds of the states. Horowitz judges this system favorably, but argues that its application to parliamentary elections raises a number of serious practical problems. He also admires the Lebanese formula of requiring all states to be ethnically mixed – thus guaranteeing a high degree of proportionality in the representation of the ethnic minorities – but he points out that it requires the official predetermination of groups. This feature, he correctly observes, makes the adoption of such a system unacceptable in South Africa.

The single transferable vote (STV) is a form of PR that differs from the more common list PR, in which parties present lists of candidates to the voters and the voters choose from among these lists (sometimes with an opportunity to express preferences for individual candidates on the lists). In STV systems, voters vote for individual candidates whom they rank order according to their preferences. In this respect, STV resembles AV, but it differs from AV in that it is not a majoritarian but a PR system and that candidates need not attain a majority to be elected but only a quota based on the number of seats at stake in a constituency. For instance, in elections to the Irish lower house – the best-known example of STV – a candidate needs only slightly more than 20 percent of the vote in order to be elected in a four-member district.[7] As in AV, second and lower preferences may be transferred, but not only from the weakest to stronger candidates but also from those candidates who have surplus votes, that is, more votes than the quota needed for election. In Australia, AV is known as the majority-preferential method and STV as the quota-preferential method – perhaps better terms because they clearly specify both the main similarity and the main difference between AV and STV.

What Horowitz likes about STV is its preferential character which gives parties and candidates an incentive to bid for second and third preferences and to make agreements with other parties and candidates to exchange reciprocally such lower preferences that may still help candidates to be elected. But, he points out, this incentive is weak "since a fraction of the total vote [is] enough to reach a candidate's quota" (p. 174). He therefore prefers AV with its "majority threshold for victory" and hence a much stronger incentive for vote pooling (p. 189).

The question now becomes: since AV is a majoritarian electoral method and hence not suitable for a divided society, is STV a more attractive form of PR than list PR? Horowitz clearly believes that this is the case: "If the choice for a divided society is between list-system PR and the single trans-ferable vote, STV is a far better choice than list-system PR" (p. 173). But STV has several serious disadvantages for plural societies:

1 Because it requires the voters to rank order the candidates, it is not a practical method for districts that elect more than about five or six representatives. Such relatively small districts can be gerrymandered, which is highly undesirable in divided societies. List PR can easily be applied in much larger districts that are immune to gerrymandering.
2 As indicated earlier, in PR systems the proportionality of the electoral outcome depends on the number of representatives per district. The small size of STV districts has an adverse effect on proportionality and minority representation, which is harmful in divided societies.
3 STV is considerably more complicated for the voters than list PR; this is only a slight problem in advanced industrial societies, but a considerable problem in developing societies with large numbers of illiterate or semi-literate voters.
4 STV requires the expression of intra-party preferences for individual candidates. As Richard S. Katz (1980: 53–58) has shown, intra-party choice negatively affects party cohesion, which in turn negatively affects interparty negotiations. In list PR, the degree of intra-party choice can vary from closed lists without any intra-party choice (as in Israel) to complete determination of the order in which candidates are elected by the voters who support the list (as in Finland). This range of options makes it possible for constitutional engineers to decide on the desired degree of intra-party choice.

These many disadvantages of STV clearly outweigh the advantage of reci-procal interparty agreements to exchange second preferences. However, Horowitz is wrong in claiming that "STV permits a measure of interethnic vote pooling that list-system PR completely precludes" (pp. 172–73). This benefit can be added to list PR by a provision that allows parties to present "connected lists," as in the Dutch and Swiss electoral laws. The gain for political parties is that for the purpose of the initial allocation of seats to party lists, a connected list will be regarded as a single list. In list PR systems treating larger parties slightly more favorably, such as the most commonly used d'Hondt system, this may give parties connecting their lists a few extra seats – and hence also an incentive to signal an accommodative attitude to each other. This "vote pooling" is probably only a marginal advantage, but for analysts like Horowitz who do consider it of major importance, it should not be a reason to prefer STV to list PR.

Conclusion

Horowitz's proposals courageously challenge the scholarly consensus favoring PR and parliamentary government for divided societies, but, however courageous, his challenge does not deserve to succeed. There is no significant difference between AV and FPTP (and the majority-runoff method) as far as incentives to compromise and the disproportionality of election results are concerned, and AV is only slightly more conducive to multipartism than FPTP. If FPTP is as harmful for divided societies – "the surest way to kill ... democracy" – as Sir Arthur Lewis (1965: 71) maintains, and as both Horowitz and I agree it is, AV is equally harmful. A presidential system of government with AV election of the president increases the danger, as does the introduction of multimember districts for parliamentary elections.

One positive lesson that has emerged from our analysis of Horowitz's proposals and his emphasis on the role that electoral systems may play in encouraging interparty cooperation is the possibility of "connected lists" in list PR systems. This is a recommendation without disadvantages, but also without anything more than a marginal advantage. For the rest, we must revert to the conclusion that list PR and parliamentary government offer the most favorable options for democracy in divided societies. They do not guarantee democratic success, of course, and democrats everywhere can only welcome suggestions to improve the chances for democracy in divided societies. But AV cannot do the trick. For South Africa and other divided societies, the alternative of AV is not a realistic alternative.

Abbreviations

AV	alternative vote (majority-preferential system).
FPTP	first-past-the-post (plurality, relative majority).
PR	proportional representation.
STV	single transferable vote (quota-preferential system).

Notes

1 This paper first appeared in *Politikon*, vol. 18, no. 2, June 1991.
2 Because I shall have to cite Horowitz's 1991 book frequently, I shall henceforth merely indicate the page numbers from which citations are taken.
3 Most democracies fit one of these two categories, but there are a few exceptions that may be regarded as intermediate between presidentialism and parliamentarism: for instance, the French Fifth Republic, which has both a "presidential" president popularly elected for a seven-year term and a "parliamentary" cabinet responsible to the National Assembly, and Switzerland, which has a collegial executive elected by the legislature (two parliamentary characteristics) but elected for a fixed four-year term (a presidential characteristic).
4 There is yet a fourth mainly majoritarian method – also often called the double-ballot or two-ballot method – used for National Assembly elections in France. It is identical with majority-runoff with regard to the first round of voting; after the first round of voting, the weakest candidates are eliminated (those with less than roughly 17 percent of the vote) and other candidates may voluntarily withdraw, but there may be as many as four or five candidates left on the second ballot; in the second round, the winner is the candidate with the most, though not necessarily a majority, of the votes.
5 The situation may be slightly more complicated, as shown by the following example: candidates A, B, C, and D have the support of 41 percent, 29 percent, 16 percent, and 14 percent of the electorate. In a majority-runoff system, A and B will be in the runoff and one of them will win. Under the usual AV method, the weakest candidates are eliminated sequentially. This means that the ballots with D as their top preference will be transferred first; if all of these ballots have C as their second preference, C will have 30 percent of the vote, B (instead of C) will be eliminated, and either A or C will be the winner. AV is therefore a more sensitive method for finding the candidate with the strongest support. Horowitz provides two definitions of AV, one of which entails the simultaneous elimination of all but the top two candidates; here the only difference with the majority-runoff method is that only one round of voting is required. What he calls "another variant of AV," with sequential elimination and vote transfers, is actually the more common – and a clearly superior – form (pp. 188–89).
6 Horowitz's third major proposal is federalism (pp. 214–26), which is perfectly compatible with PR and parliamentary government.
7 Horowitz's statement that "if there are four seats in a constituency, a candidate *could* win with about a fourth of the vote" (p. 172, emphasis added) is technically not quite correct. With as much as a fourth of the vote, victory is *guaranteed* and, in fact, surplus votes are available for transfer to other candidates.

Bibliography

Horowitz, Donald L. 1991. *A Democratic South Africa? Constitutional Engineering in a Divided Society.* Berkeley CA: University of California Press.
—— 1985. *Ethnic Groups in Conflict.* Berkeley CA: University of California Press.
Katz, Richard S. 1980. *A Theory of Parties and Electoral Systems.* Baltimore MD: Johns Hopkins University Press.
Lewis, W. Arthur. 1965. *Politics in West Africa.* London: Allen and Unwin.
Lijphart, Arend. 1991. "Constitutional Choices for New Democracies." *Journal of Democracy* vol. 2, no. 1 (winter): 72–84.

Linz, Juan J. 1990. "The Perils of Presidentialism." *Journal of Democracy* vol. 1, no. 1 (winter): 51–69.

Rae, Douglas W., 1967. *The Political Consequences of Electoral Laws.* New Haven CT: Yale University Press.

Rokkan, Stein. 1970. *Citizens, Elections, Parties: Approaches to the Comparative Study of the Processes of Development.* Oslo: Universitetsforlaget.

Sartori, Giovanni. 1968. "Political Development and Political Engineering." *Public Policy* no. 17 (John D. Montgomery and Alfred O. Hirschman, eds). Cambridge MA: Harvard University Press.

Wright, Jack F. H. 1986. "Australian Experience with Majority-Preferential and Quota-Preferential Systems." *Electoral Laws and Their Political Consequences* (Bernard Grofman and Arend Lijphart, eds). New York: Agathon Press.

14 Five exemplary devices for electoral reform

The empirical links between the electoral system dimensions on the one hand and disproportionality and multipartism on the other constitute the most important practical information for electoral engineers. In addition, however, there are a number of specific devices used in some of our electoral systems that appear to work particularly well and that deserve to be recommended as models for electoral engineers elsewhere. I shall make three major and two minor recommendations. The major recommendations are the establishment of two-tier districting for PR systems, two-tier districting of a different type for plurality and majority systems, and national legal thresholds. The two less important bits of advice concern vote transferability and *apparentement*.

Two-tier districting in PR systems

As discussed in Chapter 2 of Lijphart, *Electoral Systems and Party Systems*, several PR countries have used two-tier districting during the entire 1945–90 period (Austria, Belgium, Denmark, Germany, Iceland, Italy), but there were quite a few more who adopted it towards the end of the period (Greece, Malta, Norway, Sweden), and none that abolished it.[1] Two-tier districting is a particularly attractive way of combining the advantage of close representative-voter contact in low-magnitude districts with the greater proportionality of high-magnitude districts.

To get the full advantage of two-tier arrangements, the upper-level district should be an at-large national district and the lower-tier districts should be either single-member districts or low-magnitude multimember districts. Most of the two-tier districting systems have in fact used a single national district at the higher level; the exceptions are Austria, Belgium, and Greece. But the lower-tier districts are often still surprisingly large, especially in the different Italian electoral systems, including the Euro-election system, and in Austria since 1971, where the average magnitudes have ranged from 16.20 to 20.33 seats. Only Germany has consistently used single-member districts at the lower level. Because STV asks the voters to rank order the candidates, high-magnitude districts are impractical – which necessarily puts severe restrictions on the proportionality of the overall election result. Hence the establishment of a national upper-tier district could be of special benefit to the Irish and Maltese STV systems.[2] Malta has in fact already established such a national district but, as we have seen, only on a contingency basis and only to convert a popular majority into a parliamentary majority.[3]

National at-large districts at the upper level – especially in adjustment-seats rather than remainder-transfer systems and assuming that enough adjustment seats are available – have the added advantage that they entirely eliminate any problems of malapportionment and gerrymandering. Malapportionment has been a special problem in plurality and other single-member district systems, but it can and has occurred in PR systems, too. Malapportionment is logically precluded in electoral systems with a national upper tier of the kind described above – and, of course, also in one-tier systems with only one nationwide district (such as in Israel, the Netherlands, and most of the Euro-election systems). Gerrymandering is a particularly strong temptation in single-member districts, but it rapidly becomes more difficult with increasing district magnitude; it is safe to say that it is impractical in districts with more than five or six seats. A nationwide upper-tier district (or again a nationwide district in a single-tier system) entirely eliminates the temptation and the problem of gerrymandering.

Two-tier districting does have the disadvantage that it makes the electoral system more complex – but two-tier systems need not be extremely complex. The German, Danish, and Swedish examples show that all that is needed is a simple national translation of votes into seats, and the allocation of the adjustment seats to parties in such a way that nationwide proportionality (except for legal thresholds) is achieved.

Two-tier districting for plurality systems

Two-tier districting has been used only by PR systems and is usually only discussed as a possible reform for PR systems. However, it is an equally attractive possibility for plurality systems. As emphasized earlier, the plurality rule has a very strong tendency to produce parliamentary majorities – but such majorities are not produced with absolute certainty, and it can also happen that the second largest party wins a majority of the seats (as in Britain in 1951 and in New Zealand in 1978 and 1981). A perfect solution for these problems is to institute a national upper-tier district with sufficient adjustment seats to translate a plurality of the vote into a parliamentary majority of, say, a minimum of 55 percent of the seats.[4] The remaining seats could then be allocated proportionally to the other parties. If not just a parliamentary majority for one party, but also a strong opposition, is desired, three alternative rules could be introduced: the largest party could be limited to 55 percent of the seats (even if it has won more than 55 percent of the votes) and/or the second party could be given a minimum of, say, 35 percent of the seats with the remaining 10 percent going to the smaller parties, or the second party could be given all of the remaining 45 percent of the seats.

In the French and Australian majoritarian systems, similar rules could be introduced to guarantee that either an inter-party alliance or an unallied party, which would get, respectively, the largest number of votes nationwide or the largest number of first preferences, would receive a minimum of again 55 percent of the seats in parliament. There are obviously very many other ways to write the specific rules for two-tier districting and adjustment seats in plurality and other majoritarian systems. My main point is not to make a detailed recommendation but to point out to plurality advocates (and proponents of other majoritarian systems) that, if they regard the creation of a parliamentary majority and a clear two-party (or two-bloc) configuration in parliament as the principal objective of their favorite electoral system, two-tier districting can guarantee this result – which is merely probable but not certain without two-tier districting.

Another advantage, similar to that in PR systems but of much greater importance for majoritarian systems, is that two-tier districting with a single nationwide upper district would eliminate the problems of malapportionment and gerrymandering. Moreover, it would solve another great problem from which political parties in majoritarian systems suffer: their tendency not to make serious efforts to win in areas where they are weak, since spending a great deal of time, energy, and money in districts where they have little chance of winning tends to be regarded as a waste of scarce resources. Counting the votes nationwide and translating national vote totals into national seat totals – not proportionally but according to majoritarian rules – obviously introduces a strong incentive to try to gain as many votes as possible everywhere, including in districts that are safe for other parties.

National legal thresholds stated in terms of a percentage of the total national vote

The two basic methods of erecting barriers against the representation of small parties are high district magnitudes and legal thresholds, but there is a great variety of these legal thresholds: at the national, regional, and local levels; stated in terms of a minimum number of votes or a minimum percentage of the vote; predicated (in two-tier systems) on winning at least a seat or a particular quota or part of a quota in a lower-level district; and so on and so forth. For the analysis of this book, I converted all of these magnitudes and thresholds into effective thresholds with functionally equivalent consequences for disproportionality and multipartism.

This does not mean, however, that all these effective thresholds are equally desirable from the point of view of electoral reform. All legal thresholds as well as the thresholds implied by district magnitudes except national legal thresholds stated in terms of a percentage of the total national vote are arbitrary and haphazard because they will bar parties not just on the basis of their lack of a minimum of popular support but also on the basis of how their support and the support of other parties are distributed. Their general bias favors small parties with regionally concentrated support. The only way to avoid this problem is to measure party support nationally and to do so in terms of a particular percentage of the vote, such as 1 percent in Israel, 2 percent in Denmark, 4 percent in Norway, Sweden, and the Dutch Euro-elections, and 5 percent in the German parliamentary and Euro-elections and in the French Euro-elections.[5] Another advantage of these legal thresholds is their simplicity compared with legal thresholds that are formulated in various other ways. (Legal thresholds based on a particular minimum number rather than a minimum percentage of votes are arbitrary in a different way: they are affected by overall voter turnout.)

Such minimum national percentages can only be used in one-tier systems that use a single national district, or in two-tier districting systems. Since one-tier national districts tend to be very large, the desirability of using minimum national percentages as thresholds adds another argument in favor of two-tier districting systems.

One disadvantage is that the transition from no representation to full representation may be considered too sudden and sharp. In Germany between 1957 and 1987, for instance, a party with just below 5 percent of the national votes would not get any seats, whereas a party with exactly 5 percent or a bit more would be awarded about twenty-five seats; in principle, one extra vote could spell the winning of twenty-five seats! In most other types of systems, the threshold is a range from a lower threshold where a party may receive some representation, but is still severely underrepresented, to an upper threshold where full representation is achieved. However, if such a sliding scale is regarded as desirable, the same can be done – much less haphazardly – with national percentages. For instance, a minimum of 1 percent national support could be considered sufficient for token representation, a minimum of 3 percent for representation at half-proportionality, and a minimum of 5 percent for fully proportional representation.

Transferability of votes

STV achieves as much proportionality as it does (in spite of its relatively small district magnitude) because neither surplus votes of successful candidates nor the votes of unsuccessful candidates are completely wasted. In other words, the proportionality of STV depends on the transferability of votes from both successful and defeated candidates to candidates that are still in the running. It is the non-transferability of votes in SNTV that makes it into a semi-PR instead of a regular PR system. In practice, Japanese SNTV has operated much like STV and in districts with similar magnitudes. But an obvious improvement in the system is to make the votes transferable, that is, to change from SNTV to STV. One objection would be that, as pointed out in Chapter 2 of Lijphart, *Electoral Systems and Party Systems*, SNTV's lack of proportionality hurts the larger instead of the smaller parties. But if the object is to help the smaller parties, it would make more sense to apply STV in larger districts – or, even better, with a national upper-tier district and adjustment seats – than to retain SNTV.

A similar reform is worth considering in the Finnish list PR system, in which the voters vote for one candidate of one party and where the election of individual candidates depends on how many votes they have individually received; for instance, if a party is entitled to three seats, the three candidates with the highest individual vote totals are elected. This means that *within the party* an SNTV system is used. Here, too, using within-list STV instead of within-list SNTV would yield more accurate and less haphazard results.[6]

Apparentement

Finally, another minor recommendation concerns an advantage that is sometimes, mistakenly, attributed exclusively to STV in contrast with list PR systems: its encouragement of alliances among parties. For instance, Donald L. Horowitz observes correctly that STV encourages agreements among parties to engage in "vote pooling" by reciprocally asking their voters to cast their highest preferences for candidates of their own party but their next preferences for the candidates of the other party. Such agreements may well develop into durable alliances. Horowitz is wrong, however, when he argues that "STV permits a measure of ... vote pooling that list-system PR completely precludes."[7] As I pointed out at the end of the previous chapter, the possibility of *apparentement* may be added to any form of list PR, and it gives the linked parties the same advantage of vote pooling and hence the same incentive to form inter-party alliances. Since STV has some distinct disadvantages – such as its small district magnitude (unless alleviated by an upper-tier district) and the negative effects of intra-party competition between candidates on party cohesion – list PR with the possibility of *apparentement* may be a more attractive way of encouraging inter-party alliances than STV.

Notes

1 The higher-level seats in the multiple-tier system in Greece, used in the first elections after redemocratization, were not adjustment seats (see Chapter 2 in Lijphart, *Electoral Systems and Party Systems*); however, multiple tiers and adjustment seats were used in several pre-Second World War elections.

2 A valid objection to this proposal for Ireland, where transfers often cross party lines, is that it would count the votes of some small-party supporters twice: these votes may be transferred to, and help elect, a major-party candidate in the district, but also work for the small party itself at the national level.

3 The Maltese arrangement is reminiscent of, but different from, the Scelba Law which was in effect for the 1953 election in Italy but never became operative: it provided that any party or alliance winning more than 50 per cent of the vote would get a huge "working majority" of almost 65 per cent of the seats; see W. J. M. Mackenzie, *Free Elections: An Elementary Textbook* (London: Allen and Unwin, 1958), 91–92.

4 To my knowledge, the only previous proposal of this kind was made by Ferdinand A. Hermens, "Representation and Proportional Representation," in Arend Lijphart and Bernard Grofman (eds) *Choosing an Electoral System: Issues and Alternatives* (New York: Praeger, 1984), 29.

5 An element of arbitrariness obviously remains in that the exact percentage that is selected entails an arbitrary choice. Even when, say, an approximately 4 percent threshold is generally regarded as fair, should the threshold be exactly 4 percent, or rather 3.75 or 4.5 percent, or still another percentage?

6 This suggestion could be extended to all except closed-list PR systems if, in practice, the voters effectively decide which individual candidates are elected.

7 Donald L. Horowitz, *A Democratic South Africa: Constitutional Engineering in a Divided Society* (Berkeley CA: University of California Press, 1991), 172–73.

Part VI

Conceptual links to the fields of political behavior, foreign policy, and comparative methodology

15 Unequal participation
Democracy's unresolved dilemma

Low voter turnout is a serious democratic problem for five reasons: (1) It means unequal turnout that is systematically biased against less well-to-do citizens. (2) Unequal turnout spells unequal political influence. (3) US voter turnout is especially low, but, measured as percentage of voting-age population, it is also relatively low in most other countries. (4) Turnout in mid-term, regional, local, and supranational elections – less salient but by no means unimportant elections – tends to be especially poor. (5) Turnout appears to be declining everywhere. The problem of inequality can be solved by institutional mechanisms that maximize turnout. One option is the combination of voter-friendly registration rules, proportional representation, infrequent elections, weekend voting, and holding less salient elections concurrently with the most important national elections. The other option, which can maximize turnout by itself, is compulsory voting. Its advantages far outweigh the normative and practical objections to it.

Equality versus participation

Political equality and political participation are both basic democratic ideals. In principle, they are perfectly compatible. In practice, however, as political scientists have known for a long time, participation is highly unequal. And unequal participation spells unequal influence – a major dilemma for representative democracy in which the "democratic responsiveness [of elected officials] depends on citizen participation" (Verba 1996, 2), and a serious problem even if participation is not regarded mainly as a representational instrument but as an intrinsic democratic good (Arendt 1958; Barber 1984; Pateman 1970). Moreover, as political scientists have also known for a long time, the inequality of representation and influence are not randomly distributed but systematically biased in favor of more privileged citizens – those with higher incomes, greater wealth, and better education – and against less advantaged citizens.

This systematic class bias applies with special force to the more intensive and time-consuming forms of participation. Steven J. Rosenstone and John Mark Hansen (1993, 238) found that, in the United States, the smaller the number of participants in political activity, the greater the inequality in participation. In other countries, too, it is especially the more advantaged citizens who engage in these intensive modes of participation – both conventional activities such as working in election campaigns, contacting government officials, contributing money to parties or candidates, and working informally in the community (Verba *et al.* 1978, 286–95) and unconventional activities like participation in demonstrations, boycotts, rent and tax strikes, occupying buildings, and blocking traffic (Marsh and Kaase 1979, 100, 112–26).

Voting is less unequal than other forms of participation, but it is far from unbiased. The bias is especially strong in the United States where "no matter which form citizen participation takes, the pattern of class equality is unbroken," and where, over time, the level of voting participation and class inequality are strongly and negatively linked:

> When [relatively] many citizens turn out to vote, they are more representative of the electorate than when fewer people vote. ... Class inequality in participation was greatest in the high-turnout elections of the 1960s and least in the low-turnout elections of the 1980s. As turnout declined between 1960 and 1988, class inequalities multiplied.
> (Rosenstone and Hansen 1993, 238, 241; see also Burnham 1980; 1987)

Although generally not as strong, the same pattern of inequality can be seen in other democracies.

It is interesting to note that, at the end of the nineteenth and the beginning of the twentieth century, when universal suffrage was being adopted in many countries, political analysts tended to assume that it would be the better educated and more prosperous who would make the rational choice not to bother to vote. As a French observer put it in 1896, "The intellectual elite of the people asks itself whether it is worthwhile to cast a vote which is doomed to drown among the votes of the great crowd" (cited in Tingsten 1937, 184). But empirical studies soon showed that socioeconomic status and voting were positively, not negatively, linked. In his study of voting in the 1924 presidential election in the city of Chicago, Harold F. Gosnell (1927, 98) found that turnout increased with economic status and that "the more schooling the individual has the more likely he [or she] is to register and vote in presidential elections." In an article in the *American Political Science Review* two years earlier, the same clear pattern was reported on the basis of a voting study in the small Ohio town of Delaware (Arneson 1925). Herbert Tingsten (1937, 155) reviewed a large number of voting studies in Switzerland, Germany, Denmark, Austria, the United States, and Sweden, conducted between 1907 and 1933, and formulated "the general rule that the voting frequency rises with rising social standard."

Can the democratic dilemma of unequal participation be resolved? With the possible exception of financial contributions,[1] little can be done to equalize participation in the more intensive activities; mobilizing more people to participate appears to be of little help because, as Verba (1996, 7) laments, "for most activity, the forces of mobilization bring in the same people who would be active spontaneously." But a partial solution to the dilemma is to make the most basic form of participation, namely voting, as equal as possible – especially important as a "democratic counterweight" (Teixeira 1992, 4) to other forms of participation which are bound to remain unequal. And the obvious way to make voting more equal is to maximize voting turnout. The democratic goal should be not just universal *suffrage* but universal or near-universal *turnout* – in line with Tingsten's (1937, 230) "law of dispersion," which states that the probability of differences in voting turnout "is smaller the higher the general participation is. ... The chances of dispersion ... are inversely proportional to the electoral participation."[2]

On the basis of studies from the 1930s (Gosnell 1930; Tingsten 1937) to the 1980s and 1990s (Franklin 1996; Franklin *et al.* 1996; Jackman 1987; Jackman and Miller 1995; Powell 1980; 1986), we know a great deal about the institutional mechanisms that can increase turnout, such as user-friendly registration rules, proportional election formulas, relatively infrequent elections, weekend voting, and compulsory voting. And all of these studies, from the 1930s on, have found that compulsory voting is a particularly effective method to achieve high turnout – in spite of generally low penalties (comparable to a fine for parking violations), lax enforcement (more lenient than the enforcement of parking rules), and the secrecy of the ballot which means that an actual vote cannot be compelled in the first place.

Compulsory "voting" is therefore a misnomer: All that can be required in practice is attendance at the polls; hence the least intrusive, but sufficient, form of compulsory voting is the requirement to appear at the polling station on election day without any further duty to mark a ballot or even to accept a ballot. This was the rule in the Netherlands from 1917 until the abolition of compulsory voting in 1970 (Adviescommissie Opkomstplicht 1967; Irwin 1974, 313).[3] More democracies have used the compulsory vote than is commonly recognized: Australia, Italy, Greece, Belgium, the Netherlands, Luxembourg, Austria (several *Länder*), Switzerland (a few cantons), and most Latin American countries (Fernández Baeza forthcoming; Fornos 1996; Hirczy 1994; Ochoa 1987, 866–67).[4]

In addition to being an effective enhancer of turnout in practice, the basic logic of compulsory voting as an egalitarian instrument is also strong. As Sidney Verba *et al.* (1978, 6) argue, to make political participation perfectly equal, one needs both a "ceiling" – a prescribed maximum – and a "floor" – a prescribed minimum – for activities of various kinds. For voting participation this means that

> each citizen is allowed one and only one vote. ... Such a *ceiling* goes a long way toward equalizing political participation, but it does not eliminate the possibility that citizens will differ in their use of the

franchise. Turnout is usually related to socioeconomic status. Thus it may be necessary to place *a floor* under political activity as well, *to make it compulsory.* (emphasis added)

Unequal turnout and unequal influence

Before turning to the various institutional methods for raising turnout, including compulsory voting, let me first review the empirical evidence and theoretical arguments concerning the problems of low voter turnout and class bias. There are several serious reasons why democrats should worry about these problems.

First of all, as already indicated, low voter turnout means unequal and socioeconomically biased turnout. This pattern is so clear, strong, and well known in the United States that it does not need to be belabored further. Compared with the United States, the class bias in other democracies tends to be weaker – leading some analysts to regard it as an almost unique American phenomenon (Abramson 1995, 918; Piven and Cloward 1988a, 117–19). There is, however, abundant evidence of the same class bias, albeit usually not as strong, in other democracies. In Switzerland, the other major example of a Western democracy with low levels of turnout, the participation gap between the least and most highly educated citizens in the March 1991 referendum was 37 percentage points; Wolf Linder (1994, 95–96) calls this a "typical profile of a popular vote," and concludes that "especially when participation is low, the choir of Swiss direct democracy sings in upper-or middle-class tones." In survey data covering referenda between 1981 and 1991, the gap was almost 25 percentage points (Mottier 1993, 134). The class bias in turnout also affects Swiss parliamentary elections (Farago 1996, 11–12; Sidjanski 1983, 107).

In countries with higher turnout, as expected, the link between socioeconomic status and turnout tends to be less strong, often not strong enough to be statistically significant and sometimes even negative. However, G. Bingham Powell, Jr. (1986, 27–28) combined data for seven European nations and Canada and found a consistent effect of the level of education on turnout: a difference of 10 percentage points between the lowest and highest of five education levels and a consistent increase of 2 to 3 percentage points at each higher level in the averages of eight nations. A similar study of six Central American countries also reports mixed results, but these averages show similar turnout increases at higher educational levels and a difference of 12 percentage points between the highest and lowest levels, with the "more dramatic differences ... found in countries with lower turnout rates" (Seligson *et al.* 1995, 166–71).

Richard Topf (1995, 48–49), who surveys data from sixteen European countries in six periods since 1960, finds several instances in which the least educated cohorts actually have slightly higher turnouts than the most highly educated – contrary to the expected pattern – and concludes that there is "no generalized education effect for voting." His own figures, however, show that the instances of the expected positive link between educational level and turnout are four times more numerous than the deviant instances; without the countries with compulsory voting the ratio is almost five to one. Similarly, a study of the 1989 European Parliament elections in the twelve member countries finds several negative correlations between levels of education, income, and social class on the one hand and voting turnout on the other, but positive correlations prevail by a better than two-to-one ratio; without the four countries with compulsory voting, the ratio is higher than three to one (Oppenhuis 1995, 186–90). The same expected, but not huge, class bias is also the usual finding in Russell B. Dalton's (1996, 57–58) comparative analysis of the United Kingdom, France, and Germany, as well as in single-country studies of these countries plus Spain and the Netherlands (Denters 1995; Denver 1995; Font and Virós 1995; Justel 1995; Särlvik and Crewe 1983, 79; Schultze 1995).

A slight class bias sometimes still turns up even in countries with compulsory voting, and hence high turnout. For instance, even in Australia where about 95 percent of the registered voters usually vote, Ian McAllister (1986) finds that slightly higher turnouts give a perceptible boost to the Labor Party and that slightly lower turnouts benefit the parties of the right; he also estimates that the hypothetical abolition of compulsory voting would strengthen this pattern and would give the political right "an inbuilt advantage." In the well known graph in the first chapter of their *Participation and Political Equality*, Verba *et al.* (1978, 7) strikingly illustrate the increase in class bias that resulted from the abolition of compulsory voting in the Netherlands in 1970. For five educational groups, the reported turnout rates varied between 66 and 87 percent. Compared with these unequal turnouts, the last parliamentary election that was still conducted under compulsory voting, in 1967, showed turnouts for all groups above 90 percent – but there was still a slight class bias: turnouts increased gradually from 93 percent in the lowest educational group to 98 and 97 percent in the two groups with the most education.

In Belgium, surveys have found little or no relationship between educational level and voting participation. However, they have also discovered that, if compulsory voting were abolished, turnout would drop from well over 90 percent to about 60 percent, resulting in a strong class bias from which the more conservative parties would benefit (Ackaert and De Winter 1993, 77–79; 1996; De Winter and Ackaert 1994, 87–89). Similarly, Venezuela had high turnouts in its elections under compulsory voting until the mid-1980s and, like Belgium, relatively little class bias in turnout. Here, too, however, a survey found that, under voluntary voting, turnout would decline dramatically, to 48 percent, and that "electoral demobilization would introduce socioeconomic distinctions in voting turnout" (Baloyra and Martz 1979, 71; see also Molina Vega 1991).

In the early 1960s, two authoritative volumes summarized the most important findings of political scientists and sociologists. On the subject of voter turnout, Seymour Martin Lipset (1960, 182) stated that "patterns of voting participation are strikingly the same in various countries: Germany, Sweden, America, Norway, Finland, and many others for which we have data. ... The better educated [vote] more than the less educated ... higher-status persons, more than lower." Similarly, one of the findings in Bernard Berelson and Gary A. Steiner's (1964, 423) *Inventory of Scientific Findings* was that "the higher a person's socioeconomic and educational level – especially the latter – the higher his [or her] political interest, participation, and voting turnout." More than three decades later, these conclusions are clearly still valid.[5]

The second reason why low and unequal voting turnout should be a serious concern is that who votes, and who doesn't, has important consequences for who gets elected and for the content of public policies. What is the significance, V. O. Key (1949, 527) asked, of group differences in voting and nonvoting? And he answered: "The blunt truth is that politicians and officials are under no compulsion to pay much heed to classes and groups of citizens that do not vote." More recently, Walter Dean Burnham (1987, 99) emphasized again that "the old saw remains profoundly true: if you don't vote, you don't count." Voice and exit are often alternative ways of exerting influence (Hirschman 1970), but with regard to voting the exit option spells no influence; only voice can have an effect.

In addition to the clear connection between socioeconomic status and turnout, there are two further important links. One is the clear nexus between socioeconomic status on the one hand and party choice and the outcome of elections on the other; in Lipset's (1960, 220) famous formulation, elections are "the expression of the democratic class struggle." The second crucial link is that between types of parties, especially progressive versus conservative parties, and the policies that these parties pursue when they are in power. There is an extensive comparative literature about welfare, redistribution, full employment, social security, and overall government spending policies that is unanimous in its conclusion that political parties do matter (Blais *et al.* 1996; Castles 1982; Castles and McKinlay 1979; King 1981; Klingemann *et al.* 1994; Tufte 1978). Douglas A. Hibbs' (1977, 1467) conclusion represents the broad consensus very well: "Governments pursue ... policies broadly in accordance with the objective economic interests and subjective preferences of their class-defined core political constituencies."

Skeptics have raised two critical questions about the strength of the above links. One has to do with the supposed decline in class voting. Even Lipset (1960, 220) who originally proclaimed that "on a world scale, the principal generalization which can be made is that parties are primarily based on either the lower classes or the middle and upper classes," retreated from this conclusion in the updated version of *Political Man* (Lipset 1981, 503): on the basis of American, British, German, and Swedish data, he concluded that his original generalization "has become less valid" (see also Dogan 1995; Franklin 1992). Other analysts have argued, however, that class voting is changing – especially from a dichotomous working- versus middle-class contrast to more complex and multifaceted class differences – instead of declining (Andersen 1984; Hout *et al.* 1995; Manza *et al.* 1995). These authors also emphasize, and the supporters of the thesis of the decline in class voting admit, that this decline does not mean that class voting has vanished. This is also the conclusion of a study of class voting in twenty democracies from 1945 to 1990 by Paul Nieuwbeerta (1995, esp. 46–51). He finds a "substantial decline" in class voting in many countries, but the decline is strong enough to be statistically significant in only about half of his countries. In about a third of the countries he finds an opposite trend or no trend. Most important, in none of the countries has class voting disappeared altogether.

The second doubt about the nexus between social class, voting turnout, party choice, and public policy is raised by studies that show nonvoters not to be different from voters, especially in the United States, regarding policy preferences and candidate and party preferences. Ruy A.Teixeira (1992, 100) sums up the conclusions of a large number of studies in the following words: They

> all tell a similar story: nonvoters are somewhat more liberal than voters on policy issues concerning the economic role of government ... and all agree that the magnitude of these differences is not large and that therefore the absence of nonvoters from the voting pool probably has little immediate effect on the policy output of government.

(See also Gant and Lyons 1993, Shaffer 1982, and, for a similar British study, Studlar and Welch 1986.)[6] For election outcomes, the story is basically the same. For instance, if all nonvoters had voted in the 1980 presidential election, Reagan would have received only 2 percent fewer votes and would still have won the election; in 1984 and 1988, winners Reagan and Bush would actually have received a *higher* vote percentage (Bennett and Resnick 1990, 795; see also Petrocik 1987).

There are, however, several problems with Teixeira's (1992, 96–97) conclusion, based on the above studies, that "most electoral outcomes are not determined in any meaningful sense by turnout." Nonvoters who are asked their opinions on policy and partisan preferences in surveys are typically citizens who have not given these questions much thought, who have not been politically mobilized, and who, in terms of social class, have not developed class consciousness. It is highly likely that, if they were mobilized to vote, their votes would be quite different from their responses in opinion polls. The usual surveys, while "more representative than any of the modes of citizen activity" and hence "rigorously egalitarian" (Verba 1996, 3–4), fall short of discovering people's true opinions and preferences; only James S. Fishkin's (1991, 1995) "deliberative opinion polls" and Robert A. Dahl's (1989, 340; 1970, 149–50) randomly selected "minipopulus" of about one thousand citizens, who would meet and deliberate for an extended period of time, combine representativeness with well formed policy and political preferences.[7]

Furthermore, the few studies that attempt the difficult task of directly testing the link between voter turnout, on the one hand, and tax and welfare policies, on the other, all find compelling evidence that unequal voting participation is associated with policies that favor privileged voters over underprivileged nonvoters (Hicks and Swank 1992; Hill and Leighley 1992; Leighley 1995, 195–96; Mebane 1994). Finally, perhaps the most persuasive evidence is the strong and direct link between turnout and support for left-of-center parties found by Alexander Pacek and Benjamin Radcliff (1995). They analyzed all national elections in nineteen industrial democracies from 1950 to 1990 and found that, as hypothesized, the vote for left parties varied directly with turnout: The left share of the total vote increases by almost one third of a percentage point for every percentage point increase in turnout.[8] In short, the overall weight of the evidence strongly supports the view that who votes and how people vote matter a great deal. Indeed, any other conclusion would be extremely damaging for the very concept of representative democracy.

Low and declining voter turnout

Additional reasons for serious worry are the low levels of electoral participation in almost all democracies – even in national elections but especially in lower-level elections – and the downward trend in turnout in most countries. That the United States ranks near the bottom of voting participation in comparative perspective is well known, and this high degree of nonvoting is often contrasted with "nonvoting levels as low as 5 percent in other democracies" (Teixeira 1992, 21). Voter turnout, however, tends to be lower in other countries than is commonly recognized. Powell's (1980, 6–8) turnout figures for thirty democracies in the 1960s and 1970s – all of the democratic countries with populations over 1 million during this period – show that not a single country had a turnout rate as high as 95 percent. The highest percentage is that of Italy, a country with compulsory voting – 94 percent; the lowest percentage is that of Switzerland – 53 percent. And the median turnout rate is only 76 percent.

The main reason for the exaggeration of voter turnout in other democracies is that their turnout rates are usually calculated as percentages of registered voters rather than percentage of voting-age population. For the United States, the latter figure is almost always used since the former would be extremely misleading, given the large numbers of eligible voters who are not registered. For most other democracies, which have automatic registration or where it is the government's responsibility to register voters, turnout percentages based on registered voters are more nearly correct – but far from completely accurate: Voter registers everywhere may fail to include all eligible voters or may include names of voters who have moved or died. Therefore, the only proper turnout percentages both in absolute terms and for comparative purposes are those based on voting-age populations.[9] Powell's percentages, cited above, are the optimally accurate figures based on voting-age population. The median of only 76 percent that he reports means that in half of the countries – including most of the most populous countries such as India, Japan, Britain, France, and, of course, the United States – fewer than about three out of every four citizens turn out to vote.[10]

All of the unimpressive turnout figures that I have mentioned so far are still deceptively favorable because they are the turnout percentages in the most salient national elections and hence the elections with the highest turnout: national parliamentary elections in parliamentary systems and presidential elections in presidential and semi-presidential systems. The vast majority of elections, however, are elections with lower salience – local, state, provincial, and off-year congressional elections, as well as the elections to the European Parliament – which are characterized by considerably lower turnout. The US off-year election turnout has only been around 35 percent, and turnout in local elections only about 25 percent in recent years (Ansolabehere and Iyengar 1995, 145–46; Teixeira 1992, 7). When lower-level elections are on the same ballot as presidential elections, voting participation improves, but there also tends to be considerable roll-off, that is, voters casting their votes for president but not for less prestigious offices. Moreover, as turnout decreases, roll-off tends to increase (Burnham 1965, 13–14), and roll-off, like nonvoting, is inversely correlated with socioeconomic status (Darcy and Schneider 1989, 360–62).[11]

In other democracies, too, lower-level elections attract fewer voters than national elections. In his classic *Why Europe Votes*, Gosnell (1930, 142–76) devoted an entire chapter to local elections in European countries and found that, in the 1920s, Europeans were more faithful voters than Americans but considerably less so in lower-level than in national elections. Average turnout rates in local elections in France and Spain, in German state elections, and in elections to the parliament of autonomous Catalonia in the 1980s and 1990s have been between 60 and 70 percent, but these averages conceal much lower turnouts in particular states and cities, such as the 54.8 percent turnout in the German state of Sachsen-Anhalt in 1994 and the 45.6 percent turnout in the French city of Saint-Martin-d'Hères in 1983 (Botella 1994; Font and Virós 1995; Hoffmann-Martinot 1994; López Nieto 1994; Schultze 1995). Average turnout rates in the English-speaking democracies tend to be much lower still: 53 percent in New Zealand; 40 percent in Great Britain, but well below 40 percent in the major urban areas; 33 percent in Canada; and about 35 percent in Australia, where at the local level there is no compulsory voting (Denver 1995; Goldsmith and Newton 1986, 145–47; Miller 1994; Rallings and Thrasher 1990). In the 1994 European Parliament elections, the average turnout in the twelve member countries was 58.3 percent but in three countries only slightly more than a third of the registered voters participated: 36.4 percent in the United Kingdom and 35.6 percent in the Netherlands and Portugal (Smith 1995, 210). Turnout in the first European Parliament election in newly admitted Sweden in 1995 was a mere 41.6 percent (Widfeldt 1996).

All of these elections have been called "second-order elections" in which less is at stake than who will control national executive power (Reif and Schmitt 1980). But while second-order elections may be less important elections, they are not entirely unimportant, even in unitary and centralized systems of government. In decentralized and federal systems such as the United States and Germany, state elections are obviously of great importance and, similarly, congressional elections should rank close to presidential ones in democracies in which the executive and legislature are coequal branches of the government. From the perspective of rational choice, it is to be expected that carefully reasoning voters will vote less in most second-order than in first-order elections, but the magnitude of the difference between the two is more difficult to explain (Feeley 1974, 241). In any case, when considering the general problem of low voter turnout, second-order elections with their often striking lower voter participation cannot be ignored.

Finally, voter turnout is not only low but also declining in most countries. In the United States, participation in presidential elections has declined from 60–65 percent in the 1950s and 1960s to 50–55 percent in the 1980s and 1990s; in Teixeira's (1992, 6) words, "a *low* turnout society ... has been turned into an *even lower* turnout society." In other industrialized democracies, the decline is also unmistakable although not as dramatic. Average turnout in twenty of these countries declined from 83 percent in the 1950s to 78 percent in the 1990s, with seventeen countries showing a lower and only three a higher turnout in the latter period (Dalton 1996, 44–45). For eighteen industrialized democracies in the shorter time span from the 1960s to the 1980s – but based on more accurate turnout rates as percentages of voting-age population – average turnout went down from 80 to 78 percent, with ten countries showing lower, four higher, and four about the same turnout in the most recent period (Jackman 1987, 420; Jackman and Miller 1995, 485). For the European democracies, the *Beliefs in Government* study reports "a decline in average participation levels over the postwar period as a whole" (Borg 1995, 441) and a drop from 85 percent in 1960–64 to 80 percent in 1985–89 (Topf 1995, 40–41; see also Flickinger and Studlar 1992).[12] In Switzerland, the European country with a long record of poor voter participation, the 42.3 percent turnout in 1995 was a new all-time low in legislative elections (Farago 1996, 11).

The pattern is similar for second-order elections. Rainer-Olaf Schultze (1995, 91–94) reports declining turnout in Germany, especially since the mid-1980s, at all four levels: local, state, national, and European Parliament elections. For all of the member countries, average turnout in the elections to the European Parliament has gone down steadily from 65.9 percent in the first elections held in 1979 to 63.8 percent, 62.8 percent, and 58.3 percent in the next three elections (Smith 1995, 210).[13]

These drops in turnout are not as drastic as in the United States, but they are especially disturbing because they have occurred in spite of dramatic increases in levels of education and economic well-being and the rise of postmaterialist values (Inglehart 1990) in all industrialized countries – factors that, at the individual level, are known to increase rather than decrease the probability of voting. Moreover, the decline in turnout has been accompanied by a "participatory revolution" in Western Europe with regard to more intensive forms of political participation in which class bias is very strong; hence, as Max Kaase (1996, 36) points out, serious concerns about political equality arise because of the skewed nature of the "active partial publics."

Frances Fox Piven and Richard A. Cloward (1988b, 869) have argued that, in the United States, "restrictive registration procedures are the functional equivalents of earlier property and literacy qualifications." Similarly, it can be argued that the logical and empirical link between low voter turnout and unequal turnout is the functional equivalent of such discriminatory qualifications – as well as the functional equivalent of two earlier proposals and practices that systematically give well-to-do and educated citizens greater voting rights than their less privileged co-citizens. One is Aristotle's suggestion that "equal blocks of property carry equal weights, though the number of persons in each block is different" (Barker 1958, 262); a version of this was Prussia's three-class system from 1849 to 1918 which entailed having each of the three classes elect one third of the deputies, but the top class consisted of only 4 percent of the voters, the middle class 16 percent, and the bottom class 80 percent (Urwin 1974, 116). The other is Mill's ([1861] 1958, 138) proposal of plural voting: "two or more votes might be allowed" on the basis of occupational status and educational qualifications. Such a system, with a maximum of three votes per voter, operated in Belgium from 1893 to 1919 (Gosnell 1930, 98–99).

All of these discriminatory rules are now universally rejected as undemocratic. Why then do many democrats tolerate the systematic pattern of low and unequal turnout that is the functional equivalent of such rules?

Institutional remedies

Voting participation depends on many factors, including the salience of the issues – note, for instance, the 93.5 percent turnout in Quebec's 1995 referendum on independence (Kennedy 1996) and the high turnouts in the final years of the Weimar Republic – the attractiveness of parties and candidates, and political culture and attitudes. When we look for remedies for nonvoting, however, institutional factors are especially important. For one thing, when we compare turnout variations among countries and across social characteristics of individuals, "the most striking message is that turnout varies much more from country to country than it does between different types of individuals" (Franklin 1996, 217–18), which suggests very strongly that in order to expand voting in a country with low turnout it is much more promising to improve the institutional context than to raise levels of education and political interest. For another, rules and institutions are, at least in principle, more amenable to manipulation than individual attitudes. Fortunately, we know a great deal about the effect of institutions on turnout, especially thanks to the impressive early studies by Harold F. Gosnell (1930) and Herbert Tingsten (1937) and the outstanding recent work of G. Bingham Powell (1986), Robert W. Jackman (1987), and Mark N. Franklin (1996).

In the United States, burdensome registration requirements have long been recognized as a major institutional deterrent to voting (Gosnell 1927, 1930, 203–5; Rosenstone and Hansen 1993, 230). Voting presents a problem of collective action that becomes more serious as the costs increase, and the costs of registration are often higher than the cost of voting itself (Wolfinger 1994, 81–83). Raymond E. Wolfinger and Steven J. Rosenstone (1980, 73, 88) found that turnout would increase by 9.1 percentage points if all states adopted completely liberalized registration rules, but they also argued that turnout could be raised substantially more by a European-style system in which registration is automatic or the government's responsibility. On the basis of his comparative analysis, Powell (1986, 36) concludes that automatic registration could boost turnout by up to 14 percentage points. Comparisons between nationwide turnout and turnout in the few states with either no registration requirement at all or same-day and same-place registration – that is, the possibility of registering at the polls on election day – show differences of about 15 percentage points (Abramson 1995, 916; Wolfinger *et al.* 1990, 564–65). Other estimates have been somewhat lower; for instance, Burnham's (1987, 108) is about 10 percent. After an extensive review of all of the evidence, Teixeira (1992, 122) concludes that the increase would be somewhere between 8 and 15 percentage points.

Fifteen percentage points appears to be the maximum benefit that thorough registration reform could achieve, and it would be only a partial remedy that would still leave the United States well below the median turnout of 76 percent in contemporary democracies. Also, it is unclear how much registration reform would contribute to turnout in off-year, state, local, and primary elections; even if the increase were as much as 15 percentage points in these elections, it would still leave turnout well below 50 percent in most. Registration reform is irrelevant for most other Western democracies where registration is not a big problem.

Another important institutional mechanism that affects turnout is the electoral system. Proportional representation (PR) tends to stimulate voter participation by giving the voters more choices and by eliminating the problem of wasted votes – votes cast for losing candidates or for candidates that win with big majorities – from which systems using single-member districts suffer; this makes it more attractive for individuals to cast their votes and for parties to mobilize voters even in areas of the country in which they are weak. This phenomenon was already highlighted by both Gosnell (1930, 201–3) and Tingsten (1937, 223–25). Recent comparative studies have estimated that the turnout boost from PR is somewhere between 9 and 12 percent (Blais and Carty 1990, 174; Burnham 1987, 106–7; Franklin 1996, 226; Lijphart 1994, 5–7; see also Amy 1993, 140–52).[14]

These estimates of PR's beneficial effect are all based on the most salient national elections. In contrast, in second-order elections using PR, the level of voter participation tends to be much less impressive. The European Parliament elections provide a striking example: Turnouts have been low even though eleven of the twelve member countries choose their representatives by PR. In the 1995 provincial elections, by PR, in the Netherlands, turnout was only 50 percent. A recent American example is the 1996 New York City school board election, one of the rare cases of PR in the United States: turnout was a mere 5 percent (Steinberg 1996).

The frequency of elections has a strongly negative influence on turnout. Boyd (1981, 1986, 1989) has convincingly demonstrated this effect for the United States, in which he estimates that, on average, voters are asked to come to the polls between two and three times each year – much more often than in all except one other democracy. The one country with even more frequent dates on which elections and referenda are conducted – about six or seven times per year – is Switzerland (Farago 1995, 121; Franklin 1996, 225, 234; Sidjanski 1983, 109). The United States and Switzerland are also the two Western democracies with by far the lowest levels of turnout. The most plausible explanation is voter fatigue (Jackman and Miller 1995, 482–83) or, in terms of rational choice, the fact that frequent elections increase the cost of voting. If frequent elections depress turnout in first-order elections, it is logical to expect that they hurt turnout in second-order elections even more. This may be the explanation for the wide gap in the United States between the first-order presidential elections, on the one hand, and the second-order – but in a system of separation and division of powers still very important – midterm congressional as well as state executive and legislative elections on the other.

Rational-choice theory also leads us to expect that concurrent elections will increase turnout since the benefit of voting now increases while the cost remains almost the same (Aldrich 1993, 261; Wolfinger 1994, 76–78). In particular, second-order elections should have better turnout when combined with first-order elections. The available evidence shows this hypothesis to be correct. The European Parliament elections in Portugal and Ireland held at the same time as national parliamentary elections, in 1987 and 1989, respectively, yielded turnouts more than 20 percent higher than the preceding and/or next separate European Parliament election in these countries (Niedermayer 1990, 47–48). The 1979 local elections in England and Wales were conducted simultaneously with House of Commons elections, and, as a result, "local election turnout soared up to parliamentary levels" (Miller 1994, 69). Combining first-order and second-order elections may even help the former to some extent: In the United States, the inclusion of a gubernatorial race can increase turnout in presidential elections by about 6 percentage points (Boyd 1989, 735–36).

In contrast, the daunting accumulation of very many elections and referendum questions on one long ballot – a phenomenon unique to the United States with its extremely large number of elective offices and primary elections (Crewe 1981, 225–32) – is generally regarded as a deterrent to turnout, although the benefits of voting would appear to keep increasing with increasing ballot length. Gosnell (1930, 186, 209) emphasizes "the old lesson of the need for a shorter ballot," and comments that European voters are "not given an impossible task to perform on election day. [They are] not presented with a huge ... ballot as are the voters in many of the American states."

Minor measures to facilitate voting, such as the availability of mail ballots and the scheduling of elections on weekends instead of weekdays, can also be a small but distinct stimulus to turnout. On the basis of a multivariate analysis of turnout in twenty-nine countries, Franklin (1996, 226–30) finds that, other factors being equal, weekend voting increases turnout by 5 to 6 percentage points and that mail ballots are worth another 4 percent in first-order elections. In the second-order European Parliament elections, weekend voting adds more than 9 percentage points to turnout.

Compulsory voting

The strongest of all the institutional factors is compulsory voting, particularly with regard to second-order elections; but let us first take a look at the most salient national elections. Gosnell (1930, 184) took special pains to examine two of the European cases of compulsory voting, and his conclusion was: "There is no doubt that compulsory voting has had a sustained stimulating effect upon voting in Belgium and in the Swiss cantons where it is used. In Belgium it has maintained the highest voting records found in Europe." Tingsten (1937, 205) gathered evidence from several additional countries – Austria, Bulgaria, Czecho-Slovakia, the Netherlands, Romania, and Australia – and, like Gosnell, he concluded

> that popular participation in elections is very high in countries with compulsory voting, that the introduction of compulsory voting everywhere has been accompanied by a remarkable rise in participation, and

that in countries where compulsory voting has been enacted in certain regions, these display more intense participation than the regions without compulsory voting.

In comparative multivariate analyses, compulsory voting has been found to raise turnout by 7 to 16 percentage points. Powell (1980, 9–10) finds a difference of about 10 percent in his study of thirty democracies. The figures reported by Jackman (1987, 412, 415–16) and Jackman and Miller (1995, 474) for the industrialized democracies in three successive decades from 1960 to 1990 are 15.0, 13.1, and 12.2 percent. Franklin's (1996, 227) finding of a 7.3 percentage point difference is the lowest that has been reported. In a study of Latin American turnout in the 1980s and early 1990s, replicating Jackman's analysis, Carolina A. Fornos (1996, 34–35) finds that compulsory voting boosted turnout by 11.4 percentage points in presidential elections and 16.5 percentage points in congressional elections.[15]

The most persuasive results are in Wolfgang Hirczy's (1994) systematic study of within-country differences – both variations over time and variations among different areas in the same country – in Australia, Austria, and the Netherlands. He concludes, in line with previous findings, that compulsory voting effectively and consistently raises turnout. His more striking conclusion, however, is that the increase in turnout depends a great deal on the baseline of participation *without* compulsory voting. Mean turnout in all three countries under mandatory voting was higher than 90 percent, but the increment due to mandatory voting in Austria was only about 3 percentage points, because turnout even under conditions of voluntary voting was well above 90 percent. In the Netherlands, the abolition of compulsory voting in 1970 caused a larger drop of about 10 percentage points to the average voluntary-voting baseline of around 84 percent. And in Australia, the mean turnout difference was even larger – more than 28 percent – because the average turnout under voluntary voting before 1925 was only about 62 percent.

Brazil and Venezuela are additional examples of low baselines and hence high turnout boosts due to compulsory voting. Average official turnout in Venezuela from 1958 to 1988 was 90.2 percent but, after the abolition of mandatory voting in 1993, turnout fell to 60.2 percent (Molina Vega 1995, 164).[16] A public opinion poll in Brazil in 1990 found that, under hypothetical conditions of voluntary voting, turnout would undergo a similar drop of about 30 percentage points from the 85 percent turnout in that year's election to 55 percent (Power and Roberts 1995, 796, 819). These examples lend further support to Hirczy's (1994, 74) observation that "the impact of mandatory voting laws should be particularly pronounced in low-turnout environments."

Hirczy's conclusion also has special significance for second-order elections because these tend to be elections with low turnout. Here, indeed, compulsory voting is strikingly effective. Franklin's (1996, 227, 230) finding of a modest 7.3 percent boost from compulsory voting in national elections, mentioned above, contrasts with a 26.1 percent increase in turnout in a similar multivariate analysis of the 1989 European Parliament elections. In all four of the European Parliament elections from 1979 to 1994, the mean turnout was 84.2 percent in the countries with compulsory voting but only 46.4 percent in those with voluntary voting – a difference of almost 38 percentage points (based on data in Smith 1995, 210).

Gosnell (1930, 155) was greatly impressed with the level of turnout in provincial and local elections in Belgium in the 1920s, which was practically the same, well above 90 percent, as in the national elections: "The device of compulsory voting in Belgium overcame that indifference toward local elections which is so marked in countries with a free voting system." The same pattern can still be seen today: Belgian local elections from 1976 to 1994 had an average turnout of 93.7 percent – almost identical with the average 93.8 percent turnout in parliamentary elections during this period (based on data in Ackaert and De Winter 1996). In Italy from 1968 to 1994, mean turnout in local elections was 84.4 percent compared with 86.2 percent in national parliamentary elections – a difference of less than 2 percentage points (Corbetta and Parisi 1995, 171). In Dutch provincial and municipal elections from 1946 until the abandonment of mandatory voting in 1970, turnout was almost always well above 90 percent, often close to 95 percent, and usually only a bit lower than that in parliamentary elections. In 1970, turnout dropped to 68.1 percent in provincial and 67.2 percent in municipal elections. After a brief improvement in turnout levels later in the 1970s, they declined even further. The 1994 and 1995 figures are 65.3 percent in municipal, 50 percent in provincial, and 35.6 percent in European elections.[17]

Students of compulsory voting have not only been impressed but also often surprised by the strong effect of the obligation to vote, especially in view of the generally low penalties for noncompliance and generally lax enforcement: "Even when the penalties for non-voting are very small, and where law and practice prescribe very wide acceptance of excuses, the growth of the poll has been perceptible" (Tingsten 1937, 205–6). In rational-choice terms, however, this phenomenon can be explained easily. Turnout is a problem of collective action, but an unusual one, because turnout entails both low costs and low benefits (Aldrich 1993); this means that the inducement of compulsory voting, small as it is, can still neutralize a large part of the cost of voting.[18]

Rational-choice theory also provides the basic normative justification for compulsory voting. The general remedy for problems of collective action is to counteract free riding by means of legal sanctions and enforcement. For the collective-action problem of turnout, this means that citizens should not be allowed to be free riders – that is, that they should be obligated to turn out to vote (Feeley 1974; Wertheimer 1975).

Compulsory voting is not the only method for assuring high voter turnout. If all the other institutional variables are favorable – automatic registration, a highly proportional electoral system, infrequent elections, and weekend voting – and in a highly politicized environment, it may be possible to have near-universal turnout without compulsory voting, as Hirczy (1995) has shown for the case of Malta. Second-order elections can have high turnout if they are conducted concurrently with first-order elections in which all the major institutional mechanisms are conducive to turnout. Compulsory voting is the only institutional mechanism, however, that can assure high turnout virtually by itself.

Voting as a duty: pros and cons

The most important argument in favor of compulsory voting is its contribution to high and relatively equal voter turnout. Three additional, more speculative, advantages of compulsory voting, however, are worth mentioning. One is that the increase in voting participation may stimulate stronger participation and interest in other political activities: "People who participate in politics in one way are likely to do so in another" (Berelson and Steiner 1964, 422). Considerable evidence exists of a spillover effect from participation in the workplace, churches, and voluntary organizations to political participation (Almond and Verba 1963, 300–374; Greenberg 1986; Lafferty 1989; Peterson 1992; Sobel 1993; Verba *et al.* 1995, 304–68; but see also Greenberg *et al.* 1996; Schweizer 1995).

Second, compulsory voting may have the beneficial effect of reducing the role of money in politics. When almost everybody votes, no large campaign funds are needed to goad voters to the polls, and, in Gosnell's (1930, 185) words, "elections are therefore less costly, more honest, and more representative." Third, mandatory voting may discourage attack advertising – and hence may lessen the cynicism and distrust that it engenders. Stephen Ansolabehere and Shanto Iyengar (1995) have found that attack ads work mainly by selectively depressing turnout among those not likely to vote for the attacker. When almost everybody votes, attack tactics lose most of their lure.[19]

Having emphasized the advantages of compulsory voting so far, I must also deal with the most important arguments that have been raised against it. One criticism has been that the compulsory vote forces to the polls people who have little political interest and knowledge and who are unlikely to cast a well considered vote: "An unwilling or indifferent vote is a thoughtless one" (Abraham 1955, 21). What this objection overlooks is that mandatory voting may serve as an incentive to become better informed. An indirect bit of evidence supporting this possibility is that, in American and European election studies, respondents interviewed prior to elections were found to vote in considerably greater numbers than expected due to the stimulation of these interviews (Popkin 1991, 235; Smeets 1995, 311–12).

Warren E. Miller's comment on this phenomenon is that such interviews are "the most expensive form of adult civic education known to mankind"![20] Compulsory voting may be able to serve as an equivalent, but much less expensive, form of civic education and political stimulation. This was an important objective when compulsory voting was introduced in both the Netherlands in 1917 and in Australia in 1924; at that time, one of its Australian proponents argued, in a highly optimistic vein, that "by compelling people to vote we are likely to arouse in them an intelligent interest and to give them a political knowledge that they do not at present possess" (cited in Morris Jones 1954, 32; see also Verplanke 1965, 81–83). Moreover, under compulsory voting, parties and candidates have a strong incentive to pay more attention and work harder to get information to previous non-voters.

Another criticism, based especially on the experience of the last years of the Weimar Republic in which increasing turnout coincided with the growth of the Nazi vote, is that high turnout may be undesirable and even dangerous. Tingsten (1937, 225; see also Lipset 1960, 140–52, 218–19) already used the Weimar example to warn that "exceptionally high voting frequency may indicate an intensification" of political conflict that may foreshadow the fall of democracy. The danger is that, in periods of crisis, sudden jumps in turnout mean that many previously uninterested and uninvolved citizens will come to the polls and will support extremist parties. This, however, is an argument for, not against, compulsory voting: instead of trying to keep turnout at steady *low* levels, it is better to safeguard against the danger of sudden sharp increases by maintaining steady *high* levels, unaffected by crises and charismatic leaders. Additional evidence that the Weimar precedent should not discourage efforts to increase turnout is Powell's (1982, 206) comparative study of twenty-nine democracies in which he found a strong association between higher voter turnout and less citizen turmoil and violence: "The data favor the theorists who believe that citizen involvement enhances legitimacy" instead of producing democratic breakdown.[21]

Compulsory voting has also been disparaged, even by those who support it in principle, on the practical grounds that the possibility of it being adopted in democracies that do not already have it are very small, that one especially big obstacle to its adoption is the opposition of conservative parties, and that, particularly in the United States – where arguably it is needed more than in most democracies given its low voter turnout at all levels – its chances of being accepted are nil. Alan Wertheimer (1975, 293) argues that mandatory voting is "a good idea whose time is either past or has not yet come. It is certainly not a good idea whose time is at hand." And Richard L.Hasen (1996, 2173) favors compulsory voting in American federal elections but concludes that it "has virtually no chance of enactment in the United States."

The very fact, however, that so many democracies do have compulsory voting, and have had it for a long time, shows that, while it may be difficult, it is clearly not an impossible task to introduce it. It is also worth noting that, in compulsory-voting countries, there is no strong trend in favor of abandoning it; the Netherlands and Venezuela are the only major examples of countries that abolished compulsory voting in recent decades. It will indeed not be easy to overcome the opposition of conservative parties in whose self-interest it is to keep turnout as low and class-biased as possible. Universal suffrage was also initially opposed by most of these parties – but eventually accepted. Like universal suffrage, mandatory voting is a moral issue, not just a political and partisan one. Indeed, compulsory voting can be regarded as a natural extension of universal suffrage.

A special impediment to mandatory voting in the United States is that it may be unconstitutional. Henry J. Abraham (1955, 31) takes this position and, in support of it, cites an 1896 opinion by the Supreme Court of Missouri that "voting is not such a duty as may be enforced by compulsory legislation, that it is distinctly not within the power of any legislative authority … to compel the citizen to exercise it." However, Hasen (1996, 2176) strongly disagrees. He argues that the only plausible constitutional objection to compulsory voting would be on the First Amendment ground of a violation of freedom of speech and that the US Supreme Court has explicitly rejected the argument that the vote may be regarded as a form of speech; moreover, he points out that the Missouri Supreme Court's 1896 decision failed to mention any particular constitutional violations. And, of course, even the courts' possible finding of unconstitutionality would not be a permanent and unsurmountable obstacle; as Gosnell (1930, 207) observes, "if the courts should interfere with the adoption of a system of compulsory voting, then the state and federal constitutions could be amended."[22] It is not entirely without precedent in the United States either: in the eighteenth century, Georgia and Virginia experimented with mandatory voting laws (Hasen 1996, 2173–74), and constitutional provisions adopted in North Dakota in 1898 and in Massachusetts in 1918 authorized their state legislatures to institute compulsory voting – but no legislative action was taken (Gosnell 1930, 206–7),

The danger of too much pessimism about the chances for compulsory voting is that it becomes a self-fulfilling prophecy. If even the supporters of compulsory voting believe that its chances are nil – and hence make no effort on behalf of it – it will indeed never be adopted!

Probably the most serious objection to compulsory voting is normative in nature: compulsory voting may be an attractive partial solution to the conflict between the democratic ideals of participation and equality, but it is often said to violate a third democratic ideal, that of individual freedom. For this reason, Abraham (1955, 33) calls compulsory voting "undemocratic," and W. H. Morris Jones (1954, 25) argues that it belongs "to the totalitarian camp and [is] out of place in the vocabulary of liberal democracy."

That compulsion of any kind limits individual freedom cannot be denied, but the duty to vote entails only a very minor restriction. It is important to remember, first of all, that compulsory "voting" does not mean an actual duty to cast a valid ballot; all that needs to be required is for citizens to show up at the polls. At that point, citizens may choose to refuse to vote; the right *not* to vote remains intact.[23] Moreover, compulsory voting entails a very small decrease in freedom compared with many other problems of collective action that democracies solve by imposing obligations: jury duty, the obligation to pay taxes, military conscription, compulsory school attendance, and many others. These obligations are much more burdensome than the duty to appear at the polls on election days. It must also be remembered that nonvoting is a form of free riding – and that free riding of any kind may be rational but is also selfish and immoral. The normative objection to compulsory voting has an immediate intuitive appeal that is not persuasive when considered more carefully.[24]

Compulsory voting cannot solve the entire conflict between the ideals of participation and equality, but by making voting participation as equal as possible, it is a valuable partial solution. In the first sentence of *Why Europe Votes*, Gosnell (1930, vii) states that the "struggle for democracy has just begun with the broadening of the franchise." After universal suffrage, the next aim for democracy must be universal or near-universal *use* of the right to vote.

Acknowledgments

Earlier versions of this address were delivered to the annual meetings of the Southern, Northeastern, Western, and Southwestern Political Science Associations on 3 and 9 November 1995, and 15 and 22 March 1996, respectively. I am very grateful for the comments that I received from participants in these meetings. I also thank the many other scholars who have generously responded to my requests for information and advice as I was preparing my address: Stephen Ansolabehere, Ken Coghill, Michael J. Coppedge, Robert Darcy, Hans Daalder, Wilfried Dewachter, Lieven De Winter, Panayote E. Dimitras, Zachary Elkins, Peter Farago, Mark N. Franklin, Richard L. Hasen, Wolfgang Hirczy, Colin A. Hughes, Luc Huyse, Galen A. Irwin, Robert W. Jackman, Gary C. Jacobson, Mark P. Jones, Richard S. Katz, Hans-Dieter Klingemann, Sanford A. Lakoff, Malcolm Mackerras, Ian McAllister, José E. Molina Vega, Timothy J. Power, Benjamin Radcliff, Robert Richie, Fred W. Riggs, Kenneth Newton, Dieter Nohlen, Anton Pelinka, Samuel L. Popkin, Ronald Rogowski, W. P.Secker, Matthew S. Shugart, Jürg Steiner, Alan Wertheimer, and Raymond E. Wolfinger.

Notes

1 Making financial contributions to campaigns, parties, and candidates is an exceptional activity in two respects. One is that it is characterized by an income bias that is greater than in all other modes of participation (Verba *et al.* 1995,

516–17). The other is that, in principle, it can be equalized by complete and exclusive public financing of political parties and campaigns – a policy that, however, is more difficult to apply in countries like the United States with its "candidate-centered politics" (Wattenberg 1991) than in countries with strong and disciplined parties.

2 Of course, another crucially important reason to aim for maximum turnout is democratic legitimacy (Hasen 1996, 2165–66; Teixeira 1992, 3, 101–2).

3 Even in Australia, where the voter is actually obligated to deposit a ballot in the ballot box, compulsory "voting" is still a misnomer. In the words of a former Australian senator and proponent of compulsory voting:

> What the law requires is that [electors] turn up at a polling booth and take a ballot paper. They are not compelled to fill in that ballot paper and have an absolute right not to vote by placing a blank or spoiled ballot paper in the ballot box. That is their unqualified right which only a small number choose to exercise.
>
> (Puplick 1995, 3–4)

4 Some Latin American democracies exempt large groups such as illiterates and people over age seventy from the obligation to vote (Nohlen 1993). The exclusion of illiterate citizens, in particular, reintroduces a significant class bias in voting.

5 The one serious doubt about the practical significance of these findings is that measures to increase turnout in the United States, such as easier registration and absentee voting rules, do not necessarily increase the proportion of the less privileged among the voters. For instance, being allowed to register as late as election day "rather than goading the disadvantaged to the polls, appears to simply provide a further convenience for those already inclined to vote by virtue of their social class position" (Calvert and Gilchrist 1993, 699; see also Oliver 1996; Wolfinger and Rosenstone 1980, 82–88). One has to keep in mind, however, that such measures result in relatively small turnout increments; more substantial increases in voting participation, in line with Tingsten's law of dispersion, are much more likely to reduce class bias. Moreover, Teixeira (1992, 112–15) presents data that directly contradict Calvert and Gilchrist's conclusion.

6 It is worth noting, however, that the usual finding is that there are only *small* differences instead of *no* differences, and that these small differences usually indicate, as expected, that less privileged citizens have more leftist opinions.

7 Teixeira (1992, 102) appears to agree at least in part with this interpretation when he argues that, in the long run, low voter turnout

> may contribute to the problem of an unrepresentative policy agenda, because nonvoters and voters do tend to differ systematically from one another in attributes that reflect individual *needs and interests,* even if their specific policy preferences within a given agenda generally do not.
>
> (emphasis added)

8 In a more controversial analysis, challenged by Erikson (1995), Radcliff (1994; 1995) found a strikingly similar pattern in the United States on the basis of state-level data from 1928 to 1980. Another similar finding is that, in New Zealand between 1928 and 1988, Labour's share of the vote increased by about a third of a percentage point for every percentage point increase in turnout (Nagel 1988, 25–29). In the United Kingdom, high turnout has meant a consistent disadvantage for the Conservatives, a modest gain for the Liberals, and no appreciable advantage for Labour – but, of course, a relative advantage for Labour as a result of the Conservatives' disadvantage (McAllister and Mughan 1986).

9 Nevertheless, in the remainder of this paper, I shall often have to cite turnout figures based on registered voters because these may be the only figures that are available. It should also be noted that percentages based on voting-age population may still contain two types of inaccuracy. One is that the voting-age population includes noncitizens, which means that turnout rates in countries with relatively large numbers of resident aliens such as the United States, Switzerland, France, Germany, and Belgium are understated (Powell 1986, 40; Teixeira 1992, 9–10). The other is that, in most countries but not in the United States, the "voters" that are counted include those who cast blank and invalid ballots (Crewe 1981, 238; Wolfinger *et al.* 1990, 570). However, these inaccuracies are not likely to affect turnout figures by more than a couple of percentage points.

10 Mark N. Franklin (1996, 218) reports turnout figures for thirty-seven countries in the 1960–95 period with a much higher median – 83 percent – but these use registered voters as the denominator.

11 One recent example is the 1990 election in Oklahoma in which 39.5 percent of the voting-age population voted for governor, but only 38.3 percent and 37.1 percent in the US senatorial and congressional races, and an average of 31.6 percent in the judicial retention choices – roll-offs of 2.9 percent, and 20 percent, respectively (calculated from data in Darcy and Vanderleeuw 1993, 3–4). Gosnell (1930, 209–10) reports that in the 1920 election in Kansas "35 percent of those who voted for president did not vote for state printer."

12 Richard Topf (1995, 40), however, belittles this decline by comparing the most recent 80 percent turnout, not with the high of 85 percent, but with the overall mean of 83 percent in the postwar period, and by arguing that "a decline of some 3 percentage points is a very small change indeed." My interpretation of the findings of the *Beliefs in Government* project also obviously differs from that of its three coordinators who conclude that "voting turnout [in Western Europe] has remained remarkably stable in the postwar period" (Kaase *et al.* 1996, 226).

13 The number of member countries has increased from nine in 1979; in 1984 there were ten member countries, and there were twelve in 1989 and 1994. It may therefore be more appropriate to examine the averages for the original nine members only: 65.9 percent (1979), 62.3 percent (1984), 63.1 percent (1989), and 59.3 percent (1994). The slight boost in 1989 can be explained in terms of the concurrence of that year's election in Ireland with a national parliamentary election (van der Eijk *et al.* 1996, 154) that raised turnout by an estimated 20 percentage points – and which therefore raised the average turnout for the nine countries by about 2 percentage points.

14 The difference between PR and single-member-district systems is roughly the same as the variable that Powell (1986) and Jackman (1987) call "nationally competitive districts," with two exceptions. One is that the latter takes into consideration three categories of proportionality in PR systems, based on the number of representatives elected per district. The other concerns presidential elections: The direct presidential elections in France, in which each vote counts nationwide, are placed in the same category as the most proportional parliamentary elections, whereas the American electoral-college system of presidential elections is scored on a par with single-member-district systems. Jackman (1987) and Jackman and Miller (1995) also find that multipartism, which is strongly associated with PR, depresses turnout – thus undoing some of PR's beneficial influence – and that bicameralism lowers turnout as well.

15 Enrique C. Ochoa (1987, 867) also notes that the Latin American countries with compulsory-voting laws "tend to have a higher participation rate. The countries with the highest voter turnout during the most recent presidential elections in the 1980s ... all have mandatory voting laws."

16 Molina Vega's (1995, 163) own, more realistic, estimates of turnout are a bit lower – a mean of 82.8 percent before and 54 percent after the abolition of compulsory voting – but the difference of almost 29 percentage points between the two is roughly similar to that between the before and after official percentages. While the obligation to vote remained formally in force in 1993, compulsory voting was effectively eliminated because all penalties for nonvoting were removed.

17 I am indebted to Galen A.Irwin for providing me with these data (personal correspondence, 5 May 1996). See also Andeweg and Irwin 1993, 83–85; Denters 1995, 118–21, 137; and Irwin 1974.

18 Some compulsory-voting laws do prescribe heavy penalties, such as up to a year's imprisonment in Greece, but this kind of sanction is never imposed. The typical penalty is a relatively small fine, similar to a fine for a parking violation, but even these are imposed on only a small fraction of the nonvoters: 4 to 5 percent in Australia, less than 1 percent in the Netherlands when it had compulsory voting, and less than one-fourth of a percent in Belgium (Adviescommissie Opkomstplicht 1967, 28; Hasen 1996, 2169–70; Mackerras and McAllister 1996). In Italy, the only penalty is the "innocuous sanction" – but still effective sanction – of noting "did not vote" on the citizen's certificate of good conduct (Corbetta and Parisi 1995, 150; but see also Lombardo 1996).

19 For countries with proportional representation, a fourth argument in favor of compulsory voting is that it is illogical to want votes to be converted proportionally into seats, but to be satisfied with a situation in which only a biased sample of the eligible electorate actually votes – which necessarily introduces considerable disproportionality after all. This was an important part of the reasoning behind the simultaneous adoption of compulsory voting and proportional representation in the Netherlands in 1917 (Andeweg and Irwin 1993, 81, 84; Daalder 1975, 228).

20 Personal correspondence, 2 July 1995. The expense of this kind of civic education is, of course, not just the cost of conducting the interviews but also the fact that it is unnecessary for those who will vote anyway and far from 100 percent effective for those less likely to vote.

21 Because Powell's conclusion is based on a number of presidential as well as parliamentary systems, his finding also assuages, at least partly, Fred W. Riggs's (1988, 263–64) fear that high turnout is a special danger in presidential regimes; Riggs regards presidentialism as inherently weak and unstable – and capable of survival only when conservative forces have predominant power.

22 However, Gosnell (1930, 192–212) was certainly not at all optimistic about the chances for mandatory voting in the United States. He begins the last chapter of *Why Europe Votes* with the question: "What use can be made of European political experience in America?" He discusses the advantages of compulsory voting at great length but quietly drops it from his final list of recommendations, which does include relatively radical proposals like proportional representation in elections to the US House of Representatives, permanent voter registration that is the government's responsibility, and adoption of the short ballot.

23 Malcolm M. Feeley (1974, 242) states that most of the objections to compulsory voting can be solved by including a "no preference" alternative – or, as others have suggested a "none of the above" choice – on the ballot. The right to refuse to accept a ballot, however, is an even more effective method to assure that the right not to vote is not infringed.

24 A logical alternative to compulsory voting is to use rewards for voting instead of penalties for nonvoting: citizens can be paid to vote. The only empirical example of this – obviously more expensive – arrangement appears to be ancient Athens (Hasen 1996, 2135, 2169; Staveley 1972, 78–82).

References

Abraham, Henry J. 1955. *Compulsory Voting*. Washington DC: Public Affairs Press.

Abramson, Paul R. 1995. "Political Participation." In *The Encyclopedia of Democracy*, ed. Seymour Martin Lipset. 4 vols. Washington DC: Congressional Quarterly.

Ackaert, Johan, and Lieven De Winter. 1993. "De afwezigen hebben andermaal ongelijk: De stemverzaking in Vlaanderen op 24 november 1991." In *Kiezen is verliezen: Onderzoek naar de politieke opvattingen van Vlamingen*, eds Marc Swyngedouw, Jaak Billiet, Ann Carton, and Roeland Beerten. Louvain: Acco.

——1996. "Electoral Absenteeism and Potential Absenteeism in Belgium." Presented at the annual meeting of the American Political Science Association, San Francisco.

Adviescommissie Opkomstplicht. 1967. *Rapport van de adviescommissie opkomstplicht*. The Hague: Staatsuitgeverij.

Aldrich, John H. 1993. "Rational Choice and Turnout." *American Journal of Political Science* 37 (February): 246–78.

Almond, Gabriel A., and Sidney Verba. 1963. *The Civic Culture: Political Attitudes and Democracy in Five Nations*. Princeton NJ: Princeton University Press.

Amy, Douglas J. 1993. *Real Choices/New Voices: The Case for Proportional Representation Elections in the United States*. New York: Columbia University Press.

Andersen, Jörgen Goul. 1984. "Decline of Class Voting or Change in Class Voting? Social Classes and Party Choice in Denmark in the 1970s." *European Journal of Political Research* 12 (September): 243–59.

Andeweg, Rudy B., and Galen A. Irwin. 1993. *Dutch Government and Politics*. New York: St. Martin's Press.

Ansolabehere, Stephen, and Shanto Iyengar. 1995. *Going Negative: How Attack Ads Shrink and Polarize the Electorate*, New York: Free Press.

Arendt, Hannah. 1958. *The Human Condition*. Chicago IL: University of Chicago Press.

Arneson, Ben A. 1925. "Non-Voting in a Typical Ohio Community." *American Political Science Review* 19 (November): 816–25.

Baloyra, Enrique A, and John D. Martz. 1979. *Political Attitudes in Venezuela: Societal Cleavages and Political Opinion*. Austin TX: University of Texas Press.

Barber, Benjamin R. 1984. *Strong Democracy: Participatory Politics for a New Age*. Berkeley CA: University of California Press.

Barker, Ernest. 1958. *The Politics of Aristotle*. New York: Oxford University Press.

Bennett, Stephen Earl, and David Resnick. 1990. "The Implications of Nonvoting for Democracy in the United States." *American Journal of Political Science* 34 (August): 771–802.

Berelson, Bernard, and Gary A. Steiner. 1964. *Human Behavior: An Inventory of Scientific Findings*. New York: Harcourt, Brace.

Blais, André, Donald Blake, and Stéphane Dion. 1996. "Do Parties Make a Difference? A Reappraisal." *American Journal of Political Science* 40 (May): 514–20.

Blais, André, and R. K. Carty. 1990. "Does Proportional Representation Foster Voter Turnout?" *European Journal of Political Research* 18 (March): 167–81.

Borg, Sami. 1995. "Electoral Participation." In *The Impact of Values*, eds Jan W. van Deth and Elinor Scarbrough. Vol. 4 of *Beliefs in Government*. Oxford: Oxford University Press.

Botella, Joan. 1994. "Local Government in Catalonia: The Making of a Local Elite, 1979–91." In *Local Elections in Europe*, ed. Lourdes López Nieto. Barcelona: ICPS.

Boyd, Richard W. 1981. "Decline of U.S. Voter Turnout: Structural Explanations." *American Politics Quarterly* 9 (April): 133–59.

——1986. "Election Calendars and Voter Turnout." *American Politics Quarterly* 14 (January-April): 89–104.

——1989. "The Effects of Primaries and Statewide Races on Voter Turnout." *Journal of Politics* 51 (August): 730–39.

Burnham, Walter Dean. 1965. "The Changing Shape of the American Political Universe." *American Political Science Review* 59 (March): 7–28.

——1980. "The Appearance and Disappearance of the American Voter." In *Electoral Participation: A Comparative Analysis*, ed. Richard Rose. Beverly Hills CA: Sage.

——1987. "The Turnout Problem." In *Elections American Style*, ed. A. James Reichley. Washington DC: Brookings Institution.

Calvert, Jerry W., and Jack Gilchrist. 1993. "Suppose They Held an Election and Almost Everybody Came!" *PS: Political Science & Politics* 26 (December): 695–700.

Castles, Francis G., ed. 1982, *The Impact of Parties: Politics and Policies in Democratic Capitalist States*. London: Sage.

Castles, Frank, and Robert D. McKinlay. 1979. "Does Politics Matter: An Analysis of the Public Welfare Commitment in Advanced Democratic States." *European Journal of Political Research* 7 (June): 169–86.

Corbetta, Piergiorgio, and Arturo M. L. Parisi. 1995. "Electoral Abstentionism in Italy." In *Electoral Abstention in Europe*, eds Joan Font and Rosa Virós. Barcelona: ICPS.

Crewe, Ivor. 1981. "Electoral Participation." In *Democracy at the Polls: A Comparative Study of Competitive National Elections*, eds David Butler, Howard R. Penniman, and Austin Ranney. Washington DC: American Enterprise Institute.

Daalder, Hans. 1975. "Extreme Proportional Representation: The Dutch Experience." In *Adversary Politics and Electoral Reform*, ed. S. E. Finer. London: Anthony Wigram.

Dahl, Robert A. 1970. *After the Revolution? Authority in a Good Society*. New Haven CT: Yale University Press.

——1989. *Democracy and Its Critics*. New Haven CT: Yale University Press.

Dalton, Russell B. 1996. *Citizen Politics: Public Opinion and Political Parties in Advanced Industrial Democracies*. 2nd edn. Chatham NJ: Chatham House.

Darcy, R., and Anne Schneider. 1989. "Confusing Ballots, Roll-Off, and the Black Vote." *Western Political Quarterly* 42 (September): 347–64.

Darcy, R., and James Vanderleeuw. 1993. *The Impact of Ballot Format on Voter Rolloff*. Stillwater OK: Department of Political Science, Oklahoma State University.

Denters, S. A.H. 1995. "Voter Turnout in Dutch Elections." In *Electoral Abstention in Europe*, eds Joan Font and Rosa Virós. Barcelona: ICPS.

Denver, David. 1995. "Non-Voting in Britain." In *Electoral Abstention in Europe*, eds Joan Font and Rosa Virós. Barcelona: ICPS.

De Winter, Lieven, and Johan Ackaert. 1994. "Abstentionnisme electoral et vote blanc ou nul: Le 'non-vote' en Wallonie." In *Elections la fêlure? Enquête sur le comportement electoral des Wallons et des Francophones*, eds André-Paul Frognier and Anne-Marie Aish-Van Vaerenbergh. Brussels: De Boeck.

Dogan, Mattei. 1995. "Erosion of Class Voting and of the Religious Vote in Western Europe." *International Social Science Journal* 146 (December): 525–38.

Erikson, Robert S. 1995. "State Turnout and Presidential Voting: A Closer Look." *American Politics Quarterly* 23 (October): 387–96.

Farago, Peter. 1995. "Wahlforschung in der Schweiz: Der Neubeginn." *Swiss Political Science Review* 1 (winter): 121–30.

——1996. *Wahlen 95: Zusammensetzung und politische Orientierungen der Wählerschaft an den eidgenössischen Wahlen 1995*. Bern: Selects.

Feeley, Malcolm M. 1974. "A Solution to the 'Voting Dilemma' in Modern Democratic Theory." *Ethics* 84 (April): 235–42.

Fernández Baeza, Mario. n.d. "El voto obligatorio en America Latina." In *Tratado de derecho electoral comparado de America Latina*, ed. Dieter Nohlen. San José: Instituto Interamericano de Derechos Humanos. Forthcoming.

Fishkin, James S. 1991. *Democracy and Deliberation: New Directions for Democratic Reform*. New Haven CT: Yale University Press.

——1995. *The Voice of the People: Public Opinion and Democracy*. New Haven CT: Yale University Press.

Flickinger, Richard S., and Donley T. Studlar. 1992. "The Disappearing Voters? Exploring Declining Turnout in Western European Elections." *West European Politics* 15 (April): 1–16.

Fornos, Carolina A. 1996. "Explaining Voter Turnout in Latin America." Master's thesis, Louisiana State University.

Font, Joan, and Rosa Virós. 1995. "Catalan Electoral Abstention: A Critical Review." In *Electoral Abstention in Europe*, eds Joan Font and Rosa Virós. Barcelona: ICPS.

Franklin, Mark N. 1992. "The Decline of Cleavage Politics." In *Electoral Change: Responses to Evolving Social and Attitudinal Structures in Western Countries*, eds Mark N. Franklin, Thomas T. Mackie, and Henry Valen. Cambridge: Cambridge University Press.

——1996. "Electoral Participation." In *Comparing Democracies: Elections and Voting in Global Perspective*, eds Laurence LeDuc, Richard G.Niemi, and Pippa Norris. Thousand Oaks CA: Sage.

Franklin, Mark N., Cees van der Eijk, and Erik Oppenhuis. 1996. "The Institutional Context: Turnout." In *Choosing Europe? The European Electorate and National Politics in the Face of Union*, eds Cees van der Eijk and Mark N. Franklin. Ann Arbor MI: University of Michigan Press.

Gant, Michael M., and William Lyons. 1993. "Democratic Theory, Nonvoting, and Public Policy: The 1972–88 Presidential Elections." *American Politics Quarterly* 21 (April): 185–204.

Goldsmith, Michael, and Ken Newton. 1986. "Local Government Abroad." In *The Conduct of Local Authority Business*, ed. Committee of Inquiry into the Conduct of Local Authority Business. London: Her Majesty's Stationery Office.

Gosnell, Harold F. 1927. *Getting Out the Vote: An Experiment in the Stimulation of Voting*. Chicago IL: University of Chicago Press.

——1930. *Why Europe Votes*. Chicago IL: University of Chicago Press.

Greenberg, Edward S. 1986. *Workplace Democracy: The Political Effects of Participation*. Ithaca NY: Cornell University Press.

Greenberg, Edward S., Leon Grunberg, and Kelley Daniel. 1996. "Industrial Work and Political Participation: Beyond 'Simple Spillover.'" *Political Research Quarterly* 49 (June): 305–30.

Hasen, Richard L. 1996. "Voting Without Law?" *University of Pennsylvania Law Review* 144 (May): 2135–79.

Hibbs, Douglas A., Jr. 1977. "Political Parties and Macroeconomic Policy." *American Political Science Review* 71 (December): 1467–87.

Hicks, Alexander M., and Duane H. Swank. 1992. "Politics, Institutions, and Welfare Spending in Industrialized Democracies, 1960–82." *American Political Science Review* 86 (September): 658–74.

Hill, Kim Quaile, and Jan E. Leighley. 1992. "The Policy Consequences of Class Bias in State Electorates." *American Journal of Political Science* 36 (May): 351–65.

Hirczy, Wolfgang. 1994. "The Impact of Mandatory Voting Laws on Turnout: A Quasi-Experimental Approach." *Electoral Studies* 13 (March): 64–76.

——1995. "Explaining Near-Universal Turnout: The Case of Malta." *European Journal of Political Research* 27 (February): 255–72.

Hirschman, Albert O. 1970. *Exit, Voice, and Loyalty: Responses to Decline in Firms, Organizations, and States.* Cambridge MA: Harvard University Press.

Hoffmann-Martinot, Vincent. 1994. "Voter Turnout in French Municipal Elections." In *Local Elections in Europe*, ed. Lourdes López Nieto. Barcelona: ICPS.

Hout, Michael, Clem Brooks, and Jeff Manza. 1995. "The Democratic Class Struggle in the United States, 1948–92." *American Sociological Review* 60 (December): 805–28.

Inglehart, Ronald. 1990. *Culture Shift in Advanced Industrial Society.* Princeton NJ: Princeton University Press.

Irwin, Galen A. 1974. "Compulsory Voting Legislation: Impact on Voter Turnout in the Netherlands." *Comparative Political Studies* 7 (October): 292–315.

Jackman, Robert W. 1987. "Political Institutions and Voter Turnout in the Industrial Democracies." *American Political Science Review* 81 (June): 405–23.

Jackman, Robert W., and Ross A. Miller. 1995. "Voter Turnout in the Industrial Democracies During the 1980s." *Comparative Political Studies* 27 (January): 467–92.

Justel, Manuel. 1995. "Electoral Abstention in Spain: Characteristics and Factors." In *Electoral Abstention in Europe*, eds Joan Font and Rosa Virós. Barcelona: ICPS.

Kaase, Max. 1996. "The Impact of Sociopolitical Change in Western Europe on Transatlantic Relations." In *Estranged Friends? The Transatlantic Consequences of Societal Change*, eds Max Kaase and Andrew Kohut. New York: Council on Foreign Relations Press.

Kaase, Max, Kenneth Newton, and Elinor Scarbrough. 1996. "A Look at the *Beliefs in Government* Study." *PS: Political Science & Politics* 29 (June): 226–28.

Kennedy, J. Ray. 1996. "Canadian Province Sees Four in October: Referendums in Quebec." *Elections Today* 5 (January): 18–19,

Key, V. O., Jr. 1949. *Southern Politics in State and Nation.* New York: Vintage Books.

King, Anthony. 1981. "What Do Elections Decide?" In *Democracy at the Polls: A Comparative Study of Competitive National Elections*, eds David Butler, Howard R. Penniman, and Austin Ranney. Washington DC: American Enterprise Institute.

Klingemann, Hans-Dieter, Richard I. Hofferbert, and Ian Budge. 1994. *Parties, Policies, and Democracy.* Boulder CO: Westview Press.

Lafferty, William M. 1989. "Work as a Source of Political Learning Among Wage-Laborers and Lower-Level Employees." In *Political Learning in Adulthood: A*

Sourcebook of Theory and Research, ed. Roberta S. Sigel. Chicago IL: University of Chicago Press.

Leighley, Jan E. 1995. "Attitudes, Opportunities and Incentives: A Field Essay on Political Participation." *Political Research Quarterly* 48 (March): 181–209.

Lijphart, Arend. 1994. "Democracies: Forms, Performance, and Constitutional Engineering." *European Journal of Political Research* 25 (January): 1–17.

Linder, Wolf. 1994. *Swiss Democracy: Possible Solutions to Conflict in Multicultural Societies*. New York: St. Martin's Press.

Lipset, Seymour Martin. 1960. *Political Man: The Social Bases of Politics*. Garden City NJ: Doubleday.

——1981. *Political Man: The Social Bases of Politics*. Expanded edn. Baltimore MD: Johns Hopkins University Press.

Lombardo, Salvatore. 1996. "Mandatory Voting and Voter Participation in Italy." Presented at the annual meeting of the American Political Science Association, San Francisco.

López Nieto, Lourdes. 1994. "Local Elections in the Spanish Political System: 1979–91." In *Local Elections in Europe*, ed. Lourdes López Nieto. Barcelona: ICPS.

Mackerras, Malcolm, and Ian McAllister. 1996. "Compulsory Voting, Party Stability and Electoral Bias in Australia." Presented at the annual meeting of the American Political Science Association, San Francisco.

Manza, Jeff, Michael Hout, and Clem Brooks. 1995. "Class Voting in Capitalist Democracies Since World War II: Dealignment, Realignment, or Trendless Fluctuation?" In *Annual Review of Sociology*, vol. 21, eds John Hagan and Karen S. Cook. Palo Alto CA: Annual Reviews.

Marsh, Alan, and Max Kaase. 1979. "Background of Political Action." In *Political Action: Mass Participation in Five Western Democracies*, eds Samuel H. Barnes and Max Kaase. Beverly Hills CA: Sage.

McAllister, Ian. 1986. "Compulsory Voting, Turnout and Party Advantage in Australia." *Politics* 21 (May): 89–93.

McAllister, Ian, and Anthony Mughan. 1986. "Differential Turnout and Party Advantage in British General Elections, 1964–83." *Electoral Studies* 5 (August): 143–52.

Mebane, Walter R., Jr. 1994. "Fiscal Constraints and Electoral Manipulation in American Social Welfare." *American Political Science Review* 88 (March): 77–94.

Mill, John Stuart. [1861] 1958. *Considerations on Representative Government*. New York: Liberal Arts Press.

Miller, William L. 1994. "Local Elections in Britain." In *Local Elections in Europe*, ed. Lourdes López Nieto. Barcelona: ICPS.

Molina Vega, José Enrique. 1991. *El sistema electoral venezolano y sus consecuencias políticas*. San José, Costa Rica: IIDH/CAPEL.

——1995. "Los venezolanos abandonan el hábito de votar: La abstención en las elecciones de 1993." *Boletín Electoral Latinoamericano* 13 (January-June): 159–79.

Morris Jones, W. H. 1954. "In Defense of Apathy: Some Doubts on the Duty to Vote." *Political Studies* 2 (1): 25–37.

Mottier, Véronique. 1993. "La structuration sociale de la participation aux votations fédérales." In *Citoyenneté et démocratie directe: Competence, participation et decision des citoyens et citoyennes suisses*, ed. Hanspeter Kriesi. Zurich: Seismo.

Nagel, Jack H. 1988. "Voter Turnout in New Zealand General Elections, 1928–88." *Political Science* 40 (December): 16–38.

Niedermayer, Oskar. 1990. "Turnout in the European Elections." *Electoral Studies 9* (March): 45–50.

Nieuwbeerta, Paul. 1995. *The Democratic Class Struggle in Twenty Countries, 1945–1990*. Amsterdam: Thesis Publishers.

Nohlen, Dieter, ed. 1993. *Enciclopedia electoral latinoamericana y del Caribe*. San José: Instituto Interamericano de Derechos Humanos.

Ochoa, Enrique C. 1987. "The Rapid Expansion of Voter Participation in Latin America: Presidential Elections, 1845–1986." In vol. 25 of *Statistical Abstract of Latin America*, eds James W.Wilkie and David Lorey. Los Angeles CA: UCLA Latin American Center Publications, University of California.

Oliver, J. Eric. 1996. "The Effects of Eligibility Restrictions and Party Activity on Absentee Voting and Overall Turnout." *American Journal of Political Science* 40 (May): 498–513.

Oppenhuis, Erik Vincent. 1995. *Voting Behavior in Europe: A Comparative Analysis of Electoral Participation and Party Choice*, Amsterdam: Het Spinhuis.

Pacek, Alexander, and Benjamin Radcliff. 1995. "Turnout and the Vote for Left-of-Centre Parties: A Cross-National Analysis." *British Journal of Political Science* 25 (January): 137–43.

Pateman, Carole. 1970. *Participation and Democratic Theory*. Cambridge: Cambridge University Press.

Peterson, Steven A. 1992. "Workplace Politicization and Its Political Spillovers: A Research Note." *Economic and Industrial Democracy* 13 (November): 511–24.

Petrocik, John R. 1987. "Voter Turnout and Electoral Preference: The Anomalous Reagan Elections." In *Elections in America*, ed. Kay Lehman Schlozman. Boston MA: Allen and Unwin.

Piven, Frances Fox, and Richard A. Cloward. 1988a. *Why Americans Don't Vote*. New York: Pantheon Books.

——1988b. "National Voter Registration Reform: How It Might Be Won." *PS: Political Science & Politics* 21 (fall): 868–75.

Popkin, Samuel L. 1991. *The Reasoning Voter: Communication and Persuasion in Presidential Campaigns*. Chicago IL: University of Chicago Press.

Powell, G. Bingham, Jr. 1980. "Voting Turnout in Thirty Democracies: Partisan, Legal, and Socioeconomic Influences." In *Electoral Participation: A Comparative Analysis*, ed. Richard Rose. Beverly Hills CA: Sage.

——1982. *Contemporary Democracies: Participation, Stability, and Violence*. Cambridge MA: Harvard University Press.

——1986. "American Voter Turnout in Comparative Perspective." *American Political Science Review* 80 (March): 17–43.

Power, Timothy J., and J. Timmons Roberts. 1995. "Compulsory Voting, Invalid Ballots, and Abstention in Brazil." *Political Research Quarterly* 48 (December): 795–826.

Puplick, Chris. 1995. "The Case for Compulsory Voting." *Elections Today* 5 (October): 3–5.

Radcliff, Benjamin. 1994. "Turnout and the Democratic Vote." *American Politics Quarterly* 22 (July): 259–76.

——1995. "Turnout and the Vote Revisited: A reply to Erikson." *American Politics Quarterly* 23 (October): 397–403.

Rallings, Colin, and Michael Thrasher. 1990. "Turnout in English Local Elections: An Aggregate Analysis with Electoral and Contextual Data." *Electoral Studies* 9 (June): 79–90.

Reif, Karlheinz, and Hermann Schmitt. 1980. "Nine Second-Order National Elections: A Conceptual Framework for the Analysis of European Election Results." *European Journal of Political Research* 8 (March): 3–44.

Riggs, Fred W. 1988. "The Survival of Presidentialism in America: Para-Constitutional Practices." *International Political Science Review* 9 (October): 247–78.

Rosenstone, Steven J., and John Mark Hansen. 1993. *Mobilization, Participation, and Democracy in America*, New York: Macmillan.

Särlvik, Bo, and Ivor Crewe. 1983. *Decade of Dealignment: The Conservative Victory of 1979 and Electoral Trends in the 1970s.* Cambridge: Cambridge University Press.

Schultze, Rainer-Olaf. 1995. "Voting and Non-Voting in German Elections." In *Electoral Abstention in Europe*, eds Joan Font and Rosa Virós. Barcelona: ICPS.

Schweizer, Steven L. 1995. "Participation, Workplace Democracy, and the Problem of Representative Government." *Polity* 27 (spring): 359–77.

Seligson, Mitchell A., Annabelle Conroy, Ricardo Córdova Macías, Orlando J. Pérez, and Andrew J. Stein. 1995. "Who Votes in Central America? A Comparative Analysis." In *Elections and Democracy in Central America, Revisited*, eds Mitchell A. Seligson and John A. Booth. Chapel Hill NC: University of North Carolina Press.

Shaffer, Stephen D. 1982. "Policy Differences Between Voters and Non-Voters in American Elections." *Western Political Quarterly* 35 (December): 496–510.

Sidjanski, Dusan. 1983. "Turnout, Stability, and the Left-Right Dimension." In *Switzerland at the Polls: The National Elections of 1979*, ed. Howard R. Penniman. Washington DC: American Enterprise Institute.

Smeets, Ingrid. 1995. "Facing Another Gap: An Exploration of the Discrepancies Between Voting Turnout in Survey Research and Official Statistics." *Acta Politica* 30 (July): 307–34.

Smith, Julie. 1995. "The 1994 European Elections: Twelve Into One Won't Go." *West European Politics* 18 (July): 199–217.

Sobel, Richard. 1993. "From Occupational Involvement to Political Participation: An Exploratory Analysis." *Political Behavior* 15 (December): 339–53.

Staveley, E. S. 1972. *Greek and Roman Voting and Elections.* Ithaca NY: Cornell University Press.

Steinberg, Jacques. 1996. "Vote Changes New York School Board Little." *New York Times* (National Edition, 12 June): B8.

Studlar, Donley T., and Susan Welch. 1986. "The Policy Opinions of British Non-voters: A Research Note." *European Journal of Political Research* 14 (1–2): 139–48.

Teixeira, Ruy A. 1992. *The Disappearing American Voter.* Washington DC: Brookings Institution.

Tingsten, Herbert. 1937. *Political Behavior: Studies in Election Statistics.* London: P. S. King & Son.

Topf, Richard. 1995. "Electoral Participation." In *Citizens and the State*, eds Hans-Dieter Klingemann and Dieter Fuchs. Vol. 1 of *Beliefs in Government.* Oxford: Oxford University Press.

Tufte, Edward R. 1978. *Political Control of the Economy.* Princeton NJ: Princeton University Press.

Urwin, Derek W. 1974. "Germany: Continuity and Change in Electoral Politics." In *Electoral Behavior: A Comparative Handbook*, ed. Richard Rose. New York: Free Press.

van der Eijk, Cees, Mark N. Franklin, and Michael Marsh. 1996. "What Voters Teach Us About Europe-Wide Elections: What Europe-Wide Elections Teach Us About Voters." *Electoral Studies* 15 (May): 149–66.

Verba, Sidney. 1996. "The Citizen as Respondent: Sample Surveys and American Democracy." *American Political Science Review* 90 (March): 1–7.

Verba, Sidney, Norman H. Nie, and Jae-On Kim. 1978. *Participation and Political Equality: A Seven-Nation Comparison.* Cambridge: Cambridge University Press.

Verba, Sidney, Kay Lehman Schlozman, and Henry E. Brady. 1995. *Voice and Equality: Civic Voluntarism in American Politics.* Cambridge MA: Harvard University Press.

Verplanke, C. J. 1965. "De opkomstplicht." *Anti-Revolutionaire Staatkunde* 35 (March): 75–98.

Wattenberg, Martin P. 1991. *The Rise of Candidate-Centered Politics: Presidential Elections of the 1980s.* Cambridge MA: Harvard University Press.

Wertheimer, Alan. 1975. "In Defense of Compulsory Voting." In *Participation in Politics,* eds J. Roland Pennock and John W. Chapman. New York: Lieber-Atherton.

Widfeldt, Anders. 1996. "The Swedish European Election of 1995." *Electoral Studies* 15 (February): 116–19.

Wolfinger, Raymond E. 1994. "The Rational Citizen Faces Election Day or What Rational Choice Theorists Don't Tell You About American Elections." In *Elections at Home and Abroad: Essays in Honor of Warren E. Miller,* eds M. Kent Jennings and Thomas E. Mann. Ann Arbor MI: University of Michigan Press.

Wolfinger, Raymond E., David P. Glass, and Peverill Squire. 1990. "Predictors of Electoral Turnout: An International Comparison." *Policy Studies Review* 9 (spring): 551–74.

Wolfinger, Raymond E., and Steven J. Rosenstone. 1980. *Who Votes?* New Haven CT: Yale University Press.

16 Types of democracy and generosity with foreign aid

An indirect test of the democratic peace proposition

Arend Lijphart and Peter J.Bowman

Because full-fledged democracy is mainly a post-1945 phenomenon and because the Cold War offers an alternative explanation for the peaceful relations among democracies, it is difficult to test the democratic peace proposition directly; most tests have therefore been indirect ones. This chapter offers another indirect test, based on the cultural and structural differences between consensus and majoritarian types of democracy – comparable to the differences between democracy and non-democracy – and based on differences with regard to one kind of peaceful foreign policy – the supply of economic development assistance. The hypothesized relationship between consensus democracy and generosity with foreign aid is strongly confirmed.

The democratic peace proposition states that democracies are more peaceful, especially in their relations with each other, than non-democratic systems. This proposition is not new; in fact, it can be traced back as far as Immanuel Kant's famous treatise *Perpetual Peace*, first published in 1795. Woodrow Wilson's aim to "make the world safe for democracy" also included the idea that a more democratic world would necessarily be a safer and more peaceful world. In the 1970s and 1980s, political scientists like Melvin Small and J. David Singer (1976) and Rudolph J. Rummel (1983) started the latest phase of scholarly attention to the democratic peace proposition, and the interest in it as well as the debate about its merits have blossomed in the 1990s.[1]

The proposition is a very strong one, especially in its dyadic form – which states that democracies do not fight *each other* – and especially for the post-World War II era. Significantly, the major exceptions to the democratic peace proposition that critics frequently mention – the War of 1812 between the United States and Great Britain, the American Civil War (1861–65), the Spanish-American War (1898), the Boer War (1899–1902), the First World War (if Germany can be regarded as democratic on account of its elected parliament), and democratic Finland's participation in the Second World War – are all pre-1945 examples (Ray 1997, 54).[2] The proposition is also important because of its extremely significant policy implications: in a world in which all states are ruled democratically, "perpetual peace" would be guaranteed.

The democratic peace proposition can take three forms: dyadic, monadic, and systemic. It is the most robust and least controversial in its dyadic form, mentioned above, which postulates that democratic states tend to be peaceful toward each other, but are not necessarily peaceful toward non-democracies. One explanation that is cited for this divergent behavior of democracies is based on internal differences between democratic and autocratic polities. Margaret G. Hermann and Charles W. Kegley (1996) argue that democracies have markedly better bargaining capabilities and superior institutional resources than autocratic states, and that it is these strengths that make them less likely to be the target of attack by other states, rather than the fact that they have democratic and liberal forms of government. Conversely, democracies themselves are often self-righteous and belligerent toward authoritarian states whose governments they regard as repugnant. In addition, Arvid Raknerud and Havard Hegre (1997) find that democracies will often join other democracies in wars against non-democratic states.

Nevertheless, several scholars – especially Kenneth Benoit (1996) and Rudolph J. Rummel (1997, 63–83) – have argued in favor of the monadic proposition: that democracies are generally more peaceful even in their relations with non-democracies. A drawback of Benoit's analysis is that his time frame pertains only to conflicts in the 1960s and 1970s and that it can therefore only make a limited contribution to determining the full scope of democratic-autocratic relations. Writings that have a broader time frame but are still limited to the Cold War era are challenged by Henry S. Farber and Joanne Gowa (1997) as well as by Paul D. Senese (1997). Their analyses look at wars in the pre-Cold War years and find that not only are there weaknesses to monadic explanations, but there are also flaws in the dyadic postulate. Farber and Gowa (1997) emphasize that wars were more likely to be fought between democratic states in the pre-1945 era before the Cold War could have a strategically unifying effect on democracies. Hence, they argue, the democratic peace was brought on by structural balance-of-power conditions, not by genuine differences in internal political dynamics. We shall give this "realist" perspective more attention later on in this chapter.

A new perspective – the third variant of the democratic peace proposition – was added by Nils-Petter Gleditsch and Havard Hegre (1997) to the theoretical debate: the systemic level. Their argument is that as more states become democratic, the international system as a whole becomes more peaceful. While Gleditsch and Hegre found that war actually increased with the advent of new democracies in the pre-Cold War era, the systemic proposition becomes more persuasive in the period of the Cold War. Here again, the Cold War is introduced as a key variable.

Testing the democratic peace proposition

In all three forms, the proposition has been difficult to test, first, because *before 1945* there were almost no full-fledged democracies and, second, because *after 1945* the democratic peace can also be explained in "realist" terms. Let us look at each of these problems in greater detail.

First, "democracy" is a controversial concept, but there is general agreement on Robert A. Dahl's (1971, 3) eight criteria for democracy: not just universal suffrage is required, but also such institutional guarantees as free and fair elections, freedom of expression, freedom to form and join organizations, and alternative sources of information. What is often neglected, however, is that while universal suffrage is not a sufficient condition for democracy, it *is* a necessary condition. The first country to meet this condition was New Zealand when it instituted truly universal suffrage, that is, the right to vote for both men and women and also for the Maori minority, in 1893.[3] This means that, before 1893, there were no full-fledged democracies at all.[4] Several countries – such as Germany, the Netherlands, and Sweden – adopted universal suffrage, including full and equal suffrage for women, after the First World War. However, in the United Kingdom women did not get the right to vote on the same basis as men until 1928, and Belgian, French, and Italian women had to wait until the end of the Second World War to become voters.

Moreover, it is difficult to accept as "democracies" those countries with large colonial possessions whose inhabitants completely lacked the right to vote; for instance, even after 1928, the vast majority of the people ruled by the British government had no say in its selection. These limitations on universal suffrage were lifted after the Second World War as a result of the rapid dissolution of the colonial empires and the near-universal adoption of full women's suffrage – the one notable exception being that Swiss women had to wait until 1971.[5] It is often said that democracy is a twentieth-century phenomenon, but it would be more accurate to call it a post-1945 phenomenon. The democratic peace proposition can therefore only be properly tested in the post-1945 era.

The second problem is that the democratic post-1945 era coincides almost exactly with the era of the Cold War and that "realists" insist that the Cold War can account for the peace among the post-1945 democratic polities as well as or even better than the fact that these polities were democratic. In the words of Farber and Gowa (1997, 393–94), "the advent of the Cold War induced strong common interests among democratic states [and these] common interests rather than common polities explain the post-1945 democratic peace." Because the Cold War pitted most of the world's democracies against the major non-democracies, the relative impacts of democracy and Cold War are almost impossible to disentangle.[6]

Indirect tests

In response to the above analytical problems, most scholarly analyses have either explicitly or implicitly – usually the latter – resorted to various forms of indirect tests. One example is James Lee Ray's (1997, 56–57) answer to the Farber-Gowa explanation. He argues that if the complete absence of wars between democracies in the Cold War era can be explained in realist terms, one would also expect the absence of wars between states in the Communist camp and the absence of wars between any of the states, including non-democracies, on the "free world" side of the struggle. As he points out, however, there were several wars of both kinds: armed conflicts within the Communist camp (the Soviet attacks on Hungary, Czecho-Slovakia, and Afghanistan, Soviet border clashes with China, and Vietnam's invasion of Cambodia) and wars involving at least one undemocratic state in the non-Communist camp (the El Salvador-Honduras war in 1969, the Greek-Turkish clash over Cyprus in 1974, and the 1982 British-Argentinian war over the Falkland Islands). Hence, he concludes, the democratic peace proposition is much more persuasive than the realist proposition.

The other indirect tests all derive further propositions from the proposition that democracies do not or rarely engage in war with each other; if the derivative propositions are validated – which is the case in the majority of studies – they lend support to the original democratic peace proposition. Four such indirect tests can be distinguished. The first explores the link between democracy and actions that fall short of full-scale war but that are clearly not pacific in nature: military interventions (Hermann and Kegley 1996), militarized disputes (Oneal and Russett 1997), and the tendency to escalate conflict (Senese 1997). The second category of indirect tests includes the many studies that focus on the period before 1945, when there were very few democracies, and the period before 1893, when there were no democracies at all; an example is the pioneering Small-Singer (1976) study which covers the period from 1815 to 1965. Here, the independent variable is not democracy but the degree of non-democracy.

The third indirect test focuses on democratizing states and hypothesizes that these states tend to become more peaceful as they democratize. This hypothesis has been partly disconfirmed in one study, which shows that states in transition to democracy are less pacific than stable polities of both the democratic and autocratic type (Mansfield and Snyder 1995), but confirmed in another (Ward and Gleditsch 1998). The fourth and final test is based on the argument that, if the democratic peace proposition is correct, we can also expect democracies to be peaceful internally and not to conduct civil wars. For instance, one skeptic (Layne 1994, 41) uses the American Civil War as a key disconfirming case – not very convincing evidence, of course, since neither side was fully democratic and one side even practiced slavery. On the basis of broad comparative evidence, Rudolph J. Rummel

(1997, 85) concludes that democracy "sharply reduces the severity of domestic collective violence, genocide, and mass murder by governments," and Ted Robert Gurr (1993, 290–92) shows that democracies have an especially good record of peacefully resolving ethnic conflicts.

Another indirect test: democracy and foreign aid

We offer still another indirect test. Our argument begins with the cultural and structural explanations of the democratic peace, which are the two most common and most plausible theoretical rationales for the phenomenon. The cultural explanation is that democracies, as noted earlier, externalize their domestic norms of settling conflicts by discussion, negotiation, and compromise instead of by force. The structural explanation is that democratic checks and balances, along with transparency and accountability, give policy-makers a political and electoral motivation to avoid the material costs of war (Chan 1997, 77; Solingen 1996, 811–82). Moreover, the cultural and structural forces for peace reinforce each other. The culture of compromise strengthens compromise-inducing institutions, and compromise-oriented structures can shape accommodating political attitudes.

Our second step is to point out that democracies differ with regard to how compromise-oriented their political cultures and structures are. The distinction here is between majoritarian and consensus democracies (Lijphart 1984; 1999). Consensus democracies are more compromise-oriented than majoritarian democracies and, according to the rationale presented above, can therefore also be expected to be more peace-oriented. In other words, we assume that there is a continuum in these respects from non-democracy to majoritarian democracy to consensus democracy instead of a simple contrast between democracy and autocracy.

Our third step is to specify a dependent variable that differs from wars or other military confrontations – since these are extremely rare among democracies – but that still captures degrees of difference in the peacefulness of foreign policies. Our choice here is the supply of foreign aid – economic development assistance, not military aid – which is arguably the most peaceful and most generous of foreign policies that nations can engage in. Our hypothesis is that consensus democracy is positively correlated with levels of foreign aid giving. If this hypothesis is correct, it indirectly strengthens the democratic peace proposition.

We focus on those countries that indisputably meet the criteria of full and consolidated democracy. The precise definition is: political systems with populations over a quarter of a million that, as of 1996, can be regarded as fully democratic according to Dahl's criteria and that had been continuously democratic since 1977 or earlier.[7] Thirty-six countries fit this definition, and twenty-one of these gave economic development assistance in the 1980s and 1990s: sixteen West European countries plus the United States, Canada, Japan, Australia, and New Zealand. These twenty-one democracies are listed in

Table 16.1, in descending order according to their degree of consensus democracy.[8]

Given the importance of the Cold War in the debate about the democratic peace, we chose two four-year periods for our examination of levels of foreign aid: 1982–85, clearly well before the end of the Cold War – when, in fact, very few people expected that the Cold War would end so soon! – and 1992–95 when the Cold War had clearly ended. We use multi-year averages in order to even out annual fluctuations in foreign aid (although, in practice, very few large fluctuations occurred). The figures presented in the second and third columns of Table 16.1 are the average annual economic development assistance as a percentage of the gross national product of each country. In the 1982–85 period, foreign aid ranged from a high of 1.04 percent of gross national product (Norway) to a low of 0.04 percent (Portugal); from 1992 to 1995, the highest percentage was 1.01 percent (Denmark

Table 16.1 Degrees of consensus democracy (1971–96), economic development assistance as a percent of GNP (1982–85 and 1992–95), and economic development assistance as a percent of defense spending (1992–95) by twenty-one democracies

	Degree of consensus democracy (1971–96)	Aid as % of GNP (1982–85)	Aid as % of GNP (1992–95)	Aid as % of defense spending (1992–95)
Switzerland	1.87	0.29	0.37	24
Finland	1.66	0.34	0.42	22
Denmark	1.45	0.79	1.01	52
Belgium	1.42	0.57	0.36	21
Netherlands	1.16	0.98	0.81	37
Italy	1.16	0.24	0.27	13
Sweden	1.04	0.88	0.94	36
Norway	0.92	1.04	1.01	34
Japan	0.85	0.31	0.28	30
Portugal	0.36	0.04	0.32	12
Luxembourg	0.29	0.08	0.34	39
Austria	0.26	0.32	0.31	35
Germany	0.23	0.47	0.34	18
Ireland	0.12	0.23	0.22	18
United States	−0.52	0.24	0.14	4
Spain	−0.59	0.09	0.26	17
Australia	−0.67	0.50	0.36	15
France	−0.93	0.59	0.60	19
Canada	−1.07	0.46	0.43	23
New Zealand	−1.12	0.26	0.24	17
United Kingdom	−1.39	0.34	0.30	9

Source: Based on data in Lijphart 1999, Appendix A; United Nations Development Programme 1994, 197; United Nations Development Programme 1995, 204, 206; United Nations Development Programme 1996, 199, 201; United Nations Development Programme 1997, 214–15.

and Norway) and the lowest 0.14 percent (the United States). For the 1992–95 period, the fourth column also presents foreign aid as a percentage of defense expenditures, as calculated by the United Nations Development Programme. The highest foreign aid as a percent of defense expenditure was Denmark's 51 percent, and the lowest that of the United States, 4 percent.

The first column of Table 16.1 shows the degree of consensus democracy of the twenty-one countries, based on five institutional characteristics in the 1971–96 period: the degree of executive power sharing, the relative power of the executive and the legislature, the party system, the electoral system, and the interest groups system. Majoritarian characteristics are one-party majority cabinets, executive dominance over the legislature, a two-party system, a disproportional electoral system, and a pluralist, competitive, free-for-all interest group system. Consensus characteristics are broad coalition cabinets, a balance of power between executive and legislature, a multiparty system, relatively proportional election outcomes, and a corporatist interest group system with frequent tripartite consultations and agreements between the government, employers, and labor unions. These five variables were measured on different scales and therefore had to be standardized before they could be averaged (and standardized again). Each unit on the standardized average score represents one standard deviation. The range is from 1.87 for highly consensual Switzerland to −1.39 for the highly majoritarian United Kingdom.[9]

It is worth highlighting that two of the five characteristics that distinguish consensus from majoritarian democracy can be extended to non-democratic forms of government – which strengthens the theoretical rationale for our assumption that there is a continuum running from consensus to majoritarian to non-democracy. First, consensus democracies tend to have relatively weak executives and relatively strong legislatures; majoritarian democracies have executives that predominate over their legislatures; and non-democracies tend to have extremely strong executive power and extremely weak legislatures or no legislatures at all. Second, the multiparty systems of consensus democracy contrast with the two-party systems of majoritarian democracy and further with the typical one-party or no-party systems of autocratic regimes.

Consensus democracies are indeed more generous

Table 16.2 presents the bivariate relationships between degree of consensus democracy and the three foreign aid variables. The estimated regression coefficient is the increase or decrease in the dependent variables (foreign aid as a percent of GNP and as a percent of defense expenditures) for each unit increase in the independent variable – in our case, each increase by one standard deviation of consensus democracy. Because the table reports bivariate regression results, the standardized regression coefficient in the second column equals the correlation coefficient. The statistical significance

Table 16.2 Bivariate regression analyses of the effect of consensus democracy on economic development assistance (as a percentage of GNP and as a percentage of defense expenditures) provided by twenty-one democracies, 1982–85 and 1992–95

	Estimated regression coefficient	*Standardized regression coefficient*	*Absolute t-value*
Aid as % of GNP (1982–85)	0.09*	0.30	1.38
Aid as % of GNP (1992–95)	0.10**	0.39	1.86
Aid as % of defense spending (1992–95)	5.94***	0.51	2.58

Notes: *Statistically significant at the 10 percent level (one-tailed test)
**Statistically significant at the 5 percent level (one-tailed test)
***Statistically significant at the 1 percent level (one-tailed test)
Source: Based on the data in Table 16.1.

of the correlations depends on the absolute t-value, shown in the third column, and the number of cases (the twenty-one countries in our analysis). Whether or not the correlations are significant is indicated by asterisks; three levels of significance are reported, including the least demanding 10 percent level.

The range in degrees of consensus democracy is 3.26 standard deviations. Most democracies are not in extreme positions, however, and it would be more accurate to say that the "typical" consensus democracy and the "typical" majoritarian democracy are roughly two standard deviations apart. This means, for instance, that, based on the value of 5.94 percent in the first column, the economic development assistance (expressed as a percentage of defense expenditure) provided by the typical consensus democracy was almost 12 percentage points higher than the aid given by the typical majoritarian democracy.

In the bivariate regression analysis, consensus democracy is significantly correlated with all three foreign aid variables, albeit at different levels; the strongest correlation, at the 1 percent level, is with aid as a percentage of defense spending. Figures 16.1 and 16.2 present the scattergrams for the relationships between the degree of consensus democracy and foreign aid as a percent of GNP and as a percent of defense spending, both in the most recent period. The scattergrams for the relationship between consensus democracy and aid as a percent of GNP in 1982–85 and in 1992–95 are very similar and, in order to save space, we are not showing the scattergram for the earlier period. The close similarity between the patterns in the two periods is theoretically very significant, of course: it shows that the end of the Cold War had relatively little influence on the relative levels of foreign aid given by our twenty-one countries.

Figure 16.1 shows that the Netherlands and three of the Nordic countries Denmark, Norway, and Sweden – are the countries that are mainly responsible for the high average level of foreign aid that the consensus democracies

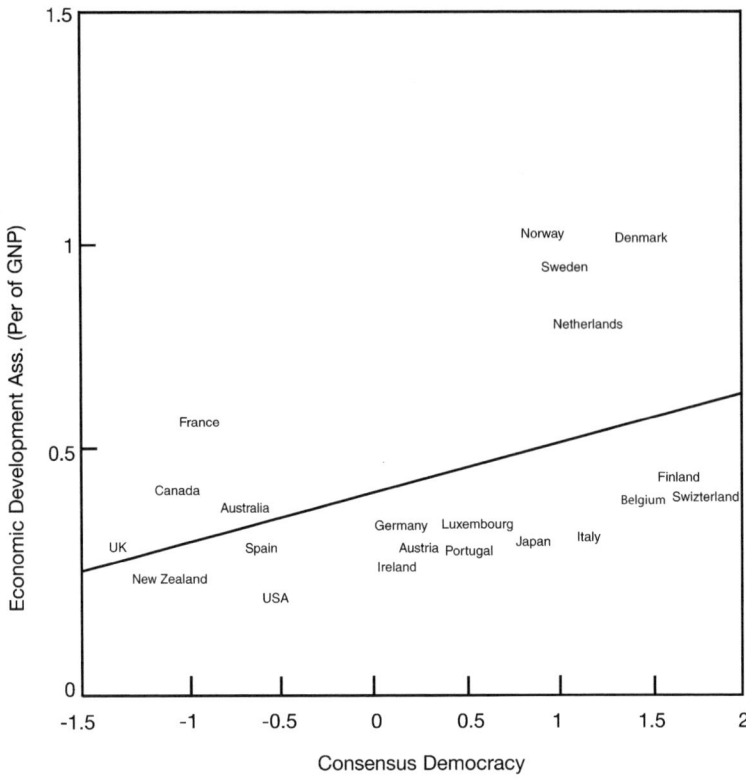

Figure 16.1 The relationship between consensus democracy and economic development assistance (as percentage of GNP), 1992–9

dispense. This generosity is neither a general Nordic characteristic nor a general Benelux quality: Finland and Belgium are also consensus democracies and Luxembourg partly so, and these three countries do not supply unusually high levels of aid. On the majoritarian (left) side of the scatter-gram, five Anglo-Saxon countries and Spain are located in close proximity to each other, all with foreign aid levels below 0.5 percent of GNP. France is the exceptional case of a majoritarian country with considerably greater gener-osity (0.60 percent of GNP) – in fact, the fifth highest level among the twenty-one democracies. There is clearly also a contrast between the more generous Continental European countries, including France, on the one hand, and the less generous countries with a British political heritage, including Ireland, on the other. The average aid levels for the fourteen Continental European countries is 0.53 percent – almost double the average of 0.28 percent for the six Anglo-Saxon countries (which is also Japan's percentage).

Figure 16.2 relates the degree of consensus democracy to foreign aid as a percent of defense spending, and the scattergram resembles that of Figure 16.1 in most respects. The same three Nordic countries and the Netherlands

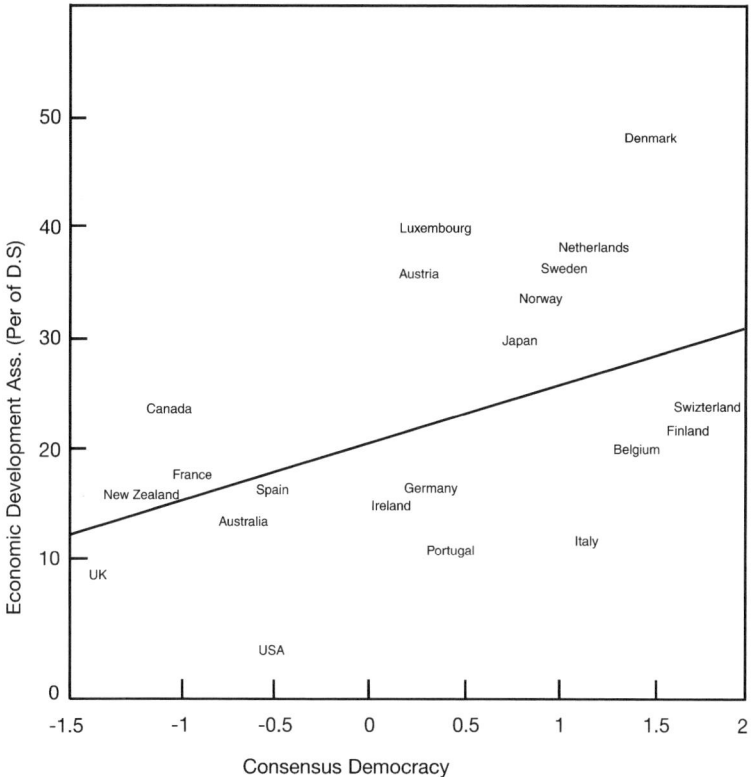

Figure 16.2 The relationship between consensus democracy and economic development assistance (as percentage of defense spending), 1992–95

are again in high positions, but they are now joined above the regression line by consensual Japan and moderately consensual Austria and Luxembourg. On the majoritarian side, France is no longer an outlier, and the United States – already the least generous democracy in Figure 16.1 – is now in an even more pronounced low position.

These findings clearly support our hypothesis concerning the relationship between type of democracy and economic development assistance. Before we declare this hypothesis confirmed, however, two important controls need to be introduced. First, since wealthier countries can better afford to give foreign aid than less well-to-do countries, the level of development should be controlled for. We used the United Nations Development Programme's (1997, 46–48) broadly based "human development index" as our measure of development.[10] The bivariate correlations between level of development and foreign aid all have positive signs, indicating that the richer countries indeed give more foreign aid than the less rich ones. However, only one of the correlations, between development level and foreign aid in 1982–85, is strong enough to be statistically significant (at the 5 percent level).

Second, since large countries tend to assume greater military responsibilities and hence tend to have larger defense expenditures, which can be expected to limit their ability and willingness to provide foreign aid, population size (logged) should be used as a control variable.[11] Here again, the bivariate correlations all have the expected sign – in this case, a negative sign: population size and foreign aid are indeed inversely related to each other. The correlation between population and aid as a percent of defense spending is very strong and highly significant (at the 1 percent level), but the other two negative correlations are not statistically significant.

When these three variables are simultaneously entered into the multiple regression equations, they all turn out to have a strong impact on levels of foreign aid: with just one exception (the influence of population size on aid in 1982–85), all of the correlations are now statistically significant. For the purposes of this study, it is especially important to note that, with population size and development level controlled for, the correlations between consensus democracy and the three measures of foreign aid remain significant – now all at the same 5 percent level. With the controls in place, the typical consensus democracy gave about 0.20 percentage points more of its GNP in foreign aid than the typical majoritarian democracy in both periods – the relationship was only fractionally stronger in the Cold War years – and its aid as a percent of defense spending was about 9.5 percentage points higher.

Conclusion

On the basis of the evidence presented above, we can conclude that type of democracy and foreign aid are closely related. We have assumed a continuum from consensus democracy to majoritarian democracy to non-democracy. This assumption is highly plausible and, if it is correct, it means that the difference in peaceful orientations that we found between consensus and majoritarian democracies can be extrapolated to non-democratic forms of government. Hence our analysis offers indirect support to the democratic peace proposition – somewhat more indirect support than that offered by the other indirect tests described earlier, but nevertheless very strong and persuasive support.

Notes

1 For excellent reviews of the literature, see Chan (1997), Maoz (1997), and Ray (1997).
2 As we shall argue below, most of the participants in these wars cannot be regarded as truly democratic.
3 However, women did not have the right to be candidates for public office in New Zealand until 1919.
4 In Samuel P. Huntington's (1991, 13–16) well known identification of three waves of democratization, he sees the first wave starting much earlier: in 1828. However,

he uses a much too lenient definition of universal suffrage: the right to vote for at least 50 percent of adult males. This means that he accepts as democratic a system in which 75 percent of all adult citizens do not have the right to vote.

5 Moreover, Australian Aboriginals (about 2 percent of the population) could not vote in federal elections until 1962, and universal suffrage in the United States was not fully established until the passage of the Voting Rights Act in 1965.

6 One example of an attempt to disentangle the variables is Erik Gartzke's (1998). He contends that similar preferences among nations (measured by means of roll-call votes in the United Nations General Assembly from 1950 to 1985) takes precedence over the degree of democracy in these nations: it is their similar preferences rather than their shared democracy that makes democratic states unwilling to go to war with each other.

7 Our reliance on Dahl's criteria differs from the reliance by most democratic peace researchers on the Polity II and Polity III data sets (see Jagger and Gurr 1995). However, our set of democracies largely coincide with the countries that receive the top ratings on the Polity II and III measures.

8 The other fifteen democracies are the Bahamas, Barbados, Botswana, Colombia, Costa Rica, Greece, Iceland, India, Israel, Jamaica, Malta, Mauritius, Papua New Guinea, Trinidad and Tobago, and Venezuela.

9 These five characteristics jointly constitute the executives-parties dimension of the contrast between consensus and majoritarian democracy. There is a second dimension to this contrast – the federal-unitary dimension – also based on five characteristics, such as federal and decentralized versus unitary and centralized government and strong bicameralism versus unicameralism (see Lijphart 1999). In this chapter, we focus exclusively on the executives-parties dimension.

10 The index is based on three main variables: income, life expectancy, and educational attainment.

11 Robert A. Dahl and Edward R. Tufte (1973, 122–23) found a strong link between population size and defense spending.

References

Benoit, Kenneth (1996). "Democracies Really Are More Pacific (in General): Reexamining Regime Type and War Involvement," *Journal of Conflict Resolution*, vol. 40, no. 4, pp. 636–57.

Chan, Steve (1997). "In Search of the Democratic Peace: Problems and Promise," *Mershon International Studies Review*, vol. 41, no. 1, pp. 59–91.

Dahl, Robert A. (1971). *Polyarchy: Participation and Opposition*, New Haven CT: Yale University Press.

Dahl, Robert A. and Edward R. Tufte (1973). *Size and Democracy*, New Haven CT: Yale University Press.

Farber, Henry S. and Joanne Gowa (1997). "Common Interests or Common Polities? Reinterpreting the Democratic Peace," *Journal of Politics*, vol. 59, no. 2, pp. 393–417.

Gartzke, Erik (1998). "Kant We All Just Get Along? Opportunity, Willingness and the Origins of the Democratic Peace," *American Journal of Political Science*, vol. 42, no. 1, pp. 1–27.

Gleditsch, Nils-Petter and Havard Hegre (1997). "Peace and Democracy: Three Levels of Analysis," *Journal of Conflict Resolution*, vol. 41, no. 2, pp. 283–310.

Gurr, Ted Robert (1993). *Minorities at Risk: A Global View of Ethnopolitical Conflicts*, Washington DC: United States Institute of Peace Press.

Hermann, Margaret G. and Charles W. Kegley (1996). "Ballots, a Barrier Against the Use of Bullets and Bombs: Democratization and Military Intervention," *Journal of Conflict Resolution*, vol. 40, no. 3, pp. 436–60.

Huntington, Samuel P. (1991). *The Third Wave: Democratization in the Late Twentieth Century*, Norman OK: University of Oklahoma Press.

Jaggers, Keith and Ted Robert Gurr (1995). "Tracking Democracy's Third Wave with the Polity III Data," *Journal of Peace Research*, vol. 32, no. 4, pp. 469–82.

Layne, Christopher (1994). "Kant or Cant: The Myth of Democratic Peace," *International Security*, vol. 19, no. 2, pp. 5–49.

Lijphart, Arend (1984). *Democracies: Patterns of Majoritarian and Consensus Government in Twenty-One Countries*, New Haven CT: Yale University Press.

——(1999). *Patterns of Democracy: Government Forms and Performance in Thirty-Six Countries*, New Haven CT: Yale University Press.

Mansfield, Edward D. and Jack Snyder (1995). "Democratization and the Danger of War," *International Security*, vol. 20, no. 1, pp. 5–38.

Maoz, Zeev (1997). *Regional Security in the Middle East, Past, Present and Future*, London: Frank Cass.

Oneal, John R. and Bruce Russett (1997). "The Classical Liberals Were Right: Democracy, Interdependence, and Conflict, 1950–85," *International Studies Quarterly*, vol. 41, no. 2, pp. 267–94.

Raknerud, Arvid and Havard Hegre (1997). "The Hazards of War: Reassessing Evidence of the Democratic Peace," *Journal of Peace Research*, vol. 34, no. 4, pp. 385–404.

Ray, James Lee (1997). "The Democratic Path to Peace," *Journal of Democracy*, vol. 8, no. 2, pp. 49–64.

Rummel, Rudolph J. (1983). "Libertarianism and International Violence," *Journal of Conflict Resolution*, vol. 27, no. 1, pp. 27–71.

——(1997). *Power Kills: Democracy as a Method of Nonviolence*, New Brunswick NJ: Transaction Publishers.

Senese, Paul D. (1997). "Between Dispute and War: The Effect of Joint Democracy on Interstate Conflict Escalation," *Journal of Politics*, vol. 59, no. 1, pp. 1–27.

Small, Melvin and David Singer (1976). "The War-Proneness of Democratic Regimes, 1816–1965," *Jerusalem Journal of International Relations*, vol. 1, no. 4, pp. 50–69.

Solingen, Etel (1996). "Democracy, Economic Reform, and Regional Cooperation," *Journal of Theoretical Politics*, vol. 8, no. 1, pp. 79–115.

United Nations Development Programme (1994). *Human Development Report 1994*, New York: Oxford University Press.

——(1995). *Human Development Report 1995*, New York: Oxford University Press.

——(1996). *Human Development Report 1996*, New York: Oxford University Press.

——(1997). *Human Development Report 1997*, New York: Oxford University Press.

Ward, Michael D. and Kristian S. Gleditsch (1998). "Democratizing for Peace," *American Political Science Review*, vol. 92, no. 1, pp. 51–61.

17 Comparative politics and the comparative method

Among the several fields or subdisciplines into which the discipline of political science is usually divided, comparative politics is the only one that carries a methodological instead of a substantive label. The term "comparative politics" indicates the *how* but does not specify the *what* of the analysis. The label is somewhat misleading because both explicit methodological concern and implicit methodological awareness among students of comparative politics have generally not been very high.[1] Indeed, too many students of the field have been what Giovanni Sartori calls "unconscious thinkers" – unaware of and not guided by the logic and methods of empirical science, although perhaps well versed in quantitative research techniques. One reason for this unconscious thinking is undoubtedly that the comparative method is such a basic, and basically simple, approach, that a *methodology* of comparative political analysis does not really exist. As Sartori points out, the other extreme – that of the "overconscious thinkers," whose "standards of method and theory are drawn from the physical paradigmatic sciences" – is equally unsound.[2] The purpose of this paper is to contribute to "conscious thinking" in comparative politics by focusing on comparison as a method of political inquiry. The paper will attempt to analyze not only the inevitable weaknesses and limitations of the comparative method but also its great strengths and potentialities.

In the literature of comparative politics, a wide variety of meanings is attached to the terms "comparison" and "comparative method." The comparative method is defined here as one of the basic methods – the others being the experimental, statistical, and case study methods – of establishing general empirical propositions. It is, in the first place, definitely a *method*, not just "a convenient term vaguely symbolizing the focus of one's research interests."[3] Nor is it a special set of substantive concerns in the sense of Shmuel N. Eisenstadt's definition of the comparative approach in social research: he states that the term does not "properly designate a specific method ... but rather a special focus on cross-societal, institutional, or macrosocietal aspects of societies and social analysis."[4]

Second, the comparative method is here defined as *one* of the basic scientific methods, not *the* scientific method. It is, therefore, narrower in scope than what Harold D. Lasswell has in mind when he argues that "for anyone with a scientific approach to political phenomena the idea of an independent comparative method seems redundant," because the scientific approach is "unavoidably comparative."[5] Likewise, the definition used here differs from the very similar broad interpretation given by Gabriel A. Almond, who also equates the comparative with the scientific method: "It makes no sense to speak of a comparative politics in political science since if it is a science, it goes without saying that it is comparative in its approach."[6]

Third, the comparative method is here regarded as a *method of discovering empirical relationships among variables*, not as a method of measurement. These two kinds of methods should be clearly distinguished. It is the latter that Kalleberg has in mind when he discusses the "logic of comparison." He defines the comparative method as "a form of measurement"; comparison means "nonmetrical ordering," or in other words, ordinal measurement.[7] Similarly, Sartori is thinking in terms of measurement on nominal, ordinal (or comparative), and cardinal scales when he describes the conscious thinker as "the man that realizes the limitations of not having a thermometer and still manages to say a great deal simply by saying hot and cold, warmer and cooler."[8] This important step of measuring variables is logically prior to the step of finding relationships among them. It is the second of these steps to which the term "comparative method" refers in this paper.

Finally, a clear distinction should be made between *method* and *technique*. The comparative method is a broad-gauge, general method, not a narrow, specialized technique. In this vein, Gunnar Heckscher cautiously refers to "the method (or at least the *procedure*) of comparison,"[9] and Walter Goldschmidt prefers the term comparative *approach*, because "it lacks the preciseness to call it a method."[10] The comparative method may also be thought of as a basic research *strategy*, in contrast with a mere tactical aid to research. This will become clear in the discussion that follows.

The experimental, statistical, and comparative methods

The nature of the comparative method can be understood best if it is compared and contrasted with the two other fundamental strategies of research; these will be referred to, following Neil J. Smelser's example, as the *experimental* and the *statistical* methods.[11] All three methods (as well as certain forms of the case study method[12]) aim at scientific explanation, which consists of two basic elements: (1) the establishment of general empirical relationships among two or more variables,[13] while (2) all other variables are controlled, that is, held constant. These two elements are inseparable: one cannot be sure that a relationship is a true one unless the influence of other variables is controlled. The *ceteris paribus* condition is vital to empirical generalizations.

The experimental method, in its simplest form, uses two equivalent groups, one of which (the experimental group) is exposed to a stimulus while the other (the control group) is not. The two groups are then compared, and any difference can be attributed to the stimulus. Thus one knows the relationship between two variables – with the important assurance that no other variables were involved, because in all respects but one the two groups were alike. Equivalence – that is, the condition that the *cetera* are indeed *paria* – can be achieved by a process of deliberate randomization. The experimental method is the most nearly ideal method for scientific explanation, but unfortunately it can only rarely be used in political science because of practical and ethical impediments.

An alternative to the experimental method is the statistical method. It entails the conceptual (mathematical) manipulation of empirically observed data – which cannot be manipulated situationally as in experimental design – in order to discover controlled relationships among variables. It handles the problem of control by means of *partial correlations*. For instance, when one wants to inquire into the relationship between political participation and level of education attained, one should control for the influence of age because younger generations have received more education than older generations. This can be done by partialing – dividing the sample into a number of different age groups and looking at the correlations between participation and education within each separate age group. Paul F. Lazarsfeld states that this is such a basic research procedure that it "is applied almost automatically in empirical research. Whenever an investigator finds himself faced with the relationship between two variables, he immediately starts to 'cross-tabulate,' i.e., to consider the role of further variables."[14]

The statistical method can be regarded, therefore, as an approximation of the experimental method. As Ernest Nagel emphasizes, "every branch of inquiry aiming at reliable general laws concerning empirical subject matter must employ a procedure that, if it is not strictly controlled experimentation, has the essential logical functions of experiment in inquiry."[15] The statistical method does have these essential logical functions, but it is not as strong a method as experimentation because it cannot handle the problem of control as well. It cannot control for all other variables, merely for the other *key* variables that are known or suspected to exert influence. Strictly speaking, even the experimental method does not handle the problem of control perfectly, because the investigator can never be completely sure that his groups are actually alike in every respect.[16] But experimental design provides the closest approximation to this ideal. The statistical method, in turn, is an approximation – not the equivalent – of the experimental method. Conversely, one can also argue, as Lazarsfeld does, that the experimental method constitutes a special form of the statistical method, but only if one adds that it is an especially potent form.[17]

The logic of the comparative method is, in accordance with the general standard expounded by Nagel, also the same as the logic of the experimental method. The comparative method resembles the statistical method in all respects except one. The crucial difference is that the number of cases it deals with is too small to permit systematic control by means of partial correlations. This problem occurs in statistical operations, too; especially when one wants to control simultaneously for many variables, one quickly "runs out of cases." The comparative method should be resorted to when the number of cases available for analysis is so small that cross-tabulating them further in order to establish credible controls is not feasible. There is, consequently, no clear dividing line between the statistical and comparative methods; the difference depends entirely on the number of cases.[18] It follows that in many research situations, with an intermediate number of cases, a combination of the statistical and comparative methods is appropriate. Where the cases are national political systems, as they often are in the field of comparative politics, the number of cases is necessarily so restricted that the comparative method has to be used.

From the vantage point of the general aims and the alternative methods of scientific inquiry, one can consider the comparative method in proper perspective and answer such questions as the following, raised by Samuel H. Beer and by Harry Eckstein: Can comparison be regarded as "the social scientist's equivalent of the natural scientist's laboratory?"[19] and: "Is the comparative method in the social sciences … really an adequate substitute for experimentation in the natural sciences, as has sometimes been claimed?"[20] The answer is that the comparative method is not the equivalent of the experimental method but only a very imperfect substitute. A clear awareness of the limitations of the comparative method is necessary but need not be disabling, because, as we shall see, these weaknesses can be minimized. The "conscious thinker" in comparative politics should realize the limitations of the comparative method, but he should also recognize and take advantage of its possibilities.

The comparative method: weaknesses and strengths

The principal problems facing the comparative method can be succinctly stated as: many variables, small number of cases. These two problems are closely interrelated. The former is common to virtually all social science research regardless of the particular method applied to it; the latter is peculiar to the comparative method and renders the problem of handling many variables more difficult to solve.

Before turning to a discussion of specific suggestions for minimizing these problems, two general comments are in order. First, if at all possible one should generally use the statistical (or perhaps even the experimental) method instead of the weaker comparative method. But often, given the inevitable scarcity of time, energy, and financial resources, the intensive comparative analysis of a few cases may be more promising than a more superficial statistical analysis of many cases. In such a situation, the most fruitful approach would be to regard the comparative analysis as the first stage of research, in which hypotheses are carefully formul; statistical analysis as the second stage, in which these hypoth in as large a sample as possible.

In one type of comparative cross-national research, it is lc and may be advantageous to shift from the comparative to ـ method. Stein Rokkan distinguishes two aims of cross-national analysis. ▭.. is the testing of "*macro* hypotheses" concerning the "interrelations of structural elements of total systems"; here the number of cases tends to be limited, and one has to rely on the comparative method. The other is "*micro* replications," designed "to test out in other national and cultural settings a proposition already validated in one setting."[21] Here, too, one can use the comparative method, but if the proposition in question focuses on individuals as units of analysis, one can also use the statistical method; as Merritt and Rokkan point out, instead of the "one-nation, one-case" approach, nationality can simply be treated as an additional variable on a par with other individual attributes such as occupation, age, sex, type of neighborhood, etc.[22] Terence K. Hopkins and Immanuel Wallerstein make a similar distinction between truly "cross-national studies" in which total systems are the units of analysis, and "multi-national but *cross-individual* research."[23]

The second general comment concerns a dangerous but tempting fallacy in the application of the comparative method: the fallacy of attaching too much significance to negative findings. The comparative method should not lapse into what Johan Galtung calls "the traditional quotation/illustration methodology, where cases are picked that are in accordance with the hypothesis – and hypotheses are rejected if one deviant case is found."[24] All cases should, of course, be selected systematically, and the scientific search should be aimed at probabilistic, not universal, generalizations. The erroneous tendency to reject a hypothesis on the basis of a single deviant case is rare when the statistical method is used to analyze a large sample, but in the comparative analysis of a small number of cases even a single deviant finding tends to loom large. One or two deviant cases obviously constitute a much less serious problem in a statistical analysis of very many cases than in a comparative study of only a few – perhaps less than ten – cases. But it is nevertheless a mistake to reject a hypothesis "because one can think pretty quickly of a contrary case."[25] Deviant cases weaken a probabilistic hypothesis, but they can only invalidate it if they turn up in sufficient numbers to make the hypothesized relationship disappear altogether.[26]

After these introductory observations, let us turn to a discussion of specific ways and means of minimizing the "many variables, small N" problem of the comparative method, These may be divided into four categories:

1 *Increase the number of cases as much as possible.* Even though in most situations it is impossible to augment the number of cases sufficiently to shift to the statistical method, any enlargement of the sample, however small, improves the chances of instituting at least some control.[27]

Modern comparative politics has made great progress in this respect as a result of the efforts of the field's innovators to fashion universally applicable vocabularies of basic politically relevant concepts, notably the approaches based on Parsonian theory and Gabriel A. Almond's functional approach.[28] Such a restatement of variables in comparable terms makes many previously inaccessible cases available for comparative analysis. In addition to extending the analysis geographically, one should also consider the possibilities of "longitudinal" (cross-historical) extension by including as many historical cases as possible.[29]

It was the promise of discovering universal laws through global and longitudinal comparisons that made Edward A. Freeman enthusiastically espouse the comparative method almost a century ago. In his *Comparative Politics*, published in 1873, he called the comparative method "the greatest intellectual achievement" of his time, and stated that it could lead to the formulation of "analogies ... between the political institutions of times and countries most remote from one another." Comparative politics could thus discover "a world in which times and tongues and nations which before seemed parted poles asunder, now find each one its own place, its own relation to every other."[30] The field of comparative politics has not yet achieved – and may never achieve – the goals that Freeman set for it with such optimism. But his words can remind us of the frequent utility of extending comparative analyses both geographically and historically. (The value of this suggestion is somewhat diminished, of course, because of the serious lack of information concerning most political systems; for historical cases in particular this problem is often irremediable.)

2 *Reduce the "property-space" of the analysis.* If the sample of cases cannot be increased, it may be possible to combine two or more variables that express an essentially similar underlying characteristic into a single variable. Thus the number of cells in the matrix representing the relationship is reduced, and the number of cases in each cell increased correspondingly. Factor analysis can often be a useful technique to achieve this objective. Such a reduction of what Lazarsfeld calls the "property-space" increases the possibilities of further cross-tabulation and control without increasing the sample itself.[31] It may also be advisable in certain instances to reduce the number of classes into which the variables are divided (for instance, by simplifying a set of several categories into a dichotomy), and thus to achieve the same objective of increasing the average number of cases per cell. The latter procedure, however, has the disadvantage of sacrificing a part of the information at the investigator's disposal, and should not be used lightly.

3 *Focus the comparative analysis on "comparable" cases.* In this context, "comparable" means: similar in a large number of important characteristics (variables) which one wants to treat as constants, but dissimilar as far as those variables are concerned which one wants to relate to each

other. If such comparable cases can be found, they offer particularly good opportunities for the application of the comparative method because they allow the establishment of relationships among a few variables while many other variables are controlled.[32] As Ralph Braibanti states, "the movement from hypothesis to theory is contingent upon analysis of the total range of political systems,"[33] but it is often more practical to accord priority to the focus on a limited number of comparable cases and the discovery of *partial* generalizations.

Whereas the first two ways of strengthening the comparative method were mainly concerned with the problem of "small N," this third approach focuses on the problem of "many variables." While the total number of variables cannot be reduced, by using comparable cases in which many variables are constant, one can reduce considerably the number of *operative* variables and study their relationships under controlled conditions without the problem of running out of cases. The focus on comparable cases differs from the first recommendation not only in its preoccupation with the problem of "many variables" rather than with "small N," but also in the fact that as a by-product of the search for comparable cases, the number of cases subject to analysis will usually be *decreased*. The two recommendations thus point in fundamentally different directions, although both are compatible with the second (and also the fourth) recommendation.

This form of the comparative method is what John Stuart Mill described as the "method of difference" and as the "method of concomitant variations." The method of difference consists of "comparing instances in which [a] phenomenon does occur, with instances in other respects similar in which it does not." The method of concomitant variations is a more sophisticated version of the method of difference: instead of observing merely the presence or absence of the operative variables, it observes and measures the quantitative variations of the operative variables and relates these to each other. As in the case of the method of difference, all other factors must be kept constant; in Mill's words, "that we may be warranted in inferring causation from concomitance of variations, the concomitance itself must be proved by the Method of Difference."[34]

Mill's method of concomitant variations is often claimed to be the first systematic formulation of the modern comparative method.[35] It should be pointed out, however, that Mill himself thought that the methods of difference and of concomitant variations could not be applied in the social sciences because sufficiently similar cases could not be found. He stated that their application in political science was "completely out of the question" and branded any attempt to do so as a "gross misconception of the mode of investigation proper to political phenomena."[36] Durkheim agreed with Mill's negative judgment: "The absolute elimination of adventitious elements is an ideal which cannot really be attained ... one can never be even approximately certain that two societies agree or differ

in all respects save one."[37] These objections are founded on a too exact-
ing scientific standard – what Sartori calls "overconscious thinking." It is
important to remember, however, that in looking for comparable cases,
this standard should be approximated as closely as possible.

The area approach appears to lend itself quite well to this way of applying the comparative method because of the cluster of characteristics that
areas tend to have in common and that can, therefore be used as controls.[38] But opinions on the utility of the area approach differ sharply:
Gunnar Heckscher states that "area studies are of the very essence of
comparative government," and points out that "the number of variables,
while frequently still very large, is at least reduced in the case of a happy
choice of area."[39] Roy C. Macridis and Richard Cox also argue that if
areas are characterized by political as well as non-political uniformities,
"the area concept will be of great value, since certain political processes
will be compared between units within the area against a common
background of similar trait configuration"; they cite Latin America as an
example of an area offering the prospect of "fruitful intra-area comparison."[40] On the other hand, Dankwart A. Rustow declares in a recent
article that area study is "almost obsolete," and he shows little faith in it
as a setting for "manageable comparative study." He argues that "mere
geographic proximity does not necessarily furnish the best basis of comparison," and furthermore that "comparability is a quality that is not
inherent in any given set of objects; rather it is a quality imparted to
them by the observer's perspective."[41] This is a compelling argument that
should be carefully considered.

It is not true that areas reflect merely geographic proximity; they tend to
be similar in many other basic respects. By means of an inductive
process – a factor analysis of fifty-four social and cultural variables on
eighty-two countries – Bruce M. Russett discovered socio-culturally
similar groupings of countries, which correspond closely to areas or
regions of the world as usually defined.[42] Comparability is indeed not
inherent in any given area, but it is more likely within an area than in
a randomly selected set of countries. It seems unwise, therefore, to give
up the area approach in comparative politics. But two important
provisos should be attached to this conclusion. First, the area approach
can contribute to comparative politics if it is an aid to the comparative method, not if it becomes an end in itself. Otherwise, area study
may indeed become "a form of imprisonment."[43] It is against this danger
that the thrust of Rustow's argument is directed. Second, the area
approach should not be used indiscriminately, but only where it offers
the possibility of establishing crucial controls. In this respect, some of the
smaller areas may offer more advantages than the larger ones – Scandinavia, for example, which has barely been exploited in this manner, or
the Anglo-American countries, which have received greater comparative
attention (but which do not constitute an area in the literal sense).[44]

An alternative way of maximizing comparability is to analyze a single country diachronically. Such comparison of the same unit at different times generally offers a better solution to the control problem than comparison of two or more different but similar units (e.g. within the same area) at the same time, although the control can never be perfect; the same country is not really the same at different times. A good example of diachronic comparative analysis is Charles E. Frye's study of the empirical relationships among the party system, the interest group system, and political stability in Germany under the Weimar and Bonn republics. Frye argues that "for the study of these relationships, Weimar and Bonn make a particularly good case [strictly speaking, *two* cases] because there are more constants and relatively fewer variables than in many cross-national studies. Yet the differences could hardly be sharper."[45]

Unless the national political system itself constitutes the unit of analysis, comparability can also be enhanced by focusing on intra-nation instead of inter-nation comparisons. The reason is again the same: comparative intra-nation analysis can take advantage of the many similar national characteristics serving as controls.[46] Smelser illustrates the utility of this strategy with the example of a hypothetical research project on industrialization in Germany and Italy:

> For many purposes it would be more fruitful to compare northern Italy with southern Italy, and the Ruhr with Bavaria, than it would be to compare Germany as a whole with Italy as a whole. These two countries differ not only in level of industrialization, but also in cultural traditions, type of governmental structure, and so on.

The advantage of intra-unit comparison is that inter-unit differences can be held constant. "Then, having located what appear to be operative factors in the intra-unit comparisons, it is possible to move to the inter-unit comparisons to see if the same differences hold in the large."[47]

As Juan J. Linz and Amando de Miguel point out, a particularly promising approach may be the combination of intra-nation and inter-nation comparisons: "The comparison of those sectors of two societies that have a greater number of characteristics in common while differing on some crucial ones may be more fruitful than overall national comparisons."[48] An illustrative example of this approach in the political realm is suggested by Raoul Naroll:

> If one wishes to test theories about the difference between the cabinet and the presidential systems of government ... one is better advised to compare Manitoba and North Dakota than to compare Great Britain and the United States, since with respect to all other variables

Manitoba and North Dakota are very much alike, while Great Britain and the United States have many other differences.[49]

4 *Focus the comparative analysis on the "key" variables.* Finally, the problem of "many variables" may be alleviated not only by some of the specific approaches suggested above but also by a general commitment to theoretical parsimony. Comparative analysis must avoid the danger of being overwhelmed by large numbers of variables and, as a result, losing the possibility of discovering controlled relationships, and it must therefore judiciously restrict itself to the really key variables, omitting those of only marginal importance. The nature of the comparative method and its special limitations constitute a strong argument against what Lasswell and Braibanti call "configurative" or "contextual" analysis: "the identification and interpretation of factors in the whole social order which appear to affect whatever political functions and their institutional manifestations have been identified and listed for comparison" (Braibanti's definition).[50] Lasswell argues that the comparative method as usually applied has been insufficiently configurative, and calls for the exploration of more variables: the entire context – past, present, and future – "must be continually scanned."[51]

Scanning all variables is not the same as *including* all variables, of course, as long as one is on one's guard against an unrealistic and eventually self-defeating perfectionism. Comparative politics should avoid the trap into which the decision-making approach to the study of international politics fell, of specifying and calling for the analysis of an exhaustive list of all variables that have any possible influence on the decision-making process.[52] Parsimony suggests that Joseph LaPalombara's call for a "segmented approach" aiming at the formulation of middle-range propositions concerning partial systems makes a great deal of sense.[53] Similarly, Eckstein's urgent call for greater manageability of the field should be carefully heeded:

> The most obvious need in the field at present is simplification – and simplification on a rather grand scale – for human intelligence and scientific method can scarcely cope with the large numbers of variables, the heaps of concepts, and the mountains of data that seem at present to be required, and indeed to exist, in the field.[54]

It is no accident that the most fruitful applications of the comparative method have been in anthropological research. In primitive societies, the number of variables is not as bewilderingly large as in more advanced societies. All relevant factors can therefore be more easily surveyed and analyzed. In this respect, anthropology can be said to provide "almost a laboratory for the quasi-experimental approach to social phenomena."[55] Political science lacks this advantage, but can approximate it by focusing attention on the key variables in comparative studies.

A final comment is in order about the relationship of comparative politics as a substantive field and comparison as a method. The two are clearly not coterminous. In comparative politics, other methods can often also be employed, and the comparative method is also applicable in other fields and disciplines. A particularly instructive example is James N. Rosenau's study of the relative influence of individual variables (personal policy beliefs and "personalizing tendencies") and role variables (party role and committee role) on the behavior of United States senators during two similar periods: the "Acheson era," 1949–52, and the "Dulles era," 1953–56. Rosenau argues that these two eras were characterized by a generally similar international environment and that the two secretaries of state conducted similar foreign policies and also resembled each other in personal qualities. He terms the method that he uses in his analysis the method of "quantitative historical comparison." One of its basic characteristics is the testing of hypotheses by comparing two eras (cases) that are "essentially comparable ... in all respects except for the ... variables being examined." The method is called "quantitative" because the variables are operationally defined in quantitative terms, and "historical" because the two cases compared are historical eras.[56] The method is, therefore, a special form of the comparative method. It illustrates one of very many ways in which an imaginative investigator can devise fruitful applications of the comparative method.[57]

The comparative method and the case study method

The discussion of the comparative method is not complete without a consideration of the case study method. The statistical method can be applied to many cases, the comparative method to relatively few (but at least two) cases, and the case study method to one case. But the case study method can and should be closely connected with the comparative method (and sometimes also with the statistical method); certain types of case studies can even be considered implicit parts of the comparative method.

The great advantage of the case study is that by focusing on a single case, that case can be intensively examined even when the research resources at the investigator's disposal are relatively limited. The scientific status of the case study method is somewhat ambiguous, however, because science is a generalizing activity. A single case can constitute neither the basis for a valid generalization nor the ground for disproving an established generalization.

Indirectly, however, case studies can make an important contribution to the establishment of general propositions and thus to theory-building in political science. Six types of case studies may be distinguished. These are ideal types, and any particular study of a single case may fit more than one of the following categories:

1   Atheoretical case studies;
2   Interpretative case studies;
3   Hypothesis-generating case studies;
4   Theory-confirming case studies;
5   Theory-infirming case studies;
6   Deviant case studies.

Cases may be selected for analysis because of an interest in the case per se or because of an interest in theory-building. The first two types of cases belong to the former category. *Atheoretical case studies* are the traditional single-country or single-case analyses. They are entirely descriptive and move in a theoretical vacuum: they are neither guided by established or hypothesized generalizations nor motivated by a desire to formulate general hypotheses. Therefore, the direct theoretical value of these case studies is nil, but this does not mean that they are altogether useless. As LaPalombara emphasizes, the development of comparative politics is hampered by an appalling lack of information about almost all of the world's political systems.[58] Purely descriptive case studies do have great utility as basic data-gathering operations, and can thus contribute indirectly to theory-building. It can even be claimed that "the cumulative effect of such studies will lead to fruitful generalization," but only if it is recognized that this depends on a theoretically oriented secondary analysis of the data collected in atheoretical case studies.[59]

As indicated earlier, the atheoretical case study and the other types of case studies are ideal types. An actual instance of an atheoretical case study probably does not exist, because almost any analysis of a single case is guided by at least some vague theoretical notions and some anecdotal knowledge of other cases, and usually results in some vague hypotheses or conclusions that have a wider applicability. Such actual case studies fit the first type to a large extent, but they also fit one or more of the other types (particularly the third, fourth, and fifth types) at least to some extent.

Interpretative case studies resemble atheoretical case studies in one respect: they, too, are selected for analysis because of an interest in the case rather than an interest in the formulation of general theory. They differ, however, in that they make explicit use of established theoretical propositions. In these studies, a generalization is applied to a specific case with the aim of throwing light on the case rather than of improving the generalization in any way. Hence they are studies in "applied science." Since they do not aim to contribute to empirical generalizations, their value in terms of theory-building is nil. On the other hand, it is precisely the purpose of empirical theory to make such interpretative case studies possible.[60] Because of the still very limited degree of theoretical development in political science, such case studies are rare. One interesting example is Michael C. Hudson's imaginative and insightful case study of Lebanon in the light of existing development theories, in which he discovers a serious discrepancy between the country's socioeconomic and political development.[61]

The remaining four types of case studies are all selected for the purpose of theory-building. *Hypothesis-generating case studies* start out with a more or less vague notion of possible hypotheses, and attempt to formulate definite hypotheses to be tested subsequently among a larger number of cases. Their objective is to develop theoretical generalizations in areas where no theory exists yet. Such case studies are of great theoretical value. They may be particularly valuable if the case selected for analysis provides what Naroll calls a sort of "crucial experiment" in which certain variables of interest happen to be present in a special way.[62]

Theory-confirming and *theory-infirming case studies* are analyses of single cases within the framework of established generalizations. Prior knowledge of the case is limited to a single variable or to none of the variables that the proposition relates. The case study is a test of the proposition, which may turn out to be confirmed or infirmed by it. If the case study is of the theory-confirming type, it strengthens the proposition in question. But, assuming that the proposition is solidly based on a large number of cases, the demonstration that one more case fits does not strengthen it a great deal, Likewise, theory-infirming case studies merely weaken the generalizations marginally. The theoretical value of both types of case studies is enhanced, however, if the cases are, or turn out to be, extreme on one of the variables: such studies can also be labeled "crucial experiments" or crucial tests of the propositions.

Deviant case analyses are studies of single cases that are known to deviate from established generalizations. They are selected in order to reveal why the cases are deviant – that is, to uncover relevant additional variables that were not considered previously, or to refine the (operational) definitions of some or all of the variables.[63] In this way, deviant case studies can have great theoretical value. They weaken the original proposition, but suggest a modified proposition that may be stronger. The validity of the proposition in its modified form must be established by further comparative analysis.[64]

Of the six types of case studies, the hypothesis-generating and the deviant case studies have the greatest value in terms of their contribution to theory. Each of these two types, however, has quite different functions in respect to theory-building: The hypothesis-generating case study serves to generate new hypotheses, while the deviant case study refines and sharpens existing hypotheses. The deviant case study – as well as the theory-confirming and theory-infirming case studies – are implicitly comparative analyses. They focus on a particular case which is singled out for analysis from a relatively large number of cases and which is analyzed within the theoretical and empirical context of this set of cases. The deviant case may be likened to the "experimental group" with the remainder of the cases constituting the "control group." Just as the analytical power of the comparative method increases the closer it approximates the statistical and experimental methods, so the analytical power of the case study method increases the more it approximates the comparative method in the form of deviant case analysis. Such case analysis requires, of course, that the position of the deviant case on the variables under consideration, and consequently also its position relative to the other cases, are clearly defined.

The different types of cases and their unequal potential contributions to theory-building should be kept in mind in selecting and analyzing a single case. Some of the shortcomings in Eckstein's otherwise insightful and thought-provoking case study of Norway may serve as instructive examples.[65] Eckstein argues that the Norwegian case deviates from David B. Truman's proposition concerning "overlapping memberships,"[66] because Norway is a stable democracy in spite of the country's deep and non-overlapping geographic, economic, and cultural cleavages. But he fails to place the case of Norway in relation to other cases. In fact, although he describes Norway's divisions as "astonishingly great, sharp, and persistent," he explicitly rules out any comparison with the cleavages in other countries. This exclusion seriously weakens the case study. Furthermore, instead of trying to refine Truman's proposition with the help of the deviant findings, Eckstein simply drops it. In terms of the sixfold typology of case studies discussed above, his analysis of the Norwegian case is only a theory-infirming one and is not made into a deviant case study.

From then on, the case study becomes a theory-confirming one. Eckstein finds that the Norwegian case strikingly bears out his own "congruence" theory, which states that governments tend to be stable if there is considerable resemblance (congruence) between governmental authority patterns and the authority patterns in society.[67] He demonstrates persuasively that both governmental and social patterns of authority are strongly democratic in Norway and thus highly congruent. The problem here is not that the Norwegian facts do not fit the theory, but that they fit the theory too perfectly. The perfect fit strengthens the theory marginally, but does not contribute to its refinement. The theory does not hold that complete congruence of authority patterns is required for stable democracy. In his original statement of the congruence theory, Eckstein himself points out the necessity of further work on the important questions of how much disparity can be tolerated and how degrees of congruence and disparity can be measured.[68] Because the Norwegian case turns out to be a perfect theory-confirming one, it cannot be used to *refine* the theory in any of these respects. Therefore, Eckstein was unlucky in his selection of this case as far as the development of his congruence theory is concerned, and he fails to take full advantage of the case study method in analyzing the case in terms of Truman's theory of overlapping memberships.

The comparative method and the case study method have major drawbacks. But precisely because of the inevitable limitations of these methods, it is the challenging task of the investigator in the field of comparative politics to apply these methods in such a way as to minimize their weaknesses and to capitalize on their inherent strengths. Thus, they can be highly useful instruments in scientific political inquiry.

Acknowledgments

This article is a revised version of a paper presented to the Round Table Conference on Comparative Politics of the International Political Science Association, held in Turin, Italy, 10–14 September 1969. I am very grateful to David E. Apter, Donald T. Campbell, Robert A. Dahl, Giuseppe Di Palma, Harry Eckstein, Lewis J. Edinger, Samuel E. Finer, Galen A. Irwin, Jean Laponce, Juan J. Linz, Stefano Passigli, Austin Ranney, Stein Rokkan, Dankwart A. Rustow, and Kurt Sontheimer for their comments and suggestions on earlier drafts of the paper, which were very helpful in the preparation of the revision.

Notes

1 The reverse applies to the relatively new field of "political behavior": its name indicates a substantive field of inquiry, but especially the derivative "behaviorism" has come to stand for a general approach or set of methods. See Robert A. Dahl, "The Behavioral Approach in Political Science: Epitaph for a Monument to a Successful Protest," *American Political Science Review*, 55 (December 1961), pp. 763–72.

2 Giovanni Sartori, "Concept Misformation in Comparative Politics," *American Political Science Review*, 64 (December 1970), p. 1033.

3 Arthur L. Kalleberg, "The Logic of Comparison: A Methodological Note on the Comparative Study of Political Systems," *World Politics*, 19 (October 1966), p. 72.

4 Shmuel N. Eisenstadt, "Social Institutions: Comparative Study," in David L. Sills, ed., *International Encyclopedia of the Social Sciences* (New York: Macmillan/Free Press, 1968), vol. 14, p. 423. See also Eisenstadt, "Problems in the Comparative Analysis of Total Societies," *Transactions of the Sixth World Congress of Sociology* (Evian: International Sociological Association, 1966), vol. 1, esp. p. 188.

5 Harold D. Lasswell, "The Future of the Comparative Method," *Comparative Politics*, 1 (October 1968), p. 3.

6 Gabriel A. Almond, "Political Theory and Political Science," *American Political Science Review*, 60 (December 1966), pp. 877–78. Almond also argues that comparative politics is a "movement" in political science rather than a subdiscipline. See his "Comparative Politics," in *International Encyclopedia of the Social Sciences*, vol. 12, pp. 331–36.

7 Kalleberg, op. cit., pp. 72–73; see also pp. 75–78.

8 Sartori, op. cit., p. 1033. See also Paul F. Lazarsfeld and Allen H. Barton, "Qualitative Measurement in the Social Sciences: Classification, Typologies, and Indices," in Daniel Lerner and Harold D. Lasswell, eds, *The Policy Sciences: Recent Developments in Scope and Method* (Stanford CA: Stanford University Press, 1951), pp. 155–92.

9 Gunnar Heckscher, *The Study of Comparative Government and Politics* (London: Allen and Unwin, 1957), p. 68 (italics added).

10 Walter Goldschmidt, *Comparative Functionalism: An Essay in Anthropological Theory* (Berkeley CA: University of California Press, 1966), p. 4. Oscar Lewis argues that "there is no distinctive 'comparative method' in anthropology," and that he therefore prefers to discuss "comparisons in anthropology rather than the comparative method." See his "Comparisons in Cultural Anthropology" in William L. Thomas, Jr., ed., *Current Anthropology* (Chicago IL: University of Chicago Press, 1956), p. 259.

11 For the idea of discussing the comparative method in relation to these other basic methods, I am indebted to Neil J. Smelser's outstanding and most enlightening article "Notes on the Methodology of Comparative Analysis of Economic Activity," *Transactions of the Sixth World Congress of Sociology* (Evian: International Sociological Association, 1966), vol. 2, pp. 101–17. For other general discussions of the comparative method, see Léo Moulin, "La Méthode comparative en Science Politique," *Revue Internationale d'Histoire Politique et Constitutionelle*, 7 (January-June 1957), pp. 57–71; S. F. Nadel, *The Foundations of Social Anthropology* (London: Cohen and West, 1951), pp. 222–55; Maurice Duverger, *Méthodes des Sciences Sociales* (3rd edn, Paris: Presses Universitaires de France, 1964), pp. 375–99; John W. M. Whiting, "The Cross-Cultural Method," in Gardner Lindzey, ed., *Handbook of Social Psychology* (Reading MA: Addison-Wesley, 1954), vol. 1, pp. 523–31; Frank W. Moore, ed., *Readings in Cross-Cultural Methodology* (New Haven CT: HRAF Press, 1961); Adam Przeworski and Henry Teune, *The Logic of Comparative Social Inquiry* (New York: Wiley-Interscience, 1970); and Robert T. Holt and John E. Turner, "The Methodology of Comparative Research," in Holt and Turner, eds, *The Methodology of Comparative Research* (New York: Free Press, 1970), pp. 1–20.

12 The case study method will be discussed below.

13 Eugene J. Meehan, *The Theory and Method of Political Analysis* (Homewood IL: Dorsey Press, 1965). He expresses this idea in three short sentences: "Science seeks to establish relationships" (p. 35); "Science ... is empirical" (p. 37); "Science is a generalizing activity" (p. 43).

14 Paul F. Lazarsfeld, "Interpretation of Statistical Relations as a Research Operation," in Lazarsfeld and Morris Rosenberg, eds, *The Language of Social Research: A Reader in the Methodology of Social Research* (Glencoe IL: Free Press, 1955), p. 115. However, control by means of partial correlations does not allow for the effects of measurement error or unique factor components: see Marilynn B. Brewer, William D. Crano and Donald T. Campbell, "Testing a Single-Factor Model as an Alternative to the Misuse of Partial Correlations in Hypothesis-Testing Research, *Sociometry*, 33 (March 1970), pp. 1–11. Moreover, partial correlations do not resolve the problem of the codiffusion of characteristics, known in anthropology as "Galton's problem"; see Raoul Naroll, "Two Solutions to Galton's Problem," *Philosophy of Science*, 28 (January 1961), pp. 15–39, and Przeworski and Teune, op. cit., pp. 51–53.

15 Ernest Nagel, *The Structure of Science* (New York: Harcourt, Brace and World, 1961), pp. 452f.

16 For instance, if the groups are made equivalent by means of deliberate randomization, the investigator knows that they are alike with a very high degree of probability, but not with absolute certainty. Moreover, as Hubert M. Blalock, Jr., states, so-called "forcing variables" cannot be controlled by randomization. See his *Causal Inferences in Nonexperimental Research* (Chapel Hill NC: University of North Carolina Press, 1964), pp. 23–26. In general, Blalock emphasizes "the underlying similarity between the logic of making causal inferences on the basis of experimental and nonexperimental designs" (p. 26).

17 Lazarsfeld, "Interpretation of Statistical Relations as a Research Operation," p. 119. Talcott Parsons makes a similar statement with regard to the comparative method: "Experiment is ... nothing but the comparative method where the cases to be compared are produced to order and under controlled conditions." See his *The Structure of Social Action* (2nd edn, New York: Free Press, 1949), p. 743. Another advantage of the experimental method is that the time variable is controlled, which is especially important if one seeks to establish causal relationships. In statistical design, this control can be approximated by means of the panel method.

18 In order to highlight the special problems arising from the availability of only a small number of cases, the comparative method is discussed as a distinct method. Of course, it can be argued with equal justice that the comparative and statistical methods should be regarded as two aspects of a single method. Many authors use the term "comparative method" in the broad sense of the method of multivariate empirical, but nonexperimental, analysis, i.e. including both the comparative and statistical methods as defined in this paper. This is how A. R. Radcliffe-Brown uses the term when he argues that "only the comparative method can give us general propositions." (Brown, "The Comparative Method in Social Anthropology," *Journal of the Royal Anthropological Institute of Great Britain and Ireland*, 81 [1951], p. 22.) Emile Durkheim also follows this usage when he declares that "comparative sociology is not a particular branch of sociology; it is sociology itself, in so far as it ceases to be purely descriptive and aspires to account for facts." (Durkheim, *The Rules of Sociological Method*, translated by Sarah A. Solovay and John H. Mueller, [8th edn, Glencoe IL: Free Press, 1938], p. 139.) See also the statements by Lasswell and Almond cited above. Rodney Needham combines the two terms, and speaks of "large-scale statistical comparison," i.e. the statistical method. (Needham, "Notes on Comparative Method and Prescriptive Alliance," *Bijdragen tot de Taal-, Land-en Volkenkunde*, 118 [1962], pp. 160–82.) On the other hand, E. E. Evans-Pritchard uses exactly the same terminology as used by Smelser and as adopted in this paper, when he makes a distinction between "small-scale comparative studies" and "large-scale statistical ones." See his *The Comparative Method in Social Anthropology* (London: Athlone Press, 1963), p. 22.

19 Samuel H. Beer, "The Comparative Method and the Study of British Politics," *Comparative Politics*, 1 (October 1968), p. 19.

20 Harry Eckstein, "A Perspective on Comparative Politics, Past and Present," in Eckstein and David E. Apter, eds, *Comparative Politics: A Reader* (New York: Free Press of Glencoe, 1963), p. 3.

21 Stein Rokkan, "Comparative Cross-national Research: The Context of Current Efforts," in Richard L. Merritt and Rokkan, eds, *Comparing Nations: The Use of Quantitative Data in Cross-National Research* (New Haven CT: Yale University Press, 1966), pp. 19–20. Rokkan specifically recommends the use of "paired comparisons" for this purpose; see his "Methods and Models in the Comparative Study of Nation-Building," in *Citizens, Elections, Parties: Approaches to the Comparative Study of the Processes of Development* (Oslo: Universitetsforlaget, 1970), p. 52.

22 Merritt and Rokkan, op. cit., p. 193.

23 Terence K. Hopkins and Immanuel Wallerstein, "The Comparative Study of National Societies," *Social Science Information*, 6 (October 1967), pp. 27–33 (italics added). See also Przeworski and Teune, op. cit., pp. 34–43.

24 He adds: "This is a very naive conception of social science propositions; if only perfect correlations should be permitted social science would not have come very far." Johan Galtung, *Theory and Methods of Social Research* (Oslo: Universitetsforlaget, 1967), p. 505. The functions of deviant case analysis will be discussed below.

25 W. J. M. Mackenzie, *Politics and Social Science* (Harmondsworth, UK: Penguin Books, 1967), p. 52. I have been guilty of committing this fallacy myself. In my critique of Giovanni Sartori's proposition relating political instability to extreme multipartism (systems with six or more significant parties), one of my arguments consists of the deviance of a single historical case: the stable six-party system of the Netherlands during the interwar years. See Arend Lijphart, "Typologies of Democratic Systems," *Comparative Political Studies*, 1 (April 1968), pp. 32–35.

26 It is clearly incorrect, therefore, to argue that on logical grounds a probabilistic generalization can *never* be invalidated; cf. Guenter Lewy's statement:

> To be sure, a finding of a very large number of ... [deviant cases] would cast doubt upon the value of the proposition, but logically such evidence would not compel its withdrawal. The test of the hypothesis by way of a confrontation with empirical or historical data remains inconclusive.
> (Lewy, "Historical Data in Comparative Political Analysis: A Note on Some Problems of Theory," *Comparative Politics*, 1 [October 1968], p. 109)

27 Furthermore, unless one investigates all available cases, one is faced with the problem of how representative one's limited sample is of the universe of cases.

28 On the necessity of establishing general concepts not tied to particular cultures, see Smelser, op. cit., pp. 104–9; Nadel, op. cit., pp. 237–38; Douglas Oliver and Walter B. Miller, "Suggestions for a More Systematic Method of Comparing Political Units," *American Anthropologist*, 57 (February 1955), pp. 118–21; and Nico Frijda and Gustav Jahoda, "On the Scope and Methods of Cross-Cultural Research," *International Journal of Psychology*, 1 (1966), pp. 114–16. For critiques of recent attempts at terminological innovation in comparative politics, see Sartori, "Concept Misformation in Comparative Politics"; Robert T. Holt and John M. Richardson, Jr., *The State of Theory in Comparative Politics* (Minneapolis MN: Center for Comparative Studies in Technological Development and Social Change, 1968); Robert E. Dowse, "A Functionalist's Logic," *World Politics*, 18 (July 1966), pp. 607–23; and Samuel E. Finer, "Almond's Concept of 'The Political System': A Textual Critique," *Government and Opposition*, 5 (winter 1969–70), pp. 3–21.

29 Michael Haas, "Comparative Analysis," *Western Political Quarterly*, 15 (June 1962), p. 298n. See also Lewy, op. cit., pp. 103–10.

30 Edward A. Freeman, *Comparative Politics* (London: Macmillan, 1873), pp. 1, 19, 302. See also Gideon Sjoberg's argument in favor of global comparative research: "The Comparative Method in the Social Sciences," *Philosophy of Science*, 22 (April 1955), pp. 106–17.

31 Lazarsfeld and Barton, op. cit., pp. 172–75; Barton, "The Concept of Property-Space in Social Research," in Lazarsfeld and Rosenberg, op. cit., pp. 45–50.

32 Smelser, op. cit., p. 113. Holt and Turner refer to this strategy as the process of "specification" (op. cit., pp. 11–13). It is probably also what Eisenstadt has in mind when he mentions the possibility of constructing "special intensive comparisons of a quasi-experimental nature" (op. cit., p. 424). See also Erwin K.Scheuch, "Society as Context in Cross-Cultural Comparison," *Social Science Information*, 6 (October 1967), esp. pp. 20–23; Mackenzie, op. cit., p. 151; Fred Eggan, "Social Anthopology and the Method of Controlled Comparison," *American Anthropologist*, 56 (October 1954), pp. 743–63; and Erwin Ackerknecht, "On the Comparative Method in Anthropology," in Robert F. Spencer, ed., *Method and Perspective in Anthropology* (Minneapolis MN: University of Minnesota Press, 1954), pp. 117–25.

33 Ralph Braibanti, "Comparative Political Analytics Reconsidered," *Journal of Politics*, 30 (February 1968), p. 36.

34 John Stuart Mill, *A System of Logic* (8th edn, London: Longmans, Green, Reader, and Dyer, 1872), book III, chapter 8.

35 Nadel, op. cit., pp. 222–23; Kenneth E. Bock, "The Comparative Method of Anthropology," *Comparative Studies in Society and History*, 8 (April 1966), p. 272.

36 Mill, op. cit., book VI, chapter 7; see also book III, chapter 10.

37 Durkheim, op. cit., pp. 129–30. But he hailed the method of concomitant variations, which he evidently interpreted to mean a combination of the statistical and

comparative methods, as "the instrument par excellence of sociological research" (p. 132). See also François Bourricaud, "Science Politique et Sociologie: reflexions d'un sociologue," *Revue Française de Science Politique*, 8 (June 1958), pp. 251–63.

38 If the *area* approach is often preferable to research efforts with a global range in order to maximize comparability, the *era* approach may be preferable to longitudinal analysis for the same reason. Cf. the following statement by C. E. Black:

> There is much greater value in comparing contemporary events and institutions than those that are widely separated in time. The comparison of societies or smaller groups that are concerned with reasonably similar problems is more likely to lead to satisfactory conclusions than comparisons between societies existing many centuries apart.
> (Black, *The Dynamics of Modernization: A Study in Comparative History* [New York: Harper and Row, 1966], p. 39)

39 Heckscher, op. cit., p. 88.

40 Roy C. Macridis and Richard Cox, "Research in Comparative Politics," *American Political Science Review*, 47 (September 1953), p. 654. See also John D. Martz, "The Place of Latin America in the Study of Comparative Politics," *Journal of Politics* 28 (February 1966), pp. 57–80.

41 Dankwart A. Rustow, "Modernization and Comparative Politics: Prospects in Research and Theory," *Comparative Politics*, 1 (October 1968), pp. 45–47. Area study may also be criticized on the ground that, in the words of Dell G. Hitchner and Carol Levine, in *Comparative Government and Politics* (New York: Dodd, Mead, 1967): "Its very method of delimitation puts emphasis on what may be particular to a limited group of states, as opposed to the universal generalizations which fully comparative study must seek" (pp. 7–8). This argument has been answered above in terms of the need for partial generalizations as a first step. See also Braibanti, op. cit., pp. 54–55.

42 Bruce M. Russett, "Delineating International Regions," in J. David Singer, ed., *Quantitative International Politics: Insights and Evidence* (New York: Free Press, 1968), pp. 317–52. See also Russett, *International Regions and the International System* (Chicago IL: Rand McNally, 1967).

43 George I. Blanksten, "Political Groups in Latin America," *American Political Science Review*, 53 (March 1959), p. 126. See also Sigmund Neumann, "The Comparative Study of Politics," *Comparative Studies in Society and History*, 1 (January 1959), pp. 107–10; and I. Schapera, "Some Comments on the Comparative Method in Social Anthropology," *American Anthropologist*, 55 (August 1953), pp. 353–61, esp. p. 360.

44 See Seymour Martin Lipset, "The Value Patterns of Democracy: A Case Study in Comparative Analysis," *American Sociological Review*, 28 (August 1963), pp. 515–31; Robert R. Alford, *Party and Society: The Anglo-American Democracies* (Chicago IL: Rand McNally, 1963); Leslie Lipson, "Party Systems in the United Kingdom and the Older Commonwealth: Causes, Resemblances, and Variations," *Political Studies*, 7 (February 1959), pp. 12–31.

45 Charles E. Frye, "Parties and Pressure Groups in Weimar and Bonn," *World Politics*, 17 (July 1965), pp. 635–55 (the quotation is from page 637). The postwar division of Germany also offers the opportunity of analyzing the effects of democratic versus totalitarian development against a similar cultural and historical background. See Ralf Dahrendorf, "The New Germanies: Restoration, Revolution, Reconstruction," *Encounter*, 22 (April 1964), pp. 50–58. See also Sylvia L. Thrupp, "Diachronic Methods in Comparative Politics," in Holt and Turner, eds, *The Methodology of Comparative Research*, pp. 343–58.

46 Heckscher, p. 69; Heinz Eulau, "Comparative Political Analysis: A Methodological Note," *Midwest Journal of Political Science*, 6 (November 1962), pp. 397–407. Rokkan, too, warns against the "whole nation" bias of comparative research ("Methods and Models," p. 49).

47 Smelser, op. cit., p. 115.

48 Juan J. Linz and Amando de Miguel, "Within Nation Differences and Comparisons: The Eight Spains," in Merritt and Rokkan, op. cit., p. 268.

49 Naroll, "Scientific Comparative Politics and International Relations," in R. Barry Farrell, ed., *Approaches to Comparative and International Politics* (Evanston IL: Northwestern University Press, 1966), pp. 336–37.

50 Braibanti, op. cit., p. 49. In this context, "configurative" analysis is not synonymous with the traditional single-country approach, as in Eckstein's definition of the term: "the analysis of particular political systems, treated either explicitly or implicitly as unique entities" ("A Perspective on Comparative Politics," p. 11).

51 Lasswell, op. cit., p. 6.

52 See Richard C. Snyder, H. W. Bruck, and Burton Sapin, eds, *Foreign Policy Decision-Making* (New York: Free Press of Glencoe, 1962).

53 Joseph LaPalombara, "Macrotheories and Micro-applications in Comparative Politics," *Comparative Politics*, 1 (October 1968), pp. 60–77. As an example he cites Robert A. Dahl, ed., *Political Oppositions in Western Democracies* (New Haven CT: Yale University Press, 1966), esp. chapters 11–13. See also LaPalombara, "Parsimony and Empiricism in Comparative Politics: An Anti-Scholastic View," in Holt and Turner, eds, *The Methodology of Comparative Research*, pp. 123–49.

54 Eckstein, "A Perspective on Comparative Politics," p. 30.

55 Nadel, op. cit., p. 228.

56 James N. Rosenau, "Private Preferences and Political Responsibilities: The Relative Potency of Individual and Role Variables in the Behavior of U.S. Senators," in Singer, ed., *Quantitative International Politics*, pp. 17–50, esp. p. 19. Rosenau adds that if "the findings are not so clear as to confirm or negate the hypotheses unmistakably, then of course the analyst moves on to a third comparable period" (p. 19). If such a third or even more periods can be found – which seems unlikely in the case of Rosenau's particular research problem – they should be included regardless of the outcome of the analysis of the first two eras (if the available resources permit it, of course).

57 See also the proposed use of "multiple comparison groups," as an approximation of the experimental method, by Barney G. Glazer and Anselm L. Strauss, "Discovery of Substantive Theory: A Basic Strategy Underlying Qualitative Research," *American Behavioral Scientist*, 8 (February 1965), pp. 5–12.

58 LaPalombara, "Macrotheories and Microapplications," pp. 60–65.

59 See Michael Curtis, *Comparative Government and Politics: An Introductory Essay in Political Science* (New York: Harper and Row, 1968), p. 7. See also Macridis, *The Study of Comparative Government* (New York: Random House, 1955).

60 As Przeworski and Teune state: "The main role of a theory is to provide explanations of specific events. These explanations consist of inferring, with a high degree of probability, statements about particular events from general statements concerning classes of events" (p. 86).

61 Michael C. Hudson, "A Case of Political Under-development," *Journal of Politics*, 29 (November 1967), pp. 821–37. See also Beer, "The Comparative Method and the Study of British Politics," pp. 19–36.

62 Naroll, "Scientific Comparative Politics and International Relations," p. 336. An example of such a case study is my analysis of the determinants of Dutch colonialism in West Irian. In most cases, both objective (especially economic) and subjective factors can be discerned, but the case of West Irian is unique because

of the complete absence of objective Dutch interests in the colony. See Lijphart, *The Trauma of Decolonization: The Dutch and West New Guinea* (New Haven CT: Yale University Press, 1966).

63 See Patricia L. Kendall and Katherine M. Wolf, "The Analysis of Deviant Cases in Communications Research," in Lazarsfeld and Frank Stanton, eds, *Communications Research: 1948–49* (New York: Harper, 1949), pp. 152–57; Sjoberg, op. cit., pp. 114–15; and Lijphart, *The Politics of Accommodation: Pluralism and Democracy in the Netherlands* (Berkeley CA: University of California Press, 1968), chapter 10.

64 This process of refining generalizations through deviant case analysis is what Robert M. Marsh calls "specification." See his article "The Bearing of Comparative Analysis on Sociological Theory," *Social Forces*, 43 (December 1964), pp. 191–96. Specification should therefore definitely not be regarded as "the garbage bin" of comparative research; see Conrad Phillip Kottak, "Towards a Comparative Science of Society," *Comparative Studies in Society and History*, 12 (January 1970), p. 102. See also Milton M. Gordon, "Sociological Law and the Deviant Case," *Sociometry*, 10 (August 1947), pp. 250–58; and André J. F. Köbben, "The Logic of Cross-Cultural Analysis: Why Exceptions?", in Rokkan, ed., *Comparative Research Across Cultures and Nations* (Paris: Mouton, 1968), pp. 17–53.

65 Eckstein, *Division and Cohesion in Democracy: A Study of Norway* (Princeton NJ: Princeton University Press, 1966), esp. pp. 60–77, 177–201. Part of the critique which follows is included in my review of this book in the *Journal of Modern History*, 41 (March 1969), pp. 83–87.

66 David B. Truman, *The Governmental Process: Political Interests and Public Opinion* (New York: Knopf, 1951).

67 In one respect, it is not altogether correct to call the Norwegian case study a theory-confirming study. Because the congruence theory has a rather narrow empirical basis, consisting chiefly of only two cases (Britain and Germany), it is a hypothesis rather than an established theory. The case study of Norway is, of course, not a hypothesis-generating study either. Perhaps it should be called a "hypothesis-strengthening" case study or, as Eckstein himself suggests, a "plausibility probe" (oral comment at the IPSA Round Table Conference in Turin, Italy, September 1969).

68 Eckstein, *A Theory of Stable Democracy*, Research Monograph no. 10 (Princeton NJ: Center of International Studies, 1961).

Part VII
Conclusion

18 Conclusion

Power sharing, evidence, and logic

How strong is the evidence supporting power sharing theory? This is a crucial question in two respects. First, a theory can only be regarded as a valid empirical theory if its propositions are in accordance with the facts, and if empirical tests are able to confirm their accuracy. Second, power sharing theory is not only an empirical but also a prescriptive theory: it recommends consensus democracy to any country that aims at establishing a democratic system of government or that wants to change its form of democracy, and it recommends consociationalism for deeply divided countries. Such policy advice based on power sharing theory is justified only if we can be reasonably sure that the underlying theory is valid.

In this concluding chapter, my focus will be on this crucial question of the evidence that supports power sharing theory. In separate sections, I shall focus on the effects of consensus democracy and those of consociational democracy. The evidence concerning consensus democracy is quite clear and unambiguous, mainly because the variables can all be operationalized and quantified, and statistical tests can be used to assess the strength of their interrelationships. The situation is more complicated for consociational democracy, because the main variables – the degree of consociationalism versus majoritarianism, the degree to which a society is deeply divided, and democratic stability and survival – are much more difficult to measure. However, I shall show that, on balance, the evidence gives strong support to consociational theory, and hence that there is no reason to be hesitant about recommending a consociational form of democracy to deeply divided countries. In addition, consociationalism as policy advice is strengthened by its inherent logic. This logic is so compelling that time and again political leaders of deeply divided societies have spontaneously turned to consociationalism as the most obvious way to solve their conflicts. Another part of this logic is that all of the alternatives are unworkable, so that consociation remains as the only practical solution.

Consensus democracy, effective government, and democratic quality

The empirical evidence concerning the effect of consensus democracy on democratic quality and on "kinder and gentler" public policies is presented at length in Chapter 6 of this volume, and its influence on effective policy-making is summarized in the Introduction (Chapter 1). This evidence is extraordinarily strong – and, in fact, much stronger than I had originally expected myself. On the basis of theoretical arguments in the political science literature as well as some preliminary empirical tests, my thinking was that consensus democracy (on the executives-parties dimension) would have a substantial advantage over majoritarian democracy with regard to democratic quality, and that it would be roughly equal in terms of effective government, although I anticipated that majoritarian democracy might have a slight edge. In both respects, the evidence turned out to be much more favorable to consensus democracy. It is consensus rather than majoritarian democracy that has the slight edge with regard to effective policy-making, and the performance of consensus democracy with regard to the indicators of democratic quality is not just superior, but vastly superior – confirmed by clear results of statistical tests.

These findings are not only extremely strong but also highly robust, because I generally used two or three operational indicators for each conceptual variable and data for as many countries as possible – in fact, all of the available relevant data. My results have not been widely challenged, but two critiques, one methodological and one substantive, should be mentioned here. The methodological critic, Klaus Armingeon (2002), has argued that it would have been better to focus exclusively on the more highly developed (OECD) countries instead of my thirty-six countries which represent very different levels of socioeconomic development. One response is that it is not difficult to control for the level of socioeconomic development, and that I consistently did so in my multivariate statistical analyses. Second, I have been a strong advocate myself of the comparative method which entails the selection of comparable cases for analysis in order to mitigate the small N/large number of variables problem (see Chapter 17). This approach is especially advisable if a large number of variables can simultaneously be held constant and if the number of cases does not have to be reduced too drastically. But Armingeon gains the advantage of having one less (albeit undoubtedly important) variable to worry about, at the cost of having thirteen fewer cases – which strikes me as a questionable sacrifice of a lot of degrees of freedom. Of course, I often do report results for the OECD countries only – by necessity rather than as a conscious choice – for all those dependent variables on which no reliable data were available for non-OECD countries (e.g. differential satisfaction with democracy and government-voter proximity) or on which more reliable information could be found for the OECD countries than for my full set of countries. In the latter situation, I presented the results for both the full set and the OECD subset (e.g. income inequality).

What I easily could have done in addition, and what in retrospect I believe I should have done, is to systematically present the correlations for both the full set and the OECD subset even when the same data were used.

Let me make up for this omission here for six key dependent variables for which I originally reported the correlations only for the full (or almost full) set of thirty-six countries. For the twenty-three OECD countries, the effect of consensus democracy on women's parliamentary representation is stronger and the effect on women's cabinet participation a great deal stronger (significant at the 1 percent and close to the 1 percent level, respectively). The effect on voter turnout, with compulsory voting and frequency of voting controlled for, is weaker, but still significant at the 10 percent level. The correlations with the democratic-quality indicators of popular cabinet support and the John Stuart Mill Criterion are very much stronger among the OECD countries (both significant at the 5 percent level). Finally, the correlation with energy efficiency is almost as strong and highly significant at the 1 percent level. In short, the overall picture does not change much when the focus is exclusively on the OECD countries – and the robustness of my results showing that consensus democracy makes a positive difference is enhanced.

My substantive critic, Rudy B. Andeweg (2001, 124), points to a dependent variable that I did not consider: the strength of right-wing populism. He worries that, during the 1990s, "extreme right-wing populism has clearly been a more significant electoral phenomenon in consensus democracies than in majoritarian democracies," and he attributes it to dissatisfaction with the absence of competition among the major parties. I concede the strength of this correlation, although it is by no means a perfect one since there are three deviant cases among the thirteen countries that he discusses (consensual Finland and the Netherlands without, and majoritarian France with a significant populist right). However, I think that it is not so much the lack of partisan opposition that fed these right-wing parties as the chance that PR offers them to get elected. I also believe that the dangers posed by the populist parties should not be exaggerated.

First of all, from a normative democratic perspective, one can argue that all parties, even distasteful ones, should have the right to compete and to be represented, with the possible exception of parties that are clearly and unquestionably committed to the overthrow of democracy. Second, it is probably also healthier for such parties to be represented rather than be suppressed. They only become dangerous when they become very large and especially if they are included in the government. But even then, the danger should not be overstated. For instance, the inclusion of the ultra-right Freedom Party as a junior partner in the Austrian cabinet in 2000 had the dual favorable effect of moderating its outlook and reducing its popular support. Finally, it is hard to justify the abolition of PR – and hence the denial of representation to all small parties, even perfectly pro-democratic parties but also more extreme but not anti-democratic parties – just to prevent small anti-democratic parties from gaining a foothold in parliament.[1] This means that, in my opinion, the electoral strength of extreme right-wing parties is not an appropriate indicator of democratic quality.

So far, I have focused on the evidence in favor of consensus democracy reported in my own writings. This evidence is reinforced by the findings of several other scholars. In a series of articles, Markus M. L. Crepaz and his collaborators (Crepaz and Birchfield 2000, Crepaz and Moser 2004) find that consensual decision-making has stronger positive effects on macroeconomic policy-making than I have found. In particular, they have investigated an important indicator of effective socioeconomic policy-making that I had not included in my analysis: the capacity of democratic governments to deal with the pressures exerted on national economies by economic globalization. They find that these pressures are managed more effectively and responsibly by consensus than majoritarian democracies.[2]

Similar supporting evidence can be found in a large-scale study of between 77 and 126 democracies that contrasts "centripetal" and "decentralist" democracies by John Gerring *et al.* (2005). These scholars analyze the effects of centripetal democracy on eight variables in three broad policy areas: political development (e.g. the institutional strength and quality of the civil service), economic development (e.g. the safety of potential investors of acquiring a stake in a country's economy), and human development (infant mortality, life expectancy, and illiteracy). They show that centripetalism, defined in terms of three components – parliamentary government, PR, and unitary government – is strongly correlated with positive policy outcomes in all of the policy areas.[3]

These findings offer significant support to mine because centripetalism is very similar to consensus democracy (on the executives-parties dimension). In the Introduction, I have already repeatedly emphasized the importance of parliamentarism and PR for both consensus and consociational democracy. In the final chapter of *Patterns of Democracy* (Lijphart 1999, 303–4), I raise the specific question of how constitution-makers can design a consensual form of democracy. The answer is that the combination of PR and parliamentary government virtually guarantees that a democracy will become consensual (on the executives-parties dimension). This means that, if I were to try to measure consensus democracy for a very large number of countries (as Gerring and his co-authors do), for which it would be too difficult to do all of the complex measurements of the five components of the first dimension of consensus democracy, the combination of parliamentary government and PR could serve as a very good and more easily measurable proxy. Hence the only difference is that Gerring and his collaborators find that unitarism has a positive influence, whereas in my analysis the roughly comparable federal-unitary dimension is neutral in its effects. But the fact that among a much larger set of democracies – obviously defined according to more permissive criteria than I have used – and with quite different indicators of good government, the same positive influence of parliamentary government and PR elections was found, is a major reinforcement of my evidence in favor of consensus democracy.

Finally, Josep M. Colomer (2001) lends further support to these conclusions. He uses social choice theory to determine which are the most "socially efficient" institutions, that is, which institutions maximize political satisfaction. He argues that this quality can be measured in terms of whether the party of the median voter is included among the winners and in the executive. According to his logic, the best systems are the parliamentary-PR ones. He then tests his conclusions by means of a quantitative analysis, which strongly supports his theoretical arguments.

Consociational democracy, stability, and survival

It is much harder to find similarly hard evidence for the proposition that consociational democracy can produce democratic stability and survival in deeply divided societies. I agree with Brendan O'Leary's (2005, 36) observation that the rival evaluations of consociation may simply not be "amenable to decisive confirmation or falsification by evidence." The main reason is that both the independent and dependent variables are much more difficult to operationalize and to measure precisely. The problems already begin with the definition and measurement of deeply divided – or what I have also called *plural* – societies. I have not been able to devise a more exact measurement than a threefold classification into plural, semi-plural, and non-plural societies – and other scholars have not been able to improve on this. As I have mentioned in the Introduction and in several chapters in Part II, consociational democracy is defined in terms of four characteristics, none of which are subject to precise measurement either. I have used the term "semi-consociational" for countries like Canada and Israel, but I have not attempted to use the implied threefold classification into consociational, semi-consociational, and majoritarian democracies for systematic statistical analysis.

Even trickier is the problem of defining stability and survival. How long does a consociational democracy have to endure to qualify for "survival"? Does the "end" of a consociation necessarily mean failure? The Austrian and Dutch examples suggest the opposite. Austria shifted from grand coalition cabinets to one-party majority cabinets in 1966, but this was not because consociational cooperation had failed but because it had been so successful in alleviating the tensions between the religious-ideological segments that further consociational measures had become superfluous. The same conclusion applies to the more gradual shift away from consociationalism in the Netherlands. Another striking example of this difficulty is Suriname. This plural society was governed by a consociational system headed by a grand coalition cabinet of leaders of the two largest ethnic groups, Creoles and East Indians, from 1958 to 1973. From 1973 to 1980, a mainly Creole cabinet replaced the grand coalition, and the East Indian community was excluded from power. Democracy was upset by a military coup in 1980 – but can this case be counted as a failure of consociational democracy? There are two opposite answers to this question. The most straightforward answer is that the coup represented the failure of majoritarian democracy, which had been in operation for seven years, rather than the failure of consociationalism; this is, in my opinion, the most credible interpretation. But one can also argue that the very shift to majoritarianism demonstrates a failure of the consociational system, and that the coup was essentially a delayed consequence of this earlier failure.

In spite of these problems, a few scholars have attempted large-scale statistical analyses, which, on balance, strengthen the case for consociational democracy. Wolf Linder and André Bächtiger (2005, 875) develop a nine-point Power Sharing Index based on the four basic principles of consociational democracy, and they apply it in a multivariate statistical analysis of the relative success of democratization in sixty-two African and Asian countries between 1965 and 1995. Their conclusion is that

> Lijphart's concept of power sharing turned out to be one of the strongest predictors for democratization. ... Our systematic analysis confirms the favorable influence of power sharing that Lijphart has illustrated in case studies of third world countries such as Malaysia, Lebanon and India.

Three other aspects of their findings are worth highlighting. The first is that consociationalism is one of only two strong predictors of successful democratization. The other is the negative influence of strong family and kinship ties which tend to prevent the development of cooperative civic networks. Second, rather unexpectedly, the level of socioeconomic development turned out not to be even a weak predictor. Finally, Linder and Bächtiger make a distinction between horizontal power sharing (based on the consociational principles of grand coalition, proportionality, and minority veto) and vertical power sharing (based on the consociational concept of cultural autonomy). They find that it is the former rather than the latter that promotes democratization. This result parallels my conclusions about the favorable effects of consensus democracy: it is the horizontal (executives-parties) dimension that produces strong positive effects for democratic government, whereas the vertical (federal-unitary) dimension is largely neutral in its consequences.

Additional supportive evidence is provided by Ted Robert Gurr's (1993) book *Minorities at Risk* – especially significant because Gurr does not take his inspiration from consociational theory. It is an extremely large-scale multivariate statistical study, accurately described in the book's subtitle as a "global view of ethnopolitical conflicts." Gurr pursues a relentlessly inductive strategy which is so full of detailed operational definitions and explanations that most readers probably fail to reach the two concluding chapters that make up the final tenth of the text. This is very unfortunate because these final chapters contain a series of significant conclusions about the possibilities of settling ethnic conflicts. The overall evidence shows that (1) such conflicts are by no means intractable; (2) that they can usually be accommodated by "some combination of the policies and institutions of *autonomy* and *power sharing*"; and (3) that democracies have an especially good record of ethnic accommodation (Gurr 1993, 290–92, emphasis added). These are exactly the claims that consociational theory also makes.

Just about all of the above conclusions and findings are challenged by a recent volume that includes a large-scale statistical study of 658 different ethnic groups in 153 states during nine successive five-year periods from 1955 to 1999, yielding an impressive total of 8,074 cases for analysis. The editors, Philip G. Roeder and Donald Rothchild (2005, 5–6), who are also the authors of the book's first chapter, begin by acknowledging that power sharing (in the sense of consociationalism) "has become the international community's preferred remedy for building peace and democracy after civil wars." They also concede that consociation can work well in the short run. Their big disagreement with consociational thinking is that they believe that "the very same institutions that provide an attractive basis to end a conflict in an ethnically divided country are likely to hinder the consolidation of peace and democracy over the long run." What they recommend instead of power sharing is power *dividing*, inspired by the American constitutional model: separation of powers, checks and balances, and civil liberties guaranteed by strong judicial guarantees. Their recommendations are largely supported by the statistical test that they perform (Roeder 2005). It is worth emphasizing the big difference between these conclusions and my findings in *Patterns of Democracy*: the latter show that it is precisely among the *long-term* democracies that power sharing institutions (the executives-parties dimension) rather than power-dividing institutions (the federal-unitary dimension) produce better policy-making.

It is difficult to reconcile Roeder and Rothchild's findings with Gurr's, Linder's, Bächtiger's, and my own. It would require a detailed critique and re-analysis, for which this chapter is not the appropriate place. Obviously, a great deal depends on how particular cases are interpreted and classified. For instance, Roeder (2005, 65–67) sees a lot of division of power in Belgium, Switzerland, and India, which I have described as classic cases of consociational power sharing. Two other prominent cases of consociational democracy, Lebanon and Cyprus, appear to confirm the pattern described by Roeder and Rothchild: power sharing worked reasonably well for about three years in Cyprus (1960–63) and for more than thirty years in Lebanon (1943–75), but ended in civil wars in both countries. The correct interpretation, however, is that these were failures not of consociational democracy per se, but of seriously flawed consociational designs: especially too extensive minority veto powers in Cyprus; the rigid Lebanese election system that was only partly proportional and continued to give the

Christian sects a legislative majority although Muslims had become the popular majority; and strong presidencies in both countries.

Let me add a bit of indirect evidence based on the data on thirty-six countries in *Patterns of Democracy* (Lijphart 1999, 248–52). The evidence is indirect because I use consensus democracy as a rough proxy for consociational democracy, although, as I have emphasized in the Introduction, the two overlap a great deal but are not identical. The hypothesis is that, because it is much more difficult to maintain majoritarian democracy in plural than in non-plural societies, we can expect to find that stable democracies in plural societies tend to be consensus democracies. If continuous democracy between 1977 and 1996 is accepted as evidence of democratic stability, there is indeed, among the thirty-six democracies so defined, a strong correlation between the degree of pluralism (measured on a three-point scale) and the degree of consensus democracy on both the executives-parties and federal-unitary dimensions: the correlation coefficients are 0.32 and 0.40, statistically significant at the 5 and 1 percent level respectively. Another way to read this evidence is to compare the eighteen plural and semi-plural societies with the eighteen non-plural societies and to dichotomize both the executives-parties and federal-unitary dimensions. In the group of eight democracies that are consensual on both dimensions, seven are plural or semi-plural: *88 percent*. In the group of sixteen that are consensual on one of the two dimensions, eight are plural or semi-plural: *50 percent*. In the group of twelve democracies that are majoritarian on both dimensions, only three are plural or semi-plural: *25 percent*.

Presidentialism/parliamentarism, stability, and survival

Testing the proposition that presidential government is negatively related to democratic stability and survival runs into the same problem of measuring the dependent variables, and the independent variable – the contrast between presidential and parliamentary government – is also more difficult to measure than appears at first blush. For instance, although a threefold classification of presidential versus semi-presidential versus parliamentary government is widely used, there is considerable disagreement about the countries that fit the semi-presidential category. Moreover, as I argue in Chapter 9, it makes more sense to classify countries into presidential, parliamentary, and several "mixed" categories without using a semi-presidential category at all.

Nevertheless, there have been many attempts at large-scale statistical tests of the relative success of presidentialism and parliamentarism in maintaining democracy. Fred W. Riggs (1988) was the pioneering scholar in this respect, and he found presidentialism to be extremely prone to failure and hence a highly "problematic regime type." Of the several later studies that have come to the same conclusion, the two by Axel Hadenius and by Alfred Stepan and Cindy Skach are the best known and most persuasive. Hadenius

(1994, 81) concludes that "the positive effect of parliamentarism ... emerges as the key institutional precondition for the upholding of political democracy." Similarly, Stepan and Skach (1994, 132) write that parliamentarism presents "a more supportive evolutionary framework for consolidating democracy" than presidential government. There have also been a few empirical studies that show no significant differences between the two types (e.g. Power and Gasiorowski 1997), but, very significantly, not a single study has been produced that show that presidentialism actually works better than parliamentarism.

Let me add the relevant numbers that I encountered in *Patterns of Democracy* (Lijphart 1999, 48–55). I defined as stable democracies all countries (with populations of at least 250,000) that had been continuously democratic from 1977 to 1996, a period of almost twenty years. Of the thirty-six countries that fit these criteria, only five are presidential: the United States, Costa Rica, Colombia, Venezuela, and France – a very small percentage (about 14 percent) that contrasts sharply with the roughly 3:2 ratio of presidential to parliamentary systems in the world (Derbyshire and Derbyshire 1996). Extending the period to 2007, that is, defining democratic stability somewhat more strictly in terms of thirty years of continuous democracy reduces the set of stable democracies to thirty-four. Significantly, the two countries that have to be dropped are Colombia and Venezuela. Now there are only three presidential systems in the total set of thirty-four stable democracies – about 9 percent. Can this pattern be explained by the fact that two thirds of these stable democracies are developed countries (members of the OECD) and that presidentialism is more prevalent in the Third World? If this were the case, we would expect presidentialism in our set of stable democracies to be concentrated in the non-OECD democracies, but the ratios are almost exactly the same: only one presidential system (Costa Rica) among the thirteen non-OECD democracies, and two (the United States and France) among the twenty-three OECD members – about 8 and 9 percent, respectively.

Presidentialism means separation of powers, which is a key element in the divided-power institutions that Roeder and Rothchild (2005) favor. Hence the empirical findings reported in this section – which show, in Juan J. Linz and Arturo Valenzuela's (1994) terms, "the failure of presidential democracy" – also throw further doubt on the conclusions and recommendations by Roeder and Rothchild.

The logic of consociational democracy

Is the evidence supporting consociational power sharing strong enough that we can confidently recommend it to divided societies? I strongly believe it is. Moreover, it is reinforced by the fundamental *logic* of consociationalism. This logic is demonstrated by the crucial decisions to establish power sharing in some of the clearest examples of deeply divided societies on which my work has focused: in the United Province of Canada in 1840, in the Netherlands in 1917, both in Lebanon and in Switzerland in 1943, in Austria in 1945, in India in 1947, in Malaysia in 1955, in Colombia in 1958, in Cyprus in 1960, in Belgium in 1970, in Czecho-Slovakia in 1989, and in South Africa in 1994.

Four aspects of these decisions by the political leaders in divided societies are worth highlighting. First, most of these decisions were made in situations of great tension and of potential or even actual violence. Second, the power sharing systems that were set up followed all or most of the four basic consociational principles. Third, these decisions were made in different parts of the world and at widely different times: the countries that I have listed are located in five different continents, and there is more than a century and a half between the first and the last case. Finally, these decisions were made completely independently of each other. With the exception of South Africa, where great efforts were made to examine the potential relevance of consociational and other theories as well as foreign examples, none of the consociational agreements were inspired by the example of an earlier agreement of this kind; each time, consociationalism was newly invented. For instance, in 1958 the Colombian peacemakers were totally ignorant of, and hence could not learn any lessons from the so-called Peaceful Settlement in the Netherlands or the 1943 Lebanese National Pact.

The widely different times and places of these decisions to institute consociational government and their complete independence from each other rule out any explanations based on cultural differences or the diffusion of knowledge. Instead, the above pattern shows that consociationalism was invented and re-invented time and again because of its compelling logic. It was the most rational choice to be made in the circumstances of potential or actual civil strife.

Another striking example of consociational democracy as a rationally invented model can be found in Sir Arthur Lewis's (1965) *Politics in West Africa*. Lewis was an economist, born in St. Lucia in the Caribbean and of African descent. He served as an economic adviser to several of the governments of West Africa from 1953 to 1965, and he observed and deplored the breakdown of democracy that was occurring in these countries. His diagnosis of this failure was that the West African ethnically divided countries had not adopted the right *kind* of democracy upon independence. What they needed, he argued, was broad inter-ethnic coalitions, elections by PR, and ethnic group autonomy. He did not attach a comprehensive label to these proposals, but they clearly add up to consociational democracy. He did not mention any empirical examples of consociationalism either, and he appears not to have known of the Colombian, Lebanese, Dutch, and other precedents. Hence, in contrast to political scientists like Gerhard Lehmbruch and myself who *discovered* consociationalism a few years later, Lewis *invented* it by trying to think what would be the logical solution to the problems in West Africa. This is another example of consociationalism as a creative invention and rational choice – especially significant because, as I already mentioned in the Introduction, Lewis was the first modern scholar to identify the consociational model of democracy.

Another part of the logic behind consociationalism as a recommendation for deeply divided societies is that all of the potential alternative proposals – integration, partition, Horowitz's alternative-vote plan, and the Roeder-Rothchild power-dividing proposal – have serious drawbacks and cannot be regarded as realistic options. Consociationalism is therefore the only realistic possibility. Integration – creating greater trust and mutual understanding among people in ethnically and religiously divided societies and making these societies less plural and more homogeneous – is a long-term effort and cannot serve as an immediate solution to potential or actual civil strife. Of course, it can be the *result* of an extended period of successful power sharing, as in the cases of Austria and the Netherlands, mentioned earlier.

The biggest problem of partition (or secession) is that ethnic and religious groups are usually geographically intermixed to a considerable extent, and that it is therefore usually not possible to draw clear and clean boundary lines between them. Hence, in order to create homogeneous territorial units, partition has to be accompanied by a large-scale exchange of populations – a process that is very costly in both economic and human terms. Another drawback is the difficulty of effecting a partition that divides the land and natural resources fairly among the contending groups. The only useful function that partition can perform is as a solution of last resort in case power sharing fails. Clearly, however, power sharing is vastly preferable and should always be tried first.

In Chapter 5, I have already shown the fatal flaws in Horowitz's alternative-vote proposal as well as the extremely low probability that it would be accepted in a negotiated transition to peace and democracy. It is hard to imagine that in a situation where one or more relatively small minorities face a majority or several large groups, the minorities will be willing to accept a system that does not offer them the chance to be represented by their own leaders but merely by the more moderate leaders of the majority or the larger groups. Apart from the dubious intrinsic merits of the Roeder-Rothchild power-diving plan, it suffers from the same low likelihood of being accepted in a negotiated settlement. The representatives of groups that are in conflict with each other will surely be deterred by the uncertainties inherent in complex separation-of-power and checks-and-balances arrangements, and are much more likely to opt for the simplicity and clarity of sharing power.

Mainly because of measurement problems that have not been solved so far, the evidence supporting consociational democracy is not as strong and convincing as the hard evidence behind consensus democracy. Nevertheless, with the evidence that we do have, combined with the strong logic of consociationalism, its validity as an empirical theory is beyond reasonable doubt. Hence we do not need to be doubtful either about recommending consociational democracy as a practical solution for deeply divided societies.

Notes

1 A better way to bar anti-democratic parties, it seems to me, is a judicial proce-dure that permits democracies to outlaw parties that are clearly aimed at the abolition of democracy.
2 Crepaz and his co-authors use the term "collective veto points" (inspired by the so-called veto-points literature), which is roughly identical to consensus democ-racy on the executives-parties dimension.
3 Gerring and his collaborators specify not just PR, but closed-list PR. This is not a significant limitation because almost all PR systems use list PR, and list PR with lists that are completely or mainly open are very rare.

References

Andeweg, Rudy B. 2001. "Lijphart versus Lijphart: The Cons of Consensus Democracy in Homogeneous Societies." *Acta Politica* 36, 2 (summer): 117–39.

Armingeon, Klaus. 2002. "The Effects of Negotiation Democracy: A Comparative Analysis." *European Journal of Political Research* 41, 1 (January): 81–105.

Colomer, Josep M. 2001. *Political Institutions: Social Choice and Democracy.* Oxford: Oxford University Press.

Crepaz Markus M. L., and Vicki Birchfield. 2000. "Global Economics, Local Poli-tics: Lijphart's Theory of Consensus Democracy and the Politics of Inclusion." In Markus M. L. Crepaz, Thomas A. Koelble, and David Wilsford (eds) *Democracy and Institutions: The Life Work of Arend Lijphart*, pp. 197–224. Ann Arbor MI, University of Michigan Press.

Crepaz, Markus, M. L., and Ann W. Moser. 2004. "The Impact of Collective and Competitive Veto Points on Public Expenditures in the Global Age." *Comparative Political Studies* 37, 3 (April): 259–85.

Derbyshire, J. D., and Ian Derbyshire. 1996. *Political Systems of the World.* New York: St. Martin's Press.

Gerring, John, Strom C. Thacker, and Carola Moreno. 2005. "Centripetal Demo-cratic Governance: A Theory and Global Inquiry." *American Political Science Review* 99, 4 (November): 567–81.

Gurr, Ted Robert. 1993. *Minorities at Risk: A Global View of Ethnopolitical Con-flicts.* Washington DC: United States Institute of Peace Press.

Hadenius, Axel. 1994. "The Duration of Democracy: Institutional vs. Socio-Eco-nomic Factors." In David Beetham (ed.) *Defining and Measuring Democracy*, pp. 63–88. London: Sage.

Lewis, W. Arthur. 1965. *Politics in West Africa.* London: Allen and Unwin.

Lijphart, Arend. 1999. *Patterns of Democracy: Government Forms and Performance in Thirty-Six Countries.* New Haven CT: Yale University Press.

Linder, Wolf, and Andre Bächtiger. 2005. "What Drives Democratisation in Asia and Africa?" *European Journal of Political Research* 44, 6 (October): 861–80.

Linz, Juan J., and Arturo Valenzuela (eds) 1994. *The Failure of Presidential Democ-racy.* Baltimore MD: Johns Hopkins University Press.

O'Leary, Brendan. 2005. "Debating Consociational Politics: Normative and Expla-natory Arguments." In Sid Noel (ed.) *From Power Sharing to Democracy: Post-Conflict Institutions in Ethnically Divided Societies*, pp. 3–43. Montreal and King-ston: McGill-Queen's University Press.

Power, Timothy J., and Mark J. Gasiorowski. 1997. "Institutional Design and Democratic Consolidation in the Third World." *Comparative Political Studies* 30, 2 (April): 123–55.

Riggs, Fred W., 1988. "The Survival of Presidentialism in America: Para-Constitutional Practices." *International Political Science Review* 9, 4 (October): 247–78.

Roeder, Philip G., 2005. "Power Dividing as an Alternative to Ethnic Power Sharing," In Philip G. Roeder and Donald Rothchild (eds) *Sustainable Peace: Power and Democracy after Civil Wars*, pp. 51–82. Ithaca NY: Cornell University Press.

Roeder, Philip G., and Donald Rothchild. 2005. "Dilemmas of State-Building in Divided Societies." In Philip G. Roeder and Donald Rothchild (eds) *Sustainable Peace: Power and Democracy after Civil Wars*, pp. 1–25. Ithaca NY: Cornell University Press.

Stepan, Alfred, and Cindy Skach. 1994. "Presidentialism and Parliamentarism in Comparative Perspective." In Juan J. Linz and Arturo Valenzuela (eds) *The Failure of Presidential Democracy*, pp. 119–36. Baltimore MD: Johns Hopkins University Press.

Bibliography
The complete scholarly writings of Arend Lijphart

Books

The Trauma of Decolonization: The Dutch and West New Guinea, New Haven CT: Yale University Press, 1966.

The Politics of Accommodation: Pluralism and Democracy in the Netherlands, Berkeley CA: University of California Press, 1968; 2nd edn, 1975.

Verzuiling, pacificatie en kentering in de Nederlandse politiek, Amsterdam: De Bussy, 1968; 2nd edn, 1976; 3rd edn, 1979; 4th edn, 1982; 5th edn, 1984; 6th edn, 1986; 7th edn (Haarlem: Becht), 1988; 8th edn, 1990; 9th edn, 1992.

Democracy in Plural Societies: A Comparative Exploration, New Haven CT: Yale University Press, 1977; paperback edition, 1980; reprinted by Popular Prakashan, Bombay, India, 1989; reprinted by University Press Limited, Ibadan, Nigeria, 1990; Japanese translation by Hideo Uchiyama, *Tagenshakai no demokrasii*, Tokyo: Sanichi Syoboo, 1979; Arabic translation by Evelyne Abou Mitry Messarra, *al-Dîmuqrâtiyya fî al-mujtamac al-mutac addid: Dirâsa muqârana*, Beirut: Librairie Orientale, 1984; Spanish translation by Susana Serdán Vázquez, *Democracia en las sociedades plurales: Una investigación comparativa*, Mexico City: Ediciones Prisma, 1988; Croatian translation by Božica Jakovlev, *Demokracija u pluralnim društvima*, Zagreb: Globus, 1992; Polish translation of chapters 1–3 by Jerzy Szczupaczynski, "Democracja w społeczeństwach sfragmentaryzowanych," in Anna Raciborska (ed.) *Elity, demokracja, wybory*, Warsaw: Agencja Scholar, 1993, pp. 87–100, and in Hanna Kalińska, Anita Witkowska, and Ludwik Krasucki (eds) *Władza i społeczeństwo: Antologia tekstów z zakresu socjologii polityki*, Warsaw: Wydawnictwo Naukowe Scholar, 1995, pp. 39–49; Russian translation by B. I. Makarenko, *Demokratiia v mnogosotavnykh obshchestvakh: Sravnitel'noe issledovanie*, Moscow: Aspekt Press, 1997; Romanian translation by Adriana Bargan, *Democraţia în societăţile plurale*, Iaşi: Polirom, 2002; Chinese translation by Hui-Chih Cang, *Tuo yuan sheh hui te min chu*, Taipei: Laureate Book Company, 2003.

The Requirements for Stability and Development in KwaZulu and Natal (with members of the Buthelezi Commission), Durban: H and H Publications, 1982.

Democracies: Patterns of Majoritarian and Consensus Government in Twenty-One Countries, New Haven CT: Yale University Press, 1984; Korean translation by Myung Chey, *Minju kukka ron*, Seoul: Pubmunsa, 1985; French translation by Evelyne Abou Mitry Messarra, *Démocraties: Les modèles majoritaire et consensuel dans vingt et un pays*, Beirut: Librairie Orientale, 1986; Chinese translation by Kun-sen Chen, *Dangdai minzhu leishi yu zhengzhi*, Taipei: Laureate

Book Company, 1993; Burmese translation by Tet Toe, *Demoekaraysi*, Rangoon: USIS Rangoon, 1994; Romanian translation by Ştefan Lupu, *Democraţii: Modele de guvernare majoritară şi consensuală în douăzeci şi una de ţări*, Chişinău: Sigma IG Press, 1999.

Power-Sharing in South Africa, Policy Papers in International Affairs, no. 24, Berkeley CA: Institute of International Studies, University of California, 1985; Dutch translation by A. P. Daalder-Neukircher, *Machtsdeling: De oplossing voor Zuid-Afrika?*, Haarlem: Becht, 1987.

Las democracias contemporáneas: Un estudio comparativo (with Thomas C. Bruneau, P. Nikiforos Diamandouros, and Richard Gunther; Spanish translation by Elena de Grau), Barcelona: Editorial Ariel, 1987; Turkish translation by Ergun Özbudun and Ersin Onulduran, *Çagdas demokrasiler: Yirmibir ülkede çogunlukçu ve oydasmaci yönetim öröntüleri*, Ankara: Turkish Democracy Foundation and Political Science Association, 1988; Italian translation by Maria Teresa Brancaccio, *Le democrazie contemporanee*, Bologna: Il Mulino, 1988; Portuguese translation by Alexandre Correia and Francisca Bagio, *As democracias contemporâneas*, Lisbon: Gradiva, 1989.

Electoral Systems and Party Systems: A Study of Twenty-Seven Democracies, 1945–1990, Comparative European Politics Series, Oxford: Oxford University Press, 1994; paperback edition, 1995; Spanish translation by Fernando Jiménez Sánchez, *Sistemas electorales y sistemas de partidos: Un estudio de veintisiete democracias, 1945–1990*, Madrid: Centro de Estudios Constitucionales, 1995; Korean translation by Jushil Suh, *Seungojedou wa jeungdangje*, Seoul: Samjiwon Press, 1997; Chinese translation by Hui-Chih Chang, *Hsuan chu chih tu yu jeng tang ti hsi*, Taipei: Laureate Book Company, 2003.

Patterns of Democracy: Government Forms and Performance in Thirty-six Countries, New Haven CT: Yale University Press, 1999; Spanish translation by Carme Castellnou, *Modelos de democracia: Formas de gobierno y resultados en treinta y seis países*, Barcelona: Editorial Ariel, 2000; Romanian translation by Cătălin Constantinescu, *Modele ale democraţiei: Forme de guvernare şi funcţionare în treizeci şi şase de ţări*, Iaşi: Polirom Press, 2000; Italian translation by Luca Verzichelli, *Le democrazie contemporanee*, Bologna: Il Mulino, 2001; Chinese translation by De-Yuan Kao, *Min chu lei hsiang: San shih liu ke hsien tai min chu kuo chia te cheng fu lei hsiang yu piao hsien*, Taipei: Laureate Book Company, 2001; Portuguese translation by Roberto Franco, *Modelos de democracia: Desempenho e padrões de governo em 36 países*, Rio de Janeiro: Editora Civilização Brasileira, 2003; Russian translation of Chapter 7 by T. Mosentseva, in *Oikumena* (Kharkiv, Ukraine), no. 2, fall-winter 2004, pp. 107–29; Japanese translation by Yuko Kasuya, *Minshushugi tai minshushugi: Tasuuketsugata to konsensasu gata no sanjuu roku kakoku hikaku kenkyu*, Tokyo: Keiso Shobo, 2005; Turkish translation by Güneş Ayas and Umut Utku Bulsun, *Demokrasi Motifleri: Otuz Altı Ülkede Yönetim Biçimleri ve Peformansları*, Istanbul: Salyangoz Yayınları, 2006; Chinese translation (simplified characters) by Chen Qi, *Min chu te mo shih: San shih liu ke min chu kuo chia te cheng fu hsing shih ho cheng fu chi hsiao*, Beijing: Peking University Press, 2006.

Edited volumes (books and special issues of journals)

World Politics: The Writings of Theorists and Practitioners, Classical and Modern, Boston MA: Allyn and Bacon, 1966; 2nd edn, 1971.

Politics in Europe: Comparisons and Interpretations, Englewood Cliffs NJ: Prentice-Hall, 1969; Korean translation by Che-sung U, *Kuju cheguk ui chongch'i chedo*, Seoul: Kukhoe Tosogwan, Ippop Chosaguk, 1973.

Symposium on Comparative Methodology (with James A. Caporaso), in *Comparative Political Studies*, vol. 8, no. 2 (July 1975), pp. 131–99.

Conflict and Coexistence in Belgium: The Dynamics of a Culturally Divided Society, Berkeley CA: Institute of International Studies, University of California, 1981.

Symposium on Reapportionment (with Bernard Grofman, Robert McKay, and Howard Scarrow), special issue #3 of *Policy Studies Journal*, vol. 9, no. 6 (1980–81), pp. 817–948.

Representation and Redistricting Issues (with Bernard Grofman, Robert B. McKay, and Howard A. Scarrow), Lexington MA: Lexington Books, 1982.

Choosing an Electoral System: Issues and Alternatives (with Bernard Grofman), New York: Praeger, 1984.

New Approaches to the Study of Cabinet Coalitions, special issue of *Comparative Political Studies*, vol. 17, no. 2 (July 1984), pp. 155–279.

Electoral Laws and Their Political Consequences (with Bernard Grofman), New York: Agathon Press, 1986.

Parliamentary versus Presidential Government, Oxford, Oxford University Press, 1992; Korean translation by Hae Kyung Cho, *Naegakjae dae daetongryungjae*, Seoul: Yijin Publishing Co., 1999.

Post-Communist Transformation in Eastern Europe (with Beverly Crawford), special issue of *Comparative Political Studies*, vol. 28, no. 2 (July 1995), pp. 171–314.

The Encyclopedia of Democracy (with Seymour Martin Lipset *et al.*), 4 vols, Washington DC: Congressional Quarterly, 1995.

Institutional Design in New Democracies: Eastern Europe and Latin America (with Carlos H. Waisman), Boulder CO: Westview Press, 1996.

25th Anniversary Issue (with Michael Laver and Peter Mair), special issue of the *European Journal of Political Research*, vol. 31, nos. 1–2 (February 1997), pp. 1–255.

Liberalization and Leninist Legacies: Comparative Perspectives on Democratic Transitions (with Beverly Crawford), Berkeley CA: International and Area Studies, University of California, 1997.

Les démocraties consociatives (with Julian T. Hottinger), special issue of the *Revue Internationale de Politique Comparée*, vol. 4, no. 3 (December 1997), pp. 527–697.

International Encyclopedia of Elections (with Richard Rose *et al.*) Washington DC: CQ Press, 2000.

The Evolution of Electoral and Party Systems in the Nordic Countries (with Bernard Grofman), New York: Agathon Press, 2002.

Articles, chapters, research notes, monographs, etc.

"The Indonesian Image of West Irian," *Asian Survey*, vol. 1, no. 5 (July, 1961), pp. 9–16.

"De Nederlandse publieke opinie inzake het Nieuw-Guineavraagstuk medio 1961," *Internationale Spectator*, vol. 16, no. 13 (July 8, 1962), pp. 311–25.

"The Analysis of Bloc Voting in the General Assembly: A Critique and a Proposal," *American Political Science Review*, vol. 57, no. 4 (December 1963), pp. 902–17.

"Tourist Traffic and Integration Potential," *Journal of Common Market Studies*, vol. 2, no. 3 (March 1964), pp. 251–62.

"Typologies of Democratic Systems," *Comparative Political Studies*, vol. 1, no. 1 (April 1968), pp. 3–44; reprinted in Arend Lijphart (ed.) *Politics in Europe:*

Comparisons and Interpretations (Englewood Cliffs NJ: Prentice-Hall, 1969), pp. 46–80; and in Roy C. Macridis and Bernard E. Brown (eds) *Comparative Politics: Notes and Readings* (Homewood IL: Dorsey Press, 5th edn, 1977), pp. 133–47; Italian translation, "Tipologie dei sistemi democratici," in Marila Guadagnini (ed.) *I sistemi di partito* (Milan: Franco Angeli, 1986), pp. 247–91.

"Consociational Democracy," *World Politics*, vol. 21, no. 2 (January 1969), pp. 207–25; reprinted in Robert J. Jackson and Michael B. Stein (eds) *Issues in Comparative Politics: A Text with Readings* (New York: St. Martin's Press, 1971), pp. 222–34; in Kenneth McRae (ed.) *Consociational Democracy: Political Accommodation in Segmented Societies* (Toronto: McClelland and Stewart, 1974), pp. 70–89; in Mark O. Dickerson, Thomas Flanagan, and Neil Nevitte (eds) *Introductory Readings in Government and Politics* (Scarborough: Nelson Canada, 3rd edn, 1991), pp. 270–83; and in Robert A. Dahl, Ian Shapiro, and José Antonio Cheibub (eds) *The Democracy Sourcebook* (Cambridge MA: MIT Press, 2003), pp. 142–46; French translation, "La démocratie consociative," in Mattei Dogan and Dominique Pelassy (eds) *La comparaison internationale en sociologie politique: Une sélection de textes sur la démarche du comparatiste* (Paris: Librairies Techniques, 1980), pp. 210–16; Chinese translation, "Hsieh ho min chu," *Hsien cheng shih ch'ao*, no. 67 (September 1984), pp. 127–35.

"Kentering in de Nederlandse politiek," *Acta Politica*, vol. 4, no. 3 (April 1969), pp. 231–47.

Paradigmata in de Leer der Internationale Betrekkingen (Amsterdam: De Bussy, 1969).

"Political Science Versus Political Advocacy," *Acta Politica*, vol. 5, no. 2 (January 1970), pp. 165–71.

"Op weg naar een presidentieel stelsel?" *Socialisme en Democratie*, vol. 27, no. 3 (March 1970), pp. 137–43.

"Doelstellingen van de leer der internationale betrekkingen," *Oost-West*, vol. 9, no. 6 (June 1970), pp. 226–29.

"Cultural Diversity and Theories of Political Integration," *Canadian Journal of Political Science*, vol. 4, no. 1 (March 1971), pp. 1–14.

Class Voting and Religious Voting in the European Democracies: A Preliminary Report, Occasional Paper Number 8, University of Strathclyde, Survey Research Centre, 1971; reprinted in *Acta Politica*, vol. 6, no. 2 (April 1971), pp. 158–71.

"Politieke verandering en politieke vernieuwing: Enkele kanttekeningen," *Civis Mundi*, vol. 10, no. 7–8 (July–August 1971), pp. 346–48.

"Il metodo della comparazione," *Rivista Italiana di Scienza Politica*, vol. 1, no. 1 (April 1971), pp. 67–92.

"Verzuiling," in Andries Hoogerwerf (ed.) *Verkenningen in de politiek* (Alphen aan den Rijn: Samsom, 1971; 2nd edn, 1973), vol. 2, pp. 24–37; 3rd edn, 1976, vol. 2, pp. 26–38.

"Comparative Politics and the Comparative Method," *American Political Science Review*, vol. 65, no. 3 (September 1971), pp. 682–93; reprinted in Louis J. Cantori (ed.) *Comparative Political Systems* (Boston MA: Holbrook Press, 1974), pp. 58–79; in Roy C. Macridis and Bernard E. Brown (eds) *Comparative Politics: Notes and Readings* (Homewood IL: Dorsey Press, 5th edn, 1977), pp. 50–66; and in Alan Sica (ed.) *Comparative Methods in the Social Sciences* (New Delhi: Sage Publications India, 2005), vol. 3, pp. 73–95; French translation, "Comment, en considérant les analogies, mettre en évidence les différences," in Mattei Dogan and Dominique Pelassy (eds) *La comparaison internationale en sociologie politique:*

Une sélection de textes sur la démarche du comparatiste (Paris: Libraries Techniques, 1980), pp. 168–71; Italian translation, "Caratteri del metodo comparato," in Domenico Fisichella (ed.) *Metodo scientifico e ricerca politica* (Rome: La Nuova Italia Scientifica, 1985), pp. 269–83.

"Toward Empirical Democratic Theory: Research Strategies and Tactics," *Comparative Politics*, vol. 4, no. 3 (April 1972), pp. 417–32.

"Hervorming van het parlement in vergelijkend perspectief," *Socialisme en Democratie*, vol. 30, no. 7–8 (July–August 1973), pp. 311–18.

"The Netherlands: Continuity and Change in Voting Behavior," in Richard Rose (ed.) *Electoral Behavior: A Comparative Handbook* (New York: Free Press, 1974), pp. 227–68.

"The Structure of the Theoretical Revolution in International Relations," *International Studies Quarterly*, vol. 18, no. 1 (March 1974), pp. 41–74.

"International Relations Theory: Great Debates and Lesser Debates," *International Social Science Journal*, vol. 26, no. 1 (1974), pp. 11–21; French translation, "La théorie des relations internationales: Grandes controverses et controverses mineures," *Revue Internationale des Sciences Sociales*, vol. 26, no. 1 (1974), pp. 11–22.

"Kiesstelsels voor universitaire verkiezingen: Dimensies, varianten en beoordelingscriteria," *Universiteit en Hogeschool*, vol. 21, no. 2 (October 1974), pp. 65–84.

"The Northern Ireland Problem: Cases, Theories, and Solutions," *British Journal of Political Science*, vol. 5, no. 1 (January 1975), pp. 83–106.

"De paradox van Condorcet en de Nederlandse parlementaire praktijk," *Acta Politica*, vol. 10, no. 2 (April 1975), pp. 188–98.

"Hervorming van het kiesstelsel: Partijbelang en landsbelang," *Liberaal Reveil*, vol. 16, no. 2 (spring 1975), pp. 16–19.

"The Comparable-Cases Strategy in Comparative Research," *Comparative Political Studies*, vol. 8, no. 2 (July 1975), pp. 158–77; reprinted in Louis J. Cantori and Andrew H. Ziegler, Jr. (eds) *Comparative Politics in the Post-Behavioral Era* (Boulder CO: Lynne Rienner, 1988), pp. 54–71; Italian translation, "Strategia dei casi comparabili," in Domenico Fisichella (ed.) *Metodo scientifico e ricerca politica* (Rome: La Nuova Italia Scientifica, 1985), pp. 283–92.

"Repliek," *Acta Politica*, vol. 11, no. 1 (January 1976), pp. 78–84.

"Fragmentaciones lingüísticas, sociales y políticas: Bélgica, Canadá y Suiza," *Revista Mexicana de Sociología*, vol. 38, no. 3 (July–September 1976), pp. 707–27.

"Political Theories and the Explanation of Ethnic Conflict in the Western World: Falsified Predictions and Plausible Postdictions," in Milton J. Esman (ed.) *Ethnic Conflict in the Western World* (Ithaca NY: Cornell University Press, 1977), pp. 46–64.

"Thresholds and Payoffs in List Systems of Proportional Representation" (with Robert W. Gibberd), *European Journal of Political Research*, vol. 5, no. 3 (September 1977), pp. 219–44.

"Dutch Universities in the Seventies," *International Council on the Future of the University Newsletter*, vol. 4, no. 1 (November 1977), pp. 1, 4–7.

"Majority Rule versus Democracy in Deeply Divided Societies," *Politikon*, vol. 4, no. 2 (December 1977), pp. 113–26; reprinted in Nic Rhoodie (ed.) *Intergroup Accommodation in Plural Societies* (London: Macmillan, 1978), pp. 27–43.

"Emergency Powers and Emergency Regimes: A Commentary," *Asian Survey*, vol. 18, no. 4 (April 1978), pp. 401–7.

"Lingua, religione, classe e preferenze politiche: analisi comparata di quattro paesi," *Rivista Italiana di Scienza Politica*, vol. 8, no. 1 (April 1978), pp. 77–111.

"The Dutch Electoral System in Comparative Perspective: Extreme Proportional Representation, Multipartism and the Failure of Electoral Reform," *Netherlands Journal of Sociology*, vol. 14, no. 2 (December 1978), pp. 115–33; French translation, "Représentation proportionnelle extrême, multipartisme et réforme électorale aux Pays-Bas," in Jacques Cadart (ed.) *Les modes de scrutin des dix-huit pays libres de l'Europe occidentale, leurs résultats et leurs effets comparés: Elections nationales et européennes* (Paris: Presses Universitaires de France, 1983), pp. 247–64.

"Religious vs. Linguistic vs. Class Voting: The 'Crucial Experiment' of Comparing Belgium, Canada, South Africa, and Switzerland," *American Political Science Review*, vol. 73, no. 2 (June 1979), pp. 442–58; reprinted in John T. S. Madeley (ed.) *Religion and Politics* (Aldershot: Ashgate, 2003), pp. 397–413.

"Nomination Strategies in the Irish S.T.V. System: The Dail Elections of 1969, 1973, and 1977" (with Galen A. Irwin), *British Journal of Political Science*, vol. 9, no. 3 (July 1979), pp. 362–69.

"Consociation and Federation: Conceptual and Empirical Links," *Canadian Journal of Political Science*, vol. 12, no. 3 (September 1979), pp. 499–515; reprinted in Nic J. Rhoodie (ed.) *Conflict Resolution in South Africa: The Quest for Accommodationist Policies in a Plural Society* (Pretoria: Institute for Plural Societies, University of Pretoria, 1980), pp. 29–41.

"Federal, Confederal, and Consociational Options for the South African Plural Society," in Robert I. Rotberg and John Barratt (eds) *Conflict and Compromise in South Africa* (Lexington MA, Lexington Books, 1980), pp. 51–75; Japanese translation, "Minami Afrika tagen shakai ni taisuru sentakushi to siteno renpoo, rengoo, takyoku kyooson," *Hoogaku Kenkyu: Journal of Law and Politics of the Faculty of Law, Keio University*, vol. 53, no. 5 (May 1980), pp. 1–34.

"The Structure of Inference," in Gabriel A. Almond and Sidney Verba (eds) *The Civic Culture Revisited* (Boston MA: Little, Brown, 1980; Newbury Park CA, Sage, 1989), pp. 37–56.

"A Crucial Test of Alphabetic Voting: The Elections at the University of Leiden, 1973–78" (with Eric A. Bakker), *British Journal of Political Science*, vol. 10, no. 4 (October 1980), pp. 521–25.

"Preface: Minority Rights, Autonomy and Power-Sharing," in Georgina Ashworth (ed.) *World Minorities in the Eighties* (Sunbury: Quartermaine House, 1980), pp. x–xvii.

"Language, Religion, Class and Party Choice: Belgium, Canada, Switzerland and South Africa Compared," in Richard Rose (ed.) *Electoral Participation: A Comparative Analysis* (London: Sage, 1980), pp. 283–327.

"Karl W. Deutsch and the New Paradigm in International Relations," in Richard L. Merritt and Bruce M. Russett (eds) *From National Development to Global Community: Essays in Honor of Karl W. Deutsch* (London: Allen and Unwin, 1981), pp. 233–51.

"Political Parties: Ideologies and Programs," in David Butler, Howard R. Penniman, and Austin Ranney (eds) *Democracy at the Polls: A Comparative Study of Competitive National Elections* (Washington DC: American Enterprise Institute, 1981), pp. 26–51; reprinted in Peter Mair (ed.) *The West European Party System* (Oxford: Oxford University Press, 1990), pp. 253–65.

"De theorie van de pacificatie-democratie," in J. J. A. Thomassen (ed.) *Democratie: Theorie en praktijk* (Alphen aan den Rijn: Samsom, 1981), pp. 128–45.

"Consociational Theory: Problems and Prospects," *Comparative Politics*, vol. 13, no. 3 (April 1981), pp. 355–60.

"Power-Sharing versus Majority Rule: Patterns of Cabinet Formation in Twenty Democracies," *Government and Opposition*, vol. 16, no. 4 (autumn 1981), pp. 395–413.

"Comparative Perspectives on Fair Representation: The Plurality-Majority Rule, Geographical Districting, and Alternative Electoral Arrangements," *Policy Studies Journal*, vol. 9, no. 6 (1980–81), pp. 899–915; and in Bernard Grofman, Arend Lijphart, Robert McKay, and Howard Scarrow (eds) *Representation and Redistricting Issues* (Lexington MA: Lexington Books, 1982), pp. 143–59.

"Consociation: The Model and Its Applications in Divided Societies," in Desmond Rea (ed.) *Political Co-operation in Divided Societies: A Series of Papers Relevant to the Conflict in Northern Ireland* (Dublin: Gill and McMillan, 1982), pp. 166–86.

"Governing Natal-KwaZulu: Some Suggestions," in Buthelezi Commission, *The Requirements for Stability and Development in KwaZulu and Natal* (Durban: South Africa, H and H Publications, 1982), vol. 2, pp. 76–84.

"If First It's Tried in Natal-Zululand," *New York Times* (27 May 1982), p. A31.

"The Relative Salience of the Socio-Economic and Religious Issue Dimensions: Coalition Formations in Ten Western Democracies, 1919–79," *European Journal of Political Research*, vol. 10, no. 3 (September 1982), pp. 201–11.

"Os modelos majoritário e consociacional da democracia: Contrastes e ilustrações," in Bolivar Lamounier (ed.) *A ciência política nos anos 80* (Brasília: Editora Universidade de Brasília, 1982), pp. 95–115.

"University 'Democracy' and the Decline of Academic Standards in the Netherlands," in John Chapman (ed.) *The Western University on Trial* (Berkeley CA: University of California Press, 1983), pp. 212–30.

"The Politics of Accommodation: Reflections – Fifteen Years Later," *Acta Politica*, vol. 19, no. 1 (January 1984), pp. 9–18.

"Advances in the Comparative Study of Electoral Systems," *World Politics*, vol. 36, no. 3 (April 1984), pp. 424–36; Spanish translation, "Avances en el estudio comparativo de los sistemas electorales," *Boletín Electoral Latinoamericana*, no. 5 (January-June 1991), pp. 65–78.

"Trying to Have the Best of Both Worlds: Semi-Proportional and Mixed Systems," in Arend Lijphart and Bernard Grofman (eds) *Choosing an Electoral System: Issues and Alternatives* (New York: Praeger, 1984), pp. 207–13.

"A Note on the Meaning of Cabinet Durability," *Comparative Political Studies*, vol. 17, no. 2 (July 1984), pp. 163–66.

"Measures of Cabinet Durability: A Conceptual and Empirical Evaluation," *Comparative Political Studies*, vol. 17, no. 2 (July 1984), pp. 265–79.

"The Pattern of Electoral Rules in the United States: A Deviant Case Among the Industrialized Democracies," *Government and Opposition*, vol. 20, no. 1 (winter 1985), pp. 18–28; Spanish translation, "El patrón de normas electorales en los Estados Unidos: Un caso modelo o un caso fuera de lo común," in Nerio Rauseo (ed.) *Simposio sistemas electorales comparados con especial referencia a nivel local* (Caracas: Consejo Supremo Electoral, 1984), pp. 85–96.

"The Field of Electoral Systems Research: A Critical Survey," *Electoral Studies*, vol. 4, no. 1 (April 1985), pp. 3–14; Japanese translation, "Senkyo seido kenkyo no bunya: Hihanteki gaikan," *Nihon Senkyo Gakukai*, no. 6 (November 1984), pp. 1–20.

"Non-Majoritarian Democracy: A Comparison of Federal and Consociational Theories and Practices," *Publius*, vol. 15, no. 2 (spring 1985), pp. 3–15.

"From the Fourth to the Fifth Republic – and to the Sixth? A Note on Regime Change and Regime Continuity," *French Politics and Society*, no. 11 (September 1985), pp. 24–31.

"Proportional Tenure *vs* Proportional Representation: Introducing a New Debate" (with Peter J. Taylor), *European Journal of Political Research*, vol. 13, no. 4 (December 1985), pp. 387–99.

"Political Parties," in Adam Kuper and Jessica Kuper (eds) *The Social Science Encyclopedia* (London: Routledge and Kegan Paul, 1985), pp. 574–76; 2nd edn, 1996, pp. 589–91; 3rd edn, 2004, pp. 705–8.

"Proportionality by Non-PR Methods: Ethnic Representation in Belgium, Cyprus, Lebanon, New Zealand, West Germany, and Zimbabwe," in Bernard Grofman and Arend Lijphart (eds) *Electoral Laws and Their Political Consequences* (New York: Agathon Press, 1986), pp. 113–23.

"The Limited Vote and the Single Nontransferable Vote: Lessons from the Japanese and Spanish Examples" (with Rafael López Pintor and Yasunori Sone), in Bernard Grofman and Arend Lijphart (eds) *Electoral Laws and Their Political Consequences* (New York: Agathon Press, 1986), pp. 154–69.

"Degrees of Proportionality of Proportional Representation Formulas," in Bernard Grofman and Arend Lijphart (eds) *Electoral Laws and Their Political Consequences* (New York: Agathon Press, 1986), pp. 170–79; Italian translation, "Sul grado di proporzionalità di alcune formule elettorali," *Rivista Italiana di Scienza Politica*, vol. 13, no. 2 (August 1983), pp. 295–305.

"A Democratic Blueprint for South Africa" (with Diane R. Stanton), *Business and Society Review*, no. 57 (spring 1986), pp. 28–32; reprinted in S. Prakash Sethi (ed.) *The South African Quagmire: In Search of a Peaceful Path to Democratic Pluralism* (Cambridge MA: Ballinger, 1987), pp. 89–98.

"Consociational Democracy: The Examples of Belgium and the Netherlands," in Theodor Hanf, Antoine N. Messarra, and Hinrich R. Reinstrom (eds) *La société de concordance: Approche comparative* (Beirut: Librairie Orientale, 1986), pp. 35–49.

"Das Parteiensystem der Bundesrepublik im Vergleich: Zwischen 'Konkurrenzdemokratie' und 'Konkordanzdemokratie'," *Das Parlament*, vol. 36, no. 37–38 (September 13–20, 1986), p. 6; reprinted in Peter Haungs and Eckhard Jesse (eds) *Parteien in der Krise?* (Cologne: Verlag Wissenschaft und Politik, 1987), pp. 47–51.

"De pacificatietheorie en haar critici," *Acta Politica*, vol. 22, no. 2 (April 1987), pp. 181–225.

"The Demise of the Last Westminster System? Comments on the Report of New Zealand's Royal Commission on the Electoral System," *Electoral Studies*, vol. 6, no. 2 (August 1987), pp. 97–103.

"Bicameralism: Canadian Senate Reform in Comparative Perspective," in Herman Bakvis and William M. Chandler (eds) *Federalism and the Role of the State* (Toronto: University of Toronto Press, 1987), pp. 101–12.

"Communal Representation," in Vernon Bogdanor (ed.) *The Blackwell Encyclopaedia of Political Institutions* (Oxford: Basil Blackwell, 1987), p. 121.

"Consociational Democracy," in Vernon Bogdanor (ed.) *The Blackwell Encyclopaedia of Political Institutions* (Oxford: Basil Blackwell, 1987), pp. 137–39.

"Pillarization," in Vernon Bogdanor (ed.) *The Blackwell Encyclopaedia of Political Institutions* (Oxford: Basil Blackwell, 1987), pp. 423–24.

Choosing an Electoral System for Democratic Elections in South Africa: An Evaluation of the Principal Options, Critical Choices for South African Society, no. 2

(Rondebosch: Institute for the Study of Public Policy, University of Cape Town, 1987); reprinted in Robert Schrire (ed.) *Critical Choices for South Africa: An Agenda for the 1990s* (Cape Town: Oxford University Press, 1990), pp. 2–13.

"A Mediterranean Model of Democracy? The Southern European Democracies in Comparative Perspective" (with Thomas C. Bruneau, P. Nikiforos Diamandouros, and Richard Gunther), *West European Politics*, vol. 11, no. 1 (January 1988), pp. 7–25.

"Democratización y modelos alternativos de democracia," *Opciones*, no. 14 (May–August 1988), pp. 29–42; also published as "Democratización y modelos democráticos alternativos," in Consejo para la Consolidación de la Democracia, *Presidencialismo vs. parlamentarismo: Materiales para el estudio de la reforma constitucional* (Buenos Aires: Editorial Universitaria de Buenos Aires, 1988), pp. 5–18.

"Alphabetic Bias in Partisan Elections: Patterns of Voting for the Spanish Senate, 1982 and 1986" (with Rafael López Pintor), *Electoral Studies*, vol. 7, no. 3 (December 1988), pp. 225–31.

"From the Politics of Accommodation to Adversarial Politics in the Netherlands: A Reassessment," *West European Politics*, vol. 12, no. 1 (January 1989), pp. 139–53; reprinted in Hans Daalder and Galen A. Irwin (eds) *Politics in the Netherlands: How Much Change?* (London: Frank Cass, 1989), pp. 139–53.

"Democratic Political Systems: Types, Cases, Causes, and Consequences," *Journal of Theoretical Politics*, vol. 1, no. 1 (January 1989), pp. 33–48; reprinted in Anton Bebler and James H. Seroka (eds) *Contemporary Political Systems: Classifications and Typologies* (Boulder CO: Lynne Rienner, 1990), pp. 71–87.

"The Ethnic Factor and Democratic Constitution-Making in South Africa," in Edmond J. Keller and Louis A. Picard (eds) *South Africa in Southern Africa: Domestic Change and International Conflict* (Boulder CO: Lynne Rienner, 1989), pp. 13–24.

"The Southern European Examples of Democratization: Six Lessons for Latin America," *Government and Opposition*, vol. 25, no. 1 (winter 1990), pp. 68–84; reprinted in Geoffrey Pridham (ed.) *Transitions to Democracy* (Aldershot: Dartmouth, 1995), pp. 173–89; and in Joshua Cohen and Archon Fung (eds) *Constitution, Democracy and State Power: The Institutions of Justice* (Cheltenham: Edward Elgar, 1996), vol. 1, pp. 428–44.

"The Political Consequences of Electoral Laws, 1945–85," *American Political Science Review*, vol. 84, no. 2 (June 1990), pp. 481–96; reprinted in Pippa Norris (ed.) *Elections and Voting Behaviour: New Challenges, New Perspectives* (Aldershot: Ashgate, 1998), pp. 227–42; Spanish translation, "Las consecuencias políticas de las leyes electorales: 1945–85," *Estudios Públicos*, no. 46 (autumn 1992), pp. 109–34; and in *Zona Abierta*, nos. 110/111 (2005), pp. 105–32.

"The Power-Sharing Approach," in Joseph V. Montville (ed.) *Conflict and Peacemaking in Multiethnic Societies* (Lexington MA: Lexington Books, 1990), pp. 491–509: Spanish translation, "El enfoque del poder compartido para sociedades multiétnicas," *Autodeterminación*, no. 12 (July 1994), pp. 159–83.

"The Cleavage Model and Electoral Geography: A Review," in R. J. Johnston, F. M. Shelley, and P. J. Taylor (eds) *Developments in Electoral Geography* (London: Routledge, 1990), pp. 143–50.

"Foreword: One Basic Problem, Many Theoretical Options – And a Practical Solution?", in John McGarry and Brendan O'Leary (eds) *The Future of Northern Ireland* (Oxford: Clarendon Press, 1990), pp. vi–viii.

"Size, Pluralism, and the Westminster Model of Democracy: Implications for the Eastern Caribbean," in Jorge Heine (ed.) *A Revolution Aborted: The Lessons of*

Grenada (Pittsburgh PA: University of Pittsburgh Press, 1990), pp. 321–40; Spanish translation, "Tamaño, pluralismo y el modelo Westminster de democracia: Implicaciones para el Caribe Oriental," in Jorge Heine (ed.) *Revolución e intervención en el Caribe: Las Lecciones de Granada* (Buenos Aires: Grupo Editor Latinoamericano, 1990), pp. 363–84.

"Constitutional Choices for New Democracies," *Journal of Democracy*, vol. 2, no. 1 (winter 1991), pp. 72–84; reprinted in Larry Diamond and Marc F. Plattner (eds) *The Global Resurgence of Democracy* (Baltimore MD: Johns Hopkins University Press, 1993), pp. 146–58; 2nd edn, 1996, pp. 162–74; and in Larry Diamond and Marc F. Plattner (eds) *Electoral Systems and Democracy* (Baltimore MD: Johns Hopkins University Press, 2006), pp. 73–85; Chinese translation, "Xin xing minzhu guojia de xian zheng xuanze," *Lilun yu Zhengce*, vol. 6, no. 3 (April 1992), pp. 75–84; Russian translation, "Konstitucionnye al'ternativy dlja novyh demokratij," *Polis*, no. 2 (1995), pp. 135–46; also in *Sovremennaia stravnitel'naia politologiia: Khrestomatiia* (Moscow: Moskovskii Obshchestvennyi Nauchnyi Fond, 1997), pp. 324–42.

"Double-Checking the Evidence," *Journal of Democracy*, vol. 2, no. 3 (summer 1991), pp. 42–48; reprinted in Larry Diamond and Marc F. Plattner (eds) *The Global Resurgence of Democracy* (Baltimore MD: Johns Hopkins University Press, 1993), pp. 171–77; 2nd edn, 1996, pp. 187–93; and in Larry Diamond and Marc F. Plattner (eds) *Electoral Systems and Democracy* (Baltimore MD: Johns Hopkins University Press, 2006), pp 98–104.

"Corporatism and Consensus Democracy in Eighteen Countries: Conceptual and Empirical Linkages" (with Markus M. L. Crepaz), *British Journal of Political Science*, vol. 21, no. 2 (April 1991), pp. 235–46.

"The Alternative Vote: A Realistic Alternative for South Africa?", *Politikon*, vol. 18, no. 2 (June 1991), pp. 91–101.

"Majority Rule in Theory and Practice: The Tenacity of a Flawed Paradigm," *International Social Science Journal*, no. 129 (August 1991), pp. 483–93; French translation, "Théorie et pratique de la loi de la majorité: La ténacité d'un paradigme imparfait," *Revue Internationale des Sciences Sociales*, no. 129 (August 1991), pp. 515–26; Spanish translation, "El gobierno de la mayoría en la teoría y en la práctica: Persistencia de un paradigma viciado," *Revista Internacional de Ciencias Sociales*, no. 129 (August 1991), pp. 507–18.

"Consideraciones sobre alternativas semipresidenciales y parlamentarias de gobierno" (with Giovanni Sartori, Enrique Barros B., Raúl Bertelsen, Bernardino Bravo Lira, Humberto Nogueira, Santiago Nino, and Arturo Valenzuela), *Estudios Públicos*, no. 42 (autumn 1991), pp. 7–44.

"The World Shops for a Ballot Box: A Comparative Perspective on Democratization," *Political Science and International Studies* (October 1991), pp. 12–15.

"Maatschappelijke voorwaarden voor democratische stelsels" (with Hendrik Spruyt), in J. J. A. Thomassen (ed.) *Hedendaagse democratie* (Alphen aan den Rijn: Samsom H. D. Tjeenk Willink, 1991), pp. 148–62.

"Self-Determination Versus Pre-Determination of Ethnic Minorities in Power-Sharing Systems," in David Schneiderman (ed.) *Language and the State: The Law and Politics of Identity* (Cowansville: Editions Yvon Blais, 1991), pp. 153–65; reprinted in Will Kymlicka (ed.) *The Rights of Minority Cultures* (Oxford: Oxford University Press, 1995), pp. 275–87.

"Foreword: 'Cameral Change' and Institutional Conservatism," in Lawrence D. Longley and David M. Olson (eds) *Two Into One: The Politics and Processes of National Legislative Cameral Change* (Boulder CO: Westview Press, 1991), pp. ix–xii.

"Presidentialism and Majoritarian Democracy: Theoretical Observations," in György Szoboszlai (ed.) *Democracy and Political Transformation: Theories and East-Central European Realities* (Budapest: Hungarian Political Science Association, 1991), pp. 75–93; also published in Juan J. Linz and Arturo Valenzuela (eds) *The Failure of Presidential Democracy* (Baltimore MD: Johns Hopkins University Press, 1994), pp. 91–105; Italian translation, "Presidenzialismo e democrazia maggioritaria," *Rivista Italiana di Scienza Politica*, vol. 19, no. 3 (December 1989), pp. 367–84; Spanish translation, "Presidencialismo y democracia de mayoría," in Oscar Godoy Arcaya (ed.) *Hacia una democracia moderna: La opción parlamentaria* (Santiago: Ediciones Universidad Católica de Chile, 1990), pp. 109–28; Portuguese translation, "Presidencialismo e democracia majoritária," in Bolívar Lamounier, *A opção parlamentarista* (Sao Paulo: Editora Sumaré, 1991), pp. 121–37.

"Democratization and Constitutional Choices in Czecho-Slovakia, Hungary, and Poland, 1989–91," *Journal of Theoretical Politics*, vol. 4, no. 2 (April 1992), pp. 207–23; also in Ian Budge and David McKay (eds) *Developing Democracy: Research in Honour of J. F. P. Blondel* (London: Sage, 1994), pp. 202–17; in György Szoboszlai (ed.) *Flying Blind: Emerging Democracies in East-Central Europe* (Budapest: Hungarian Political Science Association, 1992), pp. 99–113; and in Wladyslaw W. Adamski and Edmund Wnuk-Lipinski (eds) *Sisyphus: Social Studies* (Warsaw: Polish Academy of Sciences, 1992), vol. 1, pp. 87–102; Spanish translation, "Democratización y opciones constitucionales en Checo-Eslovaquia, Hungría y Polonia, 1989–91," *Cuadernos de la Cátedra Fadrique Furió Ceriol*, no. 5 (autumn 1993), pp. 7–29.

"Verzuiling en pacificatie als empirische en normatieve modellen in vergelijkend perspectief," in *Uitreiking van de Dr. Hendrik Muller-Prijs voor Gedrags-en Maatschappijwetenschappen* (Amsterdam: Koninklijke Nederlandse Akademie van Wetenschappen, 1992), pp. 6–13; also in *Acta Politica*, vol. 27, no. 3 (July 1992), pp. 323–32.

"Forms of Democracy: North-South and East-West Contrasts," in Wolfgang Reinhard and Peter Waldmann (eds) *Nord und Süd in Amerika: Gegensätze, Gemeinsamkeiten, Europäischer Hintergrund* (Freiburg: Rombach, 1992), vol. 2, pp. 933–42.

"The Electoral Systems Researcher as Detective: Probing Rae's Suspect 'Differential Proposition' on List Proportional Representation," in Dennis Kavanagh (ed.) *Electoral Politics* (Oxford: Clarendon Press, 1992), pp. 234–46.

"Power-Sharing, Ethnic Agnosticism, and Political Pragmatism," *Transformation*, no. 21 (1993), pp. 94–99.

"The Politics of Transition in South Africa: Report on a Faculty Seminar," *PS: Political Science & Politics*, vol. 26, no. 3 (September 1993), pp. 534–35.

"Democratisering en etnische conflicten in de jaren negentig," *Filosofie & Praktijk*, vol. 14, no. 3 (fall 1993), pp. 113–21.

"Separation of Powers and Cleavage Management" (with Ronald Rogowski and R. Kent Weaver), in R. Kent Weaver and Bert Rockman (eds) *Do Institutions Matter? Government Capabilities in the United States and Abroad* (Washington DC: Brookings Institution, 1993), pp. 302–44.

"Consociational Democracy," in Joel Krieger (ed.) *The Oxford Companion to Politics of the World* (New York: Oxford University Press, 1993), pp. 188–89; 2nd edn, 2001, p. 172.

"Israeli Democracy and Democratic Reform in Comparative Perspective," in Ehud Sprinzak and Larry Diamond (eds) *Israeli Democracy Under Stress* (Boulder CO: Lynne Rienner, 1993), pp. 107–23.

"Downsian Logic and the Comparative Study of Party Systems," in Bernard Grofman (ed.) *Information, Participation and Choice: An Economic Theory of Democracy in Perspective* (Ann Arbor MI: University of Michigan Press, 1993), pp. 231–38.

"Democracies: Forms, Performance, and Constitutional Engineering," *European Journal of Political Research*, vol. 25, no. 1 (January 1994), pp. 1–17; reprinted in Joachim Jens Hesse and Theo A. J. Toonen (eds) *The European Yearbook of Comparative Government and Public Administration*, vol. 2 (Baden-Baden: NOMOS, 1996), pp. 207–24.

"On S. E. Finer's Electoral Theory," *Government and Opposition*, vol. 29, no. 5 (special issue 1994), pp. 623–36.

"Prospects for Power-Sharing in the New South Africa," in Andrew Reynolds (ed.) *Election '94 South Africa: The Campaigns, Results and Future Prospects* (London: James Currey, 1994), pp. 221–31.

"Linking and Integrating Corporatism and Consensus Democracy: Theory, Concepts and Evidence" (with Markus M. L. Crepaz), *British Journal of Political Science*, vol. 25, no. 2 (April 1995), pp. 281–88.

"Explaining Political and Economic Change in Post-Communist Eastern Europe: Old Legacies, New Institutions, Hegemonic Norms, and International Pressures" (with Beverly Crawford), *Comparative Political Studies*, vol. 28, no. 2 (July 1995), pp. 171–99; reprinted in Stephen White and Daniel Nelson (eds) *The Politics of the Post-Communist World* (Aldershot: Ashgate, 2001), pp. 127–58.

"Civic Politics and Democratic Institutions: A Plea for the (Re-)Introduction of Compulsory Voting," in M. L. J. Wissenburg (ed.) *Civic Politics and Civil Society: Proceedings* (Nijmegen: Department of Political Science, University of Nijmegen, 1995), pp. 13–28.

"The Virtues of Parliamentarism: But Which Kind of Parliamentarism?", in H. E. Chehabi and Alfred Stepan (eds) *Politics, Society, and Democracy: Comparative Studies* (Boulder CO: Westview Press, 1995), pp. 363–73.

"Electoral Systems," in Seymour Martin Lipset *et al.* (eds) *The Encyclopedia of Democracy* (Washington DC: Congressional Quarterly, 1995), vol. 2, pp. 412–22.

"Proportional Representation," in Seymour Martin Lipset *et al.* (eds) *The Encyclopedia of Democracy* (Washington DC: Congressional Quarterly, 1995), vol. 3, pp. 1010–16.

"Multiethnic Democracy," in Seymour Martin Lipset *et al.* (eds) *The Encyclopedia of Democracy* (Washington DC: Congressional Quarterly, 1995), vol. 3, pp. 853–65; Russian translation, "Polietnicheskaya demokratija," in Algis Prazauskas (ed.) *Etnos i politika: Khrestomatiya* (Moscow: URAO, 2000), pp. 287–99.

"The Puzzle of Indian Democracy: A Consociational Interpretation," *American Political Science Review*, vol. 90, no. 2 (June 1996), pp. 258–68; reprinted in Niraja Gopal Jayal (ed.) *Democracy in India* (New Delhi: Oxford University Press India, 2001), pp. 326–57.

"The Framework Document on Northern Ireland and the Theory of Power-Sharing," *Government and Opposition*, vol. 31, no. 3 (summer 1996), pp. 267–74.

"Compulsory Voting Is the Best Way to Keep Democracy Strong," *Chronicle of Higher Education*, vol. 43, no. 8 (October 18, 1996), pp. B3–B4; reprinted in Robert E. DiClerico (ed.) *Political Parties, Campaigns, and Elections* (Upper

Saddle River NJ: Prentice-Hall, 2000), pp. 148–51; and in Robert E. DiClerico and Allan S. Hammock (eds) *Points of View: Readings in American Government* (New York: McGraw-Hill, 8th edn, 2001), pp. 74–77.

"Reflections on the First Twenty-Five Years of the *European Journal of Political Research*," *European Journal of Political Research*, vol. 31, nos. 1–2 (February 1997), pp. 5–16.

"Trichotomy or Dichotomy?", *European Journal of Political Research*, vol. 31, nos. 1–2 (February 1997), pp. 125–28.

"Dimensions of Democracy," *European Journal of Political Research*, vol. 31, nos. 1–2 (February 1997), pp. 195–204.

"Unequal Participation: Democracy's Unresolved Dilemma," *American Political Science Review*, vol. 91, no. 1 (March 1997), pp. 1–14; reprinted in Pippa Norris (ed.) *Elections and Voting Behaviour: New Challenges, New Perspectives* (Aldershot: Ashgate, 1998), pp. 355–68.

"The Difficult Science of Electoral Systems: A Commentary on the Critique by Alberto Penadés," *Electoral Studies*, vol. 16, no. 1 (March 1997), pp. 73–77; Spanish translation, "La difícil ciencia de los sistemas electorales: Un comentario a la crítica de Alberto Penadés," *Revista Española de Investigaciones Sociológicas*, no. 74 (April–June 1996), pp. 443–48.

"Hap-ui-je-wa han-guk-ui kwon-ryok-gu-jo (The Consensus Model and Korean Democracy)" (with Chae-Han Kim), *Korean Political Science Review*, vol. 31, no. 1 (spring 1997), pp. 99–120.

"Disproportionality under Alternative Voting: The Crucial – and Puzzling – Case of the Australian Senate Elections, 1919–46," *Acta Politica*, vol. 32, no. 1 (spring 1997), pp. 9–24.

"Changement et continuité dans la théorie consociative," *Revue Internationale de Politique Comparée*, vol. 4, no. 3 (December 1997), pp. 679–97.

"About Peripheries, Centres, and Other Autobiographical Reflections," in Hans Daalder (ed.) *Comparative European Politics: The Story of a Profession* (London: Cassell, 1997), pp. 241–52.

"Back to Democratic Basics: Who Really Practices Majority Rule?", in Axel Hadenius (ed.) *Democracy's Victory and Crisis: Nobel Symposium no. 93* (Cambridge: Cambridge University Press, 1997), pp. 143–60.

"Reforming the House: Three Moderately Radical Proposals," *PS: Political Science & Politics*, vol. 31, no. 1 (March 1998), pp. 9–11; reprinted in Joseph F. Zimmerman and Wilma Rule (eds) *The U.S. House of Representatives: Reform or Rebuild?* (Westport CT:, Praeger, 2000), pp. 135–40; and in Gregory M. Scott and Loren Gatch (eds) *21 Debated Issues in American Politics* (Englewood Cliffs NJ: Prentice-Hall, 2000), pp. 151–56; 2nd edn, 2004, pp. 147–52.

"Consensus and Consensus Democracy: Cultural, Structural, Functional, and Rational-Choice Approaches," *Scandinavian Political Studies*, vol. 21, no. 2 (1998), pp. 99–108.

"South African Democracy: Majoritarian or Consociational?" *Democratization*, vol. 5, no. 4 (winter 1998), pp. 144–50.

"First-Past-the-Post, PR, Michael Pinto-Duschinsky, and the Empirical Evidence," *Representation*, vol. 36, no. 2 (summer 1999), pp. 133–36.

"Australian Democracy: Modifying Majoritarianism?", *Australian Journal of Political Science*, vol. 34, no. 3 (November 1999), pp. 313–26; also in Marian Sawer and Sarah Miskin (eds) *Representation and Institutional Change: 50 Years of Proportional*

Representation in the Senate, Papers on Parliament, no. 34 (Canberra: Department of the Senate, 1999), pp. 55–69.

"Types of Democracy and Generosity with Foreign Aid: An Indirect Test of the Democratic Peace Proposition" (with Peter J. Bowman), in Erik Beukel, Kurt Klaudi Klausen, and Poul Erik Mouritzen (eds) *Elites, Parties and Democracy: Festschrift for Professor Mogens N. Pedersen* (Odense: Odense University Press, 1999), pp. 193–206.

"SNTV and STV Compared: Their Political Consequences in Japan, Ireland, and Malta," in Bernard Grofman, Sung-Chull Lee, Edwin A. Winckler, and Brian Woodall (eds) *Elections in Japan, Korea, and Taiwan under the Single Non-Transferable Vote: The Comparative Study of an Embedded Institution* (Ann Arbor MI: University of Michigan Press, 1999), pp. 289–99.

"The Future of Democracy: Reasons for Pessimism, but Also Some Optimism," *Scandinavian Political Studies*, vol. 23, no. 3 (2000), pp. 265–73.

"Varieties of Non-Majoritarian Democracy," in Markus M. L. Crepaz, Thomas A. Koelble, and David Wilsford (eds) *Democracy and Institutions: The Life Work of Arend Lijphart* (Ann Arbor MI: University of Michigan Press, 2000), pp. 225–45.

"Party Systems and Issue Dimensions: Israel and Thirty-five Other Old and New Democracies Compared" (with Peter J. Bowman and Reuven Y. Hazan), *Israel Affairs*, vol. 6, no. 2 (winter 2000), pp. 29–51; also in Reuven Y. Hazan and Moshe Maor (eds) *Parties, Elections and Cleavages: Israel in Comparative and Theoretical Perspective* (London: Frank Cass, 2000), pp. 29–51.

"Definitions, Evidence, and Policy: A Response to Matthijs Bogaards' Critique," *Journal of Theoretical Politics*, vol. 12, no. 4 (October 2000), pp. 425–31.

"Apparentement," in Richard Rose *et al.* (eds) *International Encyclopedia of Elections* (Washington DC: CQ Press, 2000), pp. 16–17.

"Turnout," in Richard Rose *et al.* (eds) *International Encyclopedia of Elections* (Washington DC: CQ Press, 2000), pp. 314–22.

Democracy in the Twenty-First Century: Can We Be Optimistic?, Uhlenbeck Lecture 18 (Wassenaar: Netherlands Institute for Advanced Study in the Humanities and Social Sciences, 2000); also in *European Review*, vol. 9, no. 2 (May 2001), pp. 169–84; and in Norbert Kersting and Lasse Cronqvist (eds) *Democratization and Political Culture in Comparative Perspective* (Wiesbaden: VS Verlag für Sozialwissenschaften, 2005), pp. 37–56.

"Foreword," in Jaap Woldendorp, Hans Keman, and Ian Budge, *Party Government in 48 Democracies (1945–1998): Composition, Duration, Personnel* (Dordrecht: Kluwer, 2000), pp. vii–viii.

"Constructivism and Consociational Theory," *APSA-CP*, vol. 12, no. 1 (winter 2001), pp. 11–13.

"The Pros and Cons – but Mainly Pros – of Consensus Democracy," *Acta Politica*, vol. 36, no. 2 (summer 2001), pp. 129–39.

"Cheong-pa-jeok sa-hoe han-guk-eui kwon-ryeok chip-jung/pun-san (Power Concentration/Sharing in Korea as a Divided Society)" (with Chae-Han Kim), in Chae-Han Kim (ed.) *Pun-yeol-eui min-ju-ju-eui* (Seoul: Sowha, 2001), pp. 259–90.

"Democracy, Southern European Style" (with Thomas C. Bruneau, P. Nikiforos Diamandouros, Richard Gunther, Leonardo Morlino, and Risa A. Brooks), in P. Nikiforos Diamandouros and Richard Gunther (eds) *Parties, Politics, and Democracy in the New Southern Europe* (Baltimore MD: Johns Hopkins University Press, 2001), pp. 16–82.

"Consensus Democracy," in Paul Barry Clarke and Joe Foweraker (eds) *Encyclopedia of Democratic Thought* (London: Routledge, 2001), pp. 90–91.

"Majoritarianism," in Paul Barry Clarke and Joe Foweraker (eds) *Encyclopedia of Democratic Thought* (London: Routledge, 2001), pp. 427–29.

"Australian Democracy in Comparative Perspective," in Marian Sawer (ed.) *Elections: Full, Free & Fair* (Leichhardt NSW: Federation Press, 2001), pp. 189–201.

"Negotiation Democracy versus Consensus Democracy: Parallel Conclusions and Recommendations." *European Journal of Political Research*, vol. 41, no. 1 (January 2002), pp. 107–13.

"Hoe moet de Europese Unie geregeerd worden? Doe maar gewoon … ," *Beleid en Maatschappij*, vol. 29, no. 1 (2002), pp. 4–7.

"Dupliek," *Beleid en Maatschappij*, vol. 29, no. 1 (2002), pp. 25–26.

"The Evolution of Consociational Theory and Consociational Practices, 1965–2000," *Acta Politica*, vol. 37, nos. 1–2 (spring–summer 2002), pp. 11–22.

"Europe, the European Union, and Democracy," *NIAS Newsletter*, no. 28 (spring 2002), pp. 20–23.

"The Wave of Power-Sharing Democracy," in Andrew Reynolds (ed.) *The Architecture of Democracy: Constitutional Design, Conflict Management, and Democracy* (Oxford: Oxford University Press, 2002), pp. 37–54; Italian translation, "L'ondata di democrazie a potere condiviso," in Arend Lijphart, Raffaele De Mucci, and Luigi Di Gregorio, *Democrazie in transizione*, Collana di studi metodologici diretta da Dario Antiseri, no. 10 (Rome: Luiss Edizioni, 2002), pp. 19–48.

"Foreword: The Value of Within-Nation Comparative Analysis," in Adrian Vatter, *Kantonale Demokratien im Vergleich: Entshtehungsgründe, Interaktionen und Wirkungen politischer Institutionen in den Schweizer Kantonen* (Opladen: Leske und Budrich, 2002), pp. 13–15.

"Revisiting Khizr Tiwana's Career: Power-Sharing, Federalism and Political Development in South and South-East Asia," in Ian Talbot, *Khizr Tiwana: The Punjab Unionist Party and the Partition of India* (Karachi: Oxford University Press, 2002), pp. 237–45.

"Foreword: Democracy Versus Majority Rule," in P. J. Emerson, *Defining Democracy: Decisions, Elections and Good Governance* (Belfast: De Borda Institute, 2002), pp. xii–xiii.

"Measurement Validity and Institutional Engineering: Reflections on Rein Taagepera's Meta-Study," *Political Studies*, vol. 51, no. 1 (March 2003), pp. 20–25.

"Majoritarianism and Democratic Performance in the Fifth Republic," *French Politics*, vol. 1, no. 2 (2003), pp. 225–32.

"Constitutional Design for Divided Democracies," *Journal of Democracy*, vol. 15, no. 2 (April 2004), pp. 96–109; reprinted (under the title "The Case for Power Sharing") in Larry Diamond and Marc F. Plattner (eds) *Electoral Systems and Democracy* (Baltimore MD: Johns Hopkins University Press, 2006), pp. 42–55; Spanish translation, "Diseño constitucional para sociedades divididas," *Acta Republicana* (Guadalajara), vol. 4, no. 4 (2005), pp. 3–11.

"Commentary," in Wayne A. Cornelius, Takeyuki Tsuda, Philip L. Martin, and James F. Hollifield (eds) *Controlling Immigration: A Global Perspective* (Stanford CA: Stanford University Press, 2nd edn, 2004), pp. 293–95.

"Foreword," in Michael Gallagher and Paul Mitchell (eds) *The Politics of Electoral Systems* (Oxford: Oxford University Press, 2005), pp. vii–x.

"The New Institutionalism and Constitutional Design," *Perspectives on Politics*, vol. 3, no. 2 (June 2005), pp. 322–25.

"Foreword: The Resilience of the Welfare State," in Markus M. L. Crepaz, *Trust Beyond Borders: Immigration, the Welfare State, and Identity in Modern Societies* (Ann Arbor MI: University of Michigan Press, 2007), pp. vii–ix.

"Introduction: The Importance of the India-United States Comparison for Political Science," in K. Shankar Bajpai (ed.) *Democracy and Diversity: India and the American Experience* (New Delhi: Oxford University Press, 2007), pp. 1–13.

"Democratic Institutions and Ethnic/Religious Pluralism: Can India and the United States Learn from Each Other – and from the Smaller Democracies?", in K. Shankar Bajpai (ed.) *Democracy and Diversity: India and the American Experience* (New Delhi: Oxford University Press, 2007), pp. 14–49.

Index